lonely

Bali, Lombok
& Nusa Tenggara

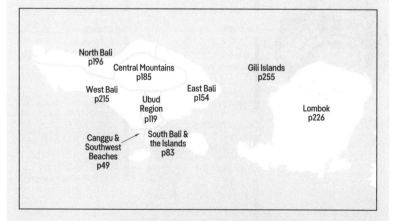

Nusa Tenggara
p268

North Bali
p196

Central Mountains
p185

Gili Islands
p255

West Bali
p215

Ubud
Region
p119

East Bali
p154

Lombok
p226

Canggu &
Southwest
Beaches
p49

South Bali &
the Islands
p83

**Narina Exelby, Anna Kaminski,
Sarah Lempa, Ryan Ver Berkmoes**

CONTENTS

Traditional offerings

Pura Tanah Lot (p222)

Sumbawa (p285)

Toolkit

Storybook

DUDAREV MIKHAIL/SHUTTERSTOCK ©

Snorkelling, Gili Trawangan (p259)

BALI, LOMBOK & NUSA TENGGARA
THE JOURNEY BEGINS HERE

In 1993, I visited Bali and Lombok for the first time. When I went through immigration at Bali's then tiny airport, the officer glanced at my passport and said in the sweetest voice possible: 'Have a wonderful birthday on Bali.' Who wouldn't fall in love? Since then, I've lived in Bali at various times in my life, and I've travelled across all of Nusa Tenggara, where the diversity of places, people and, yes, beaches is astonishing.

In Bali, much is made of the extreme rate of change. But this vibrancy and dynamism is part of its allure. Yes, many of these places have changed greatly, but their essence still evokes love.

Ryan Ver Berkmoes

@ryanverberkmoes
Ryan has travelled the world for his writing, which comprises over 150 guidebooks.

My favourite experience is sunset on the beach at Pemuteran (p207) as the kids play pick-up football in the sand, and residents and visitors mingle and stroll the shore together.

WHO GOES WHERE

Our writers and experts choose the places which, for them, define Bali, Lombok and Nusa Tenggara.

Sumba (p298) is beguiling. There's surfing, laid-back Waingapu and Tambolaka, ikat textiles in Nusa Tenggara, jungle hikes to pristine waterfalls, and villages with their welcoming residents. You may witness an animal sacrifice, watch a traditional roof getting repaired, or chew the fat (and some betel nut) with the village priest.

Anna Kaminski

@anna.cohen.kaminski
Anna is a writer who covers travel, culture and cuisine.

Lombok's **Southwestern Peninsula** (p249) is home to the 'Secret Gilis', a relatively undiscovered chain of tiny islands that is sleepy in the best way possible. Glide from one tiny jewel of an island to the next while peering through glassy waters to an impressive labyrinth of coral, where fish easily outnumber people.

Sarah Lempa

@travelempa
Sarah writes about travel, psychology and a list of things in between.

The sacred rainforest at **Danau Tamblingan** (p191) is a part of Bali that has remained unchanged for centuries. There are nettle and ficus trees that have stood watch over this intricate ecosystem for more than 600 years. The forest is protected and it's reassuring to know that however much Bali changes, this will remain.

Narina Exelby

@narina.exelby
Narina is a writer based between South Africa and Indonesia.

Pulau Menjangan, Pemuteran

Jump right in for Bali's best diving (p210)

Pantai Suluban, Uluwatu

Take on Southeast Asia's most legendary surf (p98)

Ubud

Watch mesmerising dance performances in Ubud centre (p126)

Sidemen

Stroll east Bali's magnificent rice fields (p166)

Lovina

Watch dolphins at lovely Lovina (p201)

Finns Beach Club, Canggu

Party with the best at this famous club (p60)

Klungkung

Visit one of east Bali's best markets (p160)

Seminyak

Browse the famous shops along Jl Kayu Aya (p65)

See Bali and Lombok

INDIAN OCEAN

Bali Sea

Bali and Lombok

6

Komodo National Park, Flores

Spot the world's largest lizard (p282)

Flores Sea

Komodo
National
Park

Reo
Golo
Torongkoe
Pota
Wolo
Mesa
Olaia
Seso
Roa
Kotadirumali

Wolo
Hangabera
Kolisia
Talibura
Ili
Berapun

Adonara
Sagu
Balauring
Pulau
Marisa

Tapowolo
Lewoleba

Lembata

G. Sirung

Labuan
Bajo
Poco
Dedeng
Pangga
Golo
Mori
Repi
Bamo
Flores

West Sumba

Witness Asia's most extravagant harvest festival (p303)

Sawu Sea

INDONESIA

TIMOR-LESTE

Naikliu

Kapan

Taemaman

G. Fatuleu

Timor

Tambolaka

Waikabuk

Sumba

Waingapu

West Sumba

Melolo

G. Ngadu
Langgi

Baing

Teluk
Kupang

Semau

Akle

Oesao

Kupang

Sabu

Rote

Nemberala

Sama Sama, Gili Trawangan

Revel in the party scene 'til dawn (p258)

Gunung Rinjani, Senaru

Take on Indonesia's second-tallest volcano (p246)

INDIAN OCEAN

Nusa Lembongan

Dive the underwater world of the Coral Triangle (p106)

Desert Point, Southwestern Peninsula

Surf the best at Lombok's famous break (p251)

Pantai Mawun, Kuta

Enjoy Kuta's sandy crescent of heaven (p232)

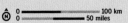

0   100 km
0   50 miles

BEACHY DELIGHTS

Indonesia's 17,000+ islands are blessed with countless beaches. Many of the very best can be found on Bali, Lombok and Nusa Tenggara. The huge swathe of Kuta Beach was the original lure for tourists to Bali. Since then, generations of travellers have discovered the endless diversity of beaches throughout the region. Pick your allure: buzzing parties or secluded isolation; mellow waves or pounding surf; gleaming white sand or elegant black. There's one for every whim.

Dreamy Sunsets

Any beach with a view west will likely enjoy one of Indonesia's famous technicolour sunsets; residents and visitors alike gather for the show.

Drink Up

At all but the most remote beaches, you'll likely find at least one drinks vendor nearby with an icy Bintang. Simple cafes are also common.

Not Hanging Out

Whether you're on Bali, the Gilis, Sumbawa or anyplace else, nude and topless sunbathing are offensive to residents. And remember to cover up away from the sand.

BEST BEACHY EXPERIENCES

Feel the energy of ❶ **Kuta Beach** (p75) – the original magnet for visitors – that runs to Seminyak and beyond.

Descend 130 steps to isolated ❷ **Thomas Beach** (p98), the secluded pocket of white sand on Bali's Bukit Peninsula.

Follow the ring of powdery sand around the coast of ❸ **Gili Air** (p264) and try to decide on your favourite spot.

Shade your eyes at ❹ **Pantai Mawun** (p232), a gleaming crescent of white sand flanked by rolling hills that's only 20 minutes from Lombok's Kuta.

Luxuriate on the dreamy sweeps of pastel sand that are the pink beaches of ❺ **Pulau Padar** (p282), the small island that's part of Komodo National Park.

JAVARMAN/SHUTTERSTOCK ©

Rice fields, Sidemen (p165)

MAGNIFICENT NATURE

From bewildering cliffs and cerulean seas to astounding peaks and dizzying terraces of jade, the natural beauty of Bali, Lombok and Nusa Tenggara knows no bounds. Witness gorgeous vistas, feel the cool mist of jungle waterfalls, amble through famed rice fields or leap out of your comfort zone and climb an active volcano.

Climb Every Volcano

Active volcanoes can be found on most major islands. Imposing icons such as Bali's Gunung Agung and Lombok's Gunung Rinjani are legendary and challenging climbs.

Discover Waterfalls

Waterfalls lace the mountains, their thundering white streaks plunging to green rainforests. In Bali, local communities have recently permitted access to previously hidden wonders.

BEST NATURE EXPERIENCES

Find new words for green when strolling the rice fields of ❶ **Sidemen** (p166), the serene escape of east Bali.

At the base of Danau Tamblingan, trek through the ancient, sacred ❷ **rainforest** (p191).

Gaze upon Lombok's picture-perfect ❸ **Selong Belanak** (p233) bay, framed by rolling hills.

Witness the impossibly beautiful ❹ **Gunung Kelimutu** (p281) volcano in Flores – with three different-coloured lakes.

Hike through jungle to ❺ **Air Terjun Wai Marang** (p302) in Sumba, with a pristine swimming hole.

FLORA & FAUNA

Bali, Lombok and Nusa Tenggara boast an array of creatures, from primeval dragons to one of the world's rarest birds. Off the coasts, the waters teem with myriad species, from small fish to leaping dolphins. Nesting on beaches, sea turtles bridge these worlds. And take time to smell the flowers, which grow everywhere in profusion.

❶ ❹ ❷   ❸   ❺

Rich Waters

A rich variety of coral, seaweed, fish and other marine life thrive off the islands, and all of Indonesia is a manta-ray sanctuary.

Travelling Turtles

One hawksbill turtle that visited Bali was tracked the following year. He travelled to Java, Kalimantan, Australia (Perth and much of Queensland!), and then back to Bali.

Mind Your Banana

Troupes of chattering, frolicking (and, yes, thieving) monkeys are found everywhere, from Bali temples to remote bends in the road deep in Nusa Tenggara.

BEST FLORA & FAUNA EXPERIENCES

Spot the rare Bali starling – an iconic white bird with black accents and a distinctive bright-blue mask – in ❶ **West Bali National Park** (p209).

In the central mountains, wander the vast ❷ **Bali Botanic Garden** (p191), which celebrates the islands' 2400 floral species.

Traverse the trails leading to Lombok's ❸ **Gunung Rinjani** (p246), and you'll spot the dozens of species that enliven the rainforest.

Stay alert for dolphins frolicking in the wake of your boat on a tour of ❹ **Lovina** (p201).

Don't get bit by the world's largest lizard, and the star of ❺ **Komodo National Park** (p282).

11

SACRED CULTURE

Bali's creative heritage is everywhere, and it is deeply tied to the culture and Hindu faith. Temples, or *pura*, are the epicentre of spiritual activity, featuring dance and musical performances that are the result of an ever-evolving culture with a centuries-long legacy. Precise choreography and discipline are hallmarks of the beautiful, captivating and ethereal Balinese dance. Balinese music is played by an ensemble called a gamelan, who create unforgettable melodies on various bamboo and bronze instruments.

Thousands of Temples

With over 10,000 temples (or possibly double that – they're hard to count), Bali has a variety that makes them difficult to categorise. (Pictured: Pura Ulun Danu Bratan, p190.)

Bali's Daily Processions

The peal of the gamelan will halt traffic for a temple procession, that disappears as suddenly as it appeared, leaving only a trail of hibiscus petals in its wake.

Mesmerising Music & Dance

Balinese dance features mystical music, dancers with hypnotic grace and chants that tell stories rich with the essence of Hindu beliefs and lore.

❶
❸ ❹
❺
❷

BEST CULTURAL EXPERIENCES

See nightly Balinese ❶ **dance performances** (p126) in a variety of styles in over half a dozen venues in Ubud.

Head to the ancient village of ❷ **Boti** (p292) on West Timor for ikat-weaving, traditional dance and royal rituals.

Learn the story of Nyepi at the ❸ **Saka Museum** (p101) in Jimbaran, with displays of extraordinary Ogoh Ogoh – huge, cartoonish figurines crafted for Nyepi.

Catch the worm at Lombok's ❹ **Bau Nyale Festival** (p232), held each year during the harvest of the prized *nyale* (sea worm).

Witness the ❺ **Pasola** (p303), the horse-riding fighting festival in West Sumba that's one of Asia's most extravagant harvest festivals.

DANISLH/SHUTTERSTOCK ©

Nest (p261), Gili Meno

GREAT ESCAPES

From the serene corners of Bali, then east through Lombok and to Nusa Tenggara, sublime refuge awaits in quiet, often artful guesthouses and small resorts, replete with the gracious and convivial welcome for which the region is lauded. The untrodden beach, thundering waterfall, and grand, green vistas are here.

Bali's Quiet Corners

Away from the frenzy of the south, you'll find plenty of blissful escapes on Bali. Consider Sidemen, Amed, Munduk and Medewi Beach, among many others.

Discovering Isolation

Relatively isolated and delightfully funky resorts can be found in the quiet corners of Bali, and at the sparse beaches and jungle-clad volcanoes further east.

BEST ESCAPIST EXPERIENCES

Head into the hills of **① Tanglad** (p112) in Nusa Penida to watch traditional weavers at work.

Do nothing at the beach of **② Pantai Umeanyar** (p206) near Seririt – a quiet stretch of coast in north Bali.

Leave life behind at **③ Sekaroh** (p235), the remote Lombok beach town famed for its pink sand.

Snorkel to the world-famous underwater sculpture of **④ Nest** (p261) at Gili Meno.

Explore the traditional Ngada village of **⑤ Bena** (p277), perched on the side of a forested volcano.

BALI'S GLORIOUS RESORTS

Whether you need a total fix for the soul or desire a pampering stay, you can indulge at a luxurious Bali resort. Unplug at palatial retreats perched above dazzling white sands or in idyllic river valleys. The design and architecture win international acclaim, the service is lavish and the opulent spas divine.

BEST RESORT EXPERIENCES

Sit on the beach at ❶ **Como Uma Canggu** (p81), an ultra-luxurious resort with a superb spa.

Discover Bali's artistic side at ❷ **Tugu Bali** (p55), a series of traditional buildings redolent with gracious charm and artful collections.

Take in the phenomenal views at ❸ **Anantara Uluwatu** (p116), a lavish resort built on a cliff edge, in sight of legendary surf breaks.

Lose yourself in green at ❹ **Mandapa** (p153), a renowned resort with a striking design set in Ubud's Sungai Valley.

Experience Ubud's traditional welcome at ❺ **Ibah** (p153), a vintage retreat that sits at the nexus of rivers, temples and hiking trails.

Finding Bali's Best

Some of the world's top resort hotels can be found around Ubud and in the south, from Canggu and Kerobokan to the Bukit Peninsula's south coast.

Yes, Sire

Set on a white crescent of sand that could almost be the fourth Gili, Sire is a luxurious enclave on Lombok that's home to palatial resorts.

Lost in Sumba

Already far off the beaten path, Sumba is home to two noted and luxurious resorts: surfer-friendly NIHI Sumba and the Sanubari.

UNDERWATER WONDERS

Encircled by magnificent reefs, Bali, Lombok and Nusa Tenggara have oodles of places to slip on fins and a mask and enter beautiful underwater worlds. There is a huge variety of coral and colourful fish and mammals of all sizes in the pristine waters that lap these islands. Scuba diving and snorkelling are huge draws: for some, slipping beneath the waves is part of a larger trip; for others, it's the whole point.

Scuba Diving

Good dive operators are found throughout the region. Try out the sport on a discovery dive, enjoy a day cruise (or longer), or get certified.

Snorkelling

There is no shortage of places on Bali's coast to don a mask and fins and explore the delights underwater, such as Tulamben, with its sunken freighter.

Freediving

Ready for something deeper? Plunge to depths of 30m and beyond on a single breath. Bali's Amed is a centre for freediving.

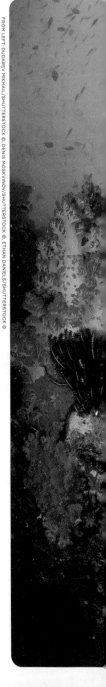

BEST UNDERWATER EXPERIENCES

Revel in Bali's best diving at ❶ **Pulau Menjangan** (p210), which is lauded for its amazingly varied diving and snorkelling.

Explore the ❷ **Coral Triangle** (p106) at Nusa Lembongan, right at the centre of a marine region revered for its remarkable biodiversity.

Choose from oodles of dive locations in the ❸ **Gilis** (p255). There's underwater statues off Meno, shipwrecks everywhere and coral walls.

Don't just come for the dragons, ❹ **Komodo National Park** (p282) is also famed for numerous dive sites and live-aboard holidays.

Invest the time to reach the remote ❺ **Alor Archipelago** (p295), where there's serious dive culture, a healthy reef and large pelagics.

BALI'S FOOD & DRINK

Bali excels at sublime eating and drinking. Seminyak boasts an array of restaurants and bars; Kerobokan is the go-to for stylish and uperb eateries; Denpasar cafes serve exceptional local fare in relaxed surrounds; Canggu sees interesting cafes and hip restaurants opening weekly; while Ubud is a profusion of creative eateries, many healthy, all delicious.

BEST EATING & DRINKING EXPERIENCES

Get intimate at Canggu's **❶ Skool Kitchen** (p53), with a high-concept menu centred on ancient wood-fired cooking traditions.

Dine well at **❷ Ijen** (p65), an earth-conscious restaurant using local seafood and produce in creative dishes.

Have the Indonesian-archipelago-inspired tasting menu at **❸ Rumari** (p101), the sophisticated restaurant at the Raffles Bali resort.

Ride the trendsetting wave at **❹ Locavore NXT** (p128), the influential Ubud restaurant located in its own farm fantasyland. Book months ahead.

Enjoy the eating and drinking delights at **❺ Room4Dessert** (p134), the top-end bistro run by chef Will Goldfarb in Ubud.

Brilliant Local Fare

Superb warungs (food stalls) serving exceptional Balinese and Indonesian cuisine are found across the island. Many are family-run affairs; peak opening hours are midday.

Bali Booze

Bali's craft breweries include Black Sand and South+East. The burgeoning wine scene boasts Hattan and Sababay wineries. And don't miss *arak* – the ceremonial spirit.

Sizzling Street Food

At night markets like those in Sanur, Sayan and Gianyar, you can graze on exceptional street food. Find staples like *sate* (satay) and *pisang goreng* (fried banana).

RADITYA/SHUTTERSTOCK ©

Potato Head (p67)

BEST PARTYING EXPERIENCES

Pick the all-day Canggu party at ❶ **Finns Beach Club** (p60), where days and nights of pure hedonism await.

Feel famous at high-concept beach clubs such as ❷ **Potato Head** (p67), with stylish bites and hip tunes.

Gird yourself for nights out in ❸ **Kuta** (p67), the centre for anything-goes boozy nights.

Watch the last surfers of the day at sunset from ❹ **Single Fin** (p99) and other beach joints near Uluwatu's Pantai Suluban.

Survive the frenetic scene at ❺ **Sama Sama** (p258) on party island Gili Trawangan.

ENDLESS PARTIES

It starts with beach cafes and clubs. Maybe mellow daytime cocktails at one and wild antics at the other. It segues to sunset drinks and continues through high-energy restaurants amid post-sunset glow and pulsing house beats. Later, world-class clubs draw you in, with international DJs spinning sets to packed dance floors.

Bali's Crescent of Delights

Starting at Canggu's beaches, Bali's party action follows the sand round via Kerobokan, Seminyak, Legian and Kuta, before heading to the Bukit Peninsula and Uluwatu.

Sandy Brews

If there's a beach and tourists, you'll find genial vendors dispensing Bintangs while you recline on loungers, cheap plastic chairs or right on the sand.

SURFING THE CURL

In Bali, Lombok and Nusa Tenggara, you have dozens of great breaks on almost every island. You can spend a lifetime here riding the waves – and some do. Surfers buzz around the islands on motorbikes with board racks, looking for the next great wave and soaking up the pervasive surf vibe that permeates the beaches.

BEST SURFING EXPERIENCES

Marvel at ❶ **Kuta Beach** (p72), the vast sweep of sand where surfers of all skills enjoy nonstop waves.

Find some of Southeast Asia's most legendary surfing at ❷ **Uluwatu** (p98). It's the climax of the breaks along the Bukit Peninsula.

Spend days riding the waves at ❸ **Pantai Jungutbatu** (p108) off Nusa Lembongan. Breaks are offshore, past the reefs. Watch the action from beachside cafes.

Trek out to semi-remote ❹ **Desert Point** (p251) on Lombok. It's a tough break, even for the experienced.

Win your stripes at ❺ **Pantai Lakey** (p285) in Sumbawa, where international championship surfers come year-round.

Bali's Surf Seasons

From September to December, go east; during the other months, go west. And most of the time, you can also go south.

Surf Schools & Gear

Board rental, repair and sales are found at popular breaks. Lessons for everyone, from enthusiastic kids through tentative adults, are easily arranged at the beaches.

Black-Sand Breaks

Escape the crowds at the beaches along Bali's east and west coasts. Try Pantai Keramas along the former and Balian and Medewi along the latter.

Klungkung market (p160)

BEST SHOPPING EXPERIENCES

Browse the shops of **❶ Seminyak** (p65), especially the famous ones along Jl Kayu Aya.

Get your textiles fix with renowned ikat expert **❷ Pak Haji Noer** (p291) in Sumba's Kupang.

Bring an extra bag to **❸ Ubud** (p140) and nearby villages for local handicrafts, art and fashion.

Get lost in **❹ Klungkung market** (p160), a warren of buildings and one of east Bali's best markets.

Explore Lombok's retail hub **❺ Mataram** (p242). Besides malls, you'll find Pasar Cakranegara market and handicraft-filled Mataram Mall.

SHOPPING MECCA

Some consider Bali a great shopping destination; for others, it's their destiny. The island draws creative designers from across Indonesia and the world, and inspires local talent. Major brands of today and the famous names of tomorrow are found in boutiques and shops. Across the region, markets are unmissable experiences.

Bargain Hunts

In markets, stalls and shops without fixed prices in Indonesia, bargaining is part of the purchasing process. Just don't stress about saving one last rupiah.

Local Markets

Residents bargain for flowers, baskets, fruit and ornaments used in temple offerings at spirited, sprawling markets (*pasars*). Other stalls sell clothing, curios and daily essentials.

21

REGIONS & CITIES

Find the places that tick all your boxes.

North Bali

ADVENTURE AND NATURE ALONG THE COAST

Far from the hubbub of Bali's south, the island's north encompasses history, culture, a national park, reef-protected beaches and sensational diving and snorkelling. Singaraja is the island's second city and has an array of museums, and nearby Lovina is a dolphin-watching hub. Hillside hikes lead to dozens of pounding waterfalls.

West Bali

BEACHES, NATURE AND TEMPLES

Seaside Pura Tanah Lot marks the end – for now – of Bali's wild development in the southwest. To the west are untrodden charcoal-sand beaches interspersed with the low-key surfing villages of Balian Beach and Medewi. The region's main hub, Tabanan, is close to Bali's rice-growing traditions and the incredible temple of Pura Taman Ayun.

Canggu & Southwest Beaches

BEACHES AND A BLISSFUL HOLIDAY VIBE

Bali's magnificent sweep of sand stretches in an arc across the southwest coast. These beaches lure the majority of Bali's visitors, from the original tourist town of Kuta through Legian, Seminyak, Kerobokan and buzzing Canggu, all pulsing with cafes, clubs, restaurants, shops, surf and round-the-clock fun.

South Bali & the Islands

IDYLLIC BEACHES AND A RELAXED ISLAND VIBE

Family-friendly Sanur is the gateway to the blissful islands of Nusa Lembongan and Nusa Penida. Both offer an escape from Bali's clamour and boast incredible beaches and superb diving. Denpasar is Bali's commercial centre, while the Bukit Peninsula holds cloistered Nusa Dua and the popular beaches and surf spots of Uluwatu.

Central Mountains

VOLCANOES, FORESTS AND BEAUTIFUL MOUNTAIN VIEWS

Misty hikes to waterfalls and trees groaning with low-hanging fruit are highlights of Bali's central mountains, which include the unmissable Munduk village. Higher up the slopes, the evocative Pura Luhur Batukau attracts worshippers, and the sacred crater lakes of Danau Tamblingan and Danau Buyan shimmer amid their volcanic calderas to the awe of sunrise hikers.

Ubud Region

CULTURE, BEAUTY AND PLEASURE

Bali's remarkable culture is celebrated in Ubud, where art, dance and religion bloom. Ever-popular, the village of Ubud is a tantalising mix of chill cafes, vegan fare, yoga studios, creative shops, family-run guesthouses and memorable walks through lush rice fields. Nearby, ancient temples, artisans' studios, village markets and white-water adventures beckon.

North Bali
p196

West Bali
p215

Lombok

BALI'S LESSER-TRAVELLED NEIGHBOUR

Lombok has much to love. Surfers adore the southern coast and Kuta for its uncrowded breaks, while others laze away on the dozens of wide-open beaches. High above the waves, Gunung Rinjani – the iconic active volcano – is a draw for hikers. The island's Sasak culture infuses the main city of Mataram, a cultural melting pot.

Nusa Tenggara

TIMELESS CULTURE, EPIC NATURE AND BIG WAVES

Nusa Tenggara is the great adventure east of Lombok. See dragons at Komodo National Park, laze at pink-sand beaches and enjoy buzzy Labuan Bajo, the tourist centre of fascinating Flores. Other major islands include Sumbawa with its surf breaks; Timor-Leste with its ancient villages; and Sumba with its artisans and indigenous culture.

Nusa Tenggara
p268

East Bali

SACRED TEMPLES, VERDANT HIKES, HISTORICAL ADVENTURE

Bali's east offers one delight after another. The ancient royal cities of Klungkung and Amlapura speak to the island's rich history. Bali's tallest volcano, sacred Gunung Agung, is the site of its holiest temple, Pura Besakih, while the compelling coast includes sights in and around Padang Bai, Amed, Tulamben and beyond.

Gili Islands

CRYSTAL-CLEAR WATERS AND LAID-BACK LIVING

Just off Lombok are three islands with three personalities: Gili Trawangan is the largest, busiest and most popular with partiers. Gili Meno is the smallest, quietest and a haven for visitors seeking solitude. Gili Air melds the two in one family-friendly, enjoyable island. Offshore, fantastic snorkelling and diving await.

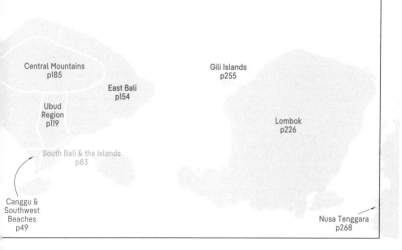

Central Mountains
p185

East Bali
p154

Ubud
Region
p119

South Bali & the Islands
p83

Canggu &
Southwest
Beaches
p49

Gili Islands
p255

Lombok
p226

Nusa Tenggara
p268

ITINERARIES

Bali to Nusa Tenggara

Allow: 6 weeks   **Distance:** 1600km

Mix the offbeat with the sublime. Start in Indonesia's heart of tourism, Bali, before hitting the Gilis and Lombok. Then, it's the islands of Nusa Tenggara province: many travellers will know parts of Flores, but Sumbawa, Sumba, West Timor etc. are little-visited and reward every single day spent exploring.

❶ BALI ⏱1 WEEK

Start in **Bali** for culture and nightlife: watch the surf and hang out in the waterfront guesthouses and cafes of **Uluwatu** (p96). Head north for the 'other' Bali – the culture, temples and rich history of **Ubud** (p122). Check out the lush beauty and historic sites in **east Bali** (p154) on your way to **Padang Bai** (p170, pictured) and the fast boat to the Gilis.

❷ GILIS & LOMBOK ⏱1 WEEK

Bounce around the paradise beaches and aquamarine water of the **Gilis** (p255). Join the parties on **Gili Trawangan** (p258) and soak off the night before on chill **Gili Air** (p264, pictured). Take the ferry to Lombok and enjoy the mellow vibes in **Kuta** (p230). Explore the wild beaches of south Lombok and consider a trek up **Gunung Rinjani** (p246), Indonesia's second-highest volcano. Catch the ferry at Labuhan Lombok.

❸ SUMBAWA ⏱1 WEEK

Admire the beautiful coastline and surf breaks that dot conservative **Sumbawa** (p285), an island of volcanic ridges, dry expanses and sheltered bays. **Pantai Lakey** (p285) is a great beach town and a surfers' mecca, with cool guesthouses and cafes overlooking awesome surf: Lakey Peak and Lakey Pipe are hallowed names here. Catch a ferry from Sape to Flores.

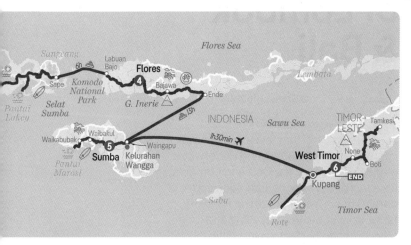

④ FLORES ⏱ 1 WEEK

Flores is a rugged volcanic island with thriving ancient cultures and dramatic terrain. **Labuan Bajo** (p272) is the fast-growing hub in west Flores for exploring the dragons (pictured) and pink-sand beaches of **Komodo National Park** (p282). Visit **Bajawa** (p278) to explore the Ngada villages of **Bena** (p277) and **Luba** (p277) on the slopes of **Gunung Inerie** (p277). At the old trading port of **Ende** (p279), catch the ferry to Sumba.

⑤ SUMBA ⏱ 1 WEEK

Step outside your comfort zone in isolated and timeless **Sumba** (p298), with its ancient villages, ancestral spirits and animist rituals. Tour the traditional villages of **Waikabubak** (p302, pictured) and **Waibakul** (p306), where the peaked thatched roofs and ancient traditions will have you wide-eyed. Catch the waves on white-sand **Pantai Marosi** (p306), one of Sumba's many superb beaches that is slowly attracting attention. Fly to West Timor.

⑥ WEST TIMOR ⏱ 1 WEEK

Ease into the off-the-grid feel of **West Timor** (p287) at **Kupang** (p288). Visit entrancing ancient villages like **None** (p290), where heads were still hunted up two generations ago. At **Boti** (p292), see how residents follow their nine-day week and in **Tamkesi** (p291, pictured), climb a sacred mountain for a view over a centuries-old village. Then jump over to **Rote** (p297) for powdery white-sand beaches and epic surf.

ITINERARIES

Beaches of Lombok & Bali

Allow: 2 weeks   **Distance:** 400km

You'll visit five islands and countless beaches on a trip that takes in the most interesting sandy shores and underwater places across Bali, the Gilis and Lombok. It's a mix of the famous, infamous and barely known, with something for every taste, from sublime snorkelling and long days lazing to perfect wave-riding.

❶ CANGGU ⏱ 2 DAYS

The series of long beaches collectively known as **Canggu** (p52) is the heart of Bali's hippest scene. Boho cafes mix with simple beach bars and pulsing, high-profile clubs. Alternate relaxation with high-energy parties and surf.

↪ **Detour:** *Foray to cliffside **Bingin** (p105) on the **Bukit Peninsula** (p100), where the vibe is even more alternative. Pocket-sized beaches of powdery sand here reward exploration.*

❷ MENGWI ⏱ 2 DAYS

This is the home of the surfing hotspot of **Pantai Medewi** (p223) and its much-vaunted long left-hand wave – rides of up to 500m are common. The immediate beach is a stretch of huge, smooth grey rocks interspersed among round black pebbles. Just west is the long swath of wide and sandy **Pantai Yeh Sumbul** (p223), with a smattering of cool beachy guesthouses – and no crowds.

❸ PEMUTERAN ⏱ 3 DAYS

Bali's best diving and snorkelling is found at **Pemuteran** (p207, pictured) on the northwest coast. A short boat ride brings you to the underwater wonders of **Pulau Menjangan** (p210), part of West Bali National Park. Surrounding this deserted island are over a dozen superb dive sites that include sunken boats, reef walls and beautiful coral. Above the water, the island has barely trodden beaches.

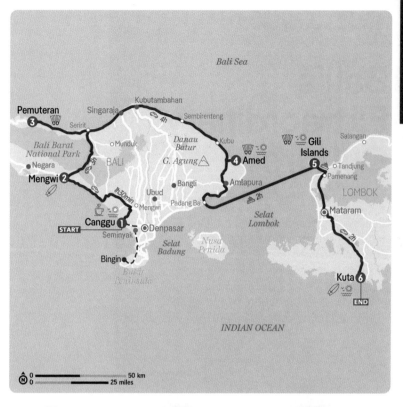

④ AMED ⏱ 2 DAYS

Get all the beach time you need at the succession of scalloped bays lined with beaches in the region known as **Amed** (p178). Little seaside villages such as **Jemeluk** (p179, pictured) and **Lipah** (p179) have boutique guesthouses where yoga seems to always be on offer. Just north is the diving and snorkelling centre of **Tulamben** (p181), with a shipwreck you can reach right from the shore.

⑤ GILI ISLANDS ⏱ 3 DAYS

These three little dots of white sand off Lombok could easily occupy your entire trip. Get to grips with island life on chill **Gili Air** (p264). Next up is **Trawangan** (p258), where there's much more action (and parties). The perfect day here can include diving, napping, swimming, lazing and drinking – all before noon. Last is **Gili Meno** (p261), where there's little to do except ponder the peace.

⑥ KUTA ⏱ 2 DAYS

The south coast near Lombok's **Kuta** (p230) has stunning beaches and surfing to reward the intrepid. Beaches just don't get much better than this: the water is warm, striped turquoise, and curls into barrels; the sand is silky and snow white, framed by massive headlands and sheer cliffs. Typical is **Selong Belanak** (p233, pictured), which has the kind of beach you fly to Indonesia for.

ITINERARIES

Bali's Extraordinary Culture

Allow: 3 weeks   **Distance:** 390km

The Balinese have a deep cultural heritage and belief systems that are an integral part of life across the island. Religion plays a role in so much of what makes the island appealing to visitors, the temples, art, music, offerings, architecture, processions and more. Get ready to dive right in.

❶ UBUD ⏱1 WEEK

Explore the temples in **Ubud** (p122) and attend Balinese dance performances (pictured). Then venture to nearby sites such as those in **Pejeng** (p147), where treasures include one of Bali's oldest artefacts. Just south are the mysteries at **Goa Gajah** (p148). To the north, Tegallalang has ancient sites like the wondrous **Gunung Kawi** (p144) and the rushing waters of **Pura Tirta Empul** (p144).

❷ SIDEMEN ⏱4 DAYS

The green cradle of **Sidemen** (p165) is an ideal base for visiting some of east Bali's holiest places. To the north is Bali's mother volcano, **Gunung Agung** (p168). On the slopes is the island's most sacred place, the **Pura Besakih** (p167, pictured) complex. Get your head above the clouds at **Pura Pasar Agung** (p168). South, don't miss Klungkung's royal compound of **Puri Agung Semarapura** (p158).

❸ TIRTA GANGGA ⏱3 DAYS

On your way to **Tirta Gangga** (p177), pause to contemplate the mysteries of **Pura Goa Lawah** (p172, pictured), the site of a *taman* (ornamental garden) – built for the enjoyment of the last king of the Karangasem regency – with brilliant rice-terrace vistas. Then head to the heavens of **Pura Lempuyang** (p181), the series of mountain-top temples – marvel at the views on a magical uphill trek.

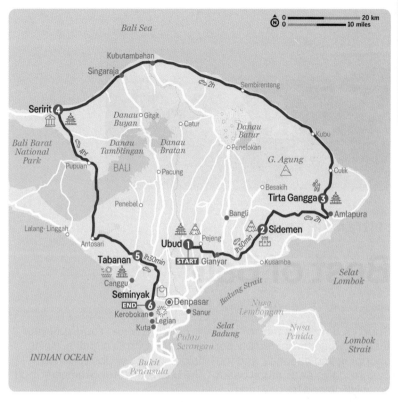

SERIRIT ⏱ 2 DAYS

Looping around Bali's east coast, stop at Yeh Sanih for interesting temples that include **Pura Maduwe Karang** (p203) and its unusual carvings. In the city of **Singaraja** (p202), don't miss important museums like **Gedong Kirtya Library** (p203). Spend the night at a beachside spot near **Seririt** (p206). Further west, the troika of temples anchored by **Pura Pulaki** (p208, pictured) is an important stop-off.

TABANAN ⏱ 1 DAY

Continue around the coast, exploring the wilds and black beaches of west Bali. **Pura Gede Perancak** (p224) is close to mangrove forests, while **Pura Rambut Siwi** (p224) is an important sea temple. Stay around **Tabanan** (p218) and hit the oceanfront **Pura Tanah Lot** (p222, pictured) early in the day, to avoid the sunset crowds. Save time for the sublime **Pura Taman Ayun** (p218) too.

SEMINYAK ⏱ 4 DAYS

One of south Bali's top destinations, **Seminyak** (p63), with its shops and nightlife, may not seem spiritual, but it is. **Pura Petitenget** (p67, pictured) is located on a beautiful stretch of beach and is the scene of frequent ceremonies – look for offerings in the sand. Make a day trip south to the popular – and vital – temple of **Pura Luhur Ulu Watu** (p99) with its views across the Indian Ocean.

FUNTASY DEVELOPER/SHUTTERSTOCK ©

Jimbaran (p100)

ITINERARIES

Best of Bali

Allow: 1 week   **Distance:** 230km

Short on time? This trip covers Bali's best in a week. You'll split your time between the incredibly popular south, with its nightlife, dining, shopping and beaches; and the hillside charms of Ubud, with its culture, cafes and natural beauty. The bases of Kerobokan and Ubud are well-placed for day trips.

❶
KEROBOKAN ⏱ 1 DAY

Start at a beachside hotel or resort in **Kerobokan** (p69) – there are many to choose from. Spend your first day in languid pursuits: head towards **Seminyak** (p63, pictured) for Bali's best shopping. Prowl the streets, watching for a likely lunch from many choices. Watch the sunset from a beach spot serving drinks. At night, pop out your frilly frocks for a stylish night out.

❷
CANGGU ⏱ 1 DAY

Canggu (p52), north and west of Kerobokan, is Bali's fastest-growing area and makes a fine day trip. The beaches are dotted with high-profile clubs (pictured) interspersed with humble beer vendors. Great strands include **Batu Bolong** (p61), which is a great scene year-round. Inland amid a maze of too-narrow lanes, you'll find creative cafes, trendy restaurants and appealing shops.

❸
NUSA LEMBONGAN ⏱ 1 DAY

Take a day trip across the waves from the fast boat dock at **Sanur** (p86) to **Nusa Lembongan** (p106). Go on an underwater adventure at **Manta Point** (p107) and **Pura Ped** (p109) and then hang out at **Pantai Jungutbatu** (p108).

↝ **Detour:** *Consider adding on time at Lembongan's much larger neighbour, **Nusa Penida** (p112). Take in the amazing vistas from its cliffs and trek down to one of its hidden beaches.*

FROM LEFT: BMPHOTOGRAPHER/SHUTTERSTOCK ©, PRATANDA N RESPATI/SHUTTERSTOCK ©, KJERSTI JOERGENSEN/SHUTTERSTOCK ©

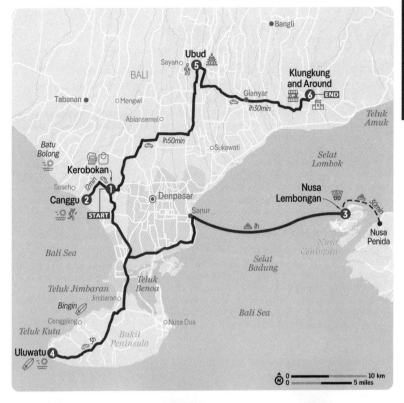

④ ULUWATU ⏱ 1 DAY

Starting at **Jimbaran** (p100, pictured), there are beautiful beaches at the end of small roads all along the west coast of the **Bukit Peninsula** (p104), all the way to the sacred temple of **Uluwatu** (p96). Swaths of Bali's best sand edge the rocky coast. Some fine coves such as **Bingin** (p105) can be reached after hiking down a cliff face. The surfing is superb.

⑤ UBUD ⏱ 2 DAYS

Spend two full days in and around **Ubud** (p122) before heading out on a day trip. To spoil yourself, stay in one of Ubud's many hotels with views across rice fields. Visit a **spa** (p134) or **yoga studio** (p136), then try one of the myriad great restaurants. At night, you'll be captivated by dance performances (p126, pictured). Go on a tour and walk along the rice fields (p128).

⑥ KLUNGKUNG AND AROUND ⏱ 1 DAY

Take a day trip from Ubud to the palace ruins and market at **Klungkung** (p158). Then go south to the volcanic beaches along the east coast. Stop at **Pantai Lebih** (p163), which has a temple and glittering sand. Head north to **Pura Dalem Penunggekan** (p164) and **Pura Kehen** (p164) in Bangli. Next, loop west and back down through **Gianyar** (p161) to feast at the night market (pictured).

WHEN **TO GO**

There's no bad time to visit Bali, Lombok and Nusa Tenggara – there's always a dry place in rainy season and a quiet place in high season.

Being tropical, when it rains in Indonesia, the downfalls are usually only intense for a short while and are not typically widespread: if it's raining in Ubud, it may not be raining in Canggu.

Overall, Bali's shoulder season (April–June; September–October) is a wonderful time to travel. The months of May, June and September experience the best weather (drier, less humid). And don't write off the low season (January–April; October–November), as fewer crowds are a real plus.

Strategies for High Season

High season in Bali and the Gilis is July, August and the Christmas holidays. To a lesser extent, this also applies to the popular beach towns in Lombok, and Labuan Bajo in Flores. Accommodation rates increase and hotels are booked far ahead of time, as are the best restaurants. To beat the high costs, travel to areas other than those mentioned above, make your plans as early as possible and shop around.

⊚ I LIVE HERE

THE JOY OF THE DRY SEASON

Idriss is a hiking and trekking guide in west Bali (WhatsApp +62 823 4018 5768)

Some parts of Bali are crowded, like in the south. But most of the island is more natural. Even if so much is brown and there are only a few leaves on the trees, I like the dry season because it allows me to see so many more animals, including some of the over 300 species of birds – though the rainy season does mean that everything is lush.

BALI'S SURF SEASONS

In the dry season, Bali's west coast has the best breaks; this is also when Nusa Lembongan is at its best. In the rainy season (October–March), surf the eastern side of the island, from Nusa Dua to Padang Bai.

LEFT: LIGHTFIELD STUDIOS/SHUTTERSTOCK ©;
FAR RIGHT: COCOS.BOUNTY/SHUTTERSTOCK ©

Surfing, Nusa Dua (p102)

Weather through the year

JANUARY	**FEBRUARY**	**MARCH**	**APRIL**	**MAY**	**JUNE**
Ave. daytime max: **33°C**	Ave. daytime max: **33°C**	Ave. daytime max: **34°C**	Ave. daytime max: **34°C**	Ave. daytime max: **33°C**	Ave. daytime max: **31°C**
Days of rainfall: **27**	Days of rainfall: **22**	Days of rainfall: **20**	Days of rainfall: **9**	Days of rainfall: **8**	Days of rainfall: **6**

WHERE IT'S COLD(ER)

There are no true 'cold' spots. However, it can get a bit less balmy as you ascend to higher elevations. In Ubud, that simply means you don't need air-con at night. On the volcanoes, that means dawn trekking requires layers.

Essential Cultural Festivals

Nyepi (Day of Silence)
(p101) Nyepi celebrates the Balinese new year. It's marked by inactivity – a strategy to convince evil spirits that Bali is uninhabited. The island shuts down completely, including the airport. **usually around March**

Bau Nyale Festival (p232)
The ritual harvesting of *nyale* (sea worms) takes place near Lombok's Kuta. Celebrations carry on until the dawn.
February or March

Pasola (p303) Held in West Sumbanese villages, this tournament between two teams of spear-wielding horsemen is an extravagant harvest festival. **February and March**

Galungan and Kuningan
Galungan celebrates the death of the legendary tyrant Mayadenawa. Celebrations culminate with the Kuningan festival, when the Balinese thank the gods. Villages celebrate in grand style. **once or twice each year, depending on the 210-day Balinese calendar**

I LIVE HERE

THE BEAUTY OF THE RAINY SEASON

Sang Ketut Rai Wibawa, Ubud resident and cofounder of Bali Silent Retreat

I come from the Bangli area – in the lush central area of Bali – known for its rivers, temples and rice terraces. Bali's soul is linked to water. During the rainy season, rivers and waterfalls are at their peak and the land is alive with the sound of running water. It's beautiful to go out into all this green.

Waterfall near Ubud

The Biggest Events

Bali Arts Festival (p92) The premier event on Bali's cultural calendar. Held in Denpasar, the festival features traditional dances as the village-based groups compete fiercely for local pride. **mid-June to mid-July**

Bali Spirit Festival (p131) A hugely popular yoga, dance and music festival. There are more than 100 workshops, yoga classes and live music. **usually May**

Ubud Writers & Readers Festival (p131) One of Asia's premier literary events, featuring scores of writers from around the world in a celebration of writing – especially that which touches on Bali. **October**

Indonesian Independence Day
Celebrated across the nation, 17 August 1945 is when Indonesia declared its independence from the Dutch. Flags fly high, traffic is snarled by processions, and lots of fireworks are shot off. **17 August**

THE SUNNIEST BEACHES

All of the beaches across Bali, Lombok and Nusa Tenggara are the sunniest, really! There are no meaningful regional variations. If you absolutely can't abide by any rain, stick to the dry season (April–September). Otherwise, your main concern is having enough sunscreen.

JULY	**AUGUST**	**SEPTEMBER**	**OCTOBER**	**NOVEMBER**	**DECEMBER**
Ave. daytime max: **30°C**	Ave. daytime max: **30°C**	Ave. daytime max: **31°C**	Ave. daytime max: **34°C**	Ave. daytime max: **33°C**	Ave. daytime max: **33°C**
Days of rainfall: **4**	Days of rainfall: **4**	Days of rainfall: **8**	Days of rainfall: **12**	Days of rainfall: **16**	Days of rainfall: **22**

LEFT: COCOS BOUNTY/SHUTTERSTOCK ©; FAR RIGHT: CINEMATIC/ALAMY STOCK PHOTO ©

Balangan Beach (p104)

GET PREPARED FOR BALI, LOMBOK & NUSA TENGGARA

Useful things to load in your bag, your ears and your brain.

Clothes & Gear

T-shirts and shorts To keep you cool in Bali and the Gilis.

Something stylish For nights out in south Bali.

Waterproof jacket Rain can always happen.

Warm layers For high-altitude trekking.

Hiking sandals For countryside walks.

Hiking boots For mountain and volcano treks.

Modest clothes For mosque visits (and in conservative parts of Lombok and Nusa Tenggara) wear long pants/skirts and shirts that fully cover shoulders. In Bali, temple attendants have sarongs available.

Post-beach cover-ups Swimwear is only for the beach.

Modest swimwear Needed in parts of Lombok and Nusa Tenggara.

Manners

Places of worship Remove shoes, and dress modestly when visiting mosques; wear a sash and sarong at Bali's temples.

Body language Don't display affection in public or talk with your hands on your hips.

Clothing Avoid showing a lot of skin. Don't go topless on the beach if you're a woman.

Photography Before taking photos of someone, ask – or mime – for approval.

Insect spray and sunscreen Essential but can be hard to find; buy before you fly.

Small umbrella It might rain.

A water bottle For refilling.

📖 READ

Ramamayana (Valmiki; date unknown) This epic is central to Hinduism. It underpins many Balinese traditions, especially dance.

Island of Bali (Miguel Covarrubias; 1937) The classic work on Bali and its culture remains stunningly relevant today.

Secrets of Bali: Fresh Light on the Morning of the World (Jonathan Copeland & Ni Wayan Murni; 2010) About Bali, its people and its traditions.

Eat, Pray, Love (Elizabeth Gilbert; 2007) This bestseller lures believers to Bali every year, hoping to capture the book's magic.

Words

Bahasa Indonesia
'Salam' Hello.
'Selamat tinggal' Goodbye, if you're the one leaving.
'Selamat jalan' Goodbye, if you're the one staying.
'Apa kabar?' How are you?
'Kabar baik, Anda bagaimana?' I'm fine, and you?
'Permisi' Excuse me.
'Maaf' Sorry.
'Silahkan' Please.
'Terima kasih' Thank you.
'Kembali' You're welcome.
'Ya' Yes.
'Tidak' No.
'Bapak' Mr/Sir.
'Ibu' Ms/Mrs.
'Nona' Miss.
'Siapa nama Anda?' What's your name?
'Nama saya...' My name is...
'Bisa berbicara Bahasa Inggris?' Do you speak English?
'Saya tidak mengerti' I don't understand.

Balinese
'Kenken kabare?' How are you?
'Matur suksma' Thank you.
'Sire wastene?' What's your name?
'Adan tiange...' My name is...
'Tiang sing ngerti' I don't understand.
'Ne ape adane di Bali?' What do you call this in Balinese?
'Kije jalan lakar kel...?' Which is the way to...?

Sasak
'Tampak asih' Thank you.
'Saik aranm side?' What's your name?
'Arankah aku...' My name is...
'Endek ngerti' I don't understand.
'Pire ajin sak iyak?' How much is this?
'Lamun lek..., embe eak langantah?' Which is the way to...?

▶ WATCH

The Act of Killing (Joshua Oppenheimer; 2013; pictured) Documentary about the 1965 slaughter of accused Communist sympathisers in Indonesia (including Bali).

Cowboys in Paradise (Amit Virmani; 2011) Highly entertaining documentary about the male gigolos working in south Bali.

Ring of Fire: An Indonesian Odyssey (Lorne & Lawrence Blair; 1999) Five-part documentary that follows two brothers travelling across Bali and nearby islands.

The More Things Change (Gerry Lopez; 2017) Surfer and actor Gerry Lopez focuses on the legendary breaks at Uluwatu.

🎧 LISTEN

NOW! Bali Podcast (Now! Bali; ongoing) Excellent show that covers various aspects of Balinese culture, such as calendars, temples and dance.

Ancient Order of Bali (Damn Interesting; 2023) Absorbing and beautifully produced episode that explains Bali's *subak* system of rice-field irrigation.

Mawar Putih (Inul Daratista; 2017) Popular song from the star from east Java. Hugely popular and controversial for her suggestive performances and lyrics.

Sunset Di Tanah Anarki (Superman Is Dead; 2013) From the band that got their start in Kuta. Now famous across the world and known for their environmental crusades.

TRIP PLANNER

WHERE TO STAY IN SOUTH BALI

When booking accommodation in south Bali, be careful where you book. What looks good on a booking site may disappoint when you discover it's in a location you didn't want. Thankfully, it's easy to avoid.

Ayana Resort and Rock Bar (p101)

The Lowdown

MISLEADING LOCATIONS

As tourist numbers in Bali have exploded, so have the number of chain hotels. The boom in the construction of large hotels in Kuta, Legian, Seminyak, Kerobokan and Canggu is changing the area's character in fundamental ways, especially as the many cheap and cheerful family-run spots are pushed out.

While some of these hotels are appearing in traditionally popular areas of south Bali, not far from the beaches and nightlife, scores more are opening far from the areas visitors consider desirable. Many chains have properties in both appealing and unappealing areas, and it's easy to get misled about their actual location, especially on booking websites. In the tradition of real estate agents everywhere, 'Seminyak' is now the address used for hotels deep in Denpasar. Note that most of these issues also apply to villas, which are being built *everywhere*.

DO YOUR RESEARCH

The good news is that with enlightened shopping, you can usually find good deals in the most appealing parts of south Bali, and often you can end up at a small or family-run guesthouse with oodles more charm and character than a generic cheap hotel. Or you may find yourself at some creative, charming boutique property or villa.

FINDING GREAT LOCATIONS IN SOUTH BALI

Carefully consider the following when choosing your accommodation:

Kuta–Kerobokan Strip
● Anything west of the Jl Legian–Jl Seminyak–Jl Kerobokan spine will be close to beaches and nightlife.
● East of the spine, things begin to get inconvenient fast: there will be less to walk to, beaches can be far and taxis hard to come by.
● Jl Ngurah Rai Bypass and Jl Sunset are both noisy, traffic-clogged streets that lack charm and are hard to cross – many chain hotels are located right on these unpleasant thoroughfares.

● East of Jl Ngurah Rai Bypass and Jl Sunset, you are deep into Denpasar's uninteresting hinterlands.

Canggu Area
● Watch out for accommodation far from beaches. Walking (and driving) can be a chore on roads hostile to pedestrians.

Bukit Peninsula
● Ensure there's beach access; at cliffside locations such as Bingin, check how far the ocean is from your room.

Sanur
● Jl Ngurah Rai Bypass should be the absolute western border of your room hunt.

CATWALKPHOTOS/SHUTTERSTOCK ©

Canggu (p52)

Navigate Bali's Traffic

Bali traffic can be horrendous in the south, with traffic jams stretching as far as Ubud to the north, Padang Bai to the east and Gilimanuk to the west. As bad as it is, there *are* ways to navigate it without worsening the problem.

Going Nowhere

A surfer sets out from her house in Canggu for a day on the breaks at Uluwatu – a 37km journey. Two hours later, she's barely halfway there. After a 10-hour flight, honeymooners thrilled to reach Bali end up stalled for an hour trying to drive the 5km to their hotel.

These are just two of the scenarios that bedevil residents and visitors to Bali every day. The Canggu area is Ground Zero for everything that's wrong – a lack of roads and public transport, too-narrow thoroughfares, a massive influx of travellers, and too many people trying to get around. In addition, the millions of people who visit this small island every year usually use their own wheels and taxis, only adding to the traffic filling the roads.

Difficult Remedies

Solutions are complicated: Bali's reverence for private property makes it difficult for the government to acquire it for road construction; ideas for tramways and subway systems are floated but have yet to materialise; a new toll road *is* being built between Denpasar and Gilimanuk but has encountered delays; rising numbers of travellers coming to Bali every year choke up already-busy roads; and attempts at quick solutions mean pathways through rice fields get paved and are soon covered in traffic trying to navigate narrow byways.

In the meantime, the best strategies for dealing with Bali's traffic are to expect it, don't fret and try to be patient – remember that you only have to deal with the traffic for the duration of your trip, unlike the Balinese, for whom it's a little more long-term; live local, stay where you want to be, and visit what's within walking distance. Also try to keep travel to realistic timelines, maybe turning that day trip into an overnighter or weekender.

TOP TIPS

If you're going to Nusa Dua, Sanur or Ubud from the airport, ask your driver to use the toll road, bypassing the worst traffic. If they're reluctant to use the road because they don't want to pay the fare, offer to pay it yourself.

Traffic in Ubud centre can be unmoving, especially at lunchtime. Time trips outside the hours of 11am and 4pm, and try to get dropped off and picked up on the outskirts and walk in.

There's an unheralded pedestrian highway from Canggu south to Kuta: the beach. You can easily cover a long distance – and enjoy lovely views.

Babi guling

THE FOOD SCENE

A great reason to travel to Bali, Lombok and Nusa Tenggara is the food: the variety and quality here are hard to beat.

Across the popular regions of Bali, you'll find every cuisine, in every style, and for every budget. In Lombok and Nusa Tenggara, the selection is much more narrow.

Bali caters to all taste buds. The culinary centres of Seminyak, Kerobokan, Canggu and Ubud boast diverse eateries, including the hottest and best restaurants. Cafes and warungs (food stalls) across the island serve exceptional Balinese and Indonesian food in simple surroundings. There's also a profusion of creative, organic and healthy eateries. Balinese cuisine, whether truly Balinese or influenced by the rest of Indonesia and Asia, draws from the bounty of fresh local foods and is rich with spices and flavours. You can savour this fare at roadside eateries and top-end restaurants.

Food in Nusa Tenggara isn't quite as creative, but you'll have no trouble sourcing plenty of tasty meals, and more traditional options. In Lombok and the Gilis (which have their fair share of new-agey healthy-eating options), opt for simply prepared, freshly caught fish and seafood.

Flavours of Bali

Compared with elsewhere in Indonesia, Balinese food is more pungent and lively, with a multitude of layers making up a dish. A meal will contain six flavours (sweet, sour, spicy, salty, bitter and astringent), all of which stimulate the senses.

There's a predominance of ginger, chilli and coconut. The biting combination of fresh galangal (Thai ginger) and turmeric

Best Local Dishes	NASI CAMPUR	NASI GORENG	AYAM TALIWANG
	The great Balinese meal – centred on rice, with many small dishes.	Fried rice in a mix of meat and vegetables; can be spicy.	Roast chicken served with tomato, chilli and lime dip.

is matched by the heat of raw chillies; the complex sweetness of palm sugar, tamarind and shrimp paste; and the clean, fresh flavours of lemongrass, musk lime, kaffir lime leaves and coriander seeds.

Rice is the staple dish and is revered in Bali as a gift of life from the gods. It is served generously with every meal – anything not served with rice is considered a *jaja* (snack). Rice acts as the medium for the various fragrant, spiced foods – almost like condiments – that accompany it, with many ingredients chopped finely to complement the dry, fluffy grains.

Bali's Signature Dish

In Bali, food is not just about enjoyment and sustenance. Like everything here, it is an intrinsic part of the island's many daily rituals and a major aspect of ceremonies that honour the gods. The most revered dish is *babi guling*, presented during important ceremonies.

Babi guling is the quintessential Bali experience. A whole pig is stuffed with chilli, turmeric, ginger, galangal, shallots, garlic, coriander seeds and aromatic leaves, basted in more turmeric (and coconut oil), and skewered on a wooden spit over an open fire. You can enjoy *babi guling* at stands, warungs and cafes across Bali.

Nasi goreng

Lombok's Sasak Cuisine

Most of Lombok's Sasak people are Muslim, and their mains feature fish, chicken, vegetables and rice. The fact that *lombok* means 'chilli' in Bahasa Indonesia makes sense, because the Sasaks like their food spicy.

Indonesia's Meat-Free Fare

Tofu and tempeh are part of Indonesia's staple diet, and many of the tastiest dishes are vegetarian. In trendier parts of the region, there are numerous vegetarian, vegan and healthy-food cafes and restaurants.

MARKETS: FESTIVALS OF FOOD

Pasar (markets) offer a glimpse of the variety and freshness of local produce in the region, often brought from the mountains within a day or two of harvesting. The atmosphere is vibrant, with baskets loaded with fresh fruit – sample the range in Kerobokan on Intrepid Travel's **street-food tour** (p69). These markets offer mounds of vegetables, flowers, spices and varieties of red, black, yellow and white rice. There are cages of live chickens, trays of dead chickens, freshly slaughtered pigs, and sardines, eggs, cakes, offerings, and stalls selling *es cendol* (a colourful iced-coconut drink), *bubur* (rice porridge) and *nasi campur*.

There's no refrigeration, so things come in small packages. Bargaining is expected. Want a picnic? All sorts of pre-cooked food is sold ready-to-go, often in banana leaves.

Pasar Badung (p94), Denpasar

BABI GULING	SATE LILIT	SATE (SATAY)	GADO GADO	PISENG GORENG
Spiced, roasted pork is the quintessential Balinese food experience.	Fragrant combination of minced fish, chicken or pork with lemongrass.	Marinated meat grilled on a skewer, served with sauces.	Tofu, tempeh and steamed vegetables with boiled egg and peanut sauce.	Fried bananas prepared myriad ways, served from breakfast to dessert.

Specialities

Sambal

An essential part of any meal, *sambal*, the ubiquitous spicy condiment, comes in endless variations. Below are the main ones (ignoring the generically sweet commercially bottled gloop):

Sambal bajak Fried tomato-based sauce filled with crushed chillies, palm sugar and shallots.

Sambal balado Sauteed chillis, shallots, garlic and tomatoes.

Sambal matah Raw Balinese sambal made from thinly sliced shallots, tiny chillies, shrimp paste and lemongrass. Divine.

Sambal pelecing A Lombok *sambal* with hot chillies in tomato base.

Sambal taliwang Popular Lombok *sambal* made with peppers, garlic and shrimp paste.

Drinks

Jamu This ubiquitous health tonic is popular across the archipelago and was recognised by UNESCO as part of Indonesia's cultural heritage in 2023. No two versions are

Jamu

alike: ingredients can range from tamarind to bark to flowers to eggs.

Bintang Indonesia's national brand of lager is synonymous with beer. In Bali, craft breweries include Black Sand and South+East.

Wine In Bali, Hattan and Sababay wineries produce some nice drinkable wines.

Arak At social gatherings and ceremonies, Balinese might enjoy traditional *arak* (colourless, distilled palm wine). It's lately had a renaissance, and several producers are exploring the lost art of making quality *arak*.

Coffee Grown in Bali and elsewhere in Indonesia, coffee is widely served everywhere.

MEALS OF A LIFETIME

Shrimpis Diners rave about the seafood meals at this buzzy dining spot in Seminyak that has people booking far in advance. (p65)

Tanaman The famous club on the beach at Potato Head in Kerobokan offers an exceptional (and imaginative) plant-based set menu.

Locavore NXT Latest incarnation of the ground-breaking high-end food temple in Ubud. (p128)

Bali Asli Ultra-fresh *nasi campur* and spectacular views over rice terraces are on offer at this hybrid restaurant and cooking school in west Bali's Amlapura. (p177)

Dapur Bali Mula Fabulous Balinese lunches and dinners by famed Chef Yudi on Bali's northeast coast. (p182)

THE YEAR IN FOOD

RAINY SEASON (OCTOBER–MARCH)

Tropical fruit delights – rambutan, dragon fruit (pictured), salak, mangosteen, pineapple, banana, mango, guava and lychee – are lush and abundant. In October, your nose will tell you that it's durian season as the huge, odoriferous (and beloved) fruit fills market stalls. Vendors hawk the nubby orbs in town centres and along roadsides.

DRY SEASON (APRIL–SEPTEMBER)

Enjoy year-round staples like papaya (pictured) and coconut. April ushers in the Ubud Food Festival, a three-day event showcasing the diversity and innovation of Indonesian cuisine. The end of the rice-harvesting season is celebrated in Bali from 1 May to 30 June, when *subak* (the complex system of rice-field irrigation) towns raise flags, erect shrines and prepare traditional regional dishes in honour of Dewi Sri, the goddess of rice and fertility.

Traditional food, Bali

HOW TO...

Eat & Drink

Meals in Indonesia don't have the same social role as meals elsewhere. On Bali, for instance, there are already so many reasons throughout the day for friends and family to gather that meals are simply a reason to eat as opposed to an opportunity to bring people to the same table.

Indonesians usually eat with their right hand, which is used to give and receive all good things. The left hand deals with unpleasant, sinister elements (such as ablutions). It's customary to wash your hands before eating, even if you use a spoon and fork; use the sinks outside the restrooms to do this.

When to Eat

Lunch is the big meal of the day, as it provides the chance to break up the day's toil. It's also when food is freshest. The day might start with a cup of rich, sweet black coffee and a few sweet *jaja* at the market: colourful temple cakes, glutinous rice cakes, boiled bananas, *pisang goreng* (fried bananas) and *kelopon* (green rice-flour balls with a palm-sugar filling).

The famous *bubur injin* (black rice pudding with palm sugar, grated coconut and coconut milk), which is on most restaurant dessert menus, is actually a breakfast dish. A variation available at the morning market is the nutty *bubur kacang hijau* (green mung-bean pudding),

fragrantly enriched with ginger and served warm with coconut milk.

The household or warung (food stall) cook usually finishes preparing the day's dishes mid-morning, so lunch is served around 11am. Leftovers are eaten for dinner. Dessert is a rarity and mostly for special occasions; it usually consists of fresh fruit or delicious gelato-style coconut ice-cream.

Of course, for visitors there are few, if any, rules. Indonesians are used to the seemingly inexplicable habits of foreigners and handle most requests with aplomb. Traditional mealtimes are honoured, although you'll be hard-pressed to find many kitchens open late.

WHERE TO EAT

Restaurants Bali is a magnet for talented chefs, as the cost of doing business is low and the potential rewards high. South Bali and Ubud are renowned for casual, innovative eateries.

Cafes There are Western-style cafes all over Bali, Lombok and the Gilis. Coffee is often made from local beans.

Warungs Local eateries serve great-tasting fare on a budget. In Nusa Tenggara, the terms warung and *rumah makan* are often interchangeable.

Fast-food vendors All residents gather round simple food stalls in *malam* (markets) and *pasar malam* (night markets). On village streets, wave down *pedagang* (mobile traders) for snacks.

ELIZAVETA GALITCKAIA/SHUTTERSTOCK ©

Cyclist, rice fields (p128), Ubud

THE **OUTDOORS**

This region is an incredible place to get outside and play: enjoy exceptional diving, surfing and hikes through rice fields or up volcanoes.

The azure rollers of the Indian Ocean build momentum on their journey from the Antarctic, so it's no surprise that these coastlines have some truly spectacular waves. Scuba diving and snorkelling are huge draws in Bali and Nusa Tenggara, both of which are encircled by magnificent reefs that are easily accessed from the beach in many places. A walk or trek to one of the myriad waterfalls, virescent rice fields or rumbling volcanoes is a trip highlight for many.

Surfing

Surfing kick-started tourism in Bali in the 1960s. Many Balinese love to surf, and the grace of traditional dancing is said to influence their style. Surfers – local and visiting – buzz around on motorbikes with board racks, looking for the next great break. Waves blown out? Another spot is just five minutes away.

Swells come from the Indian Ocean, so the surf is on the southern side of the island. In the dry season (roughly April to September), the west coast has the best breaks. In the wet season, surf the eastern side of the island, from Nusa Dua around to Padangbai.

Lombok also has some superb surfing and the breaks are generally uncrowded. The giant bay at Gerupuk has multiple breaks, so there's always some wave action no matter the weather or tide.

Big Thrills

KITESURFING
Head to the Ekas peninsula (p235) in southwestern Lombok and to Pantai Lakey (p285) in East Sumbawa.

WILDLIFE WATCHING
Spot deer, reptiles, monkeys and hundreds of bird species, including the striking Bali starling, at West Bali National Park (p209).

CYCLING
Coast downhill through the lush countryside amidst the villages and rice terraces north of Ubud (p145).

FAMILY ADVENTURES

Hit the beach at **Kuta** (p72) where surf schools abound and at **Sanur** where there are mellow waves for swimming. **Thrill underwater** at **Pulau Menjangan** (p210) in north Bali for the best snorkelling in the region.

Splash yourself silly at Tuban's **Waterbom Park** (p76), a huge aquatic playground with water slides and features. **Explore the ancient water palace** at **Tirta Empul** (p144), north of Ubud, where kids love the Indiana Jones–like pools.

Play in the sand at **Gili Air** (p264), a delightful mix of laid-back vibes and fun-filled amenities. **Enjoy gentle waves** at **Blue Lagoon Beach** (p170) on the far side of Padang Bai's eastern headland.

Off the beaten track in Nusa Tenggara, Sumbawa's southwest coast has white beaches with renowned surf, while the southeast waves are year-round surf magnets. South of Maluk is Supersuck, consistently rated as the best left in the world.

Stunning Pantai Nemberala on remote Rote island is home to the world-renowned T-Land break.

Diving & Snorkelling

With their warm water, extensive coral reefs and abundant marine life, Bali and Nusa Tenggara offer excellent diving and snorkelling adventures. Reliable dive schools and operators throughout the region (particularly at Pemuteran and Tulamben in Bali, in the Gilis, and in Labuan Bajo in Flores) can train complete beginners or arrange challenging trips that will satisfy the most experienced divers.

Snorkelling gear is available near all the most accessible spots; bring some along when you're out exploring the less-visited parts of the coasts. Dive operators can arrange trips that include snorkellers to the main dive sites in their regions. Distances can be long, so it's better to sleep relatively close to your diving or snorkelling destination.

Walking & Hiking

You could travel through this region for a year and still not see all the islands have to offer, but their relatively small size means that you can nibble off a bit at a time, especially as day hikes and treks are easily arranged. Guides can help you summit volcanoes such as Gunung Batur (p193), while tour companies will take you to remote regions and emerald-green valleys.

You can access much on your own. Bali is very walkable, especially around Ubud, the Sidemen area and Munduk. In busy Seminyak or Canggu, you can walk to the beach, pick a direction and just take off. No matter where you're staying, ask for recommendations and set off for discoveries and adventures. Note, you'll need good boots for mountain treks and solid sandals for walks.

DUDAREV MIKHAIL/SHUTTERSTOCK ©

Hiking Gunung Batur (p193)

FREEDIVING
On Bali's far east coast, the Amed region (p179) is a base for freediving, with excellent operators and schools.

TREKKING
On Lombook, massive Gunung Rinjani (p246) has several routes to the top.

YOGA
There are many ways to relax in Bali, especially in Ubud (p134) and Canggu (p55). The Gilis (p255) are good too.

NATIONAL PARKS
Climbing, trekking, hiking, mangrove-exploring and advanced diving are all possible at West Bali National Park (p209).

ACTION AREAS

Where to find Bali, Lombok and Nusa Tenggara's best outdoor activities.

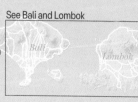

See Bali and Lombok

INDIAN OCEAN

Bond

Extreme Adventures

① Gunung Abang (p194)
② Gunung Agung (p168)
③ Gunung Rinjani (p246)
④ Gunung Batur (p193)
⑤ Amed (p178)

Surfing

① Kuta (p72)
② Batu Bolong (p52)
③ Uluwatu (p96)
④ Pantai Ketewel (p163)
⑤ Tanjung Desert (p251)
⑥ Gerupuk (p233)
⑦ Selong Belanak (p233)

Walking/Hiking

① Ubud (p122)
② Danau Tamblingan (p191)
③ Munduk (p188)
④ Sidemen (p165)
⑤ Tirta Gangga (p177)
⑥ West Bali National Park (p209)
⑦ Sendang Gile (p243)

Bali and Lombok

Flores Sea

Labuan Bajo

Golo Torongkoe

Pota

Wolo Meza

Kolisia

Talibura

Sagu

Pulau Marisa

Poco Dedeng

Pangga

Flores

Olaia

Lewoleba

Komodo National Park

Seso

Roa

Wolo Hangahera

Tapowolo

G. Sirung

Golo Mori

Repi

Bamo

Kotadirumali

Ili Berapun

INDONESIA

Sawu Sea

TIMOR-LESTE

Naikliu

mbolaka

Sumba

Waingapu

Kapan

ibakul

Melolo

Taemaman

G. Ngadu Langgi

G. Fatuleu

Timur

Teluk Kupang

Oesao

Taman Nasional Laiwangi Wanggameti

Baing

Akle

Kupang

Nemberala

Rote

INDIAN OCEAN

Snorkelling/Diving

1. Tulamben (p181)
2. Pulau Menjangan (p210)
3. Nusa Lembongan (p106)
4. Gili Air (p264)
5. Gili Meno (p261)
6. Komodo National Park (p282)
7. Alor Archipelago (p295)

Beach

1. Batu Bolong (p52)
2. Thomas Beach (p98)
3. Jungutbatu (p108)
4. Pantai Pasir Putih (p173)
5. Selong Belanak (p233)
6. Tanjung Aan (p230)

0   100 km
0   50 miles

BALI, LOMBOK & NUSA TENGGURA

THE GUIDE

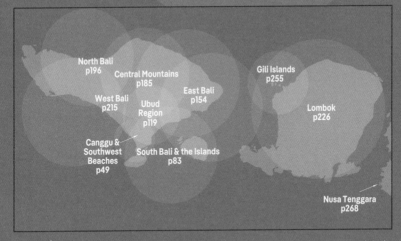

Nusa Tenggara
p268

North Bali
p196

Central Mountains
p185

East Bali
p154

West Bali
p215

Ubud
Region
p119

Gili Islands
p255

Lombok
p226

Canggu &
Southwest
Beaches
p49

South Bali & the Islands
p83

Nusa Tenggara
p268

Chapters in this section are organised by hubs and their surrounding areas. We see the hub as your base in the destination, where you'll find unique experiences, local insights, insider tips and expert recommendations. It's also your gateway to the surrounding area, where you'll see what and how much you can do from there.

Macaque on a temple statue
SONJA MACDONALD/SHUTTERSTOCK ©

Above: Seminyak, p63; Right: turtle hatchling

Canggu & Southwest Beaches

BEACHES AND A BLISSFUL HOLIDAY VIBE

Bali's dynamic southwest coastline draws the crowds with exhilarating surf breaks, tranquil spas, cute cafes, luxury boutiques and world-class restaurants.

Constantly busy and pulsing with life, the southwestern fringe of Bali's coastline – a generous arc of wide sand sweeping northwest from the airport – is the much-loved playground on the Island of the Gods. It's a region that never sleeps; where DJs at the world's most exciting beach bars spin beats late into the night, and surfers rise before dawn to ride Bali's most popular waves. The beaches, peppered with umbrellas that create an enticing kaleidoscope of colours, are the gateway to a carefree holiday where sunshine and palm trees charm languid beachgoers and gorgeous spas lull guests into a state of bliss.

With its cheeky hipster spirit, constantly evolving Canggu (pronounced *chan-goo*)

beckons surfers and digital nomads who are drawn to a scene that is as alluring by day as it is by night, when crowds transition from the beach clubs and creative cafes to trendy restaurants and sultry cocktail bars.

In Seminyak, sophistication takes centre stage as boutiques, luxury resorts and laid-back beachfront bars define the scene; the emphasis is always on fun, and this is where the well-heeled come to play. Meanwhile Kuta, a perennial favourite, remains the casual beach hub it's been for decades. While Seminyak is more cocktails and beanbags, Kuta is Bintang beers and plastic stools; it's here where laid-back surf culture meets frenetic nightlife, and the air is infused with an infectious, easy-going spirit.

YKHONGKP/SHUTTERSTOCK ©

THE MAIN AREAS

CANGGU
Cafes, cocktails and hipster hangouts.
p52

SEMINYAK
Sunsets, spas and world-class restaurants.
p63

KUTA
Beaches, surf and a carefree vibe.
p72

Find Your Way

While the coastline of this area stretches only 12km from Bali's airport, the roads around here are the island's most congested. Know that it could easily take an hour to travel 10km in a car.

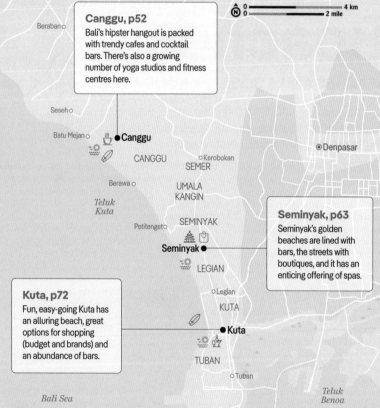

Canggu, p52
Bali's hipster hangout is packed with trendy cafes and cocktail bars. There's also a growing number of yoga studios and fitness centres here.

Seminyak, p63
Seminyak's golden beaches are lined with bars, the streets with boutiques, and it has an enticing offering of spas.

Kuta, p72
Fun, easy-going Kuta has an alluring beach, great options for shopping (budget and brands) and an abundance of bars.

MOTORBIKE

Motorbikes – everything from small mopeds to retro cafe racers – are widely available for rent, but the congested roads can be overwhelming for inexperienced drivers. Ride-hailing apps Gojek and Grab make for a safer, affordable and convenient way to travel.

PRIVATE CAR

Taxis are common, and hotels will assist if you want to hire a car with a driver. Travel time is slow and only a worthwhile option if you plan to go beyond this coastal region.

Surfing lessons (p52), Canggu

Plan Your Time

This is beach-holiday heaven, so soak up the cosmopolitan vibes and indulge in the cafes and beach clubs before connecting with Bali's culture elsewhere on the island.

Pressed for Time

Spend a thrilling morning at **Waterbom** (p76), then head across to the beach for a **surf lesson** (p72). Afterwards, release a **baby turtle** (p75), and then take a **long beach walk** (p80) before you settle on the sand to **watch the sunset** (p75). Turn your sights to Jl Legian and **shop for souvenirs after dark** (p75), then **party up a storm** (p76).

A Week-Long Stay

Settle into Canggu life by sampling a selection of the neighbourhood's **cafes** (p58) and signing up for **fitness sessions** (p62) or **yoga classes** (p55). Kick off the morning with a **beach walk** (p61) before **brunch** (p54), fill your days with **surf sessions** (p52) and your nights at **live music venues** (p56) and **cocktail bars** (p55). Be sure to book in a few **spa treatments** (p56) too.

SEASONAL HIGHLIGHTS

JANUARY
Beach clubs organise huge New Year's Eve parties. The weeks after the Christmas holidays bring fewer tourists.

MARCH
Some hotels and resorts have deals for Nyepi (Bali's Day of Silence; p33) – a special time to be on the island.

AUGUST
The height of the dry season is a particularly lively time to immerse yourself in Canggu's party vibe and surf scene.

NOVEMBER
The start of the rainy season means fewer tourists and lower prices. Rain will normally be short and sharp.

Canggu

HIP VIBE | CAFE CULTURE | SURF BREAKS

GETTING AROUND

The traffic around Canggu is notorious; on Jl Raya Canggu it will often take an hour to travel 10km in a car. By far, your quickest option to get from A to B in the Canggu area is to use a scooter from ride-hailing apps Grab or Gojek – and if you want to go further (say, to Ubud or Uluwatu), then hail one of their cars. Your hotel can also help you source a private car and driver, if you prefer. If you're going to rent your own scooter, it's best to take a scooter lesson first (see p57).

☑ TOP TIP

Beat the traffic (and work on your tan and fitness at the same time) by walking on the beach between Berawa, Canggu and Pererenan. You can then use Grab or Gojek to hail a scooter to take you to your destination.

To Bali old-timers, Canggu is still the new kid on the block, but this sprawling area has been carving out its reputation as Bali's premier beach town for about a decade. Back then, many considered its paddy-lined roads to be the wild west, but the rice fields are fast disappearing, and this once low-key coastline now has a unique cosmopolitan appeal all of its own. 'The Gu' challenges Seminyak's party zone status, boasting some of the world's most celebrated beach clubs, and there might be more hip cafes and eateries per capita here than anywhere else on the planet. Rebel child that it is, with its yoga studios and fitness centres, Canggu is making inroads into usurping Ubud's position as Bali's wellness capital. And, of course, there's the surf. Batu Bolong (often called Old Man's for the nearby iconic bar) might be Bali's most crowded break, thanks to its fairly forgiving longboarding waves.

Bali's Booming Beach Break

Surf Canggu's iconic waves

Batu Bolong might fall far short of Indonesia's finest reef-break waves but this beach break is arguably the most iconic longboarding wave in the country. Every hipster kook and nose-riding hotshot worth their salt will one day come here to catch a wave or two.

Known locally as Old Man's (for the super popular party venue a block back from the beach), Batu Bolong is a sand-bottom beach break with waves that tend to break far outside only to reform again, creating a slow, cruisy middle section (breaking left and right) that could be custom-designed for longboards. You can rent boards of all sizes on the beach – 50,000Rp for an hour and a half – and surf lessons are available from about 350,000Rp. **Mojosurf Camp** also runs intense courses that can include the full package with accommodation and transportation.

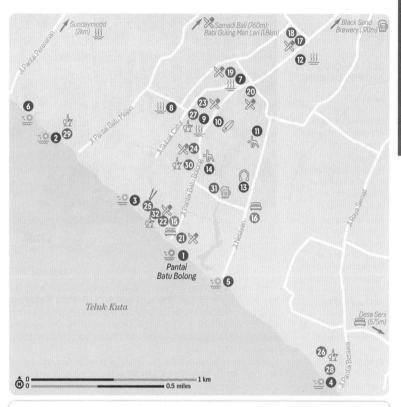

 EATING IN CANGGU: OUR PICKS

Varuna Warung
Traditional Indonesian fare – choose from the menu or Masakan Padang (buffet-style Padang cuisine). **$**

Yuki An elegant Japanese restaurant with beach views. The food at Yuki is superb, and there are delicious plant-based options, too. **$$**

Deus Cafe An absolute favourite in Canggu, the food at Deus is legendary – as is the adjacent Deus Ex Machina store. **$$**

Skool Kitchen This restaurant is based on the concept of 'primitive cooking, modern dining', and every dish served is touched by wood fire. **$$$**

BEST BEACHES AROUND CANGGU

Berawa
This wide, light-grey beach is a favourite with dog owners and sunset gazers.

Nelayan
Huts and fishing boats give relatively quiet Nelayan a distinctly local character.

Batu Bolong (p52)
Board shacks, warungs (food stalls) and umbrellas line the beach between Jl Nelayan and Jl Batu Bolong. Clustered at this busy surf spot is a collection of restaurants, including Old Man's and the Lawn.

Echo Beach
Watched over by lovely La Brisa beach club, Echo Beach boasts one of Bali's best surf spots. It's busy at sunset.

Pererenan (p62)
Relatively untouched and uncrowded (for now), with a handful of bars and warungs.

NICOLEEEEKM/SHUTTERSTOCK ©

Yoga practice

A Canggu surf experience needn't begin and end with the crowded Batu Bolong line-up, however. **Pantai Nelayan**, just half a kilometre to the east, is a favourite spot for kite-surfers (although not for beginners), but if you're learning regular surfing it could be worth visiting since the shore break is more unforgiving.

West from Batu Bolong you'll find a stretch of great waves leading up to **Munduk Catu Beach**. Here there are well-shaped waves both for longboarding and shortboard-ripping style, but it is ideally suited to more experienced surfers who are drawn by the steeper (sometimes barrelling) faces and who appreciate the fact that the fairly intimidating rocks keep crowds to an absolute minimum.

See Bali's Beaches from the Saddle

Go horse riding on Canggu's beaches

There's something irresistibly romantic about experiencing a new place from horseback, particularly when there's an end-less stretch of sand to ride on. Canggu's beaches are wonderful for this, and **Royal Sporthorse Bali** (horseridinginbali.com) has a stable of well-schooled and perfectly habituated horses that will carry you on a gentle ride along this coastline. The guides will lead you for the first half-kilometre stretch past bars,

EATING IN CANGGU: BEST BRUNCHES ———————————————— MAP p53

Avocado Factory Taking avocado toast to the next level, with options like avo pancake, avo cheese croissant and avo granola bowl. **$$**

Monsieur Spoon A popular French bakery and cafe, serving fresh and mouth-wateringly good handmade pastries. The croissants are exceptional. **$$**

Crate There's a casual warehouse vibe at Crate, where everything on the extensive brunch-focussed menu is under 60,000Rp. **$**

Buongiorno by Sa'Mesa An Italian bakery with a menu based on breads, paninis, pies and rolls. There's excellent coffee and vegan options, too. **$$**

cafes and hotels to Pantai Nelayan, and although you'll then pass busy Atlas and Finns (p60) beach clubs, the sand itself is relatively deserted so there is space for a trot or canter (depending entirely on abilities and tastes). Between their two properties (in Canggu and Nusa Dua) Royal Sporthorse Bali have more than 30 horses, so there is an animal suitable for all ages and abilities, from little Shetland and Welsh ponies through to medium-sized local horses and big powerful Danish and Dutch Warmbloods. The horses – as is usual – are typically more inspired to get into a higher gear after you turn at the halfway point of what is usually about a 4km route. An exhilarating canter along the empty waterline and across the shallow streams that run onto the beach might well be one of the highlights of your visit to Canggu.

Begin (or Deepen) Your Yoga Practice

Find a class that suits your vibe

Ubud might be revered as Bali's yoga heartland but manic Canggu doesn't fall too far behind, with its own growing offering of yoga studios. There is something for everyone here, from beginners to lifelong yogis, and hippies to hipsters. Near Pantai Nelayan, family-owned, permaculture-based **Serenity** is a down-to-earth yoga resort offering eight classes a day, including aerial yoga. Pop by for a class, workshop or wellness treatment (book all via the website), stay for a meal at Serenity's vegan restaurant, or check into the guesthouse and immerse yourself in yogic living.

You can't stay overnight at **Samadi Bali**, but you can spend all day there. This peaceful yoga and wellness centre (with a boutique and eco-conscious supermarket) on busy Jl Padang Linjong provides an opportunity to embark on a comprehensive wellness journey that will nourish both your body and mind. Up to 15 classes are held throughout the day, and Samadi also offers a series of retreat packages that include a one-day detox programme, which takes full advantage of the centre's plant-based restaurant. Every day different healers and therapists work from this dreamy, peaceful space.

From its breezy bamboo-covered rooftop location on Jl Nelayan, **Radiantly Alive** boasts urban views, so be sure to come for a sunset yoga class. Another popular space is the **Practice**, on Jl Pantai Batu Bolong. It might appear contemporary in style, but all classes here are rooted in traditional Hatha yoga. It's a calm, powerful and very grounded space. Classes range from Beginner's Hatha Yoga to Yin Yoga, and teacher training sessions are held here, too.

WHERE TO FIND BALI IN CANGGU

Canggu is a cosmopolitan, ever-changing neighbourhood that nowadays feels distinctly un-Balinese, but there is one very special enclave that stands as a bastion of tradition and culture. **Tugu Bali**, a hotel owned by an Indonesian art collector, offers a chance to connect with the history and traditions of the archipelago. Simply walking into the antique-filled property is an evocative journey into the Indonesia of old, and experiences like Balinese dance, cooking or *jamu*-making classes (*jamu* is a turmeric-based elixir), ceremonial dinners, and spa treatments rooted in beauty traditions offer a chance to connect with Balinese culture. Don't miss Bale Puputan, an extensive collection of artefacts from Bali's 1906 Puputan War with the Dutch (see p338).

DRINKING IN CANGGU: OUR PICKS

MAP p53

Barn This atmospheric British-style pub has 10 craft beers on tap and serves traditional pub fare to boot.

Lacalita Bar y Cocina A Mexican-inspired bar and restaurant with a reputation for serving Bali's best margaritas (there are eight to try on the menu).

Black Sand Brewery Craft beers are brewed on site and Black Sand's IPA, Kölsch, pilsner and ales are available on tap, along with 'guest taps'.

La Brisa This dreamy bohemian-style beach club has a good selection of wines, mocktails, cocktails, spirits, liqueurs and beers.

BEST SPAS AROUND CANGGU

Sundaymood
Designed to focus on wellness and recovery, Sundaymood uses private ice baths and infrared saunas to enhance healing and relaxation.

AMO Spa
As well as the usual spa treatments, luxurious AMO also offers IV therapy, body contouring, permanent makeup and 'pro-aging' packages.

Goldust
A signature treatment at this glamorous sanctuary is the indulgent 90-minute 24-karat gold facial (1,450,000Rp).

Ramaya Day Spa
One of the more affordable spas in the area, Ramaya is a brilliant option for massages (from 140,000Rp for an hour), as well as manis and pedis.

Espace
The aromatherapy therapeutic massages are quite sublime. Book a 'four hands massage' for added bliss.

BERNARDUS KHRISNANDA/SHUTTERSTOCK ©

Babi guling

Most studios provide mats and blocks, and you usually don't need to book a class in advance.

Feast on a Balinese Delicacy

What to expect from *babi guling*

Cafes in Bali's trendy traveller hubs are fast growing their offering of vegan dishes – but *babi guling* (spit-roasted suckling pig) remains an unapologetically carnivorous indulgence that sits as a firm favourite among the Balinese. It's an absolute delicacy on the island, and it's prepared with infusions of coriander seeds, turmeric, lemongrass and other herbs and spices. Many warungs specialise in *babi guling* (you'll recognise them from the image of the skewered pig that hangs outside), but **Babi Guling Men Lari** on Jl Bypass Tanah Lot is widely accepted by Canggu locals as one of the best in the area. The pork is prepared offsite but served as would be expected with steamed cassava leaves and rice, and a selection of meat from all parts of the pig. Crispy slices of heart, lung and skin, some crunchy crackling, tender meat, and more meat minced and prepared as satay. The folk at Men Lari don't hold back on the chilli either, so be sure to order *es jeruk* – fresh orange juice with ice.

 DRINKING IN CANGGU: BARS WITH LIVE MUSIC ———— MAP p53

Old Man's Almost on the beach at Batu Bolong, Old Man's – with its wide selection of drinks – is a favourite daytime eatery and after-dark party venue.

Lawn DJs rock the decks every day from 3pm until 10pm at this small but very chic beach club.

Baliwood Local bands take centre stage at this laid-back bar. There are open-mic nights, too.

Deus Cafe As hip as Canggu can get. Come here for live music; go home with a new haircut and fresh tattoo.

Beyond Canggu

Life slows down a little in Berawa and Pererenan, even though they're only a stone's throw from Canggu.

More a state of mind than a place, 'Canggu' has become a catch-all for the sprawling area that lies between Seminyak and Cemagi. In essence Berawa and Pererenan, which flank Canggu's central Batu Bolong area, are their own entities and offer some respite from Batu Bolong's busyness. Berawa, though, still loves to party and it's here along a road packed with laid-back cafes that you'll find the premier beach clubs Atlas (p55) and Finns (p60), which claim for themselves the titles of World's Best (Finns) and World's Biggest (Atlas). Further north, once sleepy Pererenan is today what Canggu was five years ago – the paddies are being drained and new hotels, shops and restaurants are constantly opening.

Places

North Canggu p57
Berawa p60
Pererenan p61

GETTING AROUND

Travelling by scooter is definitely your best bet and, as with the rest of the region, hailing a Gojek or Grab is by far the most convenient way to get around. Because the roads are quieter and more forgiving here, novice scooter drivers are more comfortable in these neighbourhoods (remember to wear a helmet), and apart from the heat there's nothing stopping you from walking from cafe to cafe, or to the shops and the beach.

North Canggu

TIME FROM CANGGU: **20 MINS**

Get Confident on the Roads

Taking a scooter lesson while on holiday might sound like an odd thing to do, but with the extreme traffic situation around the Canggu area it should be considered essential for anyone who wants to drive here, regardless of their driving experience. The roads are notoriously congested – scooters are usually nudged onto parts of the street that are crumbling and pot-holed – and the flow of traffic can be particularly overwhelming. From their quiet parking area about 20 minutes' drive inland from Pantai Batu Bolong, **Canggu Scooter Lessons** provide a valuable two-hour introduction to two-wheeling around the island. You'll be coached through the intricacies of driving a scooter, and will spend time getting to grips with making sharp turns, weaving around beacons, inclined stops and starts, and making emergency stops. After running through an explanation of the rules of the road, you'll then head out to drive through the streets, with your instructor sitting behind you. It's not only foreigners who come here for lessons; Indonesians from other islands come here too as they say driving in Canggu is not like driving in their own cities.

HELP ME PICK

Cafes Around Canggu

Canggu has an incredible density of cafes. In the 500m stretch from the beach up to popular Milk & Madu Beach Road on Jl Pantai Batu Bolong there are almost 20, and that's pretty typical of the whole Canggu area where, it seems, a new cafe opens almost every week. The scene is ever-changing and the locations are evergrowing, and experiencing this vast selection of eateries – whose decor is usually as appealing as the menus – is a highlight for many travellers.

Where to go for...

Cafes to work in

Zin Breezy and with large trees outside, this peaceful cafe has a free co-working space and a variety of seating areas. It's a relaxed place with gentle music and a get-work-done vibe.

Good Mantra Comfy sofas and relaxing nooks in which to chat, hold meetings or just sip great coffee. Friendly staff greet you like an old friend. Combine work with plant-based lunches or craft cocktails.

Miel Coffee An air-conditioned cafe with a light and spacious outdoorsy vibe. Numerous power sockets and comfortable seating make it a great place to work, and it's a favourite with caffeine connoisseurs

(information cards detailing origins etc come with each exquisite cup).

Speciality Coffee

Revolver Billed as Bali's first speciality coffee store (and, some say, the best on the island), Revolver has become an institution. Buy their beans in-store, or order a range of coffee and meals at the cafe.

Hungry Bird Serving coffee grown in Indonesia and abroad, Hungry Bird is invested in the fair-trade system. The coffee is excellent, as is the latte art.

Indonesian Coffee

Anomali Coffee This roasting company is known and loved for specialising in Indonesian coffee – they've garnered a reputation for serving excellent meals, too.

Kawisari Coffee Farm Shop & Eatery All coffee served here is grown on the owner's farm (established in 1870) in eastern Java. For something truly local order coffee made the traditional Indonesian way.

Satu Satu The Sudana family has been producing Bali-grown organic coffee since 1985, using agricultural traditions that date back generations. For a timeless tradition go for their Bali coffee, but for a caffeine buzz order the four-shot *cortado* or their *kopi luwak* (claimed to be '100% pure wild').

Vegetarian Treats

Oma Jamu A very affordable eatery with a good vegan breakfast buffet until 11am, and a mixed-plate offering thereafter. There is a small grocery section, too.

Bali Buda The menu at Bali's pioneering health-food restaurant is packed with nutritious, wholesome meals, smoothies and juices. Bali Buda also has a well-stocked store where you can buy organic groceries and eco-friendly household goods.

HOW TO

Go vegan Vegan milk options are often available in Canggu's 'regular' cafes – you simply need to ask.

Get a delivery You can order coffee and meals from many of Canggu's cafes via GoFood (Gojek app) and GrabFood (Grab app), Indonesia's answer to Uber Eats.

Work consistently Power points can be hard to come by in cafes, so be sure to charge your devices before you leave your accommodation.

Budget Some cafes include a tax and service charge in their prices. Check the fine print at the bottom of the menu for disclosure.

Shady Shack This destination cafe has an extensive menu of only vegan and vegetarian fare, including all-day breakfasts, share plates and a range of burgers, desserts, smoothies and coffees.

Kynd Community Super Instagrammable, Kynd is 100% plant based. Come here for breakfasts (which include vegan eggs and 'beacon'), smoothie bowls, curries, burgers and pizzas. Inspired to cook vegan at home? Check out Kynd's online plant-based cooking course.

Cafes for Families

Village A 'play cafe' with a garden playground, serving what's probably the best almond-milk cappuccino on the island.

Made's Warung Berawa

The vast indoor and outdoor playgrounds here are an absolute delight. Made's also has a daycare and hosts events for kids.

Milk & Madu Beach Road

There's a fun outdoor play space for kids, and a huge menu for the whole family, including healthy breakfast bowls, pizzas, pastas, wraps and burgers.

BEST LIVE MUSIC VENUES AROUND CANGGU

Gimme Shelter
A rock-'n-roll-style bar with live music on Wednesdays, Fridays and Saturdays and open-mic nights on Mondays.

Peels Records & Bar
An intimate bar with a 'secret' entrance, ultra-hip Peels has a distinct retro vibe.

Lusa By/Suka
There's acoustic live music on Tuesdays, Wednesdays and Saturdays, and a Pasta & Jazz night on Thursdays.

Shady Fox
This might be a clandestine cocktail parlour, but DJs and live music take centre stage.

Atlas Beach Club
(p55)
Expect world-class DJs and special events at what's billed as Bali's biggest night club.

ELIZAVETA GALITCKAIA/SHUTTERSTOCK ©

Finns Beach Club

Berawa

TIME FROM CANGGU: **15 MINS**

Party in Paradise

Located on the beach at Berawa, **Finns Beach Club** is a pulsating all-day party venue that sets the stage for unforgettable days and nights of pure hedonism. For those on the scene, this is absolute paradise – DJs and vocalists set the vibe as revellers order drinks from swim-up bars, roller-skaters wearing retro hot pants weave between Finns' four pools, and figures with glitter balls for heads dance up a storm. There's always something going on somewhere – and with up to 5000 people partying here, there's never a dull moment. Entrance is free but you will need to spend a minimum of 650,000Rp to claim a daybed; prices increase depending on the level of exclusivity you're after. The nine bars (and roaming shot-pourers) keep patrons well hydrated, while seven 'kitchens' (ranging from sushi to Mexican to pizza) and three chic party-restaurants take care of the munchies.

EATING IN BERAWA: OUR PICKS

Warung Sunshine This rooftop eatery (with an air-conditioned indoor area) serves up Indonesian classics, as well as a selection of Western dishes. **$**

Neighbourhood Food This soulful, laid-back cafe is intent on supporting local producers and artisans. There's a good selection for vegans here. **$$**

Bokashi Japanese-inspired Bokashi is an earth-conscious teahouse, cafe and grocery store. The food is excellent. **$$**

Pels Supershop A wholesome, very on-trend 100% vegan restaurant, serving cakes, bowls, tacos, soups and fritters – an absolute feast. **$$**

Pererenan

Deserted Sunrise Beach Walk

'Quiet' is not a word anyone would ordinarily use to describe the Canggu area – particularly if they've only experienced it during the day, when roads are clustered with vehicles, sidewalks become an escape route for frustrated scooter drivers, the beach is jam-packed with daybeds and the waves are streaked with surfers. But wake at dawn and head to Pantai Nelayan (p54) for a sunrise beach walk and you'll find yourself experiencing a completely different version of 'the 'Gu', one where there's an unusual sense of space and freedom. On your drive to Nelayan Beach you'll wind your way along quiet streets that are empty of traffic and frequented by joggers and people walking their dogs – something that's not possible once Canggu wakes. By the time you've parked at the beach end of Jl Nelayan and begun to walk west towards **Pantai Batu Bolong** you might have seen one or two Balinese women making offerings on the grey sand, and walked past closed-up board-rental shops where piles of daybeds are still wrapped in tarpaulins. Batu Bolong Beach is 400m west of Pantai Nelayan and here a handful of

Pantai Batu Bolong

LANYWATI/SHUTTERSTOCK ©

BERAWA AFTER DARK

Annisa Levandra, vocalist and assistant entertainment manager at Finns Beach Club. *@annisalevandra*

The vibe in Berawa is a fantastic mix of relaxed and energetic, and you can enjoy a really chill evening at beach-club bars. They're a good place to kick your night off, and they come alive at sunset. Finns Beach Club is legendary, and Caravan beach bar is super vibey for sunset drinks, too. Berawa's nightlife is pretty diverse. If you're after a more upscale experience head along Jl Berawa where you'll find stylish cocktail bars like the Shady Pig, Club Soda, Mesa and BELLA, which are all very well known for their craft cocktails and classy ambience. Note that at some places dress codes might apply.

THE GUIDE

CANGGU & SOUTHWEST BEACHES BEYOND CANGGU

DRINKING IN BERAWA AND PERERENAN: OUR PICKS

Mosto Billed as Indonesia's first natural wine bar, Mosto has an incredibly extensive menu of international wines.

Behind the Green Door An intimate, exclusive speakeasy known for beautifully presented cocktails and liqueurs, along with late-night beats.

Hippie Fish This chic beachfront restaurant with a rooftop bar has an array of international wines and a Mediterranean-inspired drinks list.

Friends A classy, cosy bar serving exceptional cocktails in a relaxed, homely atmosphere. There's karaoke on Thursdays.

FITNESS FIRST

Denis Christian, founder of **Kor Pilates** studio, names his favourite classes.

Mobility at Nirvana Life
The mobility classes focus on stretching and training strength. Nirvana offers calisthenics, gymnastics strength training and hand balancing.

CrossFit at Wanderlust Fitness Village
This big fitness facility has lots of space and equipment. CrossFit enthusiasts from all over the world train at Wanderlust.

Factory Fit at Body Factory Bali
The coaches are good here, and classes range from strength to barre to female only.

Boxing at Soma Fight Club
Soma is best for mixed martial arts (MMA) classes, which cater to levels from basic to advanced.

High-Intensity Interval Training (HIIT) at Power + Revive
The training space and equipment are good. Other classes include strength, mobility and boxing.

A.JPROJECTPHOTOS/SHUTTERSTOCK ©

La Brisa beach club

surfers will be making the most of the almost-empty waves. Just past Old Man's (p56) and the other cafes that tower from a concrete wall above the beach, the coastline starts to open up and a wonderful sense of space sets in. Laid-back **Times Beach Warung**, a locally owned cafe, opens at 6am and is a good place to grab a coffee. Kick back in one of the warung's beanbags or continue to walk west towards Pererenan. Along the way, you'll see swarms of swiftlets diving through the air above the thicket of palm trees at La Brisa (p55) beach club, and you might even walk across the tell-tale tracks of turtles who've hauled themselves across the sand to lay their eggs beyond the shoreline. You'll know you've reached **Pantai Pererenan** when you find yourself standing below the colourful statue of Dewa Baruna, ruler of the ocean, riding on Gajah Mina, the elephant-headed fish from Hindu mythology. It's an easy 2km walk from Pantai Nelayan to Pantai Pererenan.

 EATING IN PERERENAN: OUR PICKS

Rize Bali An atmospheric contemporary Indian restaurant fast becoming a favourite in Pererenan. **$$**

Arte Come for the delicious Italian food (and gelato); linger for the exhibits by local artists (all work is for sale) and the Mine is Yours library. **$$**

Zali From scrumptious breakfasts to delightful dinners, this classy Lebanese restaurant brings Mediterranean magic to Pererenan's food scene. **$$**

Pescado Bali The presentation of meals at this small Spanish seafood eatery turns dinner into a culinary experience. **$$$**

Seminyak

BEACH BARS | SUMPTUOUS SPAS | FOODIE HEAVEN

Seminyak effortlessly blends luxury with a laid-back beach vibe, and this captivating neighbourhood is a magnet for those seeking a fusion of fun, style and relaxation. It's long been an alluring destination for shoppers and there is an eclectic mix of designer boutiques and cheap and cheerful clothing stores here. The area also has a reputation for its exceptional restaurants, and the food scene is always evolving, with international chefs working alongside Balinese ones to create fusions and flavours that are out of this world. It's along Seminyak's stretch of golden beach that you'll find some of Bali's most-loved hotels and beach clubs – Potato Head, Double-Six Rooftop Sunset Bar, W Bali, Alila Seminyak and Ku De Ta. Seminyak sits on a wide, sandy beach and early mornings are a busy time as joggers and dog walkers get in their exercise. Sunset is also busy when beanbags are hauled out and strings of lights are hung beneath umbrellas, ready for the revellers.

A Feast for the Senses

Learn to prepare Balinese cuisine

Bali's tropical climate and fertile volcanic soils yield an astounding range of fruits, vegetables, herbs and spices – and enrolling in a cooking class provides you with an excellent opportunity to explore not only how these ingredients shape Balinese cuisine, but also to be immersed in a multi-layered experience that, as cliché as it sounds, really is a feast for the senses. Most cooking classes begin with a trip to a local market to shop for lemongrass, ginger, tamarind and other fresh ingredients, and it also provides an opportunity to catch a glimpse of authentic Balinese life. At **Nia Cooking Class**, which is based on the edge of the flea market on Jl Kayu Aya, the morning then evolves as you set about making the various elements of iconic Balinese dishes, like spice pastes and the delicately flavoured minced fish mix for *sate lilit ikan*

GETTING AROUND

Seminyak's sidewalks are generally in good condition, so walking is a great way to get around and explore the area, particularly if you have shopping on your mind. Much of Seminyak's beach is lined with a boardwalk and you can stroll along the paved walkway from here right through to Kuta. Scooters are readily available for rent but parking can be hard to find, so if you need to get further than your feet will take you it will be more convenient to use the ride-hailing apps Grab or Gojek than to drive yourself.

☑ **TOP TIP**

Seminyak's beach is a lovely place to spend the early morning hours. The wide stretch of sand is popular with sunrise joggers and dog walkers, and no matter the tides you can clock up way more than your allocated 10,000 steps here.

63

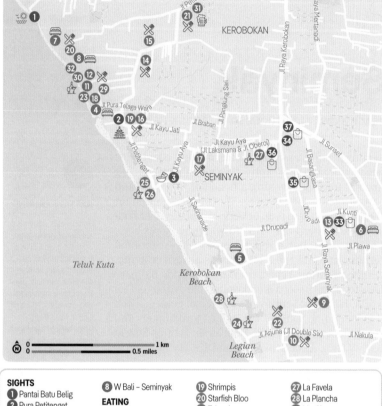

SEMINYAK

KEROBOKAN

SEMINYAK

Teluk Kuta

Kerobokan
Beach

Legian
Beach

0 ——————————— 1 km
0 ——————————— 0.5 miles

SIGHTS
1 Pantai Batu Belig
2 Pura Petitenget

ACTIVITIES
3 Nia Cooking Class

SLEEPING
4 Alila Seminyak
5 Grandmas Plus Hotel Seminyak
6 Kubu Cempaka
7 Potato Head Suites and Studios
8 W Bali – Seminyak

EATING
9 Dod's Burger
10 Felicity Espresso
11 Ijen
12 Kaum
13 Made's Warung
14 Mauri
15 Merah Putih
16 Motel Mexicola
17 Revolver
18 Seasalt
19 Shrimpis
20 Starfish Bloo
21 Takumi
22 Warung Murah Double Six

DRINKING & NIGHTLIFE
23 Beach Bar
24 Double-Six Rooftop Sunset Bar
25 Infinity
26 Ku De Ta
27 La Favela
28 La Plancha
29 Mrs Sippy
30 Potato Head
31 The Forge Gastropub
32 Woobar Bali

SHOPPING
33 BINhouse
34 I Love Bali
35 Jewel Rocks
36 Magali Pascal
37 Mercredi

DRINKING IN SEMINYAK: BARS WITH A VIBE

La Favela Magical La Favela is an enchanting bohemian blend of Indonesia's jungles, Rio's underground bars and London's art scene.

Motel Mexicola Striking combinations of bold colour and retro patterns fuel the fun, festive vibe at this Mexican bar and restaurant.

Woobar Bali (p66) Plush sofas set under strings of lights hanging beneath tall palm trees set the tone for a stylish, laid-back evening in the tropics.

Revolver With style inspiration taken from a Wild West saloon, this intimate cafe/bar is loved for its coffee. Try the espresso martini.

W Bali

SEMINYAK FOR SHOPPERS

Emmelyn Gunawan, curator and founder of luxury boutiques Canaan Studio and Escalier. *canaan-studio.com; escalier-store.com*

Seminyak is dynamic; there are new stores opening all the time. Its main shopping street is **Jl Kayu Aya**, where stores range from homeware to fashion. Some of the iconic shops here are **Magali Pascal**, the iconic French-owned boutique with Parisian-style clothing; **Mercredi**, a homeware store that's been around for years; and tiny Hawaiian-vibe **I Love Bali**, which sells beach essentials. I like to walk along **Jl Drupadi**, a quaint road with many villas and spas tucked inside, to drop into **Jewel Rocks**, which sells colourful bracelets handmade by Balinese women. And I'm often inspired by **BINhouse** next to Made's Warung (p67), which showcases exquisite Indonesian batik textiles.

(minced fish satay). Throughout the class you will learn some of the methods used to create these flavour sensations, such as how to grind ingredients on a stone pestle (which is not as simple as it sounds), and how to wrap a whole chicken in a banana leaf, which is more of an art than you'd expect. The class ends with a delicious feast – and you leave not only with a full belly, but also with a deeper understanding of the age-old culinary traditions of this island.

Seminyak's Beach Allure

Spend all day on the sand

Seminyak's stretch of beach lies halfway along the gentle arc that sweeps from the airport south of Kuta up almost to Tanah Lot, and it morphs from the umbrella-cluttered sand at Legian's Double-Six resort through more umbrellas and beach clubs to calmer **Pantai Batu Belig**. The northern section of Seminyak's beach tends to be quieter, flanked as it is by big hotels and beach clubs like W Bali (p81), Alila Seminyak, Potato Head (p67) and Ku De Ta (p66), while the vibrant southern section, between Double Six and the small inlet near Noku Beach House, draws the crowds. Here, you can rent an umbrella and sunbed

 EATING IN SEMINYAK: SEAFOOD RESTAURANTS

Shrimpis Known for their superb seafood, particularly shrimp (farmed by the restaurant) and oysters – some say the best in Bali. **$$**

Seasalt Ocean views compliment the menu, which features seafood with a Japanese touch. All fish served is wild caught and sustainably harvested. **$$$**

Ijen An earth-conscious restaurant using local produce to create innovative seafood dishes, and creating minimal waste in the process. **$$$**

Starfish Bloo Cool, breezy and stylish, beachfront Starfish Bloo uses local ingredients. The Sunday brunch is exceptionally popular. **$$$**

SEMINYAK'S FOOD SCENE

Dom Marquez-Hammond, flavour-maker and ex-head chef at Tanaman. @dom.tropical

Seminyak has long been known as a melting pot of flavours, where international chefs and mixologists bring flair and buzz to this bustling neighbourhood. We're seeing a rise of new Asian restaurants like **Takumi**, a new menu at Indonesian-inspired **Kaum**, and wood-fired seafood at **Mrs Sippy** and **Ijen** (p65).

There's now a great selection of natural wines across many menus, too. We've got all the boxes ticked here: from fine dining at restaurants like **Merah Putih** and **Mauri** to street food along **Jl Petitinget**, to beach clubs, classic pubs (the **Forge** is always popular) and everything in between. Pop-up restaurants are also becoming popular, and **Potato Head** always hosts a variety of international chefs and bartenders.

TRAVELSTOCK44/ALAMY STOCK PHOTO ©

Ku De Ta

(100,000Rp for half a day), sip on a coconut or cold Bintang beer bought from one of the small stalls that line the beach, and settle in for a day of near-constant entertainment. There's always something on the go: people learning to surf (board rental is just 50,000Rp an hour), or playing ball on the wide, flat sand beach, or taking selfies with the ocean backdrop. There are hawkers selling everything from sarongs and bracelets to speakers, card games, balloons and sunglasses. Women wander between the daybeds and offer massages (100,000Rp for an hour) and manicures, or to braid your hair. You can even get a henna tattoo. As afternoon transitions to evening, staff at the beach bars towards the Double Six end of Seminyak haul colourful beanbags onto the sand, string lights under the umbrellas, and set up small stages for a sunset show and an evening of live music.

A Beach Club with a Difference

Go on an enlightening waste tour

Seminyak is revered for its beach clubs like **Ku De Ta**, **Infinity** and **Woobar**, where you can lounge on a plush daybed beside an infinity pool and sip on fresh coconuts or tropi-

---

 DRINKING IN SEMINYAK: BEST BARS FOR SUNSETS ──────── MAP p64

Ku De Ta The evenings are ushered in by a line-up of international DJs during Ku De Ta's legendary Sunset Sessions.

Beach Bar Alila Seminyak's laid-back beachfront bar is all about the view (and great cocktails), with music by a DJ or live band setting the tone.

Double-Six Rooftop Sunset Bar Settle into a daybed surrounded by an infinity pond at one of Bali's largest rooftop bars.

La Plancha Beanbags on the beach and lights strung under umbrellas make this one of Bali's most colourful sunset spots. A DJ plays from 5pm.

cal cocktails while a DJ mixes sultry tunes. They're popular places to while away the holidays, and progressive beach club **Potato Head** takes this experience to a whole new level. The award-winning property (which is an integration of a beach club, five restaurants and two luxury hotels) is driven by the ethos 'good times, do good', and from the moment you arrive here you're made aware of how your footprint will be reduced.

Entrance to Potato Head is through 'the Womb', an enchanting 90m-long bamboo sculpture that houses display spaces showcasing how Potato Head's waste is recycled and transformed into hip decor; there's also a sustainably designed studio and streaming platform. You can take this introduction further by signing up for the inspiring (and free) 90-minute Waste Tour, which starts at 11am daily. From seeing where and how Potato Head's waste is sorted, you'll learn about the steps taken to reduce waste through the supply chains, and how the plastic is recycled and shaped into panels, furniture, beads and containers for Potato Head's amenities. You'll also see how hotel linen is given a new life as bags and clothing, and how waste cooking oil is turned into the candles the restaurants use. It's an incredibly inspiring tour that showcases what can be done when creativity meets responsibility.

A Guardian Temple
Witness traditional architecture at a Hindu temple

Standing guard on Seminyak's busy beachfront is **Pura Petitenget**, one of Bali's six sea temples built to protect the island from evil spirits. Its name translates loosely as 'magic chest' and relates back to the time, according to legend, the Hindu priest Dang Hyang Nirartha transformed Buto Ijo, a malicious beast, into the guardian of the nearby village. As Nirartha exorcised evil spirits from the area, he captured them in wooden chests, which were kept under the watch of Buto Ijo. With the iconic *candi bentar* (split gateways, see p329) at its entrance, *meru* (a multi-tiered shrine) and the intricate stone carvings on the walls and around doorways, Pura Petitenget is a fantastic example of Balinese temple architecture. To enter you'll need to wear a sarong, which you can borrow when you pay the 50,000Rp entrance fee at the southern side of the temple. Outside the northern corner of the temple and standing in a small, manicured garden is a large statue of Buto Ijo.

ALL ABOUT ARAK

Once considered backstreet hooch, *arak* (colourless, distilled palm wine) now features on many of Bali's trendy cocktail menus. Not to be confused with Middle Eastern *arak* (made from grapes and anis), Bali's *arak* can be tapped from more than a dozen different trees, most commonly the aren palm. Non-alcoholic *tuak* is the juice that is first collected; once fermented the potent *arak* is around 40% alcohol content.

You might also come across *brem* (sticky rice simmered with yeast, then fermented). *Arak* and *brem* are commonly used in the offerings placed on the ground for Bhuta Kala (the low spirits). Take care when consuming *arak* produced in village stills, as cases of methanol poisoning (leading to blindness and death) have been reported.

EATING IN SEMINYAK: CHEAP EATS

MAP p64

Warung Murah Double Six Murah means cheap, and this eatery has a very affordable menu – grilled chicken with veg and rice costs 39,000Rp. $

Felicity Espresso A lovely cafe serving Indonesian food, pizzas, pastas and sandwiches. Brilliant spot for an early breakfast; it's open for coffee from 6am. $

Dod's Burger With a reputation for making the best beef burgers in Bali, Dod's classic popular burger is just 50,000Rp. Don't skip the spicy mayo. $

Made's Warung This Bali institution is known and loved for its hearty meals. The vast menu includes Western, Thai and Indonesian options. $$

Beyond
Seminyak

Tucked between busy Seminyak and the often-frenzied Canggu area, Kerobokan and Umalas offer a welcome respite from the crowds.

Places
Kerobokan p69

GETTING AROUND

You'll need wheels to get around here. Depending on where you stay, there will likely be a warung or a cafe within walking distance, but bigger restaurants, the beach and spas will be more accessible by vehicle. You can likely arrange a scooter rental through your accommodation, and you can always call on Grab or Gojek for a taxi ride. Jl Raya Kerobokan forms part of the main thoroughfare between the airport and Canggu, so expect traffic jams.

With a miniscule stretch of coastline to claim as their own, Umalas and Kerobokan are predominantly inland neighbourhoods. Their boundaries are hard to define: little Umalas lies north of Seminyak and Kerobokan wraps around them both, forming a buffer between Seminyak and Denpasar, and nudging in between Umalas and the greater Canggu area. They take on a residential kind of vibe and it's here that many long-time expats have settled, building villas in Umalas and moving into housing complexes around Kerobokan. While Umalas has an upmarket sort of feel, Kerobokan is an interesting mix of suburb and commerce (the area is excellent for furniture, crafts and homeware). Both neighbourhoods are a treat for foodies, too.

Handicrafts, Kerobokan

Babi guling restaurant, Kerobokan

KEROBOKAN'S HOMEWARE & HANDICRAFT HOTSPOTS

Kara Home Living
Absolutely packed with locally made products, this is a convenient one-stop homeware store.

Kaula Bali
Order bespoke handmade leather products, or book a session and make your own. Workshops vary from one day to one week.

Home Basket
A myriad of styles, sizes and colours of baskets, as well as decorative tableware, is sold here.

Jonathan Lombok Pottery
Trawl the packed warehouse shelves for vases, pots and jars of all shapes and sizes.

Mercia Home Living
Gorgeous functional and decorative home decor, from rattan lampshades and baskets to cushions and accessories.

Kerobokan

TIME FROM SEMINYAK: **20 MINS**

Indulge in a Street-food Tour

Kerobokan has plenty to offer the hungry traveller, particularly in the evening when the night markets come to life. Here, the warungs and restaurants tend to cater predominantly to Indonesian patrons rather than international tourists, and so a food tour around Kerobokan is an opportunity to indulge in a culinary journey that takes in some of Indonesia's most popular dishes. **Intrepid Travel**'s street-food urban adventure (urbanadventures.com) is a fantastic way to acquaint yourself with the flavours of the island. It begins with time spent walking among the tropical fruit stalls at an afternoon market (Ever tasted snakefruit before? Here's your chance!) and sampling *jajanan*, or snacks, like *pukis* (akin to a small, fat pancake) and *lumpia* (similar to spring rolls). As the night market on busy Jl Raya Kerobokan comes to life, you'll feast on iconic Indonesian foods like *sate ikan* (fish satay) and *soto ayam* (chicken soup), as well as *es teler*. This Indonesian favourite is a taste sensation – the iced drink/dessert is a chunky combination of jelly cubes, ice, avocado, grated cheese, jackfruit, coconut milk and condensed milk. You're not done yet, though. Still to come is a stop at a popular *babi guling* (spit-roasted suckling pig) restaurant and an eatery known for its modern take on traditional desserts. Be sure to begin this tour on an empty stomach.

EATING IN KEROBOKAN AND UMALAS: OUR PICKS

Babi Guling Sari Kembar 99 People come from far and wide to feast here on the Balinese delicacy *babi guling*. **$**

Soto Ayam Surabaya Tucked into the night market along busy Jl Raya Kerobokan, this warung sells delicious *soto ayam*. **$**

Es Teler Chuy Also in Kerobokan's night market and serving the popular Indonesian dessert *es teler*, a cocktail of jelly, coconut milk, condensed milk, grated cheese and other delicacies. **$**

Naughty Nuri's A long-time favourite on the island, this high-end warung is celebrated for its signature BBQ pork ribs. **$$**

HELP ME PICK

Spas Around Seminyak

Spas are to Seminyak as cafes are to Canggu, and you can hardly wander two minutes down any busy street without a therapist waving a brochure at you. Seminyak's spa scene offers a harmonious fusion of traditional Balinese healing techniques and contemporary wellness practices, and there is something here for everyone – from absolute budget salons, where a 60-minute massage costs 100,000Rp, to ultra-luxurious destination day spas that are a sanctuary of indulgence and wellbeing.

Where to go if you're looking for...

Budget Spas

Lamora Spa Surrounded by a lovely garden, peaceful Lamora offers treatments with products like coconut or coffee scrubs made from local ingredients. Massages here are from 160,000Rp for 60 minutes.

Carla Spa Don't be fooled by the rather uninspired decor – you only need to watch people swooning out of the doors to know that the massages here (from 160,000Rp for an hour) are excellent.

Spa Bali Seminyak There's a vast array of treatments on offer, and the packages are brilliant value. The six-hour 'Ultimate' package (massage, flower bath, body scrub, mani, pedi, facial and cream bath) is 1,100,000Rp.

Day Spas

Spring Spa Located on the rooftop of Seminyak Village Mall, contemporary-style Spring offers urban views with many of its treatments. For something different, book the 45-minute sunset package (which includes a foot massage, shoulder massage and an alcoholic drink).

Lagoon Spa A light and airy luxury day spa with facilities including a swimming pool, sauna and Jacuzzi. Lagoon Spa has won multiple awards during the 20 years it has been operating.

Re Day Spa Sitting at the more affordable end of Seminyak's day spas (a 60-minute massage here is 300,000Rp), Re's treatments draw on Balinese traditions and local ingredients.

Sundari Day Spa Modern-looking Sundari is also one of the more affordable day spas. Massages here are from 90 minutes (and cost from 500,000Rp). Also, book for scrubs, manis, pedis and facials.

Natura Organics Spa This beautifully decorated tranquil oasis is an eco-friendly spa that works with natural products. Prices here are very affordable (a 60-minute massage is from 235,000Rp).

Destination Spas

Bodyworks This incredibly dreamy spa is an Instagrammer's delight. You might be tempted to come just for the gorgeous Morocco-inspired design, but the luxurious treatments are even better.

Prana Also with a Moroccan touch, simply being at Prana (pictured, left) is an experience in itself. Come for the Ayurvedic treatments, or indulge in a sublime three-hour 'Arabian Nights' package, which includes genuine pearl powder in one of the treatments and it's set in an exotic room with thrones and red drapes.

Spa Alila The opulent menu here includes 'Wellness Escapes', consisting of three hours of spa treatments of your choice, followed by a three-course spa dinner. Some of the

PEAKSTOCK/SHUTTERSTOCK ©

─── HOW TO ───

Plan your time You can walk into most budget spas and have a treatment straight away, but book ahead (sometimes a week in advance) for popular destination spas like Bodyworks and Prana.

What to wear Most spas (budget ones included) will give you disposable underwear to change into for your treatment.

Tipping Some of the larger spas might include a 10% service charge onto your bill. At the smaller spas, a tip won't often be expected but it will of course be appreciated.

Protect your skin Keep in mind that sunburns and spa treatments don't often go well together, and some spas offer soothing after-sun treatments.

treatments conclude with a blissful Vichy shower.

Speciality Spas

Jari Menari Famous for their award-winning massages conducted only by men, Jari Menari's treatments – a unique blend of massage styles – are considered by many to be the best on the island.

Glo Day Spa More on the beauty salon side of spas, Glo is revered for its tanning, tinting, waxing, lash and brow services, as well as a wide range of facials.

Chill Reflexology Specialising in reflexology and acupuncture, this peaceful contemporary spa has a brilliant reputation for its holistic treatments.

Montigo Spa Something for families – along with the regulars like wraps, facials and massages, this popular resort spa has a kiddies menu that includes Twinkle Toes pedis, facials, manis and 'Mom and I' and 'Dad and I' treatments.

Hi Sugars This specialist hair-removal salon uses natural sugar-based wax to simultaneously remove unwanted hair and exfoliate dead skin.

Aliya Bali While the spa has an extensive range of treatments for adults (from massages to pedis, waxing and even haircuts), they also offer many treatments for children, including nail art, body scrubs and lice treatment.

Kuta

BUSY BEACHES | HOLIDAY VIBES | GOOD SURF

GETTING AROUND

Few people recall the time when Kuta and Legian were separate villages. These days the urban sprawl and logjams of traffic make walking the best (and often fastest) way to get around Kuta. Taxis are widely available (cheapest if booked through the Grab or Gojek apps) and motorcycle taxis (*ojek*), the nippiest way to get around town, can also be booked through the apps. Kura-Kura Bus (kura2bus.com) runs a bus service between Kuta and Ubud. For longer trips across the island consider hiring a car and driver.

☑ TOP TIP

The sidewalks in Kuta and Legian are generally in good condition, which means they make convenient bypass routes for scooter drivers who're frustrated by slow-moving traffic. Be sure to look both ways before you step out from between stationary vehicles or onto the sidewalk as they are frequently used by scooters.

Kuta is the town that travellers often love to hate, but there is an unexpected charm here. Almost 90 years after the first hotel was built on Kuta Beach, high-rise construction is still almost absent and, from the beach, you'll rarely see buildings looming above the trees. If you've been lured to these golden beaches for sunshine, cocktails and spas, you've come to the right place – and you'll find a dose of culture here too, among the shrines and temples (Buddhist and Hindu) and in the early morning market that has changed little over the last century. The once thronging Poppies I is yet to rebound from the COVID-19 pandemic, but Jl Legian is bustling. While Seminyak and Canggu sprawl quite widely, Kuta's long-established community has retained a town centre that is still pleasantly walkable. The beach strip is lined with bars and the new promenade, and an influx of recent accommodation options makes the beachfront more appealing than ever.

Wave of the Day

Where to surf around Kuta

Kuta has drawn surfers in ever-increasing numbers since Bob Koke – Kuta's first hotelier – had his boards shipped here from Hawaii in the early 1930s, and these days with rental boards available by the hundreds and surf instructors by the score, Pantai Kuta (p75; more commonly called Kuta Beach) is one of the best places in Bali to learn how to surf. You simply need to approach one of the board-rental kiosks on the beach to set up a lesson. Although Kuta arguably sees more surfers on an average day than almost any other spot in the world, this area almost always has a wave to offer anyone who doesn't mind paddling away from the crowds or heading north to **Pantai Padma**. For uncrowded waves, typically with less power, go to **Pantai Segara** on the far southern end of the beach.

HIGHLIGHTS
1 Pantai Kuta

SIGHTS
2 Bali Sea Turtle Society
3 Memorial Wall
4 Pantai Padma
5 Pantai Segara
6 Site of Sari Club

ACTIVITIES
7 Waterbom

SLEEPING
8 Berlian Inn
9 Mamaka by Ovolo
10 Poppies Bali

EATING
11 Afterglow
12 Bella Italia
13 Bene Italian Kitchen
14 Kopi Pot
15 Kuta Social Club
16 Riva Bar and
Restaurant

17 Temple by Ginger
Moon
18 Warung Indonesia

**DRINKING
& NIGHTLIFE**
19 Boshe VVIP Club Bali
20 Bounty Discotheque
21 Don Juan Mexican
Restaurant and Bar
22 Gracie Kelly's Irish
Pub
23 Hard Rock Cafe

24 LXXY
25 Paddy's Pub
26 Stadium Cafe
27 Stark Craft Beer
Garden

SHOPPING
28 Beachwalk
29 Discovery Mall
30 Kuta Art Market
31 Lippo Mall Kuta
32 Mal Bali Galeria

KEEP BALI BEAUTIFUL

Bali (and Kuta in particular) often receives harsh media coverage because of the trash that washes up on the beaches. Some visitors assume that the beaches are permanently filthy, but they're like this particularly during the rainy season, when the rivers carry the trash accumulated along their banks during the dry months into the ocean.

One of the organisations working hard to alleviate the island's plastic problem is **Sungai Watch**, which focuses on removing plastic from the island's rivers. There are permanent teams who clean the rivers daily, but Sungai Watch also organises river clean-ups for volunteers; the schedule is on their website. Another leader in the plastic war is **Potato Head** (p67).

ANOM HARYA/SHUTTERSTOCK ©

Wood carvings for sale

Surfers with more experience might appreciate an offshore adventure at **Kuta Reef** (sometimes called Airport Reef), where turtles wallow in crystal-clear water and the reef shimmers with fish; you might think that you're out in open ocean if it weren't for the planes booming down just over your head (perhaps a unique surf experience in itself). To get to Kuta Reef look for the **Red Flag Office** on Pantai Segara and ask for a *jukung* (outrigger fishing boat) to take you and your board out to the reef (it costs 70,000Rp). Don't forget to arrange a pickup time; you then simply look for the boat with the red flag when it's time to be collected. There are several great surf spots here that put the Kuta beach break to shame, but since they all break onto relatively shallow reef they are not suitable for beginners. 'Airport Lefts' and 'Airport Rights' break either side of the rocky promontory at the end of the international runway. They can be dangerously shallow at lower tides, while the spot known simply as 'Middles' tends to break bigger and to be surfable right through the tides.

DRINKING IN KUTA: OUR PICKS

MAP p73

Gracie Kelly's Irish Pub As authentically Irish as you can get in the tropics (although the Guinness is bottled, not on tap).

Stadium Cafe A classic sports bar with multiple screens, showing rugby, cricket, tennis, boxing and football. There's a comprehensive drinks list and good pub fare.

Stark Craft Beer Garden Craft beer made in Bali, and cocktails served in a rustic-industrial setting. There's live music every night.

Don Juan Mexican Restaurant and Bar There are bar stools overlooking busy Jl Pantai Kuta – brilliant for people watching while you drink *micheladas*.

The Long Flip-Flap to Freedom

Release a baby turtle on Kuta Beach

A tiny turtle hatchling making its bid for survival is an unforgettable sight, and the **Bali Sea Turtle Society** (BSTS) gives visitors an opportunity to play a hand in releasing these near-mythical creatures. Indonesia is home to six of the world's seven marine turtle species and, while attitudes are changing, the creatures are still threatened in many areas by collectors who harvest the eggs or kill mature turtles for meat. BSTS collects the eggs from nests in insecure areas and relocates them to their hatchery on Kuta Beach. The hatching season is usually from April to October, and more than 300 baby turtles are released in the late afternoons; this doesn't happen every day so keep an eye on BSTS's Instagram page (@baliseaturtlesociety) for updates. BSTS is easy to find – simply look for the enormous fibreglass turtle off the beach just south of Jl Pantai Kuta. The event is free, but most visitors are happy to make a donation.

It's Not All Souvenirs and Singlets

Where to shop in Kuta

Whether you're looking for budget bargains or big brands, Kuta is an absolute boon for shoppers. Haggling your way through the souvenir and cheap clothing shops along Jl Legian (see p79) and at the **Kuta Art Market** makes for a fun evening out, and during the day – when a blast of air-con will be so welcome – there is no shortage of malls to trawl. Head to chic **Beachwalk** shopping centre for stores like Adidas, Deus, Kate Spade and Lacoste, or to popular **Discovery Mall** for local and international brands including Hurley and Guess, and to **Lippo Mall** and **Mal Bali Galeria** for chains and department stores. Along Jl Sunset you'll find Bali's flagship stores and outlets for Eiger, Havaianas, 69 Slam and Rip Curl. Most shops and malls often remain open until 10pm.

A Night to Remember

Watch the sunset on Kuta Beach

You might think there's not much to be said about watching the sunset on a beach, but west-facing **Pantai Kuta** is famous for dramatic sunsets, and you could write an entire book about the activity that unfolds on its three action-packed

MEMORIAL WALL

12 October 2002 is regarded as one of the darkest days in Bali's modern history. Just after 11pm a bomb exploded at **Paddy's Pub** (p76), a Kuta bar popular with backpackers, and as revellers fled to apparent safety on the street, another (bigger) bomb was detonated over the road, just outside **Sari Club**. The blasts killed 202 people, among them 38 Indonesians, 88 Australians and 23 Britons. There is now a **memorial wall** for those who lost their lives on Jl Legian, just metres from where Sari Club once stood. The victims' names are listed, and family and friends still bring flowers and photos to honour the memory of those who were killed.

 EATING IN KUTA: OUR PICKS ———— MAP p73

Warung Indonesia This popular Masakan Padang (buffet-style) restaurant – with good vegetarian dish options – is one of the best-value eateries in Kuta. $

Temple by Ginger Moon A menu designed for sharing (by acclaimed chef Dean Keddell), featuring fire-cooked dishes like rotisserie chicken, smoked duck and *babi guling*. $$

Bella Italia Absolutely delicious authentic Italian food. This stylish restaurant has an atmospheric streetside section, and air-conditioned seating indoors. $$

Kopi Pot This garden cafe on Jl Legian (great for people watching) serves tasty Indonesian dishes, as well as seafood, steaks, curries and pastas. $$

BEST CLUBS IN KUTA & LEGIAN

LXXY
The most popular club in town these days, nights at LXXY are clubbing extravaganzas. Some of Indonesia's best DJs play here.

Hard Rock Cafe
For a night out with live music, Hard Rock Cafe is always a good choice. There are plenty of options on the drinks list.

Paddy's Pub
One of the oldest bars in Kuta, Paddy's is great for a no-pretences dance-all-night kind of night.

Boshe VVIP Club Bali
This late-night club often has live bands and DJs. There are karaoke rooms too.

Bounty Discotheque
For cheap drinks and raucous nights, Bounty is the place to be. This is casual clubbing at its wildest.

kilometres of beachfront. Along here it's all about people watching, so order a Bintang beer or a fresh coconut from a beachfront vendor and settle in for the show: there are talented surfers ripping the waves and beginners getting catapulted into the shore break, dogs and children race each other across the sand, honeymooners pose for selfies, and a medley of travellers and locals work on maximising their Tik-Tok game. Watching the sunset here can also become a static spa and shopping spree – without having to move from your seat you could have your hair braided, get a fake tattoo, and enjoy a manicure and a back massage, all at the same time. From wandering hawkers you can buy kites, jewellery, sarongs, card games and bamboo blowpipes, and there's a never-ending procession of snacks and refreshments on offer. There's also now a small market under the trees and over the road from chic Beachwalk (p75) shopping centre, and a skate park (open until 10pm) that has become a favourite meeting place for children of all ages. The skate park is free, but skateboards are available for hire. When the action on Kuta's beach quietens down, take a walk along the beachfront promenade to Pantai Padma (p72), where the lively beach bars remain open until late at night.

A Wild Watery Adventure

Slip down the slides at a watery amusement park

One of the island's most popular family tourist attractions since the taps were first turned on in 1993, **Waterbom** is still regularly voted as Asia's best waterpark. Spiralling, spinning, shooting and splashing across 5 hectares of carefully landscaped tropical gardens are 26 slides, and their names alone – Smashdown 2.0, Boomerang, the Drop, Fast n Fierce – might convince you that Waterbom is not for the fainthearted. Although there's enough here to challenge even the most serious of adrenaline junkies, Waterbom's strength lies in its appeal for 'kids of all ages'. There are several beautifully designed lagoon pools with sunbeds and VIP gazebos, and a 'Lazy River', which provides sufficient excitement in the form of bridges, cascades and water jets. In September 2023 Waterbom opened the new Oasis Gardens section, which has a lagoon pool and a 20m tower with four slides featuring unnerving blackout sections, very trippy rainbow-ribboned tubes and 9m drops. Those who prefer to relax can enjoy a massage or get their nails done, and there is a choice of five restaurants when your energy needs replenishing.

EATING IN KUTA: ROOFTOP RESTAURANTS ———————— MAP p73

Kuta Social Club A relaxed rooftop pool club with a view all the way to the Bukit Peninsula; serves Mediterranean-inspired dishes. **$$**

Bene Italian Kitchen Contemporary Italian dining at the Sheraton Bali Kuta Resort. Delicious meals come with an enchanting ocean outlook. **$$**

Afterglow A casual-chic beachside restaurant with an infinity pool. Lots of choice on the menu, including salads, burgers, seafood and grills. **$$**

Riva Bar and Restaurant This a good option for an elevated sunset view over Kuta Beach. The menu has Indonesian and international options. **$$**

Beyond
Kuta

- Kerobokan
- Legian
- **Kuta**
- Tuban

Legian's warren of alleyways and magnificent stretch of beach offers an ideal one-size-fits-all introduction to this vibrant tropical island.

Despite all odds Legian – crammed in between Kuta and Seminyak – has retained something of a 'village' vibe that appeals to devotees (mainly Australians) who have returned here for decades. As a souvenir-shopping area, it's probably surpassed only by Ubud (or, if you're looking for international brands, by Seminyak). There are good bars and restaurants here catering to all tastes, and you'll find nightlife and phenomenal Balinese massages for a fraction of what you'd pay in swankier beach areas up the coast. Legian's Pantai Padma has what is probably the most vibrantly colourful beach nightlife on the island. Elsewhere, almost everything closes within an hour of sunset, but Padma's strip of beach bars stay open until midnight.

Places

Legian p78

GETTING AROUND

Legian's lanes are best explored on foot since there can be a hidden gem even down the humblest gang (alley or footpath). Jl Legian, the main street, stretches almost arrow-straight for 3km south through Kuta to what used to be called Bemo Corner – when bemos (minibuses) still plied the streets. These days, your most convenient option for getting around is by taxi, or by the nippier motorcycle taxis you can hail via the Grab and Gojek apps.

Legian

BALI'S STRIKING SPLIT GATEWAYS

If you enter **Legian Beach** from Jl Melasti, you'll walk through an ornate split gateway (called *candi bentar*) – the same sort of architectural structure you'll see at entrances to temples, palaces and other sacred sites around Bali. These traditional gateways serve as important cultural and spiritual symbols, and consist of two symmetrically shaped pillars connected by a central opening, which creates a striking entryway. The gates are typically adorned with intricate carvings and decorative motifs, and represent the division between the profane world and the sacred realm, signifying the transition from the mundane to the divine. The inside edge of the gates are always smooth – some say to cleanse the mind upon entry.

Legian

TIME FROM KUTA: **15 MINS**

Start your day in real Bali style

Legian might feel like a long way from 'traditional' Bali, but a trip to a morning market will reveal a slice of life that's remained almost unchanged for generations; it's here where fruit, vegetables, meat and spices are traded. There are two morning markets in the greater Kuta area that are well worth a visit: the popular Legian morning market (known officially as **Pasar Pagi Desa Adat Legian**) and the even more timeless **Pasar Pagi Kuta** (at the junction of Jl Raya Kuta and Jl Pantai Kuta). Legian's morning market is located in a large modern building, somewhat like a hangar inside, while Kuta's more colourful market is in a ramshackle shelter down an alleyway on the northern side of Jl Blambangan. If you're squeamish, it'll be best to avoid the butcher's section where pork, beef, chicken and a variety of fresh fish are carved up. The most lively sections of both markets are the fruit and vegetable stands, and the wonderfully colourful stalls that sell a mind-boggling selection of traditional offerings. Look out for the stalls where women sell *jamu* – this traditional elixir, a spicy turmeric-based drink, is a wonderful early morning pick-me-up. It is best to arrive early to see the markets at their most vibrant; Kuta's market opens at 4am and closes at 10am, while Legian's market opens and closes an hour later.

Feast on traditional Indonesian fare

Masakan Padang (Padang food) is probably Indonesia's most iconic cuisine. It originates from the Padang area in Sumatra and includes rich curries, spicy stir-fries, grilled meat and deep-fried delicacies – and eating at a Padang restaurant usually means you'll be sitting down to a veritable feast. A typical Padang warung will have bowls and plates stacked in the window displaying what's on offer, while larger eateries often have the food set out buffet-style behind a glass counter; there can be as many as 30 dishes to choose from, including beef rendang, sweet-and-sour chicken, grilled fish, curried eggs, corn fritters and a variety of sambal. There are two ways of serving Padang food: *pesan* is the most common, where you choose what you'd like and order this directly from the person behind the counter, while *hidang* is when plates of food are placed on your table and you're charged for those that you eat from. In Legian, **Warung Kolega** (on

 DRINKING IN LEGIAN: OUR PICKS

Sky Garden Bali Come for dinner and to party. Each floor has something different going on, and weekends are event nights.

Y Sports Bar This popular bar has good food and, of course, it shows all the big sports events. There is live music here, too.

Brother Bar With beanbags clustered on the sand, this casual on-the-beach bar is a brilliant option for sunset sessions.

Zen Bar A chilled bar on the beach, with plastic chairs set under umbrellas. It's one of the few beach bars in Legian that sells cocktails.

Sumatran food on display

WHERE TO SHOP FOR SOUVENIRS

Legian is a fantastic area for souvenir shopping, and at the small shops that line the length of Jl Legian you can hunt for bargains on Bintang T-shirts (always a popular gift), sarongs, handbags, cheap boho-style dresses and the ubiquitous penis-shaped bottle openers.

There's more of the same at **Legian Art Market** on Jl Melasti. Unless prices are set, you'll be expected to bargain; be sure to take a friendly approach and don't drive the seller into the ground. A general rule of thumb: only begin to bargain if you're a serious buyer, and begin by offering half of what the seller asks for. For set-price shopping there's **Krisna Oleh-Oleh**, a souvenir emporium on Jl Sunset.

Jl Dewi Sri) is popular, and while it's not the cheapest warung around it is still good value. Here, a heaped plate of rice, various meats and egg dishes, as well as sambal (served *pesan* style), will set you back about 70,000Rp. If you're on a tight budget, head for Warung Indonesia (p75) on Gang Ronta in Kuta, where you'll pay about 40,000Rp for a generous meal.

EATING IN LEGIAN: OUR PICKS

Warung Kampung This airy eatery serves all the popular Indonesian dishes. Tasty meals at very budget-friendly prices. **$**

Coffee Cartel A cute, contemporary cafe with an all-day breakfast menu, as well as smoothies (delicious!), burgers, bowls and salads. **$$**

Brunch Club Bali Indulge in this trendy cafe's 'porncakes' – layers of oversized pancakes with toppings like whipped cream, syrups, biscuits, berries and chocolate sauce. **$$**

Azul Beach Club An upmarket open-air restaurant and tiki bar with tropical vibes and beach views. Come for the seafood and salads. **$$$**

Kuta's beach runs for more than 5km and, with its outlying communities of Tuban (to the south) and Legian (to the north), it is surprisingly diverse. Start your walk at **❶ Pantai Jerman** (German Beach) in the south, a sheltered cove that was a haven for fishing boats long before it became a favourite beach for families. The promenade behind Discovery Mall Bali leads you to **❷ Pantai Segara**. This timeless beach is the site of the **❸ Pura Dalem** ('Death Temple', where Hindu cremations still take place). It's also the hangout of boatmen, most of whom have given up fishing in favour of shuttling surfers to Kuta Reef (p74).

After passing the **❹ Bali Sea Turtle Society**, you'll reach Kuta's lively **❺ Pantai Kuta**, where there are hawkers, surf schools and board-rental spots. From here, the shaded, newly paved promenade will lead you beyond **❻ Beachwalk** shopping centre and the **❼ skate park** to **❽ Pantai Padma**, where plastic chairs and Bintang beers are supplanted by comfy beanbags and cocktails. Around sunset the bars here come to life with fairy lights and live music. Look out for **❾ Kanoa Bali** (for a sit-down meal with your feet in the sand) and **❿ Erika Sunset Bar** (for a romantic chill spot).

Next up is **⓫ Double Six Beach** – named for the big resort, its wide beach is a favourite venue for playing beach soccer, volleyball and frisbee. At the northern edge of Double Six (where Legian was once separated from Seminyak by rice fields) is **⓬ D'Joglo** (for live music) and **⓭ La Plancha Bali**. It's a popular bar at sunset, so arrive early to snag a beanbag.

Places We Love to Stay

$ Cheap $$ Moderate $$$ Pricey

Canggu   p52 (Map p53)

Asung Guesthouse $ This simple, contemporary-style guesthouse offers good value for money. The rooms are spacious and there's a pool, too.

Serenity Eco Guesthouse $ An eco guesthouse and yoga resort close to Pantai Nelayan, with a distinctly bohemian vibe. Rooms range from dorms to singles with shared bathrooms to more luxurious en-suite doubles.

Melati Bali Homestay $$ Lovely traditional wooden rooms are surrounded by a tropical garden. The property is small but private and full of character.

Tugu Bali $$$ A hotel with lots of character and Indonesian antiques; it has many activities on offer, too. Tugu is a brilliant place to connect with Balinese culture.

Pererenan   p61

Kubudiuma $$ Each room is a wooden joglo (some antique, some new) lined along a central walkway. The bathrooms are open-air and there's a pool, too.

Ize Canggu Hotel $$$ A contemporary-style hotel halfway along Jl Pantai Pererenan; conveniently close to good restaurants and not too far from the beach.

Como Uma Canggu $$$ Sitting on a quiet stretch of beach between Canggu and Pererenan, Como is an elegant and ultra-luxurious resort. The spa here is exceptional.

Berawa   p60

Guru Canggu $$ This quiet boutique hotel has a small pool and garden. Each room is different, but there's a sweet tropical vibe and a guru 'theme' that connects them all.

Sedasa Lodge $$ Crisp, contemporary rooms, set along a pool. It feels quite contained, but the narrow rooms are large and have a sofa area.

Desa Seni $$$ This tranquil boutique resort comprises antique wooden joglos (traditional Javanese houses) sourced from around Indonesia. Yoga, wellness and community are the focus here, and it's a peaceful oasis in the very heart of the busy greater Canggu area.

Seminyak   p63 (Map p64)

Kubu Cempaka $$ Conveniently close to Jl Sunset, Kubu Cempaka is a good base from which to explore Seminyak, Canggu and the surrounds.

Grandmas Plus Hotel Seminyak $$ A hop and a skip from the beach. Rooms here are compact and contemporary, and it's a convenient base from which to explore Seminyak.

Potato Head Suites and Studios $$$ Super stylish, and there's a huge emphasis on being environmentally friendly. There is always something happening here too, from yoga classes to DJ events.

W Bali $$$ This vibrant beachfront hotel is in the very heart of Seminyak. Features include four terraced pools, seven dining areas, a sound studio and a spa.

Kuta   p72 (Map p73)

Berlian Inn $ A good budget option (with a pool) 250m from the beach. Rooms at the back have private verandas overlooking the tropical garden.

Poppies $$$ This peaceful boutique hotel has been here for 50 years. It's an atmospheric tropical-oasis escape tucked into the very heart of built-up Kuta.

Mamaka by Ovolo $$$ Kuta's chicest new hotel features a fantastic rooftop bar with a pool overlooking the beach, as well as the excellent Kupu-Kupu spa.

Legian   p78

De' Puspa Residence $$ This small homestay is tucked into a side street off Jl Arjuna. The location is excellent – on the doorstep of the beach, shops, spas and restaurants.

Puri Damai $$ This well-established homestay-style accommodation is close to Double Six Beach. It has an old Balinese atmosphere and is built around a garden of frangipani trees. It's well cared for, and it has a pool and apartment-style rooms.

Above: Surfers, Uluwatu (p98); Right: Sanur Beach (p86)

South Bali & the Islands

IDYLLIC BEACHES AND A RELAXED ISLAND VIBE

Sanur's beachfront hotels are an ideal springboard to the chic surf-havens of the Bukit Peninsula and the laid-back islands of Nusa Lembongan and its neighbours.

Just a short drive from the airport and with easy access to appealing beaches (and surf spots), south Bali is the island's premier holiday destination. It's here that trees and umbrellas muddle on white-sand beaches, and there are sprawling hotels, world-class waves, and reefs that make for exquisite diving. You'll see few reminders of rural Bali as you pass from Sanur into Denpasar (the capital) or down the main highway to the Bukit Peninsula, but Bali's rich Hindu culture remains as strong here as it does elsewhere, and the coastal communities have a tradition of hospitality that runs deep.

Some of Bali's longest-standing hotels are in Sanur and Denpasar, and have hosted celebrities and royals in their glory days.

And Sanur retains this regal appeal – its powdery beach (pictured) is fringed with well-established old trees, and a boardwalk threads past the verdant gardens of genteel properties. The calm, reef-protected waters make Sanur ideal for families.

South on the Bukit Peninsula is Uluwatu with its exceptional ocean views and legendary surf. Uluwatu is also increasingly popular with travellers who are drawn to the beaches and growing collection of yoga studios, cafes and bars. As the crow flies, Nusa Lembongan is just 18km from Sanur, but it feels a world away. The pace of life here is slow and Lembongan, revered by divers, still has that wonderful laid-back island charm.

THE MAIN AREAS

SANUR
A classic beach holiday destination.
p86

ULUWATU
Wild beaches, wonderful surf and chic cafes.
p96

NUSA LEMBONGAN
Exceptional diving and a chilled island vibe.
p106

Find Your Way

Uluwatu sits at the southern tip of the Bukit Peninsula, the bulb that 'hangs off' mainland Bali, while Sanur is on the coast that fans northeast of the airport. Nusa Lembongan is a 40-minute fast-boat trip from Sanur.

RIDE-HAILING APPS

Grab and Gojek (Asian versions of Uber) are your best options for travelling shorter distances by car or scooter. For longer journeys consider hiring a car and private driver (most hotels can assist with this).

MOTORBIKE

Motorbikes are widely available for rent and are an almost irresistible opportunity for independent exploration. South Bali's busy roads are not an ideal place to learn, and traffic police have become stricter about licences and safety rules.

Sanur, p86

With a range of accommodation options, great restaurants and a promenade along a tranquil beach, Sanur is an ideal family holiday base.

Uluwatu, p106

Dramatic cliffside beaches, trendy cafes and one of the world's most iconic temples make Uluwatu a tropical idyll.

Nusa Lembongan, p106

It's rare to find a base that offers equal appeal for surfers and divers, and Nusa Lembongan packs in much more.

0 ___ 10 km
0 ___ 5 miles

MAZUR TRAVEL/SHUTTERSTOCK ©

Kecak performance (p96), Pura Luhur Ulu Watu, Uluwatu

Plan Your Time

It's the gorgeous beaches and ocean (for diving, snorkelling and surfing) that hold the big appeal around here, but don't miss the area's beautiful temples and viewpoints.

A Day to Experience the Bukit Peninsula

The heart of the Bukit Peninsula is less than 30 minutes from Ngurah Rai airport. With a hired driver you can also explore iconic beaches like **Balangan** (p104), **Padang Padang** (p105) and **Bingin** (p105), or visit one of the celebrated beach clubs – **Sundays** (p104) – is highly recommended. In the afternoon head to spectacular **Uluwatu temple** (p99) for the enthralling sunset performance of the **Kecak dance** (p96).

A Week to Explore the South

There are fantastic restaurants in Sanur, so work up an appetite with activities like **cycling** (p86), **SUP-ing**, **kayaking** (p87) or swimming in the sheltered beach. Transfer by boat to Nusa Lembongan, the perfect low-key base for anyone who wants to **dive** (p106) and **surf** (p108), before ending your trip among the **cafes** (p99) and **bars** (p98) around Uluwatu.

SEASONAL HIGHLIGHTS

MARCH
Many people avoid Nyepi (Bali's 'Day of Silence'; p101), yet it's a uniquely thrilling and poignant time to be on the island.

MAY
Uluwatu's waves tend to be well-formed and consistent during the dry season (April to October).

JULY
The **Bali Kite Festival** (p89) takes place in the 'windy season' and is usually held around July or August.

AUGUST
The ocean temperature drops late July to early November. It is the best time to see sunfish at Nusa Lembongan.

85

Sanur

SPACIOUS RESORTS | TRANQUIL BEACH | BEACHFRONT COCKTAILS

GETTING AROUND

Cycling is not recommended here, but Sanur's promenade is an exception, as most of it has a dedicated cycle lane. For trips around the Sanur area use Gojek or Grab to hail a car or motorbike taxi. For travel beyond Sanur consider getting to a taxi – the traffic on the Ngurah Rai Bypass can be unnerving for anyone unused to motorcycle transport. Kura-Kura Bus (kura2bus.com) services connect Sanur with Kuta and Ubud.

☑ TOP TIP

Plan your beach activities according to the tide since the reef-protected shoreline (blissfully tranquil in comparison with the coast elsewhere in the south) is almost dry at low tide. Surfers will need to get beyond the barrier reef, but boatmen are always available if you want to catch uncrowded waves.

Sanur's waterfront promenade feels very laid-back compared to the beachfront bustle of Bali's southwest beaches. Whether you stay in a luxury resort or the humblest homestay, you're never far from a peaceful wander along the shaded walkway that connects several kilometres of excellent bars, restaurants and hotels – and some unexpectedly deserted sections of beach. The area's refreshingly verdant and spacious resorts (with only one sizeable concrete monstrosity to mar the skyline) means that you are more likely to find yourself in accommodation set among tropical gardens than in the sort of six-storey oceanfront hotels that line the southwestern coast.

The area's intriguing history (a Chinese junk – a type of sailing ship – that was wrecked on the reef here ultimately brought about the ritual suicide of the entire royal family) has become barely a footnote in the ongoing tourism business, but traditional daily life is still evident in the villagers who harvest seafood from the reefs and in the traditional *jukung* (outrigger fishing boats) that have goggle-eyed swordfish faces.

Cruise the Coastline

Cycle Sanur's beachfront promenade

Alongside **Sanur Beach** there is a paved, almost 6km-long promenade, and a leisurely cycle along it provides an idyllic opportunity to explore the coastline of one of Bali's most family-friendly beach towns. The bicycles available for rent are comfortable cruisers, most of which have baskets in front and a bell that should be gently pinged when you're approaching pedestrians from behind. The **Sanur beachfront promenade** has been designed with bicycles in mind, and along much of it there is a dedicated bike lane (cyclists must stick to the inland side of the path). On your ride, a very convenient place to stop for a coffee or snack is the cafe at

HIGHLIGHTS
1. Museum Le Mayeur
2. Sanur beachfront promenade

SIGHTS
3. Mertasari Beach
4. Sanur Beach

SLEEPING
5. Kubu di Kayla's
6. Laghawa Beach Inn Hotel
7. Puri Mesari
8. Segara Village Hotel
9. Tandjung Sari Hotel

EATING
10. Fisherman's Club
11. Sindhu Night Market
12. Soul on the Beach
13. Stuja di Pantai
14. Tities Warung

DRINKING & NIGHTLIFE
15. Byrd House Beach Club
16. Casablanca
17. Seagrass by the Beach
18. Shotgun Social

Laghawa Beach Inn Hotel (p116), which is about halfway along the promenade and has space to park bicycles. The promenade runs from just north of Museum Le Mayeur (p89) south to the parking lot at **Mertasari Beach**, and there are pockets of bike-rental places all along here; many have small bikes for children, too. The bikes are usually available for rent from around 7am, and the quieter early mornings make for the most carefree cycling.

Explore Bali's Barrier Reef

Kayak and SUP along Sanur's coastline

Sanur's tranquil coastline is protected by a barrier reef that stretches for 7km and creates a series of waveless beaches, which is a real novelty on Bali's south-facing coastline. Even at high tide the crystal-clear water in this 'lagoon' is rarely much over waist-level, making it an ideal playground for those who are into kayaking and stand-up paddle boarding (SUP). Even while the waves are crashing onto the outer reef, the mirror-like surface along Sanur's beachfront is so peaceful that even first timers are able to stand up on a

LOVE & DEATH IN BALI

Vicki Baum's 1937 novel *Love and Death in Bali* is far more than a beach-blanket love story; it's rooted in historic events. Set in the fishing village of Sanur, the haunting tale offers insight into life in feudal Bali and a dark period of colonial history. The fast-moving plot draws you in, and there's something timeless about the central character, rice farmer Pak.

WHY I LOVE SANUR

Narina Exelby, writer

Sanur has that lazy, languid holiday vibe that's so hard to find these days around Bali's popular areas. The promenade is an absolute boon and allows families with strollers, walkers and wheelchairs easy access to the white-sand beach, which is well-shaded in many places. The coral reef keeps the clear water calm and makes for interesting snorkelling – and it puts SUP-ing and kayaking on the holiday agenda. The beachfront is full of character – draw your gaze away from the colourful fishing boats and sea views, and you'll spy hidden beach houses, unusual shrines and beautiful temples. Throw in views of Gunung Agung at sunset and a wide selection of bars and restaurants and you have all the key ingredients for a brilliant beach holiday.

Sindhu Night Market

paddle board. You might want to crank out a few miles of ab-toning, core-tightening exercise, or (if you take one of the biggest, most stable boards) perhaps even to practise some yoga moves on your solitary floating platform. It can be a very relaxing experience simply to soak up the sun while you potter out across the reef, floating over starfish and among the anchored boats. Look out for the traditional outrigger *jukung* (unique in this part of the island), which are adorned with long swordfish 'noses' and staring eyes painted on the bows. At its widest point the lagoon is a little over 1km from the beach to the breaking waves on the outer reef. SUPs and kayaks can be rented from about 100,000Rp per hour all along the **beachfront promenade** (p86).

Feast on Indonesian Fare

Night market specialities

Sanur's atmospheric **Sindhu Night Market** (sometimes called Senggol Market) might at first glance appear small, but its food stalls offer a fantastic opportunity to sample a wide variety of tasty traditional Indonesian fare. Each stall specialises in something different, and most of the food will be prepared

---

 EATING IN SANUR: ALONG THE BEACHFRONT ———————— MAP p87

Tities Warung A good budget option on the beach, Tities serves up Indonesian classics, as well as sandwiches and snacks. $

Soul on the Beach This breezy, laid-back cafe is a beachfront fave. It has an international menu with a focus on fresh, healthy meals. $$

Stuja di Pantai All-day dining on Sanur's beachfront. Come for an early-morning coffee and one of the best pastries in Sanur. $$

Fisherman's Club A classy seafood resto on Sanur's promenade, with comfy seating on the shady beach. There's a kids menu, too. $$$

while you wait. There's everything from *sate ayam* (chicken satay), *bakso* (meatball soup) and *lumpia* (similar to spring rolls) to Masakan Padang (see p78) and *nasi campur* (rice with a choice of side dishes). The tables belong to the stalls near them, so if you want to sit down to a meal instead of take away, then be sure to use a table belonging to someone you buy food from. If you have a sweet tooth it's best to leave some room for treats like donuts, *pisang goreng* (banana fritters), and *onde-onde* (sweet rice cake balls filled with palm sugar), which are sold from a cart near the entrance to the market.

Art & Architectural Marvels

Discover Le Mayeur's life and work

Standing right on Sanur's beachfront and engulfed by modern development is a small museum that, from its gateway, appears quite unassuming. Step inside, however, and you will be treated to an astonishingly beautiful display of art and Balinese craftsmanship. The intimate **Museum Le Mayeur** is a tribute to Belgian painter Adrien-Jean Le Mayeur (1880–1958), who was revered for his mastery of colour and light. The artist moved to Bali in 1932, and he married his muse, Legong dancer Ni Pollok, a year later. The museum stands in the house that was once the artist's studio and the couple's home, and displays a remarkable collection of Le Mayeur's work, showcasing his deep affection for Bali's vibrant culture and landscapes. Almost 90 of the artist's paintings are on display; some are in good condition, while others – including those painted on rice sacks while Le Mayeur was under house arrest during WWII – have faded terribly. This doesn't detract from the experience of being here, though; the many comprehensive information cards are packed with details that provide insight into Le Mayeur's life and lifestyle. The artist invested income from the sale of his paintings into decorating his home's intricately carved doorways and window frames, as well as the bas-relief walls, which are spectacular. The museum is small but there are so many details to look at and information cards to read that you should give yourself at least an hour here. Look for the statues of the couple in the garden.

BALI KITE FESTIVAL

During the windy season Bali's sky is dominated by kites that are flown not only as a pastime, but also as a thanksgiving message to the gods for abundant harvests. For a few days, all eyes turn to **Padang Galak** (just north of Sanur), the hub of the Bali Kite Festival, as teams compete to get the most spectacular – and the most gigantic – kites soaring on the thermals. This colourful festival is usually held in July or August; the exact dates vary in order to capitalise on the favourable windy conditions that are needed to get the enormous kites (which sometimes measure more than 4m wide by 10m long) into the air.

 DRINKING IN SANUR: OUR PICKS ———————————— MAP p87

Byrd House Beach Club This elegant 'beach house' sprawls beneath towering palm trees; there's a relaxed atmosphere and a view of Gunung Agung at sunset.

Seagrass by the Beach Brilliant for sunset drinks, this laid-back beachfront restaurant has a well-priced selection of cocktails, wines and beers.

Shotgun Social With 16 craft beers on tap, an extensive cocktail menu and a large garden and play area, this hip restaurant is great for families.

Casablanca Restaurant by day, vibey club by night – with live music (usually cover bands) every night and a range of happy-hour specials.

STROLL ALONG SANUR'S BEACHFRONT

Begin at the 'top' end of Sanur Beach at ❶**Museum Le Mayeur**, which houses the work of acclaimed artist Adrien-Jean Le Mayeur. Nearby on the boardwalk there is a ❷**bicycle rental kiosk**; cycling is an easy way to get around (see p86), but it's more convenient to pop in and out of places if you're on foot. Just past ❸**Byrd House** (return for sunset cocktails) do some souvenir shopping at the entrance to ❹**Sindhu Beach**, or stop for a smoothie at ❺**Soul on the Beach**. An old coral wall further on fronts ❻**Tandjung Sari**, an old hotel full of character, and shortly after you'll reach the carved *candi bentar* (split gateway; see p329) of ❼**Pura Tanjung Sari**. Take time in the shade to admire the astounding craftsmanship of this carved temple entrance. Further along, at ❽**Pantai Karang**, you'll reach a *bale* (a stilted

shelter) on the path. Beside it is an unusual shrine made entirely from *karang* (coral). By the time you reach Andaz Bali, you'll see colourful ❾**traditional fishing boats**; notice the faces on the front, which are becoming rare these days. Pause at ❿**Seagrass by the Beach** for a drink or to rent a kayak or SUP (see p87), or indulge in a treatment at the ⓫**Nest Beachside Spa**. If you're on a tight budget continue past ⓬**Area Belanja**, where a cluster of wooden huts house warungs; 400m further on you can get a ⓭**beachfront massage** beside the boardwalk. If, after this 5km walk, you're still up for some exercise, then continue to the ⓮**Rip Curl School of Surf** for a lesson, or take a yoga class at ⓯**Power of Now Oasis**; there's also a kids play area here, under the trees and beside the beach.

Beyond Sanur

Denpasar city is a vibrant cultural and economic hub known for its lively markets, historic monuments and elaborate buildings.

Bali's busy capital city, which took over the helm from Singaraja just after WWII, is an intriguing place that's well worth a visit, even if only for a few hours. Within the sprawling tangle of streets that form the hub of Bali's trade and commerce, there lies at Denpasar's centre a district of old tree-lined roads, and manicured gardens that cluster around the bases of monuments built to honour the people and events that have shaped the island's history. From its vibrant markets and beautiful temples to a museum built more than nine decades ago, a dynamic arts festival and diverse culinary offerings, this surprisingly cosmopolitan city offers unexpected insight into Indonesian life.

Denpasar

TIME FROM SANUR: **25 MINS** 🚗

Name and Release Turtles

The well-run **Turtle Conservation and Education Centre** (TCEC) on Pulau Serangan is very active in rescuing and rehabilitating turtles, and it offers visitors the chance to play a hands-on part in preserving one of Indonesia's most iconic marine species. Here, you'll see heart-rending sights like green turtles that have lost flippers to sharks or boat engines, hawksbills that are recovering from operations to remove ingested plastic bags, and Olive Ridley turtles that were trapped in nets. You're also, however, likely to see dozens of newly hatched youngsters jostling in some of the centre's many pools. The facility is free to visit, but you can pay 230,000Rp to 'adopt' a hatchling. You'll be given a coconut shell in which to transport your turtle, and then you'll be taken by boat to the edge of the bay where you can release it. Turtles are a protected species in Indonesia, but they are traditionally used in Hindu ceremonies (as well as for food in fishing villages all over the island). The TCEC (@tcecserangan) plays a large part in educating the communities about turtle conservation, and on a busy day as many as 200 school children can pass through the facility.

Places

Denpasar p91

GETTING AROUND

As the city can be hot and dusty it's quite unpleasant to travel around by scooter; the most comfortable way to travel around is in a car. It's very easy (and cheap) to use the ride-hailing apps Grab or Gojek as the rate is set and you don't need to explain your destination to the driver. You could also hire a car and driver for the day, which is best arranged through your accommodation.

CELEBRATE BALI'S ARTISTIC HERITAGE

For one month every year, Denpasar erupts into an extravaganza of colour and costumes as Bali's rich artistic heritage is celebrated. The **Bali Arts Festival**, which is usually held around June and July, serves as a platform to showcase and preserve the island's vibrant traditional art forms.

Dance, music, visual arts and literature take centre stage, and each day performances, competitions and workshops are held at the **Taman Werdhi Budaya Art Centre**, which is the home of the festival. If you only see one thing, let it be the opening-day parade, an absolute highlight of the festival when performers wearing intricate costumes and traditional dress take to the streets of Denpasar.

LEODAPHNE/GETTY IMAGES ©

Pura Jagatnatha

A Walking Tour of Old Denpasar

Along the wide, tree-lined streets of central Denpasar are windows into the island's history and culture. There's the lively Pasar Badung (p94), the largest market on the island, and the elaborate **Pura Jagatnatha**, a recently renovated temple dedicated to the supreme god Sanghyang Widhi. There's also a historic hotel that once hosted Charlie Chaplin and Queen Elizabeth II, and the Museum Negeri Propinsi Bali (p95), which holds – among its treasures – relics of the island's Stone Age past. Simply viewing these landmarks without understanding their

EATING IN DENPASAR: OUR PICKS

Mie Goreng Makassar Pelita This popular local eatery has a small menu of Sulawesi dishes. The portions are generous. **$**

Sejak 1970 A local favourite for nasi goreng (fried rice), particularly the nasi goreng special *babi* (fried rice with pork). **$**

Kedai Emak This contemporary Javanese restaurant serves halal food, buffet style. There's fish, chicken and vegetarian options. **$**

Warung Wardani This Indonesian restaurant is known for its delicious *nasi campur* (rice with a choice of side dishes) and chicken satay. **$**

context could be quite an empty experience, but a walk with I Gusti Ngurah Parta Wijaja (WhatsApp: +62 8135 322 0414), a knowledgeable guide who has lived in Denpasar all his life, helps to put everything into perspective. Ngurah's informative three-hour walking tour of historic Denpasar is more an introduction to Balinese culture than a history lesson of the city, and therein lies the value. A visit to Pura Jagatnatha offers the opportunity not only to learn about the spatial arrangement that dictates the layout of all the temples on the island, but also a chance for Ngurah to explain some of the intriguing rituals and customs that punctuate Balinese life. A plaque showing the name of **Puputan Square**, written in Sanskrit, evolves from an explanation about the suicidal stand of Bali's royal family against the Dutch in 1906 (see p338) into a discussion of family names, Bali's caste system and the intricacies of the Balinese language. The tour covers historic sites, as well as a walk through an old residential area. It's a brilliant introduction to the island, its people and their way of life. Schedule time to do this at the beginning of your trip.

BALI'S HISTORIC HOTEL

Southeast Asia boasts some historic hotels, and although Denpasar's **Bali Hotel** cannot be compared with Singapore's grand Raffles hotel, in its heyday it hosted a number of celebrities, including Queen Elizabeth II, Charlie Chaplin, Mahatma Gandhi and Indonesia's first president, Sukarno. Bali's first international class hotel, now called **Bali Inna Heritage Hotel**, was built in 1928. It still retains much of its original Art Deco charm: tall white columns and narrow windows give its entrance a very grand appeal, and the high-ceilinged reception room is regally clad in white and brown decor. Historic photos lend some character, and the restaurant still serves *betutu* chicken and *rawon* (a strong black beef soup) with yellow rice – the favourite meals of Sukarno.

Puputan Square

MONUMENT TO THE STRUGGLE OF THE BALINESE PEOPLE

The imposing **Bajra Sandhi Monument** stands to honour the resilience of the Balinese people and their struggle for independence from the Dutch colonisers. It rises from the centre of a peaceful, carefully manicured park, and the impressively ornate structure, which was completed in 1981, is laden with symbolism. Look for the 17 stairs leading to the main entrance, then count the eight pillars inside the monument and notice that it stands 45m tall – together these elements represent 17 August 1945, which is Indonesia's Independence Day.

Inside the monument are dioramas that trace Bali's history and detail the 1906 battle with the Dutch. The park that surrounds the monument is popular with walkers and joggers.

Museum Negeri Propinsi Bali

Shop at Bali's Biggest Market

The name Denpasar translates as 'beside the market' and **Pasar Badung** (Badung Market), the largest traditional trading place on the island, is a market that never sleeps. In and around the imposing three-storey building there's always something being traded, or being prepared to be traded, and while shopping is serious business for those who work here, it's a fun and lively place to visit. The market is distinctly different on each level: there are spices on the ground floor; fruits, vegetables and meat on the second floor; and homewares and religious items on the third floor. To see the colourful produce section in full swing, aim to be at the market between 8 and 10am. By 4pm trading inside the building has almost come to an end, and it's then that the action moves to the streets outside. The southwest corner of the market has the biggest buzz, and it's here that scores of trucks laden with fresh produce brought in from around the island jostle for parking space and buyers. There are truckloads of leafy greens and heaped baskets of tomatoes and onions, and piles of dragon fruit, sweet potatoes and oranges lend colour to an already vibrant scene. It's also astounding to watch the *tukang suun*

DRINKING IN DENPASAR: COFFEE SPOTS

Bhineka Djaja This historic cafe has been serving traditional Balinese coffee since 1935. Come in for a cup and to buy a bag of Balinese coffee.

Bali Buda Renon Perfect for health-conscious travellers, Bali Buda has a wide selection of smoothies and juices, as well as various milk options for coffee.

Gula Bali the Joglo A colourful, characterful restaurant with a lovely garden area. There's lots of juices, teas and coffees (hot and cold) on the menu.

Ritual Kopi A cosy, contemporary cafe known for its excellent speciality coffees. Try the lychee tea for something different.

– the women who transport the produce on behalf of the buyers – carry heaped baskets of fruit and vegetables weighing as much as 50kg on their heads.

Visit an Upside-down House

Shift your perspective at **Upside Down World** where more than a dozen rooms have been staged as a variety of upside-down scenes. It's all about the photo ops, and the whole family can have fun snapping selfies around the house in settings that can be as strangely vertigo-inducing as they are fun. It's not always an upside-down world, though; sometimes the scenes are sideways too, like the Chinese restaurant where all of the furniture is mounted on the right-hand wall. There are enough props handy – a toilet-cleaning brush in the bathroom, for example, and a banister that is ideally located for (simulated) slides – to keep you coming up with evermore wacky poses for photos. Try to arrive early since around mid-morning tour buses roll in and you might need to line up to snap your photos.

Explore History at the Bali Museum

Bali's unique culture and traditions are so much a part of everyday life that the island's ancient history can easily be overlooked – but a record of its past is permanently on display at **Museum Negeri Propinsi Bali**, the Bali Museum, in Denpasar. Even though the information shared here is scant at best, it's interesting to wander through Gedung Timor (East Building), which houses Stone Age tools and various other artefacts from different periods of Bali's history. Information given in the museum's three other buildings is much more comprehensive: the Buleleng Building focuses on coins (their use in rituals and ceremonies, as well as trade), the displays at the Karangasem Building centre on the symbolism of the goddess Cili, and the Tabanan Building houses an impressive collection of *keris*, the daggers that carry much symbolic and spiritual value. (Neka Art Museum – p131 – in Ubud also has a large collection.)

The museum buildings themselves are interesting in that the courtyards, the gates and pavilions showcase different architectural styles from around the island. The Tabanan Pavilion is constructed from posts from the court of a nobleman from that regency, and the Karangasem Pavilion was built in the style of an audience hall at an east Bali palace. The Buleleng Pavilion was built in the style of a north Bali residence; it was originally built in 1914 for an event in Central Java and was then moved to Singaraja where it was a museum. The pavilion was reconstructed in its current location in the 1930s.

When you enter the museum compound, 'guides' will offer their services; they add very little value to a visit and you're better off reading the information panels.

TRADITIONAL-DRESS THURSDAYS

In 2018, the Balinese government passed a regulation that every Thursday – and on every full moon and new moon days – all school children, professionals and office workers around Bali should wear *pakaian adat*, the traditional clothing of the island. While the aim was to preserve and protect Bali's heritage, it also initiated a renewed appreciation for Indonesia's beautiful textiles. More than 50 kinds of traditional fabrics are produced around the archipelago, and many are sold in central Denpasar's intriguing fabric stores.

I Gusti Ayu Martiasih (@canangsari experience.bali) leads an informative walk through the textiles area; it's a wonderful way to learn about the traditions and techniques used to produce these colourful and intricately decorated fabrics.

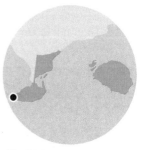

Uluwatu

CLIFFTOP VIEWS | DRAMATIC BEACHES | WORLD-CLASS SURF

GETTING AROUND

The traffic jams (especially around sunset) are enough for most visitors to travel by motorbike rather than car, and the Gojek and Grab ride-hailing apps are convenient. Motorbike rentals – from scooters to retro scramblers and Ninja sport bikes – are widely available. Traffic police can be stringent about paperwork and sometimes riders pay the ultimate penalty for ignoring safety protocols (helmets and protective clothing).

☑ TOP TIP

The monkeys around Uluwatu and the Bukit Peninsula can be malicious. They steal food and drinks, and take sunglasses right off people's heads. Keep a safe distance, secure your belongings and be aware that their bites can transmit diseases.

It's hard to imagine now that the dry Bukit Peninsula was once almost uninhabited. In the five decades since the epic wave at Uluwatu was first surfed, the ululating sound of its name has echoed around the world to sum up not only the epitome of surfing, but also as a place of pilgrimage for thousands who are drawn to the modern take on the exotic Far Eastern holiday.

Even today, Uluwatu is more a life choice than an actual place. It is hard to pin down as a destination since, apart from a small community that cared for the famous temple, there was no traditional village on what was generally considered a fairly inhospitable and spiritually intimidating location. These days 'Ulu' is far from threatening (unless you're a surfer on a big day at Outside Corner), and it's easy to see why every inbound plane is packed with travellers intent on living the Ulu dream.

A Spectacular Sunset Show

Watch the Kecak dance at Uluwatu

As the sun begins to slip below the Indian Ocean, the air around Pura Luhur Ulu Watu (p99) reverberates with the hypnotising *chak-chak-chak* chant as Kecak (pronounced *ke-chak*) performers mesmerise an audience that's gathered to watch what has become one of the most iconic displays of Balinese culture. With the majestic Uluwatu cliffs as a backdrop, the dancers enact tales from the Ramayana (one of the great Hindu holy books), and their traditional attire, the flickering flames, and rhythmic sounds and movements create a true spectacle. While the Kecak dance is performed in various locations around the island, it's the one at Uluwatu that is the most popular; its clifftop setting is hard to beat, particularly at sunset. Be prepared to sit in traffic jams (or sidestep them by using a scooter from ride-hailing apps Grab or Gojek) and aim to arrive an hour before the show starts. You can also avoid the queues and buy your ticket online at least 24 hours

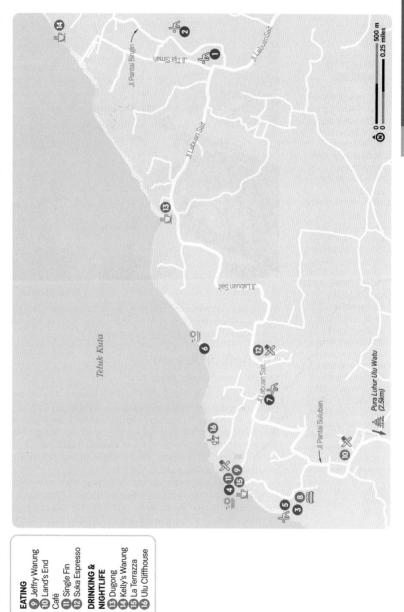

SIGHTS
1 Alchemy
2 La Tribu
3 Morning Light
4 Pantai Suluban
5 The Istana
6 Thomas Beach
7 Yoga Searcher

SLEEPING
8 Uluwatu Surf Villas

EATING
9 Jeffry Warung
10 Land's End
11 Single Fin Café
12 Suka Espresso

DRINKING & NIGHTLIFE
13 Dugong
14 Kelly's Warung
15 La Terrazza
16 Ulu Cliffhouse

500 m
0.25 miles

THE FIRST TO SURF ULUS

In 1971 movie director Albert Falzon's crew was filming footage for the iconic surf movie *Morning of the Earth* when they stumbled upon the now legendary freight-train left-handers breaking off the cliffs at Uluwatu. That was almost four decades after surfing was first introduced in Kuta and the other waves of the Bukit Peninsula had barely been discovered yet.

Australian surfer Stephen Cooney (just 15 years old at the time, and who later told his story in his book *Unearthed*) was filmed catching the first wave ever ridden at Ulu. Within a few years, Wayne 'Rabbit' Bartholomew and Hawaiian legend Gerry Lopez were photographed shooting the barrel at Ulu.

AXELLE LEVUIET/SHUTTERSTOCK ©

Pantain Suluban

in advance (kecakdancebali.com). As with all temples in Bali, you'll need to wear a sarong in order to enter; if you don't have one you'll be given a sarong at the entrance.

The Thrill of Uluwatu

Surf Bali's best-known waves

With its consistent waves and dramatic scenery, Uluwatu is considered one of the best places in the world to surf, and the cliffs here provide exceptional vantage points from which to watch the action – it's hard to beat the view from **Single Fin** and the cluster of cliffside cafes at **Pantai Suluban**. There are five peaks that comprise what is affectionately referred to as Ulus; none of these are suitable for beginners, but neighbouring **Thomas Beach** has consistently smaller waves and is better for newbies and apprehensive surfers. If you're an experienced surfer, then paddle out from the famous cave at Pantai Suluban, the entry point to Ulus, to reach Racetracks. This is the fastest section with the steepest walls and the roundest barrels; at mid to lower tides you'll have access to some of the world's most perfect tubes. Just south of the cave is the Peak, which is best avoided around low tide

DRINKING AROUND ULUWATU: CLIFFTOP COCKTAILS
MAP p97

Kelly's Warung Just above beach level with a view of the cliffs, Kelly's is gorgeous at sunset. Happy hour is 3pm to 5pm.

Dugong Look out over a curved infinity pool and across the ocean here. There's a comprehensive menu of wines, cocktails and juices.

Ulu Cliffhouse There's a relaxed but exclusive atmosphere at this upmarket boutique hotel. Settle into a plush daybed with a cocktail in hand.

La Terrazza Italian food and drinks on the cliff at Uluwatu surf break. Book a seat to nab one of the best sunset views on the Bukit Peninsula.

when it can be uncomfortably shallow; it's not for the faint-hearted, but the Peak has a forgiving take-off point. Outside Corner, where the swell can rise to triple overhead, is where the 'Balinese Pipeline' starts to work some real big-wave magic. It breaks beyond the Peak and fires right across the line of Racetracks. South of Outside Corner (and breaking even further out) is the Bombie, which can reach 40ft and should be avoided unless you're a big-wave charger of note. If you're looking for a quiet wave, then head for Temples, a relatively fickle spot south of the Peak that can break on smaller days; the longer paddle also helps to keep crowds to a minimum. For an excellent guide to the surf breaks around the Bukit Peninsula, see indonesiansurfguide.com.

A Place of Power

Visit the famous Uluwatu temple

According to ancient Balinese scripts, **Pura Luhur Ulu Watu** is a magical portal that has the potential to transport those who set eyes on it directly to heaven. It is absolutely spectacular, and even the casual observer can feel its significance; the landscape, sculpted gardens and, above all, the dramatic 70m-high cliffs that rise from the ocean amount to what would be a highly spiritual spot even without the presence of one of Bali's most important sea temples. Since it was built in the 11th century, the temple has been one of the most spiritually charged sites in all of Bali, although the crowds of selfie-hunters can make it difficult to remember that this is first and foremost a place of worship. Take time to walk along the clifftop path, which offers gorgeous views of the temple with the Indian Ocean below, but beware of the monkeys here. Some people say they are the guardians of the temple, but they really are a nuisance and behave more like bandits. They rarely miss an opportunity to make off with visitors' bags, sunglasses, cameras or phones, and researchers have established that these monkeys have learned 'bartering' skills and know that people will offer food in order to retrieve their belongings. Like Pura Tanah Lot (p222), which also has an astounding Indian Ocean vantage point and is a favourite location at sunset, Pura Luhur Ulu Watu is one of Bali's busiest tourist spots; if you want to experience sunset spirituality at an historic sea-cliff temple without the crowds, then head to the comparatively almost-unknown Pura Rambut Siwi (p224) in west Bali.

BEST YOGA STUDIOS AROUND ULUWATU

The Istana A luxurious clifftop retreat and meditation resort hosting two classes a day; drop-ins are welcome.

Morning Light Classes are held every morning in a beautiful grass-roofed yoga space, surrounded by tropical vegetation and a view of the ocean.

Yoga Searcher Choose from three classes each day at this 'eco-lodge for yoga lovers', which also holds workshops and kirtan (devotional singing) events.

Alchemy All classes here are centred on the Earth's elements. After class you can nourish your body at Alchemy's plant-based restaurant.

La Tribu With a focus on movement, La Tribu offers classes like dance, flexibility and breath work, as well as yoga. There is a schedule for kids classes, too.

 EATING IN ULUWATU: OUR PICKS ———————————— MAP p97

Jeffry Warung A good budget option at the popular surf point. Sandwiches here are under 50,000Rp. $

Single Fin A surfer bar on the cliffs overlooking the surf break. The food is tasty and the vibe is laid-back. Great spot for sunset drinks. $$

Land's End Café This daytime cafe has a good selection of smoothies, smoothie bowls and breakfasts. There are also vegan options. $$

Suka Espresso With breakfast specials for 55,000Rp, this buzzing cafe is a popular morning hangout. The lunch and dinner options are delicious, too. $$

Beyond Uluwatu

The rest of the hot and arid Bukit Peninsula, revered for its sunset views, is peppered with gorgeous beaches, famous surf breaks and cliff-top hotels.

Places

GETTING AROUND

Even the main roads on the central part of the Bukit Peninsula are more like winding (often potholed) country lanes. At busy times (particularly around sunset) it can take a long time to travel by car, and it will be quicker (and cheaper if you're travelling with friends) to hire individual Gojek or Grab motorbikes. Some riders will, for a small additional fee, allow two passengers on a bike, but beware of the safety implications of this.

It's a bizarre fact that the Bukit Peninsula, which hangs off the southern tip of Bali, is markedly less well-known than Uluwatu, its furthest point. On early Dutch maps the peninsula was marked as Tafelhoek (Table Corner) and the Bukit (pronounced *book-it*), which translates simply as 'hill', was barely inhabited thanks to its lack of permanent rivers. These days, the Bukit coastline and its luxury resort enclave of Nusa Dua host some of the world's most iconic beach clubs and hotels. You'll find accommodation to suit every budget (from US$10 dorms to Raffles' US$3500 per night villas) and beaches so varied that almost every traveller will find their piece of paradise.

Jimbaran

TIME FROM ULUWATU: **35 MINS**

Feast on Just-caught Seafood

Pantai Jimbaran is famous for the scores of seafood restaurants that line the bay and spill out onto the golden sand, and an evening spent here will give you the chance to indulge in exceptionally fresh locally caught fish that's barbecued while you soak up the laid-back tropical ambiance. As evening falls and strings of lights begin to twinkle, aromatic smoke from the restaurants' grills swirls through the air, and meandering musicians serenade diners seated at tables on the sand. Along Jimbaran's sweeping 4km beach there are three groups of restaurants. The ones on **Pantai Muaya**, in the south, are mid-range in terms of pricing and atmosphere. The cluster of 10 eateries at **Queen Beach**, the smallest section, is more basic than the others and this is reflected in the cheaper prices. **Pantai Kedonganan**, on the airport end, is the largest and busiest section; expect more neon lights and higher prices. There are around 40 restaurants in total. They're all relatively similar in that they have ice boxes and tanks of seafood at their entrance, and they sell the fish by weight (snapper is around 150,000Rp per kilogram at Pantai Muaya). The price includes rice and vegetables, and platters and set menus are available, too. While many restaurants open from late morning and take the last order at around 10pm, sunset is prime time to be here and the restaurants are all but empty by about 8pm.

Buy Seafood at Jimbaran's Market

In years gone by Jimbaran was predominantly a fishing village, and the tradition still lives on in this seaside town. Every morning from around 7am the **Kedongan Fish Market** (some call it the **Jimbaran Fish Market**), on the airport end of **Pantai Jimbaran**, swings into full gear as just-caught fish fresh off the boats is sold to shoppers, chefs and restauranteurs. It's as frenetic as it is fascinating, and the colours, shapes and sizes of the fish and shellfish on sale are mesmerising. The market is open all day, and if you buy anything the seller will scale and gut the fish, which you can then take to a warung just outside the market and, for around 20,000Rp per kilogram, have someone cook it for you.

A Museum of Mythical Monsters

The beginning of the Balinese new year, according to the Saka calendar, is **Nyepi** (Bali's 'Day of Silence'). It's a remarkable time to be on the island; a day when everything comes to a standstill and the island descends into silence. Roads are closed, lights are turned off, no fires may be made, and even the air space over Bali is shut down. The night before, however, absolute pandemonium reigns as enormous effigies of the monsters and demons from Balinese mythology are paraded through the streets, and musical instruments are banged, clattered and beaten. The effigies, called *ogoh-ogoh*, are astounding pieces of art that often stand more than 3m tall. They're made from bamboo and papier-mâché and are created over weeks (months, sometimes) by teams of men and boys. Usually the effigies are burned in the culmination of the Ngrupuk parade, so only those who are on the island around Nyepi (which usually falls in March) are treated to the *ogoh-ogoh* spectacle; however, the new **Saka Museum** at Ayana Resort in Jimbaran has changed this. It houses a collection of enormous *ogoh-ogoh* that were commissioned specifically for the display, and that were designed and made by the most revered artists in every one of Bali's nine regencies. The well-curated museum centres on Nyepi, and – through comprehensive information boards and a beautifully directed video – it transports visitors through this intriguing day. If you appreciate books, don't miss the library section of the museum, which features rare and collectable books about Bali.

THE BUKIT'S WATER WOES

If you get stuck in traffic on the Bukit Peninsula, it's quite likely that a water tanker is slowing things down; they can be an annoyance, but these vehicles have become a very necessary part of life on this arid peninsula. The Bukit has no permanent rivers and no freshwater sources of its own, and as the limestone that comprises this land is extremely porous, rainwater disappears quickly as it drains into the cracks and fissures. With all of the development on the Bukit, the existing infrastructure battles to sustain the increasing demands, particularly in the dry season, so it's worth being mindful of your water consumption when you stay in the area.

EATING ON THE BUKIT PENINSULA: OUR PICKS

Warung Local This super popular local-style eatery has an array of Indonesian dishes on offer. The food is delicious. $

Bali Buda Bukit A health-food staple on the island, Bali Buda has an eclectic menu featuring organic and locally sourced ingredients. $$

Arwana The seafood brunch is a firm favourite at this beachfront grill restaurant, which serves fresh oysters, lobsters and premium fish. $$$

Rumari Indulge in a fine-dining experience at Raffles' Rumari restaurant, where the seven-course menu is inspired by the Indonesian archipelago. $$$

INDONESIA'S TALLEST STATUE

One of the first things you'll see as you fly into Bali is the **Garuda Wisnu Kencana** (GWK) statue, which depicts the Hindu god Vishnu riding the mythical bird Garuda. It towers over the Bukit Peninsula and, standing almost 120m high, is among the tallest statues in the world. It was designed by renowned Balinese sculptor Nyoman Nuarta and comprises 3000 tonnes of copper and bronze. It is a feat of art, science and engineering, and if you go to the GWK Cultural Park (gwkbali.com), it's well worth paying the extra fee for the tour inside the statue. The displays are excellent and share interesting details on the design, engineering and construction of the statue.

DOLLY MJ/SHUTTERSTOCK ©

Nusa Dua blowhole

Nusa Dua

TIME FROM ULUWATU: **45 MINS** 🚗

Witness the Ocean's Power

The exclusive resort enclave of Nusa Dua, which flanks the northeastern peninsula of the Bukit, has its own little peninsula, **Nusa Gede Island** (sometimes called Peninsula Island). It's been tamed into a park called the **Garden of Hope**, and is fringed by dramatically ragged limestone edges that are in stark contrast to its manicured surroundings. On the east side of this peninsula, powerful waves crash against this slab of dangerously jagged rocks, and in places the water is forced up through steep, tight gaps in the limestone, creating dramatic water eruptions. For years this natural phenomenon was obscured by vegetation and the jagged limestone made it difficult (and dangerous) to get closer for a good view. Thankfully, a concrete walkway and viewing points have now been built, and the path will take you safely over the rocks and close to the blowhole. You'll have to pay to access the walkway, and the gate only opens at 9am – a pity, as sunrise here would be epic. There is a picturesque sunrise spot nearby, though, and there's another little outcrop just north of Nusa Gede Island – while you won't see the water blow here, watching the sun rise from there is something well worth waking up for.

 DRINKING ON THE BUKIT PENINSULA: OUR PICKS

Cliff Bar at Six Senses Uluwatu Unbelievable ocean views and fab cocktails – try the banana colada and chipotle margarita. The kombucha is good, too.

Rock Bar Decks jut out over the rocks, and it's spectacular for sunset drinks. Rock Bar is incredibly popular, so book a table in advance.

El Kabron An adults-only clifftop beach club with a very Mediterranean vibe and stunning Indian Ocean views. There's an extensive drinks menu.

White Rabbit Lounge A sultry speakeasy that doubles as an early-morning coffee bar. Order from the extensive cocktail menu, or build your own martini.

ART & ARCHITECTURE OF THE BUKIT PENINSULA – A SCOOTER TOUR

Start at the Garden of Hope at ❶ **Nusa Gede Island** along the Nusa Dua enclave, where the ❷ **water blow** is impressive at high tide. The next stop is ❸ **Museum Pasifika**, about 1km away, which has a permanent exhibition of more than 600 pieces of art from around the Asia Pacific region. The roads from here across the Bukit Peninsula are tangled, so use Google Maps to plot your route southwest to ❹ **Pura Dhang Kahyangan Gunung Payung**, a spacious, quiet temple complex with interesting architecture and lovely ocean views. You'll then need to skirt around a golf course to reach ❺ **Pantai Pandawa**. It's popular for its beach, but what's remarkable here are the large sculptures of characters from Hindu mythology that are set into cliffside enclaves on the steep road down to the beach. Pull into the view site parking to appreciate them. Continue east, using Google Maps to navigate, to ❻ **Pura Luhur Ulu Watu**, renowned for its spectacular architecture and clifftop location. You'll have seen the imposing Garuda statue from various spots around the Bukit; that's your next stop. Jl Raya Uluwatu Pecatu will take you from Uluwatu almost to the ❼ **GWK Cultural Park**, an old illegal quarry that now has huge sculptures set between enormous walls of cut limestone. It's worth paying the additional fee for the tour inside the Garuda statue, and to learn about the engineering work that went into constructing this 120m-high icon. The final stop is the ❽ **Saka Museum**, which has an outstanding display of *ogoh-ogoh* effigies made by some of Bali's most revered artists.

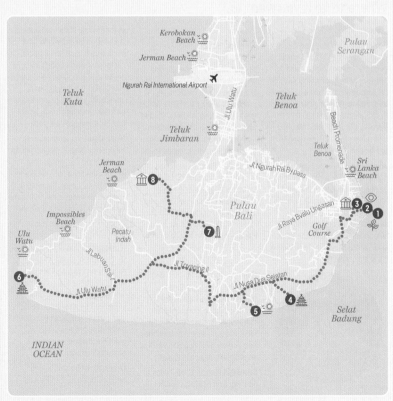

Beaches on the Bukit Peninsula

Tucked into coves and bays around the Bukit's dramatic coastline are pockets of enticing beaches – almost each one quite different from the other. Here, there is something for everyone: those seeking solitude, to swim, or to enjoy scenic spots for photographs. Generally, the beaches get busier throughout the day (sunset is a popular time to be at the west-facing beaches); expect crowds on the weekends. There is an entry fee (usually less than US$1) for most beaches.

Where to go if you want to...

Swim

Pantai Guning Payung A reef keeps the water off this small, secluded beach quite calm. There is a lifeguard, and you can rent a canoe, umbrella or sun bed. At low tide you can walk to Pandawa Beach. For 15,000Rp (return) a shuttle will take you down the steep 700m road to the beach.

Jimbaran (p100, pictured top right) With an almost 4km-long beach, it's easy to find a spot here to relax. The water is calm and great for a paddle. It's superb for plane-spotting (the airport runway flanks the beach) and, as the beach is west-facing, it's scenic at sunset.

Relax

Thomas Beach (p98) Pretty Thomas Beach can feel quite secluded, as lush vegetation shrouds its steep sides. There are some warungs here and you can swim or surf (the waves are always smaller here than at neighbouring Pantai Suluban). Access is via 130 stairs, which helps to keep the crowds away.

Balangan Beach (pictured left) A rare spot for blissful beach bumming. The row of stilted bars high over the sand (some with rooms you can stay in overnight) could be a Swiss Family Robinson backdrop.

Hang out with family

Melasti Popular Melasti Beach has been developed into a tourist area, and there are beach clubs, restaurants and sun loungers here, too. A reef forms natural pools at low tide. Kecak (see p96) is performed at an amphitheatre at sunset.

Sundays Beach Club At the eastern end of Melasti, but

inaccessible from that beach, is Sundays Beach Club. This exclusive beach has a good restaurant and various VIP areas, and lifeguards are always on duty. SUPs, kayaks and snorkelling gear are available, and the evenings bring beach bonfires and movies, too.

Nusa Dua Exclusive resorts have colonised the idyllic Nusa Dua beachfront, but you can still access the area at Nusa Gede Island (p102), near the Grand Hyatt. The water is calm and the beach sandy – lovely for kids.

Be alone

Nunggalan The 30-minute hike to the beach, along a steep, rocky trail, is strenuous but worthwhile for the solitude. The almost-2km-long beach is flanked by a reef and feels quite deserted, although some umbrellas are available. A graffiti-covered shipwreck attracts Instagrammers.

Green Bowl Beautiful, wild and secluded, Green Bowl is

YUSNIZAM YUSOF/SHUTTERSTOCK ©

HOW TO

Bay watch Keep an eye on the tides – some beaches are inaccessible when the tide is high, so be careful you don't get stranded.

Be aware Monkeys are a real menace on the Bukit. Watch your belongings and don't coax the monkeys closer.

Budget Keep small notes easily accessible as you'll need to pay 2,000Rp or 5,000Rp to access some of the beaches.

Go prepared The walk to some of the beaches can be hot and strenuous. Drinks aren't always available so take your own bottled water.

loved by surfers. There's not much beach at high tide; low tide reveals rock pools and two caves. An arduous walk to access it keeps the crowds away.

Do some people-watching

Pantai Pandawa Busy Pandawa is well developed, with canoes and bicycles for rent, and an array of restaurants and shops. Looking for a quiet patch? Walk east to Timbis Beach.

Pantai Padang Padang This tiny beach is hugely popular, and there's a lot going on: swimming, tanning, surfing

and surf lessons. There are umbrellas for rent. Market stalls are tucked into a cove, and there are some warungs here, too.

Dreamland The name alone is an irresistible drawcard and Dreamland is a lively crowd-puller for both tourists and expats (in fact everyone... and their dogs). There's even more of a show when the surf's big.

Take photographs

Pantai Suluban (p98) This beach is popular with Instagrammers, and is the spot for advanced surfers

(it's the entry point for the Ulu breaks). After weaving past cliffside cafes, you'll emerge into a limestone cove. At low tide you can access the small 'hidden beach' through a cave; it's dramatic and surrounded by craggy limestone boulders and cliffs.

Pantai Batu Barak The beach is unimpressive, but the road leading there slices dramatically between sheer-cut cliffs – good for photos.

Pantai Bingin Cliffside bars, craggy rock outcrops and picturesque traditional shrines make Bingin one of Bali's most photogenic beaches.

Nusa Lembongan

UNCROWDED SURF | WORLD-CLASS DIVING | MANGROVE FORESTS

GETTING AROUND

Boats to Nusa Lembongan leave from Sanur, Benoa or Serangan harbours. Fast-boat services take 40 minutes. Find prices at baliferries. com. Public boats leave at irregular times from the beach at Sanur, and the crossing takes 90 minutes. Grab and Gojek apps don't work here but 'taxis' (canopied pickups) ply the streets. Most visitors hire a motorbike as distances are short. Beware that maintenance might be lax and many lanes are badly potholed.

☑ TOP TIP

Pack light and be prepared to get a little wet. While departures from mainland Bali will be via jetty, most fast boats and ferries will moor off the beach at Nusa Lembongan, and you'll wade through the shallows and then carry your luggage a short distance across the beach.

Only 40 minutes from Bali by fast boat, Nusa Lembongan's rich Hindu culture and dramatic landscapes of wave-pounded cliffs and quiet mangrove forests offer a more accessible and relatively uncrowded alternative to the ever-popular Gili Islands. It's small enough to give you that feeling of being on an island, but big enough to allow for a change of scenery should you need one.

The 2km stretch of white sand that is Pantai Jungutbatu must be one of the few beaches on the planet where you can snorkel over a coral reef just 100m from surfers who are riding perfectly formed reef-break waves. Lembongan is renowned for its underwater world, and numerous dive centres offer easy access to all the best diving and snorkelling spots. The island is also the launch pad for Nusa Ceningan and Nusa Penida, but it packs in enough variety and activities to keep you inspired and exploring for a week or more.

Explore Lembongan's Underwater World

Dive or snorkel around the islands

Nusa Lembongan (along with neighbours Nusa Ceningan and Nusa Penida) falls within the **Coral Triangle**, a marine region revered for its exceptional biodiversity, and the diving and snorkelling here is absolutely sublime. The rocky shorelines and warm waters host healthy reefs and beautiful coral gardens that attract an abundance of marine life; don a mask and snorkel and you'll see schools of colourful reef fish, curious turtles and majestic manta rays gliding with the currents. The water around Lembongan, Ceningan and Penida was declared a marine protected area (MPA) in 2010, and there are said to be 296 species of coral and 576 species of fish here – it really is an underwater wonderland.

The visibility for diving is good year-round (it averages 20m, although often it can be up to 30m) and the warm water makes for pleasant snorkelling. There are more than 15

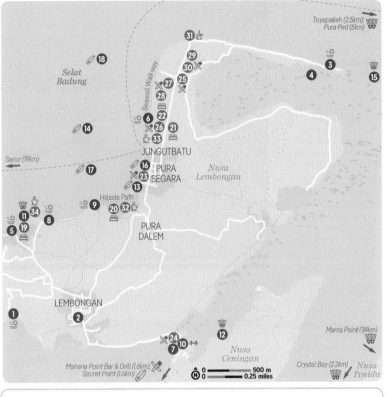

SIGHTS
1 Dream Beach
2 Gala-Gala Underground House
3 Mangrove Beach
4 Mangroves
5 Mushroom Bay
6 Pantai Jungutbatu
7 Seaweed plantations
8 Secret Beach
9 Song Lambung Beach
10 Yellow Bridge

ACTIVITIES
11 Bali Hai
12 Ceningan Divers
13 Eddy Surfboard Hire
14 Lacerations
15 Mangrove Point
16 Monkey Surfing
17 Playgrounds
18 Shipwrecks

SLEEPING
19 Bali Hai Villa
20 Batu Karang
21 Isla Indah Retreat
22 Pondok Jenggala

EATING
23 99 Meals House
24 Alponte Ristorante
25 Curry Traders
26 Fin Island
27 Koa Donuts
28 Ohana's
29 The Coconut Hut
30 The Sampan

DRINKING & NIGHTLIFE
31 The Captain Bar and Grill
32 The Deck Café and Bar
33 Tigerlillys Beach Shack
34 Why Not Mushroom

dive sites around the three islands (**Manta Point**, with its cleaning station, is a highlight for many), many of which are accessible for snorkellers, too. If you don't want to head out on a boat, then scoot around to **Mangrove Point** at the northeast of Lembongan. You can hire snorkelling gear here and swim out from the beach (at high tide is best) to explore the pretty coral gardens.

Setting up a boat-based snorkelling or diving trip from Lembongan is easy. Dive shops abound, and most homestays and guesthouses also sell trips; expect to pay from around

GIVE BACK

To get involved with beach clean-ups in Lembongan, check @lembogansurfteam, @frenchkissdivers lembongan or @ceningandiver for updates.

BEST BEACHES ON NUSA LEMBONGAN

Jungutbatu
Lembongan's busiest beach is fringed with cafes, bars and guesthouses. There are dive spots and surf breaks, and it's also great for SUP.

Mangrove Beach
Fronted by warungs, pretty Mangrove Beach offers wonderful views of Bali and Gunung Agung, particularly at sunset.

Mushroom Bay A crescent of powdery sand is fringed with old trees; boats come and go during the day, but it's serene in the late afternoons.

Secret Beach This quiet, secluded beach next to Mushroom Bay feels quite wild.

Song Lambung Beach A beautiful and justifiably popular beach tucked into a small bay. Trees offer plenty of shade.

RICHARD WHITCOMBE/SHUTTERSTOCK ©

Manta ray

150,000Rp for a three-stop snorkelling trip. If you only have one day, book a trip with long-established **Bali Hai**, who will arrange everything from your hotel pickup on Bali to boat transport, snorkelling and dive sessions, as well as lunch. If you're interested in learning more about marine life, then book a diving or snorkelling trip with eco-friendly **Ceningan Divers**, who take care to explain the role and significance of the creatures spotted underwater.

Share Waves with Mantas

Surf the breaks off Nusa Lembongan

Crashing waves are not typically conducive to the conditions that make for great diving, but Lembongan offers excellent surfing and outstanding diving on the same beach. Spectacular **Pantai Jungutbatu**, a 2km-long west-facing stretch of Lembongan's coastline, has three reefs that catch good, consistent surf on a daily basis – and, on rare occasions, you will see barrelling overhead waves. **Playgrounds** is the southernmost – and most popular – surf spot, and **Lacerations** is just a 150m paddle to the north (past Bali Hai's dive pontoon). Although some surf schools do bring their students to

 EATING IN NUSA LEMBONGAN: OUR PICKS ———————— MAP p107

99 Meals House A simple warung with a brilliant sea view, and a delicious *nasi campur* (rice with a choice of side dishes). $

Fin Island A popular cafe serving everything from soups and variations of avo toast to Mexican options, pizzas, sandwiches and rice bowls. $$

Curry Traders Quite unexpected, this dreamy restaurant is as much a feast for the eyes as it is for the tastebuds. $$

Alponte Ristorante With gorgeous views of the Yellow Bridge, seaweed farms and Nusa Ceningan, this alfresco-style restaurant serves all the Italian faves. $$

Lacerations, it might be the intimidating name that keeps the crowds away. But here beautifully peeling waves break both left and right, allowing for an easy paddle with the current back around the edge of the reef. You will sometimes see turtles and, with any luck, manta rays. Beware of surfing these breaks and the more fickle **Shipwrecks** further to the north at lower tides as the reef can become very shallow. You can paddle to these spots from the beach, or for 50,000Rp a boatman will take you out and pick you up at an arranged time. **Eddy Surfboard Hire** at the southern end of Pantai Jungutbatu has a good selection of boards for all conditions, and **Monkey Surfing** (in the middle of the beach) runs well-prepared classes for all levels.

Secret Point is the only surf spot on neighbouring Nusa Ceningan. It's a real gem for experienced surfers and is reached through a sort of cellar room under the terrace of the **Mahana Point Bar & Grill** (p113), which has phenomenal views and two high-tide cliff-jump boards.

Explore Lembongan's Most Peaceful Side

Kayak through the mangroves

The northeastern corner of Lembongan is wrapped in an immense tangle of **mangroves**, and exploring the waterways here is probably the most peaceful way to experience the island. Shady tunnels that wind through trees offer respite from the sun and – despite the shrill sounds from cicadas – the world here feels quiet, still and cool. For an extremely serene mangrove experience, hire a boatman to pole you through the waterways (expect to pay around 150,000Rp for 30 minutes). If you're up for a paddle, rent a kayak and explore on your own, or go on a guided kayak tour (around 175,000Rp for an hour).

Mangroves are exceptionally important and diverse ecosystems, and the dense forest plays a vital role in protecting land from erosion and the wrath of the waves. It's a nursery for coral reefs, and it's here that fish like snappers and tarpons come to spawn; look among the roots and you might see fiddler crabs, crab-eating frogs or, if you're lucky, an Asian water monitor. The early mornings and late afternoons are particularly rewarding if you're into birding. The metallic blue cerulean kingfisher is quite common here, as is the striated heron and the little lemon-bellied white-eye.

The mangroves cover a significant portion of Lembongan, and while most kayak and boat trips run from the northeastern stretch of the island (simply arrive and book your trip

THE ISLANDS' BEST DIVE SPOTS

Dive master **Kadek Gama**, who has worked for Bali Hai (balihaicruises.com) around Nusa Lembongan since 1999, shares his favourite dive sites.

Manta Point (p107) Throughout the year you'll find at least four or five manta rays here at the cleaning station.

Crystal Bay In the cold-water season between July and October you'll see *mola mola* (ocean sunfish) at depths of 18m to 40m.

Mangrove Point (p107) This is great for snorkelling; it's shallow and safe, the coral is beautiful and there are often turtles. If you're lucky you might see dolphins.

Toyapakeh The coral here is the best in the area but it gets very busy with boats.

Pura Ped You can usually see turtles, sunfish, pufferfish, and sometimes beautiful thresher sharks.

DRINKING IN NUSA LEMBONGAN: BARS WITH A VIEW — MAP p107

| **Deck Café and Bar** Set above Pantai Jungutbatu, the views here are a big drawcard. There's beer on tap, a good gin selection and interesting cocktails. | **Why Not Mushroom** Climb steep steps for a gorgeous sunset view over Mushroom Bay; there's a happy-hour offering and good-value cocktails. | **Tigerlillys Beach Shack** Lounge on the sand at Pantai Jungutbatu and sip on cocktails, local wines, fresh-pressed juices or coffees. | **Captain Bar and Grill** An on-the-beach restaurant near the mangroves serving cocktails, mocktails, juices and beers. |

THE OCEAN'S DAY OF SILENCE

Every year on the fourth full moon of the Balinese calendar (usually around October) the ocean surrounding Nusa Lembongan, Nusa Ceningan and Nusa Penida goes quiet. There are no ferries darting between the islands, and no fishers casting their lines. All boats remain moored for 24 hours.

The bays are also empty of surfers, snorkellers and divers, and farmers refrain from collecting seaweed. The day of stillness – Nyepi Laut (sometimes also called Nyepi Segara) – is in honour of Dewa Baruna, the god of the sea. It is observed around these three islands only, and it happens about six months after Nyepi, the 'other' day of silence celebrated on Bali to mark the new lunar year (see p101).

JOAKIMBKK/GETTY IMAGES ©

Seaweed plantation, Nusa Lembongan

from one of the numerous small-scale operators), a handful are based on the southwestern arc of the mangroves near the Yellow Bridge. The road that skirts the mangroves, Jl Raya Lembongan, makes for a peaceful drive and is worth travelling simply to experience Lembongan's wilder, quieter side.

Nusa Lembongan's Fields of Green

Learn all about seaweed farming

Much of Nusa Lembongan's coastline is dominated by a beguiling submarine patchwork of **seaweed plantations**, and while the grid-like pattern can be discerned on many reefs

EATING IN NUSA LEMBONGAN: RESTAURANTS FOR FAMILIES ——— MAP p107

Koa Donuts A take-away spot for when only something sweet will do – flavours include tiramisu, strawberry sprinkle, Nutella and custard. $

Coconut Hut While the food at this casual eatery is fantastic (there's a good kiddies menu, too), the mini-golf course is a highlight. $$

Sampan Kids have a ball at the small playground, which includes a slide and climbing ropes. This seafood restaurant and grill also serves breakfast. $$

Ohana's This slightly swanky beach club has a kids menu, its small pool has a shallow section, and the beach forms a natural play area. $$

(and even on the fringe of the mangrove forests), it is most noticeable in the shallow 600m-wide channel between Lembongan and Ceningan islands. This patchwork of plots (most of which measure around 6m by 40m) make for intriguing photos, and a trip to the farms will give you an opportunity to learn about the planting, harvesting and drying processes involved in farming this submarine crop, which sustains a large proportion of the island's population. You can visit the seaweed farms at any stage of the tide, but you will get a better understanding of the complexities of this crop when the water is lower, and (unless you have a working command of Bahasa Indonesia) if you visit with a guide (most hotels and homestays can arrange this).

The seaweed industry is relatively new to Lembongan; it was introduced by a businessman from Surabaya in 1984 and almost immediately became a major earner as the lucrative crop was used chiefly in the cosmetics and ice-cream industries. During the tourism slump of the COVID-19 pandemic, however, prices plummeted when many islanders turned their attention from hospitality to seaweed and, due to increased production, profits dropped by about 75%. Towards the end of 2023, dried seaweed was netting only about 10,000Rp per kilogram.

Island of Intrigue

Tour Lembongan by e-bike

Diving, snorkelling and surfing might be Lembongan's biggest drawcards, but there are some intriguing places to visit on the island too. Bali E-Bike Tours (baliebiketours. com) has strung together a 23km route that takes in some of these spots and makes for a fun way to get to know the island. The tour starts at Mushroom Bay (p108); the first stop is **Dream Beach** and the rugged wave-pounded chasm known as Devil's Tears; you'll then visit the unusual **Gala-Gala Underground House**, which was hand-dug into the limestone by one man in the 1960s and '70s. A cycle over the iconic (if heart-stoppingly narrow) **Yellow Bridge** will put you on Nusa Ceningan to meet with a family of seaweed farmers. The shallow water that stretches half a kilometre between Lembongan and Ceningan is almost entirely patchworked by seaweed farms, and it's insightful to learn more about the gruelling work that goes into maintaining these.

Other stops on the tour include one of the oldest and most beautiful traditional family compounds on Lembongan, a death temple (where you'll learn about the intricacies of temple architecture), and the mangroves (p109). Lembongan is not big; it measures just 5km at its widest part, and while it rises to only 50m above sea level there are some steep hills, but the Indonesian-made Polygon e-bikes make for almost effortless cruising, for any level of fitness.

A HOUSE UNDERGROUND

Gala-Gala is a 500-sq-metre 'underground house' that has become a popular attraction on Nusa Lembongan. In the early 1960s the late Made Byasa, who lived next door, began to dig when he was inspired by the Mahabharata Hindu scripts to create his own version of Gala-Gala, a forest cave that became a hiding place for the heroes of one of the Hindu epics. Despite the label it has been given, Gala-Gala is more a labyrinth of tunnels than it is a house. It was quarried by hand with only a crowbar and a pick, and it took Made Byasa 15 years to complete it. He went on to use his cave as a place for meditation.

Beyond Nusa Lembongan

Even compared with laid-back Lembongan, rural Nusa Penida and the little sliver of 4km-long Nusa Ceningan are delightfully sleepy backwaters.

Places

Nusa Penida p112

GETTING AROUND

Having your own wheels is the only way to go north of Ubud. The relentless uphill climbs make it a challenge for all but the most dedicated cyclists and hikers. Conversely, returning to Ubud is all downhill, so if you can get a ride one-way, you can cycle or walk downhill the other way. Use apps for taxi rides and consider hiring a car and driver for a day out to the top sights.

For a coral outcrop that is barely 1km wide, Nusa Ceningan offers surprisingly varied landscapes with forested hilltops, sprawling mangrove forests, dramatic cliffs and the underwater patchwork of seaweed 'fields'. There are also some lovely homestays and boutique hotels here.

A short boat ride away is Nusa Penida, by far the largest of the three islands, which rises in a series of steeply forested ridges and ravines to an elevation of 524m. It's dry and arid (at least in comparison with Bali), and Penida has remained relatively undeveloped in terms of tourism. Most visitors only do an organised day trip, while those who stay longer settle into the wonderfully slow pace of this island.

Nusa Penida   TIME FROM NUSA LEMBONGAN: **20 MINS** 🚤

Watch Penida's traditional weavers at work

High up in the hills of remote southeast Nusa Penida, at the intersection of the roads to **Pantai Suwehan** and **Teletubbies Hill**, is the village of **Tanglad**, which is revered for the weaving traditions still practised there. The skills and knowledge have been passed down through generations, and the weavers are held in high regard; the textiles that many politicians and celebrities buy for their clothing are made here.

Tanglad resident Ngurah Hendrawan is an acclaimed dyer who uses only natural ingredients to colour his threads. He makes red from the root bark of the *mengkudu* trees (*Morinda citrifolia*) he grows, and browns come from the bark of his mahogany trees. His wife weaves textiles on a backstrap loom next to their **Ngurah Gallery** shop (in the village, on the road to Suwehan Beach), where you can buy the textiles they've created. If you'd like to see his dying process, Pak Ngurah will gladly show you.

Textiles like bold, geometric *rangrang* and intricate *cepuk* are produced in other homesteads around the village, and it's mesmerising to watch the women working at their looms. If

RIC JACYNO/SHUTTERSTOCK ©

Off Nusa Penida

SECRET SPOTS ON NUSA PENIDA

Wayan Surianta, owner of Penida Colada Beach Bar, on some of Nusa Penida's lesser-known scenic spots. *@penidacolada*

Pantai Tembeling
It's cool and shady here, where tropical rainforest meets the sea, and there is a cave and refreshing spring-water pools. Do not attempt the drive down on your own; local *ojek* (motorbike taxi) drivers offer their services from the parking space at the top.

Pantai Suwehan It's quiet and stunningly beautiful here. Go at low tide; at high tide the beach disappears and waves crash against the cliff.

Pantai Lumangan
From above you overlook Manta Bay and you can often see mantas. Steps were only recently cut into the cliff, so you can now access the beach – it's worth the walk.

you're travelling independently, ask around the village and look for signs that read '*tenun*' (which means weaving). Very little English is spoken here, so to learn more about the processes take a look at the informative Threads of Life website (threadsoflife.com). Ngurah's work is sold through their Ubud-based studio, and there is a wealth of weaving information on the site.

A temple beneath the Earth

Deep in a beachside hill in Nusa Penida's Suana district there is a rather unusual temple. **Pura Goa Giri Putri** is located in a cave, and to reach it is an adventure in itself. After wrapping a sarong around you, you will need to climb 110 steps from the carpark before you are blessed by a Hindu priest in a short purification ritual. You'll then need to wriggle through a narrow gap between the boulders that form the temple's gateway. The entrance can be claustrophobic, but once inside you'll be astounded by the size of the great cavern, which

✗ EATING ON NUSA PENIDA AND NUSA CENINGAN: OUR PICKS

Three Island Bar Enjoy Indonesian classics like *sate ayam* (chicken satay) and nasi goreng. This is a great budget option. (Nusa Ceningan) **$**

Mahana Point Bar & Grill Indonesian meals, pizzas, snacks and grilled fish are served along with exceptional ocean views. (Nusa Ceningan) **$$**

Penida Colada A very eco-conscious beachfront cafe with a broad menu of healthy foods and excellent cocktails. (Nusa Penida) **$$**

Cactus Beach Club Chill beside the pool or in the breezy cafe, and feast on Asian-influenced Mediterranean dishes. (Nusa Penida) **$$**

VIEWPOINTS ON NUSA PENIDA

Kelingking (T-Rex) This is the place to be for that famous view of Nusa Penida – the arc of gorgeous white beach fringing sublimely azure waters, and the towering spine of a white limestone cliff shaped a bit like a T-Rex. Get here early to avoid the day-tripping masses.

Saren Cliff Point The rough road means you'll need to walk the last half kilometre or so, which keeps the crowds away, but views of Penida's craggy coastline and churning turquoise bays are worth the effort.

Pura Gunung Cemeng This off-the-radar temple offers unadulterated views of Penida's ragged coastline. You'll walk about 1km from Sebuluh village, and from the ridge you might spot mantas in the turquoise bay below.

KASAKPHOTO/SHUTTERSTOCK ©

Kelingking

comprises several immense galleries in a natural cave system. Electric lighting has been fitted here, but it can still be dark and spooky in parts of the almost 300m walk past the five stations of prayer in the temple.

This is an important place of pilgrimage for Balinese Hindus, and there are almost always worshippers at the shrines; while you should respect their prayers and speak quietly, you will be more than welcome to pass through. Around the cave you are likely to see swiftlets, bats, spiders, cave crickets and, if you are very fortunate, you might catch sight of a rare orange-pincered Giri Putri cave crab. Unknown to science until 1993, this critically endangered species is found nowhere else on Earth.

 ## DRINKING ON NUSA CENINGAN: OUR PICKS

Twilight The cocktails here are excellent value (70,000Rp), and can be sipped with a view across the ocean to Bali.

View Day Club The cocktail menu is modest, but the views from up here make for unforgettable sunsets.

Park Cave Ceningan A scenic spot for a Bintang beer or fruit juice. It's up on Ceningan's hill, overlooking Nusa Penida.

Sea Breeze Affordable cocktails (80,000Rp) at a casual tropical-style bar. Don't miss the two-for-100,000Rp cocktails from 4pm to 7pm.

Experience the laid-back vibe of tiny Nusa Ceningan by hanging out at some of the viewpoints around this deceptively hilly 6.5-sq-km-island. Start at the iconic **1 Yellow Bridge** that connects Nusa Lembongan and Nusa Ceningan, and head for **2 Three Island Bar** on the crest of Ceningan. The view of Nusa Penida from its infinity pool is fantastic. Ignore Google Maps, which will guide you up a particularly steep lane, and instead turn right from the bridge and then drive 750m to where the road forks and take the sharp left. This road leads up Ceningan's spine to Three Island Bar. It's good in some places and decidedly rough in others, but nothing a scooter can't handle. Head back down the way you came, then turn right at the fork. **3 The Island** beach bar (excellent cocktail menu), just 120m back along this road, has a pool and beach-club vibe, and

views of the seaweed farms and Nusa Lembongan. Next stop is **4 Twilight** near the southwest tip of the island. It's also a small restaurant with a pool, but it has a very different view as it faces west towards Bali; this is a good spot for a lazy afternoon coffee. Backtrack 200m, then wind your way towards Insta-famous **5 Blue Lagoon**. Some of the cliffs have been wrapped in concrete pillars to protect the resort built atop them, so for something more spectacular follow the signs to **6 Driftwood Bar** at Island Cove Resort, where a short zip line (not for the fainthearted!) and a restaurant overlook an impressively turbulent inlet. Final stop – exceptional for sunsets – is **7 Mahana Point**, a warung and bar perched on a clifftop. There are two cliff-jumps here (5m and 10m; high tide only) and brilliant views of the surf point below.

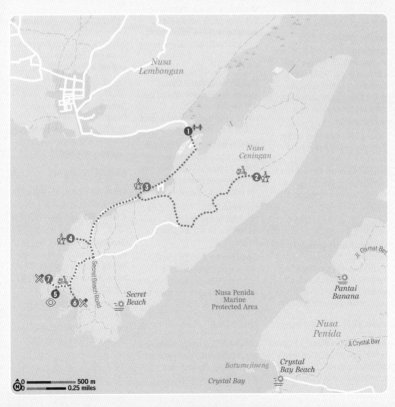

Places We Love to Stay

$ Cheap $$ Moderate $$$ Pricey

Sanur p86 (Map p87)

Kubu di Kayla $ Sanur's best-value budget rooms offer all the comforts and easy access to the beach, which is an eight-minute walk away.

Puri Mesari $$ Spacious rooms surround a pool, and there's an excellent Vietnamese restaurant on the property. It's a five-minute walk from Mertasari Beach.

Laghawa Beach Inn Hotel $$ An old Bali-style hotel with large rooms (each with a veranda) and gorgeous garden. While there is one step onto the veranda, the hotel is popular with those who have mobility issues.

Tandjung Sari Hotel $$$ This family-owned boutique hotel was built in the 1960s by an Indonesian-Dutch artist. It's on the beach, and comprises cottages surrounded by a verdant garden.

Segara Village Hotel $$$ A spacious luxury beachfront resort surrounded by large trees and a plush garden. It was established in the 1950s, but rooms are now contemporary in style.

Denpasar p91

Bali Inna Heritage Hotel (p93) $ Once host to celebrities and royalty but now past its prime, Denpasar's oldest hotel still retains some of its charm. It's a good, clean option in the city.

Uluwatu p96 (Map p97)

Uluwatu Surf Villas $$$ Loved by families, this clifftop resort comprising modern villas has outrageous views of the ocean.

A skate park and yoga shala add to the appeal.

Bingin

Temple Lodge $$ Dreamy, eclectic suites with a surf-and-yoga vibe, and sea views from Uluwatu to Kuta.

Mû Bungalows Boutique Resort $$$ This laid-back boutique-style resort is perched atop a cliff. There's a real bohemian kind of vibe here, and views from the pool and restaurant are stunning.

Anantara Uluwatu $$$ Incredible views abound from this luxury resort. It's built on the edge of Uluwatu's cliffs; some suites have infinity pools and spa baths with ocean views.

Jimbaran p100

Bali Bobo Hostel $ Clean, characterful hostel with mixed dorm rooms and a pool. There's not much around so you'll need a scooter to get to places.

Raffles Bali $$$ The ultimate in luxury and indulgence, Raffles' sublime villas have sea views, private pools and guests are allocated a private butler.

Movenpick $$$ The extensive kids club at this resort is incredible, as are the pools for kids.

Open House $$$ This neat, contemporary hotel has a laid-back beach-house vibe. It's 100m from a cluster of seafood restaurants.

Nusa Dua p102

Laguna $$$ A newly renovated beachfront resort built around seven pools. Perfect for a chilled luxury holiday.

Nusa Lembongan p106 (Map p107)

Pondok Jenggala $ Offering excellent value, this small guesthouse has large, simple rooms set around a deep pool.

Isla Indah Retreat $$ A tropical chic boutique hotel just off Pantai Jungutbatu. There is a yoga space, a surf and yoga shop, and a vegan restaurant on site.

Bali Hai Villa $$$ The luxurious two-bedroom open-air villas have a private swimming pool and lounge area.

Batu Karang $$$ With a focus on sustainability, this peaceful boutique hotel has gorgeous views over Pantai Jungutbatu and Bali's Gunung Agung.

Nusa Penida p112

Deep Roots Dive & Yoga Resort $$$ A peaceful getaway just 15 minutes from Penida's coastline. Daily yoga classes are included.

Nusa Ceningan p115

Tatak Bunut Private Villa $$ Five wooden bungalows dotted around a pool at the very top of Nusa Ceningan's tranquil hills.

Ceningan Divers $$ This small, very sustainable dive centre has six cosy bungalows. It's in a peaceful waterside setting, surrounded by mangroves.

Aurora Beach View $$ The rooms, restaurant and infinity pool have gorgeous views over the bay to Nusa Lembongan.

R.M. NUNES/SHUTTERSTOCK ©

Pura Luhur Ulu Watu (p99)

Above: *Legong* dancers (p127); Right: stone carvings, Batubulan (p152)

Ubud Region

CULTURE, BEAUTY AND PLEASURE

One of Bali's unmissable regions, Ubud has a seductive vibe accented by thrills, surprises and personal delights.

A dancer moves her hand just so and 200 pairs of entranced eyes follow the exact movement. A gamelan player hits a melodic riff and 200 pairs of feet tap along with it. The Legong goes into its second hour as the bumblebee dance unfolds with its sprightly flair and 200 back-sides forget they're stuck in rickety plastic chairs.

So another dance per-formance works its spell in Ubud, the famed town where all that is mag-ical about Bali comes together in one popular package. From night-ly cultural performances, to museums celebrating the works of artists whose creativ-ity flowered here, to the impossibly green rice fields that spill down lush hill-sides to rushing rivers below, Ubud is a feast for the soul. Personal pleasures like deli-cious dining, shopping, spas and more only add to the appeal. Ubud's full charm may be hard to detect on a quick visit, but over time its addictive vibe takes hold – the size of the town's expat community at-tests to this.

North and south of Ubud you'll discover even more enchanting sights, wheth-er it's swaths of natural beauty, famed ancient temples and archaeolog-ical sites, or traditional artisans' studios. It's a land ideal for exploring backroads shaded by bam-boo and palm trees. You can thrill to white-water rafting, downhill cycling, rural treks or just strolling through timeless villages.

THE MAIN AREAS

UBUD
The centre of it all.
p122

BEYOND UBUD (NORTH)
A lush land with ancient sites.
p142

BEYOND UBUD (SOUTH)
Handicrafts, ancient sites and villages.
p147

Find Your Way

The Ubud region stretches from near the coast to the north, up ever-steeper Mt Batur. Main roads follow the land's textures. Explore it in half a day or a week, depending on how often you stop.

WALKING

Ubud and the surrounding countryside are easily covered on foot. Villages such as Pejeng, Bedulu, Tampaksiring and Taro are also easily explored on walks. Longer distances, however, are more of a challenge owing to busy roads.

CAR OR MOTORBIKE

The region is best explored with the freedom of your own wheels, whether you or someone else does the driving. Surprises await along the roads that call for an unplanned stop and experience.

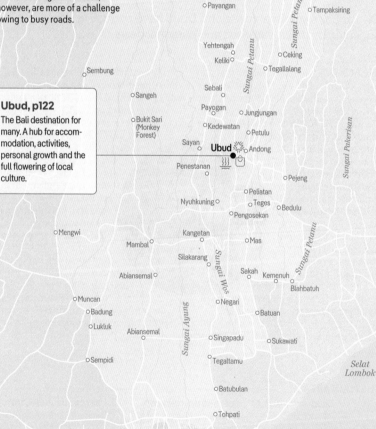

Ubud, p122

The Bali destination for many. A hub for accommodation, activities, personal growth and the full flowering of local culture.

Payangan

Sebatu

Tampaksiring

Yehtengah

Keliki

Ceking

Tegallalang

Sungai Petanu

Sungai Petanu

Sembung

Sangeh

Sebali

Payogan

Jungjungan

Sungai Pakerisan

Bukit Sari (Monkey Forest)

Kedewatan

Petulu

Sayan

Ubud

Andong

Penestanan

Pejeng

Peliatan

Nyuhkuning

Teges

Bedulu

Pengosekan

Mengwi

Kangetan

Mas

Mambal

Silakarang

Sungai Wos

Sakah

Kemenuh

Abiansemal

Blahbatuh

Sungai Petanu

Muncan

Negari

Batuan

Badung

Lukluk

Abiansemal

Sungai Ayung

Singapadu

Sukawati

Sempidi

Tegaltamu

Selat Lombok

Batubulan

Tohpati

Selat Badung

Denpasar

0   5 km
0   2.5 miles
N

IVELICHKO/SHUTTERSTOCK ©

Ubud Monkey Forest (p133)

Plan Your Time

Time in Ubud proper may become an enjoyable blur, but you'll want to save days for the many delights to the north and south.

Only One Day

Stroll the streets of Ubud starting with the **Palace** (p122) and **Monkey Forest** (p133). Pause at a **cafe** (p133) and browse the **shops** (p139) on Jl Dewi Sita and Jl Hanoman. Make time for a **museum** (p128) filled with the art for which Ubud is famous. Then venture into the verdant **rice fields** (p132). At night, enjoy a meal followed by a **dance performance** (p126).

A Week or More

During the mornings, take long walks in the countryside. In the afternoons, visit the art museums. Get in tune with Ubud's rhythm: take naps, read books, wander. Try a **course** (p137) in Balinese culture. Head north to ancient sites like **Gunung Kawi** (p144), explore the wonders of nearby **Pejeng** (p147) and **Bedulu** (p148). Prowl handicrafts villages like **Mas** (p149) and **Sukawati** (p151) in the south.

Seasonal Highlights

DECEMBER–FEBRUARY	MARCH–MAY	JUNE–AUGUST	SEPTEMBER–NOVEMBER
Peak season around the winter holidays brings visitors. Lodgings, restaurants and activities are booked solid. Rain is common.	At night, mountain breezes make air-con unnecessary, allowing you to enjoy the symphony of frogs, bugs and distant gamelan practices.	Temperatures average 30°C during the day and 20°C at night, although extremes are possible. July and Aug are peak tourism months.	From October to April the weather is cooler and wetter than in the south. In October, the Ubud Writers & Readers Festival is popular.

Ubud

ART & CULTURE | NATURE | CAFES & DINING

GETTING AROUND

From South Bali, Ubud is reached via Denpasar or Sanur. Expect the trip from the airport to take from 90 minutes to two hours or more depending on traffic. Other than the odd tourist bus, most people arrive via hired car.

Much of central Ubud is walkable, and walking is one of the top local activities. For rides further afield you will see local taxi drivers holding up signs, but these are not metered and negotiations can be a costly hassle. The ubiquitous Gojek and Grab apps provide easy access to rides on motorbikes and cars.

☑ TOP TIP

Ubud can be anything but serene at midday when traffic is calamitous and day trippers jam the centre of town and sights like the Monkey Forest. Escape to surrounding villages that are quieter, take walks in the countryside, visit a museum or shelter by the hotel pool.

Ubud is one of those places where a few days can easily turn into a stay of weeks, months or even years. Carefully developed over the decades, the town's reputation for art and culture is well deserved. This is a place where Balinese traditions imbue every waking moment, where colourful offerings adorn the streets and where the hypnotic strains of gamelan are an ever-present soundtrack to everyday life. It's also somewhere that is relentlessly on trend – a showcase of sustainable design, mindfulness, culinary inventiveness and personal development, whether it be yoga or a more esoteric pursuit.

Ubud is popular – sometimes suffocatingly so. But there's always an escape into a gallery, a rice-field path, a hidden cafe or within oneself. Ubud draws people with creative visions from across Bali and the world. Come here for relaxation, rejuvenation and self-fulfillment. And revel in all Ubud has to offer.

Visit Ubud's Palace
Wander amidst glitter and sculpture

Ubud's modest **palace** and temple, **Puri Saren Agung**, share a compound in the heart of Ubud. Most of the structures were built after the 1917 earthquake and the local royal family still lives here. Despite the name, this sprawling compound is not palatial or excessively ornate. Rather, it's a warren of courtyards and traditional Balinese buildings that extend well back from the limited area open to the public.

The stone carvings are a highlight; many are by noted Ubud artists such as I Gusti Nyoman Lempad and can be easily appreciated on a brief visit. At night, the main courtyard is a popular – and evocative – venue for dance performances. One way to gain access to the inner sanctum is to book via Airbnb one of two midrange guestrooms (called 'Saren Kauh Ubud Palace' online) hidden away inside. You can rise with the roosters in the morning and observe traditional Balinese life and feel the rhythms of the royal compound.

NOKURO/SHUTTERSTOCK ©

Puri Saren Agung

Enjoy Sacred Masterpieces

Visit Ubud's evocative temples

Ubud has dozens of temples. Most are closed to visitors; however, there are some noteworthy exceptions.

Pura Taman Saraswati is the most picturesque temple that's always open to the public. Right off Jl Raya Ubud, it provides a welcome relief from the crowded sidewalks. Waters flowing from the rear of the large site feed a pond in front, which overflows with lotus blossoms. Carvings honour Dewi Saraswati, the goddess of wisdom and the arts, who has clearly given her blessing to Ubud. Regular dance performances are staged at night.

To the east, **Pura Desa Ubud** is the main temple for the Ubud community. It's often closed and quiet. However, it comes alive for the extravagant ceremonies and processions for which Ubud is known. Stop by to see if something is on.

Continues on p128

UBUD'S ARTFUL HISTORY

Late in the 19th century, Cokorda Gede Agung Sukawati established a branch of the Sukawati royal family in Ubud and began a series of alliances and confrontations with neighbouring kingdoms. In 1900, with the kingdom of Gianyar, Ubud became (at its own request) a Dutch protectorate and was able to concentrate on its religious and cultural life.

The Cokorda descendants encouraged Western artists and intellectuals to visit the area in the 1930s, most notably Walter Spies, Colin McPhee and Rudolf Bonnet. They provided an enormous stimulus to local art, introduced new ideas and began displaying and promoting Balinese culture worldwide. As mass tourism arrived in Bali, Ubud became an attraction not for beaches or bars, but for the arts.

 EATING IN UBUD: BEST BALINESE WARUNGS ———————— MAP p124-5

In Da Compound Warung Behind a family guesthouse on delightful Jl Goutama; bargain-priced dishes burst with flavour and style. Bunnies hop about the garden. $

Mama's Warung Cheery Mama and her retinue cook up spicy Indo classics redolent with garlic. Satay peanut sauce is silky smooth, the fried sambal superb. $

Nasi Ayam Kedewatan Few residents trekking through Sayan pass without stopping. The star is *sate lilit:* minced chicken combined with spices then grilled on skewers. $

Warung Pulau Kelapa Huge menu of authentic Indonesian dishes drawn from across the archipelago. Sensational sambals; ask for dishes 'local style' to get real spiciness. $$

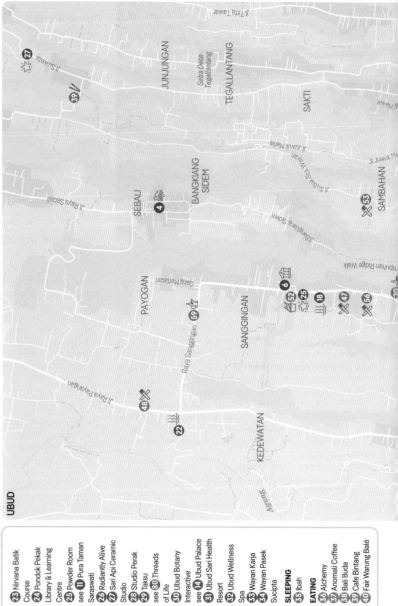

UBUD

HIGHLIGHTS
1. Casa Luna Cooking School
2. Yoga Barn

SIGHTS
3. Agung Rai Museum of Art
4. Bangkiang Sidem
5. Museum Puri Lukisan
6. Neka Art Museum
7. Pura Dalem Agung
8. Pura Dalem Ubud
9. Pura Desa Ubud
10. Pura Gunung Lebah
11. Pura Taman Saraswati
12. Puri Saren Agung
13. Ubud Monkey Forest
14. Ubud Palace

ACTIVITIES
15. ARMA
16. ARMA Open Stage
17. Bali Bird Walks
18. Bali Botanica Day Spa
19. Bali Swasthya Yoga Centre
20. Dumbo
21. Intuitive Flow
22. Mandapa Spa

23. Nirvana Batik Course
24. Pondok Pekak Library & Learning Centre
25. Powder Room
see 11 Pura Taman Saraswati
26. Radiantly Alive
27. Sari Api Ceramic Studio
28. Studio Perak
29. Taksu
see 30 Threads of Life
30. Ubud Botany Interactive
see 14 Ubud Palace
31. Ubud Sari Health Resort
32. Ubud Wellness Spa
53. Wayan Karja
54. Wayan Pasek Sucipta

SLEEPING
55. Ibah

EATING
56. Alchemy
57. Anomali Coffee
58. Bali Buda
59. Cafe Bintang
40. Fair Warung Balé

SAYAN

PENESTANAN

CAMPUAN

KUTUH

UBUD

PENGOSEKAN

NYUHKUNING

Katik Lantang

Ubud Centre

See Ubud Centre

Casa Luna Cooking School

Yoga Barn

Mandala Wisata Wenara Wana

N
0   500 m
0   0.25 miles

N
0   200 m
0   0.1 miles

41 Hujan Locale
42 In Da Compound Warung
43 Kafe
44 Locavore to Go
45 Mama's Warung
46 Moksa
47 Mozaic
48 Nasi Ayam Kedewatan
49 Nusantara
50 Pizza Bagus
51 Produce Market
52 Room4Dessert
53 Sari Organik
54 Sayuri
55 Tukies Coconut Shop
56 Warung Pulau Kelapa
57 Yellow Flower Cafe

DRINKING
58 Boliche
59 Kawi
60 Lair
61 Seniman Coffee Studio
62 Sweet Orange Warung

ENTERTAINMENT
63 Bali Culture Workshop

64 Kerta Art
65 Pondok Bamboo Music Shop
66 Pura Padang Kerta
67 Pura Penataran Kloncing
68 Puri Agung Peliatan

SHOPPING
69 Above the Clouds
70 Ananda Soul
71 Blue Stone Botanicals
72 Curative
73 Ganesha Bookshop
74 Jl Kajeng Market
75 Kado by Saraswati Paper
76 Kevala Home
77 Kou
78 Sensatia Botanicals
79 Studio K
80 Threads of Life
81 Toko Elami
82 Ubud Art Market
83 Ubud Raw Chocolate

125

JAJA/SHUTTERSTOCK ©

Scan the QR code for more info on the Cudamani gamelan troupe.

TOP EXPERIENCE

Balinese Dance

The highlight of an Ubud visit, Balinese dance flows with a hypnotic grace as dancers tell stories rich with the essence of Hindu lore. Multiple performances are staged nightly in Ubud, in a variety of styles. Gamelan music played on bamboo and bronze instruments is an integral part of many shows.

Kecak Dance

Probably the best-known dance for its spellbinding, hair-raising atmosphere, the Kecak features a 'choir' of men and boys who sit in concentric circles and slip into a trance as they chant and sing 'chak-a-chak-a-chak', imitating a troupe of monkeys. Sometimes called the vocal gamelan, this is the only music to accompany the dance re-enactment from the Hindu epic Ramayana, the familiar love story about Prince Rama and Princess Sita. The tourist version of Kecak was developed in the 1960s.

Barong & Rangda

The Barong and Rangda dance rivals the Kecak as Bali's most popular performance for tourists. Again, it's a battle between good (the Barong) and bad (the Rangda).

The Barong is a good but mischievous and fun-loving shaggy dog-lion, with huge eyes and a mouth that clacks away to much dramatic effect. Because this character is the good protector of a village, the actors playing the Barong (who are utterly lost under layers of fur-clad costume) will emote a variety of winsome antics. But as is typical of Balinese dance, it is not all lighthearted – the Barong is a very sacred character and you'll often see one in processions and rituals.

There's nothing sacred about the Barong's buddies. One or more monkeys attend to him and these characters often steal the show. Actors are given free rein to range wildly. The best aim a lot of high jinks at the audience, especially members who seem to be taking things a tad too seriously. Meanwhile, the widow-witch Rangda is bad through and through. The Queen of Black Magic, the character's monstrous persona can include flames shooting out her ears, a tongue dripping fire, a mane of wild hair and large breasts.

The story features a duel between the Rangda and the Barong, whose supporters draw their kris (traditional daggers) and rush in to help. The long-tongued, sharp-fanged Rangda throws them into a trance, making them stab themselves. It's quite a spectacle. Thankfully, the Barong casts a spell that neutralises the power of the kris so it cannot harm them.

Legong Dance

Characterised by flashing eyes and quivering hands, this most graceful of Balinese dances is performed by young girls. Their talent is so revered that in old age, a classic dancer will be remembered as a 'great Legong'. The stylised and symbolic story involves two Legong girls dancing in mirror image. They are elaborately made up and dressed in gold brocade, relating a story about a king who takes a maiden captive and consequently starts a war, in which he dies.

Kecak Fire Dance

This dance was developed to drive out evil spirits from a village. A male adult or boy dancer in a trance dances around and through a fire of coconut husks, riding a coconut palm 'hobby horse'. There are many variations of this dance, which is often included as a dramatic, flaming add-on at the end of other performances.

DANCE VENUES

Ubud Palace
Magical setting with an ornate backdrop.
Pura Dalem Ubud
A temple compound with a flame-lit backdrop.
Pura Taman Saraswati Beautiful temple setting with water features.
Arma Open Stage
Hosts top troupes.
Puri Agung Peliatan Village setting that hosts serious troupes.
Pura Padang Kerta and **Pura Penataran Kloncing** Simple, convenient venues on Jl Hanoman.

TOP TIPS

- Most performances start at 7pm or 7:30pm. Get there at least 20 minutes ahead to get a good seat. You can wait and buy tickets at the entrance.
- Snacks, water and beer are often sold inside the venue. Performances last about 90 minutes.
- Watch out for dirty costumes, disinterested orchestras, performers that tell stale jokes and other hallmarks of a cynical performance.
- Bright screens on phones are very distracting to those behind you. Leaving in the middle of a performance is rude and an insult to the performers.

Continued from p123

Just west of the centre, down by the start of Jl Raya Campuan, **Pura Gunung Lebah** sits on a jutting rock at the confluence of two tributaries of Sungai Cerik (*campuan means* 'two rivers'). Far below street level in a lush gorge, the setting is magical; listen to the rushing waters while admiring the impressive *meru* (multi-tiered shrine) and a wealth of elaborate carvings. One of Ubud's oldest temples, it's thought to date to the 8th century. You can easily spend an hour or more wandering paths around the temple, the flowing waters and the hillsides.

Go for a Walk

Explore Ubud's beautiful countryside

Walking the green hills, lush river valleys and rolling rice fields is a top Ubud activity. Surprises abound, from the idiosyncratic artists at work in a trailside hut to a sensational little juice stand where everything's organic.

A classic Ubud walking route is the **Campuan Ridge Walk**, which is popular, easy and gives a good taste of what you'll enjoy on future perambulations. Following this paved trail along a ridge between two rivers is a great sunrise and sunset activity, but can be enjoyed at any time of the day. Start at the driveway of the Ibah hotel (p153) and then follow the signs for the walk which point left, where a walkway crosses the **Sungai Wos** (Wos River) and passes the tranquil **Pura Gunung Lebah**. Continue north on the concrete path, climbing up onto the Campuan Ridge between the Wos and Cerik Rivers. Fields of elephant grass, traditionally used for thatched roofs, slope away on either side of the path and you'll be able to see the rice fields above Ubud in all of their lush green majesty. Continue uphill past rice fields to the village of **Bangkiang Sidem**, passing little warungs and low-key vendors and artists along the way. Avoid retracing your steps or braving the narrow road by summoning a ride with the Grab or Gojek apps.

Visit Ubud's Prettiest Museum

Evocative art amid gardens

The modern Balinese art movement started in Ubud when artists first began to abandon religious and royal themes for scenes of everyday life. Of the various local art museums,

EATING IN UBUD: TOP END ———————————————————— MAP p124-5

Nusantara From the legendary Locavore team, a stylish Indonesian restaurant with boldly flavoured, highly spiced dishes. $$$

Hujan Locale Chef Will Meyrick's Ubud outpost serves Indonesian with creative flair in an open-air, vintage dining room. Passion fruit cocktails are addictive. $$$

Mozaic Chris Salans oversees French fusion cuisine; the seasonal menu takes influences from tropical Asia. Tasting menus. $$$

Locavore NXT Next incarnation famous restaurant; located in its own farming fantasyland southwest of town. High prices, high concept, very hard to book. $$$

GEKKO GALLERY/SHUTTERSTOCK ©

Museum Puri Lukisan

the **Museum Puri Lukisan** is the most enjoyable to visit, even if your interest in art is limited. It's set in lovely, tiered gardens replete with water features and has four buildings displaying works from all schools and periods of Balinese art. There's a focus on modern masters including I Gusti Nyoman Lempad (1862–1978), Ida Bagus Made (1915–99) and I Gusti Made Kwandji (1936–2013). All works are labelled in English and QR codes link to excellent additional info. You can easily spend an hour or two here.

The **East Building** has a collection of early works from Ubud and surrounding villages. These include examples of classical *wayang*-style paintings (art influenced by shadow puppetry) from the 10th to 15th centuries. Note that these ancient works have a palette limited to the only five colours of pigment that could be produced at the time. Among the impressive 20th-century works is *The Death of Karna* (1935) by I Wayan Tutur.

UBUD'S FAMOUS PAINTERS

I Gusti Nyoman Lempad (1862–1978) The giant of Balinese art. Renowned for his stark ink drawings on paper, which conveyed detail and movement in a *wayang* style suggestive of shadow puppets.

Ida Bagus Made Poleng (1915–99) Won international competitions in the 1930s and went on to be renowned for his softly coloured depictions of everyday life.

Murni (1966–2006) Famed for her stark and even whimsical depictions of serious issues facing local women.

Walter Spies (1895–1942) German painter who played an important role in promoting Bali's artistic culture in the 1930s.

Arie Smit (1916–2016) The best-known Western artist in Ubud. He came to Bali in 1956. In the 1960s his influence sparked the Young Artists school of painting in Penestanan.

EATING IN UBUD: BEST CAFES

MAP p124-5

Sweet Orange Warung An idyllic location in the midst of the rice fields; walk here via the path to the right of Museum Puri Lukisan. $

Kafe Attractive decor, new-age vibe and healthy food are the hallmarks of this upscale cafe cooled by air-con; alternative healer promotions cover the bulletin board. $

Yellow Flower Cafe Perched in Penestanan along a greenery-edged path; good range of health drinks (turmeric, kombucha, chia water) and decent coffee. Great views. $

Anomali Coffee Indonesia's answer to Starbucks takes its excellent coffee seriously. Central location, ideal for watching Ubud's frenetic passing parade from the streetside tables. $

Nyoman Masriadi (b 1973) Born in Gianyar, Masriadi is the superstar of Bali's current crop of painters. He is renowned for his sharp-eyed observations of Indonesian society.

Made Djirna (b 1957) From Ubud, Djirna critiques the relationship between ostentatious money and modern Balinese religious ceremonies.

Agung Mangu Putra (b 1963) His works decry the impact of Bali's tourist boom and its uneven benefits.

Wayan Sudarna Putra (b 1976) An Ubud native, Putra uses satire to question the absurdities of current Indonesian life.

Gede Suanda Sayur (b 1980) Sayur questions the pillaging of Bali's environment. He helped create an installation in a rice field that spelt out 'Not for sale'.

Neka Art Museum

The **North Building** features fine ink drawings by I Gusti Nyoman Lempad and paintings by artists of the Pita Maha school such as Walter Spies. Don't miss *Temple Festival* (1938) by I Gusti Ketut Kobot (1917–99). Another intricately detailed masterpiece is *The Idiot Who Became King* (1932) by Ida Bagus Made Togog (1913–89), which tells the tale of a simple but honest man who became a ruler thanks to divine intervention.

The **West Building** is devoted to 20th-century Balinese painters. Look for *Barong Dance* (1970) by I Gusti Made Kwandji (1936–2013). The **South Building** is used for special exhibitions. Immediately east of the museum complex, a river path takes you to the rice fields behind the museum.

Best Serious Art Museum

See Ubud's finest masterpieces

Agung Rai Museum of Art (ARMA) is another must-see museum. Founder Agung Rai built his fortune selling Balinese artwork to foreigners in the 1970s, and during his time as a dealer he also acquired one of Indonesia's most impres-

 EATING IN UBUD: BEST FOR PICNICS ———— MAP p124-5

Locavore to Go Local meats, cheeses and bread are used for sandwiches that will have you pausing your walk early to dig in. **$$**

Pizza Bagus Not just pizza, but a full deli counter with everything for a meal on the go. Imported Italian meats and cheeses. Fresh bread. **$$**

Produce Market Ubud's traditional produce market is buried in the Ubud Art Market. Search out the vast range of local fruits plus prepared foods. **$**

Bali Buda Great source for organic produce and groceries; its baked goods – including savoury items – are varied and portable. **$**

sive private collections of art. Highlights on display include the wonderful 19th-century *Portrait of a Javanese Nobleman and His Wife* by Javanese artist Raden Saleh (1807–80).

Exhibits include classical Kamasan paintings and Batuan-style work from the 1930s and '40s. Among the artists represented are I Gusti Nyoman Lempad (1862–1978), Ida Bagus Made (1915–99), Anak Agung Gede Sobrat (1912–92) and I Gusti Made Deblog (1906–86). Works to seek out in the modern gallery are *Green Rice Paddies* (1987) by Nasjah Djamin (1924–99) and *Wild Orchids* (1988) by Widaya (1923–2002).

In the traditional gallery, look for *The Dance Drama Arja* (1990) by I Ketut Kasta (b 1945), Cremation Ceremony (1994) by I Ketut Sepi (b 1941) and the extraordinarily detailed *Wali 'Ekadesa Rudra'* (2015) by I Wayan Mardiana (b 1970). The traditional art gallery is also home to a collection of works by expat artist Walter Spies (1895–1942), who played a significant role in promoting Ubud's international artistic reputation.

During a visit of an hour or two, you might see local children learning **Balinese dance** or hear **gamelan practice**. The complex also has a hotel and cafe; it's a venue for dance performances.

Best Museum for an Overview

See how Ubud's artistic reputation grew

Well up Jl Raya Campuan, the **Neka Art Museum** offers an excellent introduction to Balinese art, with a top-notch collection displayed in a series of pavilions and halls. On a one-hour visit, don't miss the multiroom Balinese Painting Hall, which showcases *wayang* (puppet) style as well as the European-influenced Ubud and Batuan styles introduced in the 1920s and '30s. Also notable is the Lempad Pavilion, with works by the master I Gusti Nyoman Lempad, and the East-West Art Annexe, where works by Affandi (1907–90) and Widayat (1919–2002) impress.

The museum is the creation of Suteja Neka, a private collector and dealer in Balinese art, and his collection is huge. As well as works by Balinese and Indonesian artists, there are plenty of works by foreign artists who have called the island home, including Arie Smit, Johan Rudolf Bonnet, Theo Meier, Louise Garrett Koke, Donald Friend and Tay Moh-Leong.

The museum's **gift shop** offers quality local handicrafts and has a good range of books devoted to Balinese art.

UBUD'S BEST EVENTS

Ubud Writers & Readers Festival
Southeast Asia's major literary event draws writers and readers from around the world for a five-day celebration in October.

Ubud Open Studios
Two-day celebration in March of local artists, with over 70 opening their studios to visitors. Many special events.

Bali Spirit Festival
A popular yoga, dance and music festival with hundreds of workshops, concerts and more in May.

Ubud Village Jazz Festival
Annual two-day jazz festival features an international line-up of performers in late July.

Ubud Food Festival
Diverse and delicious Indonesian cuisine takes centre stage at this three-day festival in late June or July.

EATING IN UBUD: BEST VEGETARIAN ———————— MAP p124-5

Sayuri 'If we are what we eat, what food do you want to become?' Here you'll be a raw vegetable. Vegan. $$

Sari Organik In an organic farm overlooking rice terraces, with a large menu of veggie food and drink, including raw options. $

Alchemy High-concept Ubud cafe: create-your-own salads and smoothie bowls, plus raw vegan ice creams, desserts and cold-pressed juices. $$

Moksa On a permaculture farm, serves extraordinary meals created with simple vegetables. Many dishes are raw. Bucolic setting. $$

Enjoy a walk with deep forests, lush rice fields and waterfalls just north of Ubud. The 7km route is fairly level and takes two to three hours.

Head north up **❶ Jl Kajeng**, passing by the long strips of vendor stalls. Just past the **❷ Bale Banjar Ubud Kaja**, head uphill as the road becomes a path. You'll soon see a lush green vista of rice fields. Follow the path north past a few villas and vendors selling coconuts. Cement gives way to dirt and eventually becomes the top of a narrow concrete wall along a **❸ subak (irrigation) channel** on one side and a small river on the other. Palm trees and bamboo close in overhead, providing deep shade. Walk carefully until you come to a **❹ tiny footbridge** over the river followed by a narrow path up an embankment. Continue north for about 1.5km along the footpath through

the green rice fields dotted with the odd villa, drink vendor and artist studio. When you reach a **❺ road wide enough for cars**, turn east and walk down past the **❻ Cafe Bintang** to a bridge over surging waterfalls. Immediately to the east, take the **❼ small lane** that runs south through the river gorge. Fenced yards filled with ducks give way to more rice as the path rises up out of the gorge and curves back and forth south.

About 750 m after the waterfall, turn east and follow the **❽ car-capable road** down, over a bridge and back up to Jl Suweta. Walk south for 1km, past many small cafes perfect for a pause. Cross the **❾ bridge** to fairly quiet Jl Sri Wedari and walk gently downhill past little warungs and shops back to **❿ Jl Raya Ubud**.

A Forest of Monkeys & Temples
Ubud's top attraction

With its flashy theme-park-like entrance near the south end of the eponymous road, you'd be hard-pressed to realise that the **Ubud Monkey Forest** was once a shady expanse that was home to three temples and a resident troop of over 1000 well-fed and light-fingered monkeys.

It's now a top destination for day trippers from across Bali, but you can escape the crowds by visiting early and late in the day. Ignore stunts like the 'mysterious' tunnel at the entrance and follow the paths to the holiest of the temples, **Pura Dalem Agung**, where the entrance to the inner temple features Rangda figures devouring children.

You can't miss the grey-haired and greedy long-tailed Balinese macaques who are nothing like the innocent-looking, doe-eyed primates in social media shots – they can bite, so be careful. Watch all your belongings carefully, including glasses, phones, bags and anything sticking out of your pockets. Never feed them, lest you set off a frenzy.

Trails lead down a ravine to a cool and serene river valley. The attraction's app (heavily promoted at the entrance) offers little to enhance a visit. Expect to spend about an hour here.

Magical Shadow Puppets
Artistry by light at night

Look for *wayang kulit* performances in Ubud, which are attenuated to a manageable 90 minutes or less. Watching this low-tech artistry in action makes for an enthralling evening. Check schedules with the venues.

Very central, **Bali Culture Workshop** at the Oka Kartini BnB stages popular evening shows. Hidden away near the soccer field, **Kerta Art** has evening performances on the porch of the Kerta Accommodation. Short programmes are performed at **Pondok Bamboo Music Shop** at the south end of town by noted experts.

Laze Away in a Cafe
Match your mood to the spot

Scribbling in your journal, pondering your phone or just staring off into space are some of the activities that can provide hours of happy diversion in one of Ubud's myriad **cafes**. You'll find them along streets buzzing with life such as Jl Raya Ubud

SHADOW PUPPETS

Much more than sheer entertainment, *wayang kulit* (shadow puppetry) has been Bali's candlelit village cinema for centuries, embodying the sacred seriousness of classical Greek drama. Traditional performances were long and intense – lasting six hours or more and often not finishing before sunrise.

Originally used to bring ancestors back to this world, the shows feature painted buffalo-hide puppets believed to have great spiritual power, and the *dalang* (puppet master and storyteller) is an almost mystical figure. The *dalang* sits behind a screen and manipulates the puppets while telling the story, often in many dialects.

Stories are chiefly derived from the great Hindu epics like the Ramayana. You can find shortened performances nightly in Ubud.

DRINKING IN UBUD: BEST COCKTAILS
MAP p124-5

Boliche On the site of pioneering Ubud boozer Beggar's Bush, a stylish, top-end cocktail bar draws on local flavours for offbeat drinks; goes late.

Kawi Means 'poet' in Sanskrit; inventive drinks made with local ingredients like *arak* and infused with dried bananas. Narrow bar, chill garden.

Lair Look for the boho sign pointing down at the Campuan Bridge. Within earshot of the flowing river; primitive decor, sophisticated drinks and snacks.

Dumbo Music, mixology and Italian bites; drinks named after albums feature housemade cordials, bitters, accents and liquors. Always buzzy.

SEEING A *BALIAN*

Bali's traditional healers, known as *balian*, play an important part in Bali's culture by treating illnesses, removing spells and channelling information from the ancestors. Some tourists hope to visit a *balian*, which doesn't always work out due to the significant cultural differences. Consider the following before a visit: Make an appointment before visiting a *balian*. Know that English is rarely spoken. And understand what you're getting into – your treatment will be public and painful. It may include being poked with sharp sticks or having chewed herbs spat on you. Finding a *balian* can take some work. For an excellent introduction to traditional Balinese therapies, contact **I Madé Suryasa** (balihealers.com). He organises *balian* visits and helps with translation.

or Jl Hanoman. Or you might find a quieter location with a virescent view of rice fields. Still others can only be reached along walking paths that trail out into the countryside.

Organic fare might be the specialty or perhaps it's juices with purported healing qualities or just a perfect cup of coffee. The vibe can be cool and on point, stylish and luxe, or bamboo-adorned and open-air simple. Lose yourself in self-indulgent contemplation or make new friends with fellow travellers or chatty proprietors. Languid cafe interludes are an essential part of the Ubud experience.

Indulge in a Spa Day
Feel the ahhh

Like its cafes, Ubud brims with **spas** and **health salons** that come in many forms. You can heal, pamper, rejuvenate or otherwise focus on your personal needs, physical and mental. Getting a massage or treatment at an Ubud spa is at the top of many a visitor's itinerary. Expect the latest trends from many practitioners and prepare to try some new therapies. You may also wish to seek out a *balian* (traditional healer). Many spas also offer courses in therapies, treatments and activities such as yoga (p136). In addition, as you wander around town, you'll see placards offering familiar and esoteric therapies and services, from reiki to tonal therapy and beyond.

Well up from town along atmospheric Jl Kajeng, **Ubud Sari Health Resort** has fully embraced the hippie-ish Ubud vibe for decades. Amidst gardens where the herbs used in its therapies are grown, the spa offers an extensive menu of treatments, including massage, detox programmes, reflexology and beauty treatments.

Taksu is one of Ubud's most popular spas; it has a long and lavish menu of massages and beauty treatments. There are private rooms for couples massages and a healthy cafe. You can easily spend an entire day here being pampered.

To go all in for sybaritic joy, **Mandapa Spa** in Ritz-Carlton's Mandapa Resort is the place for luxurious pleasures in a lush setting on the Ayung River just west of the centre.

In Pengosekan, **Ubud Wellness Spa** is a favourite among Ubud's creative community. It concentrates on what counts, not the fru-fru. Try the 3½-hour Royal Kumkuman Body Wellness package, which includes a ritual holy bath. In Sanggingan, diminutive **Bali Botanica Day Spa** specialises in Ayurvedic treatments.

EATING IN UBUD: OFFBEAT CHOICES

MAP p124-5

Room4Dessert
Celebrity chef Will Goldfarb's top-end bistro could be a nightclub; locally sourced tasting menus mix savoury and sweet. $$$

Fair Warung Balé Run by the Swiss NGO Fair Future Foundation, it donates its profits towards local healthcare. Mostly tasty Indonesian fare. $

Cafe Bintang Hidden away in a river glen near a waterfall north of Ubud, this family-run spot mixes simple, authentic Japanese with Indonesian. $$

Tukies Coconut Shop
Housemade coconut ice cream topped with shaved coconut and coconut brittle. It's vegan, too. Sells other coconut-y delights. $

Explore the rice fields, attractions and even a few surprises on this 4.2km walk through Sanggingan, Penestanan and Campuan.

Begin at ❶ **Jl Raya Sanggingan** on the path running west into the rice fields just north of Powder Room by R4D. A patchwork of rice stretches out into the distance, often dotted with white herons. Zigzag west on the path until you reach the ❷ **Ubud Padi Villas**, then turn south. Stop to enjoy a ❸ **small waterfall** and continue south through various small turns, past ❹ **Sari Padi Warung**. After ❺ **Gioja Italian Restaurant**, turn east and follow the concrete path 175m until you see a ❻ **huge banyan tree**. Take the narrow path east downhill and past a ❼ **small temple**. The soaring bamboo architecture of Desa Alam Indah is above you to the north. Follow the sound of water into a ❽ **remarkable grotto** that's one of Ubud's most surprising sights. During the pandemic, bored local artisans carved up the stone walls with all manner of huge reliefs, from the heads of goddesses to elephants. Now covered in moss, they seem centuries old rather than just a few years. Make the short but steep climb out of the grotto to the east, then follow a path, slightly south, then east, then slightly south again until you reach the ❾ **Yellow Flower Cafe** and some surprisingly good views over Ubud.

Pause for a healthy refreshment and continue south until you arrive at a point where the path intersects with the long, concrete ❿ **Penestanan stairs** down to Jl Raya Campuhan. Follow this down and over the bridge to the ⓫ **Ibah**, which is the starting point for the iconic walk up Campuan Ridge (p128).

UBUD'S NEIGHBOURHOODS

Central Ubud
The original heart of Ubud is easily walkable and flush with businesses and attractions.

Padangtegal & Tebesaya
Conveniently located, these two areas blend into central Ubud to the west.

Sambahan & Sakti
North of Jl Raya Ubud, with rolling rice terraces and expat villas.

Nyuhkuning
A popular and quiet area just south of the Monkey Forest.

Pengosekan
South of the centre and an extension of Jl Hanoman.

Campuan & Sanggingan
Two communities strung out along a namesake road west of the centre.

Penestanan
Sitting on a plateau above Campuan, this area of cafes, guesthouses and rice fields can be a long walk to the centre.

ALEXANDERSTOCK23/SHUTTERSTOCK ©

Yoga Barn

Find Your Balance
Finding the right yoga studio

Downward facing dog and the tree pose may be an Ubud cliché, but there is no denying that yoga is part of the region's soul. Studios, practitioners, personal coaches and shops for gear abound. Some visitors come here for an intensive week-long retreat and before they know it they are scurrying to renew their 30-day visa.

The chakra for Ubud's yoga revolution is the **Yoga Barn**, which sits in its own lotus position amid trees near a river valley. The name describes exactly what you'll find: a huge space offering a vast range of classes in various yoga practices.

Radiantly Alive appeals to students looking for an intimate space and offers a mix of drop-in and long-term yoga classes in various disciplines. **Bali Swasthya Yoga Centre** is the exclusive domain of Balinese-born instructors who eschew trends and style for substance and authenticity.

Perched in Penestanan, **Intuitive Flow** offers a wide range of workshops in healing arts, although climbing the concrete stairs to get here from Campuan may well leave you too spent for a round of asanas.

To go with your renewed balance, you can tune up your yoga wardrobe at **Studio K**, a Bali-based designer of casual and workout wear that is ethically sourced and produced. The boutique is one of the highlights of a stroll along Jl Goutama.

Learn Something New

Courses in art, dance and culture

Ubud is the perfect place to develop your creative skills, discover your inner artist and plunge into the wonders of Balinese culture. The range of courses offered could keep you busy for a year.

ARMA is a veritable college of Balinese culture and creativity. Classes include painting, woodcarving, gamelan and batik as well as Balinese dance and offering-making. The other major galleries, Museum Puri Lukisan (p129) and Neka Art Museum (p131), offer similar menus of courses.

From their exquisite Jl Kajeng shop, **Threads of Life** transports students to their nearby studio to learn the traditional techniques of creating batik with natural dyes. This non-profit is renowned for its work preserving ages-old textile skills from across Indonesia.

A community treasure (and a great place to refill your water bottle), **Pondok Pekak Library & Learning Centre** is on the far side of the football field and offers a shady refuge from the tourist scrum. Its public and private courses cover Balinese dance, gamelan, carving and offering-making. No matter your age, Kerta Art (p133) has an in-depth Balinese dance class for you. Bali Culture Workshop (p133) at the Oka Kartini BnB has a range of classes from shadow puppets to various aspects of dance to offering-making.

Some of Ubud's most rewarding classes are taught by resident experts in their own homes. Abstract artist **Wayan Karja** offers intensive painting and drawing classes in the studio behind his guesthouse, Santra Putra, in Penestanan. Gamelan master **Wayan Pasek Sucipta** shares his expertise at Eka's Homestay on Jl Sriwedari. The long-running **Nirvana Batik Course** combines design skills with the personal discipline needed to craft intricate textiles.

Powder Room, the fun and idiosyncratic vendor of sweet treats, also offers regular art classes that – like their candy – break the mould. One popular class teaches how to properly paint a *barong*, the mythical king of Balinese spirits. Long-running **Sari Api Ceramic Studio** offers personalised training in ceramics at their open-air workshop and kiln.

Studio Perak specialises in Balinese-style silversmithing courses. In one three-hour lesson you'll make at least one finished piece. Classes can even be geared to children. Learn how to combine and refine locally grown plants and herbs into healthful potions and lotions at **Ubud Botany Interactive**. They also offer tours that explore Ubud's flora.

Cultivate Culinary Creations

Learn how to re-create Bali's flavours

Ubud cooking classes often start at the local produce market, which runs mornings and is set deep within the modern Ubud Art Market (p140). You'll learn about the huge range of fruits, vegetables and other foods that are part of the Balinese diet.

UBUD TIME

Ubud gets up with the roosters and the sun. Cooking fires are lit in family compounds, offerings are made and people get on with work ahead of the heat of the day. For visitors, life may understandably take on a more somnolent pattern and businesses geared towards tourists may not start serving breakfast until 9am or later. By noon, markets aimed at residents are closing and naps may be in order. Dinner comes early as many visitors attend dance performances, which start around 7pm. Most kitchens close by 9pm, so don't delay if you want to eat after a performance. Bars – like the streets – are usually quiet by 11pm. With a few exceptions, Ubud does not party late.

The famous **Casa Luna Cooking School** has a full menu of classes; half-day courses have differernt themes and cover a range of dishes. Tours of the popular Gianyar night market are offered, as is a weekly 'Food as Medicine' class in vegan cuisine.

Learn from master Balinese chef **Wayan Manis** in her home kitchen. You'll prepare iconic dishes for a dinner feast using traditional ingredients and a wood stove. Book through travelingspoon.com.

Start with the basics of Balinese spices and cuisine at two-hour courses run by the long-running **Cafe Wayan Cooking Class**. The lesson plan varies each day; afterwards, you'll get to eat your work for lunch – an inducement to excel.

The fanatics at **Seniman Coffee Studio** teach about all things Java (and Bali) at in-depth classes that cover topics such as espresso-making, latte art, manual brewing methods and cupping (the art of tasting and rating coffee).

Guided Adventures

Walking and biking tours of Ubud

Specialised tours in Ubud include thematic walks and cultural adventures. Spending a few hours exploring the area with an expert is a fabulous way to savour Ubud and its region.

Perhaps the best two to three hours you'll spend locally is on a tour with **Ubud Story Walks**. These remarkably detailed and entertaining tours cover Balinese culture and history in the region. Learn about Ubud past and present, the unsung wonders of the temples in Pejeng, the works of the legendary artist I Gusti Nyoman Lempad and more.

Spend the early morning with Agung Rai, the founder of his namesake museum ARMA, on his **Golden Hour Tour** that explores old villages and landscapes before the roar of another day begins.

Ubud native Dewa Rai of **Bali Nature Walks** conducts three- to four-hour nature walks through jungle and rice-field landscapes in the region.

Whizz downhill while enjoying day-long tours of remote villages near Ubud with **Banyan Tree Cycling Tours**. The popular tours emphasise interaction with villagers.

One of Ubud's first tourist businesses, **Bali Bird Walks** was started by the legendary Victor Mason more than 30 years ago. Although Mason has since gone on to the big nest in the sky, his legacy lives on. Tours, which include the use of binoculars, usually spot 30 to 100 species.

Ubud's Fashionable Heart

Stylish wares made in Bali

Within a few hundred metres of where Jl Dewi Sita meets Jl Hanoman are some of Ubud's most interesting and stylish shops. Barely wider than a bolt of fabric, **Above the Clouds Natural Wear** sells casual linen and cotton clothes that are designed and sewn in the villages around Ubud. Quality and service are both tops.

Rice terraces

WHERE TO SHOP

Ubud is home to a dizzying array of designer shops, boutiques and galleries and you can spend days shopping. Many stores sell items that have been created in Bali. In central Ubud, Jl Dewi Sita, Jl Goutama and the northern stretch of Jl Hanoman have the most interesting local shops.

Other good places to stroll include the small streets running north from Jl Raya Ubud. The area around the palace and south along Monkey Forest Rd is geared towards souvenir shoppers. Ubud's main strip for household shopping is found along Jl Peliatan in Tebesaya and Peliatan as well as the road to Gianyar. There are numerous craft galleries, studios and workshops in the villages to the north (p142) and south (p147).

Ananda Soul is a store with a heart. Proceeds from their locally designed and produced jewellery and a small line of resort wear support disadvantaged Balinese. **Kado by Saraswati Paper** sells high-end goods for creative pursuits, journals, cards, prints and more. Everything is made from recycled paper and produced in Bali. Right next door, **Kevala Home** is a slick shop selling stylish, locally made ceramic and porcelain goods. Browse the work of more than 30 Balinese and Indonesian jewellery, accessories and clothing designers at **Curative**. Prices are aimed at the local market, so bargains abound.

Read Up

Ubud's top bookshop

Ubud boasts Bali's best place for the printed word, **Ganesha Bookshop**. An extraordinary selection of curated new and used titles fill this compact shop. There's a huge range of books on Balinese and Indonesian culture and you'll find otherwise hard-to-locate copies of works by authors appearing at the Ubud Writers & Readers Festival.

Bali-Grown & Produced

Sample treats, potions and lotions

Boutique producers who use ingredients from the Ubud region sell a wide range of foods, drinks, cosmetics and bath items. Inside its turquoise confines, **Ubud Raw Chocolate**

THE LEGACY OF *EAT, PRAY, LOVE*

Many Ubud residents blame the book *Eat, Pray, Love* for some of the town's wild popularity. Significantly, Elizabeth Gilbert's book still resonates locally years after its 2006 publication. It chronicles the American author's search for self-fulfilment (and fulfilment of a book contract) across Italy, India and, yes, Ubud.

Some criticise Gilbert for not offering a more complete picture of Ubud life, warts and all. And they decry basic factual errors such as the evocative prose about surf spots on the north coast (there are none), which lead you to suspect plot embellishments. Still, genuine *EPL* fans continue to visit Ubud, hoping for a dose of its self-actualization, validation and, yes, love.

Ubud Art Market

is an uncompromising producer of treats made with locally grown cacao. If they don't think you're going to care for their easily melted chocolate properly, they might not sell you any (cooling packs are available).

Sniff your way to a better you at **Blue Stone Botanicals**, an aromatherapy store selling oils made in Bali and Java. Started in East Bali in 2000, **Sensatia Botanicals** is a polished and stylish vendor of cosmetics. Packaging is made from cassava starch. **Kou** sells handmade soaps redolent with the evocative scents of frangipani, tuberose, jasmine, orange and lemon.

Carnivals of Consumerism

From high end to schlock

Completed in 2023, the latest iteration of the **Ubud Art Market** is at least the fourth-generation complex to house the vast collection of shops and vendors. Occupying a prime corner plot across from Ubud Palace, the market is thronged with day-trippers to Ubud throughout the day. But its glossification has come at the cost of atmosphere, and Bali's most popular souvenir – the penis-shaped bottle opener – looks even more out of place than usual in these sterile surroundings.

Fortunately, alternatives abound. A short stroll northeast of the market, **Jl Kajeng** is lined with vendors selling all the polyester sarongs, Bintang singlets, carved wooden bowls, cheesy masks and every other bit of tourist tat you can't go home without. It's an open-air carnival of consumerism that echoes with come-ons and promises of bargains. Part of the fun – besides comparing the sizes and colours of the bottle openers – is prowling for unusual items on offer amidst the seemingly generic selection in every stall.

And don't forget to look behind the stalls on Jl Pejang as you'll find little boutiques selling goods an order of magnitude more classy. Typical is **Toko Elami**, which sells the creations of over 20 local artisans. Look for out-of-the-ordinary T-shirts, prints, games, bags, stickers and much more. Just north is **Threads of Life**, the famous purveyor of traditional textiles.

UBUD'S DELIGHTFUL HOMESTAYS

Ubud has Bali's largest concentration of family-run homestays. Offering clean, comfortable rooms (always with wi-fi and air-con) within a family compound, these places to stay are both a bargain and a part of the overall Ubud experience. Guests soon get caught up in the rhythms of family life, from offering-making to lounging around and having a chat. Friendships are formed and some guests stay at the same homestay year after year.

Most are on booking websites, but you can also just wander the streets and see what you find. There are concentrations north of Jl Raya Ubud on Jl Kajeng, Jl Sriwedari and Jl Sandat. South, look to Jl Goutama, Jl Hanoman, Jl Sugriwa, Jl Jembawan and Jl Sukma.

Masks, Ubud

ANASTASIA PELIKH/SHUTTERSTOCK ©

Beyond
Ubud (North)

The action of the south melts away as you move upslope from Ubud. It's a lush land with ancient sites.

Places

GETTING AROUND

Having your own wheels is the only way to go north of Ubud. The relentless uphill climbs make it a challenge for all but the most dedicated cyclists and hikers. Conversely, returning to Ubud is all downhill, so if you can get a ride one-way, you can cycle or walk downhill the other way. Use apps for taxi rides and consider hiring a car and driver for a day out to the top sights.

North of Ubud, Bali becomes cooler and more green. Fascinating sights and natural beauty abound in this hilly countryside where the north-south striations of river valleys abound. One easy route from Ubud northeast towards Gunung Batur passes through Tegallalang, home to the touristy Ceking rice terraces, and then continues via Tampaksiring, passing the ancient sites of Gunung Kawi Sebatu, Gunung Kawi and Tirta Empul. The scenery on this route is verdantly picturesque – you'll see farmers working in their fields, colourful flags fluttering in the wind and plenty of rice terraces and roadside shrines. Hillside villages such as Taro are timeless windows into Balinese life. Closer to Ubud is excellent handicraft shopping.

Petulu

TIME FROM UBUD: **10 MINS**

Witness the herons

Every evening after 5pm, thousands of striped white herons fly into **Petulu**, a village about 3km north of Ubud, squabbling over the prime perching places before settling into the trees beside a 400m-long stretch of road. The herons, mainly the Javan pond species, started their visits to Petulu in 1965. A local myth says that the herons are the spirits of those killed during the anti-communist massacres that swept Indonesia (and Bali) that year.

Warungs sell drinks and snacks to enjoy with the spectacle, which can be enjoyed from a raised platform in the village centre. Walk quickly under the trees if the herons are already roosting. Nesting and egg-laying begin in November, with the fledglings taking flight in March. Petulu is a pleasant walk or bicycle ride north of Ubud. Head up busy Jl Raya Gentong and then take the quieter village road. If you stay for the birds, you'll be returning in the dark, so walk one way and taxi back.

Tegallalang

TIME FROM UBUD: **30 MINS**

Those busy terrace views

Heading north from Ubud, the stupendous views of the **Ceking Rice Terraces** from Tagallalang's main road have morphed into a vast tourist circus, replete with competing

MELANI N/SHUTTERSTOCK ©

Istana Kepresidenan Tampaksiring (p144)

Instagram swings. Cafes continue to build out further over the edge of the cliff to cut off their competitors' views, which means that nowadays everyone's view is obscured. Some have even added infinity pools. Signs and touts shill for parking lots, walking tours and the inevitable coffee luwak (p146) joints.

Still, this is one of the best views of rice terraces in Bali, so the frenzy of selfies isn't surprising. Look for openings in the commercial strip not yet filled by cafes and savour the view of the sinuous ribbons of green without the hustle. Follow trails down into lush valley and expect to pay the occasional toll levied by farmers angling to get in on some of the action up the hillside.

Tampaksiring

TIME FROM UBUD: **40 MINS** 🚗

Experience echoes of Sukarno

Located in the Pakerisan Valley, 18km northeast of Ubud, the tidy town of **Tampaksiring** was the base of one of the major kingdoms during Bali's pre-colonial period. It's cleaved by the Pakerisan River, which flows through a revered valley that's home to both Pura Tirta Empul, an ancient and important water temple, and Gunung Kawi, one of the most impressive ancient sites in Bali. Terraced rice fields striate the hillsides that run down to the river and streams.

Tampaksiring is also notable for its connections to Sukarno, the legendary first president of Indonesia, who led the nation from its independence from the Dutch in 1945 until he was deposed in 1967. About 1km south of town, the privately run **Sukarno Center** is a cross between a shrine and a museum to his legacy. The walls show the fruits of Sukarno's leadership of the non-aligned movement during the Cold

RAFTING AROUND UBUD

The **Sungai Ayung** (Ayung River) is the most popular river in Bali for white-water rafting. You start north of Ubud and end in Sayan to the west. Depending on rainfall, the river can range from sedate to thrilling. Numerous companies offer these trips, which are all similar. Transport is provided from hotels and resorts in South Bali (the departure from Nusa Dua can be very early) and Ubud to a starting point off the main road north to Kintamani. Protective gear is provided, as are beverages. Some rafting packages may include lunch at tourist-group-oriented restaurants. Other possible options include short treks in the lush river valley and ecologically damaging ATV rides.

SHOPPING NORTH OF UBUD

Some of the best **handicraft and houseware shopping** around Ubud can be found on a stretch of road north to Tegallalang. The retail fun begins about 500m north of the junction with Jl Raya Ubud at the landmark statue of Dewa Indra. One interesting shop after another line the road for about 5km. Around the time you see the first Instagram swing near the Ceking Rice Terraces is when gaudy souvenirs begin taking precedence over quality merchandise.

Many of the shops double as workshops and studios where merchandise is created. Beaded handbags, intricately woven baskets, housemade *endek* textiles, artful accessories, primitive furniture, ornate wood carvings and much more are on offer. New sidewalks make it easy to wander between shops.

DOTMILLER1986/SHUTTERSTOCK ©

Pura Tirta Empul

War. Both Soviet and Western leaders regularly called on Sukarno hoping to curry allegiance; note the 1961 photo of JFK glad-handing the Indonesian president.

Sukarno had a deep affection for Bali and had a presidential palace, **Istana Kepresidenan Tampaksiring**, built in the centre of town. It's still used for functions today and was a favourite refuge for his daughter Megawati Sukarnoputri when she was president (2001–04).

Visit a lively water temple

Immediately east and in the shadow of the presidential palace, **Pura Tirta Empul** dates to 962 CE (although little remains from then). This water temple is believed to have magical powers, and the holy springs bubble up into a large pool and gush out through waterspouts into a *petirtaan* (bathing area). The site is always thronged with Balinese and visitors performing the *melukat* ritual cleansing, which is meant to assure a better future.

For a more serene setting, go downstream about 500m and take a long flight of steps down to **Pura Mengening**, a temple with a freestanding *candi* (shrine), similar in design to those at Gunung Kawi. This towering stone structure is thought to be over 1000 years old.

Explore a remarkable ancient site

One of Bali's oldest, holiest and most important monuments, the stunning river-valley complex of **Gunung Kawi** consists of 10 huge *candi* cut out of rock faces. Each is believed to be a memorial to a member of 11th-century Balinese royalty. Legends relate that the whole group was carved out of the rock in one hard-working night by the mighty finger-nails of Kebo Iwa.

The five *candi* on the eastern riverbank are probably dedicated to King Udayana, Queen Mahendradatta and their sons Airlangga, Anak Wungsu and Marakata. While Airlangga ruled eastern Java, Anak Wungsu ruled Bali. The four *candi* on the western side are, by this theory, dedicated to Anak Wungsu's chief concubines. Another theory is that the whole complex is dedicated to Anak Wungsu, his wives, concubines and, in the case of the remote tenth *candi*, to a royal minister.

Groups of *candi* and monks' cells carved into cliff faces are found throughout this area that was once encompassed by the ancient Pejeng kingdom, which stretched south along the Pakerisan River to Goa Garba (p148) and beyond.

Get to Gunung Kawi as early as possible for the best experience. If you start down the steps by 7.30am, you'll avoid some of the persistent vendors and see residents going about their morning ablutions and the cleaning of ceremonial offerings in the streams. You can hear the birds, the flowing water and your own voice going 'ooh' and 'aah' without the distractions that come later when large groups arrive. In addition, you'll still have cool air when you start back up the steep 250-step staircase.

Sebatu

TIME FROM UBUD: **45 MINS**

Purification at a temple to Vishnu

The western approach to **Pura Gunung Kawi Sebatu**, a slightly off-the-beaten-track water temple, offers wonderful views down onto the complex, which is set in a lush gorge. The temple is dedicated to Vishnu, the supreme Hindu god who protects the cosmic order and is used locally for purification rituals. Inside, spring-fed pools are set against a lush green backdrop and fat carp swim in the large decorative pond. Behind an ornate wall, you'll find two ritual bathing pools fed by water spouting from carved heads. You can take a dip in the cool, clear water.

In the surrounding small village of **Sebatu**, look for shops run by woodcarvers who create intricate decorative items from fine-grained, light albesia wood.

Taro

TIME FROM UBUD: **1 HR**

Tranquil village life

The air is noticeably cooler in this hillside village, which is 18km north of Ubud. It's compact and easily visited on foot. The community runs a useful website (desawisatataro.com) filled with info about the village (including homestay options). Start at **Pura Agung Gunung Raung**, the large temple in the centre marked by large statues of *lembu putih* (white cows, the local icon) at the entrance. The temple dates to the 17th century and is named for Gunung Raung, the active volcano in East Java where the founding priests hailed from.

About 300m north, look for signs for the **Yeh Pikat Waterfall**. There's a small cafe at the top of the privately

CYCLING NORTH OF UBUD

While you can cycle around the Ubud area, the narrow and busy roads make it a challenge. However, there are good – and thrilling – opportunities to the north. Some of the quieter roads following the terrain from north to south offer less stressful routes that run through lush and beautiful countryside.

There are numerous tour operators that transport groups to northern villages and provide a guided journey back to Ubud. The roads are rarely steep, and you can usually coast gently downhill.

On your own, you'll have to either pedal uphill or arrange a ride that will transport you and your bike. Decent mountain-bike rentals (including helmets) are easy to find in Ubud.

COFFEE LUWAK CONCERNS

Coffee luwak (*kopi luwak*) is ubiquitous and overhyped in tourist areas north of Ubud. It's named after the cat-like civet (*luwak*) indigenous to Sulawesi, Sumatra and Java, which eats ripe coffee cherries. Entrepreneurs initially collected the intact beans found in the nocturnal civet's droppings and processed them to produce a supposedly extra-piquant brew.

However, once the profit potential of exploiting coffee luwak was realised, outlets touting it proliferated. With interest in coffee luwak exceeding all reason, trouble abounds. There is *no* certification that your expensive cup of coffee actually was brewed from beans that passed through the gut of a civet. Reports of mistreatment of civets that are caged on factory farms and displayed for tourists are common.

Pura Gunung Kawi Sebatu (p145)

maintained trail down into the deep valley. There are sweeping views of the dense tropical forest. The waterfall is not high (6m) but is in a lovely spot at the confluence of two rivers and a natural spring.

About 1km south of the village just past the entrance to the private elephant park is a small community-run park where the *lembu putih* are kept. You can watch the light-coloured bovines placidly munching silage before their next call to a ceremonial procession.

Learn Balinese cooking on a farm

Spend a day out in the untrammelled countryside just north of Taro and learn how to cook Balinese food. The **Pemulan Bali Farm Cooking School** (pemulanbali.com) is run by villagers passionate about organic farming. Students learn about local produce and foods; morning courses include a visit to the local produce market. Vegan, vegetarian and omnivore courses are available. Classes are held in an open-air pavilion amidst beautiful gardens redolent with herbs. Opt for the overnight package and you'll be fully immersed in community life.

Beyond
Ubud (South)

Villages of artisans, astonishing ancient sites and plenty of places to shop for handicrafts mark the lands south of Ubud.

A remarkable artefact more than 2000 years old is but one of the highlights of the adjacent villages of Pejeng and Bedulu, once the centres of a great kingdom. The legendary Dalem Bedaulu ruled the Pejeng dynasty from here, and was the last Balinese king to withstand the onslaught of the powerful Majapahit from Java in the 14th century. They are but two of the villages dotting the drier and flatter countryside running to the coast. The roads are lined with little shops that make and sell handicrafts. Many visitors shop here as they head to and from Ubud. Places like Mas, Blahbatuh, Sukawati and Batubulan are renowned for the quality and craftsmanship of their goods.

Places

Pejeng p147
Bedulu p148
Mas p149
Blahbatuh p151
Batuan p151
Sukawati p151
Batubulan p152

Pejeng

TIME FROM UBUD: **15 MINS**

See a jaw-dropping relic

Located 5km east of central Ubud, the village of Pejeng was the capital of the Balinese Pejeng kingdom for a short period between Javanese invasions. It collapsed in 1343 when the Majapahits defeated King Dalem Bedaulu. Today, it is home to one of the region's most extraordinary but least-visited sights.

Pura Penataran Sasih was once the state temple of the Pejeng kingdom. In the inner courtyard is a remarkable treasure: a huge bronze drum known as the **Moon of Pejeng**, which is thought to date back as far as 300 BCE. The hourglass-shaped drum is 186cm high and is the largest single-piece cast drum in the world. The bronze alloy and casting technique have been traced back to the Dong Son people of ancient Vietnam, revealing a previously unknown trade route.

Visit intriguing temples

There are three other fascinating sites near Pura Penataran Sasih. **Pura Pusering Jagat** dates from 1329 and is popular with young couples, who pray at the stone lingam and yoni in hopes of fertility. Also in the grassy compound is a large stone urn, with elaborate carvings of gods and demons searching for the elixir of life in a depiction of the Mahabharata tale 'Churning the Sea of Milk'.

GETTING AROUND

Having your own wheels is the only way to go north of Ubud. The relentless uphill climbs make it a challenge for all but the most dedicated cyclists and hikers. Conversely, returning to Ubud is all downhill, so if you can get a ride one-way, you can cycle or walk downhill the other way. Use apps for taxi rides and consider hiring a car and driver for a day out to the top sights.

Pura Kebo Edan is not an imposing structure but is famous for its much-weathered 3m-high statue, known as the Giant of Pejeng, thought to be approximately 600 years old. Although generally covered, one peek at his midsection and you'll see that the giant moniker is apt.

Many of the oldest treasures have been found by farmers plowing their fields. See a range of artefacts at the **Museum Gedung Arca**. This archaeological museum has exhibits in several small buildings, including some of Bali's first pottery from near Gilimanuk, and sarcophagi dating from as early as 300 BCE. Note that Ubud Story Walks runs an excellent tour of the main Pejang sites.

Across two rivers further east, **Goa Garba** echoes the rock carvings of Gunung Kawi (p144) to the north. It's a quiet, atmospheric site far from Bali's bustle. Niches in the cliffs known as 'hermit's alcoves' are thought to date to the 11th century.

Bedulu

TIME FROM UBUD: **20 MINS** 🚗

Explore a foundational temple

Bedulu was once the capital of a great kingdom. The legendary Dalem Bedaulu ruled the Pejeng dynasty from here and was the last Balinese king to withstand the onslaught of the powerful Majapahit from Java. He was defeated by Gajah Mada in 1343. The capital shifted several times after this, first to Gelgel and then later to Klungkung (Semarapura). You can easily use a bike to visit the sights of Bedulu and nearby Pejeng.

The majestic and tranquil **Pura Samuan Tiga** (Temple of the Meeting of the Three) is on a small lane about 200m east of the Bedulu junction. The name probably refers to meetings held here in the 10th century that established that each Balinese village would have temples honouring the three Hindu deities: Pura Desa (village temple for daily worship) for Brahma, Pura Puseh (temple honouring the village's heritage) for Vishnu and Pura Dalem (temple of the dead) for Shiva. This tradition has continued ever since. What you see here today was rebuilt after the 1917 earthquake.

Revel in the mystery of Goa Gajah

Visitors enter the rock-hewn **Goa Gajah** (elephant cave) through the cavernous mouth of a demon. Inside, there are fragmentary remains of a lingam, the phallic symbol of the Hindu god Shiva, and its female counterpart, the yoni, as well as a statue of Shiva's son, the elephant-headed god

EATING SOUTH OF UBUD: OUR PICKS

Warung Makan Teges North of Mas, it serves only one dish – *nasi campur* – and it gets every element just right. $

Art Lounge Cafe Enjoy Bali chic at the Tonyraka Art Lounge Cafe for lunch, a snack or a coffee. In Mas. $$

Ka Ka Du Café Make like a rooster and say the name at this stylish outlet. Good coffee in the heart of Sukawati. $

Sayan Night Market Located southwest of Ubud, dozens of stalls sell fresh, authentic and cheap meals nightly. $

SHARON WILDIE/SHUTTERSTOCK ©

Goa Gajah

THE LEGEND OF DALEM BEDAULU

As the legend goes, the powerful Pejeng dynasty ruler **Dalem Bedaulu** possessed magical powers that allowed him to have his head removed and then put back on during meditation (Bedaulu means 'he who changed heads').

On one occasion, the king attempted to perform this unique party trick but a servant botched it, lopping off the head and accidentally dropping it in a river. As it floated away, the servant panicked and grabbed a pig, cut off its head and popped it on the king's shoulders. Thereafter, the king sat on a soaring throne and forbade his subjects to look up at his curious face.

Ganesha. Outside, two square bathing pools have water spouts held by six female figures.

There were never any elephants in Bali (until tourist attractions changed that); ancient Goa Gajah probably takes its name from the nearby Sungai Petanu (Petanu River), which at one time was known as Elephant River.

The origins of the cave are uncertain; one tale relates that it was created by the fingernail of the legendary giant Kebo Iwa (p151). It probably dates to the 11th century and was certainly in existence during the Majapahit takeover of Bali.

As it's a popular stop for large tours, try to get here before 10am. Expect to spend about an hour on-site.

Visit a hidden wonder

Set amid rice terraces, underappreciated **Yeh Pulu** is a 25m-long carved cliff face next to the Pakerisan and Petanu Rivers and is believed to be the remnants of a 14th-century hermitage. Even if your interest in carved Hindu art is minor, the site is compelling and you're likely to have it all to yourself. Apart from the figure of Ganesha, the nine scenes depict everyday life 600 years ago. There are good walks here through the surrounding rice fields. Ask directions for Goa Gajah.

Mas

TIME FROM UBUD: **20 MINS**

Discover art and commerce

Mas may mean 'gold' in Bahasa Indonesia, but woodcarving is the principal craft in this village south of Ubud. Stores and galleries line the main road, Jl Raya Mas, and workshops are located both here and along side streets. To the north, **Pipin's**

EXPLORING SOUTH OF UBUD

Khana Putri Pertiwi, tour guide and archaeology major, shares her tips for visiting the area south of Ubud.

Don't skip **Batuan** village, just 30 minutes away from Ubud. This historically rich village holds great significance as it's where the renowned American anthropologist Margaret Mead conducted most of her research on Balinese culture. On Sundays, guests can visit **Studio Gelombang** and watch the local artist Made Griyawan conducting a traditional art class for neighbourhood kids.

Nature lovers can take a refreshing dip in either of the nearby waterfalls, **Air Sumampan** or **Air Uma Anyar**. In the late afternoon, it's fun to walk along Sukawati's new '**jogging track**' through the rice fields, where residents watch the sunset from a wide open space.

Pura Puseh Batuan

Art Shop is a vast wonderland of woven goods like baskets. West of the village, **Ubud Diary** is a labour of love by a collector of Indonesian art. It's a dramatic and modern gallery with an emphasis on celebrating the Ubud school of painting.

A World of serious make-believe

One of the best museums in the Ubud area, the **Setia Darma House of Masks and Puppets** is home to more than 7000 ceremonial masks and puppets from Bali, other parts of Indonesia, Asia and beyond. All are beautifully displayed in a series of renovated historic buildings in a rural compound. Among the many treasures, look for the amazing Barong Landung puppets and the Kamasan paintings.

Some hipster spots

One of the premier galleries in the Ubud area, **Tonyraka Art Lounge** shows top-notch Balinese tribal and contemporary art. Come to browse, buy and enjoy the cafe. Learn how to make your own stencils and prints at **Black Hand Gang**, a creative compound that also features a shop, **Toko Hands**, which recalls the hip Japanese outpost Tokyu Hands. Browse wares like irreverent T-shirts designed by local artists.

Create a Balinese mask

Led by master woodcarver **Ida Bagus Anom** (balimaskmaking.com), three generations of Bali's best mask carvers will show you their secrets in the family's **Astina Mask Gallery** opposite the football field. Students can complete a simple mask or a puppet in three to four days.

Blahbatuh

Visit vital temples

Blahbatuh is known for its association with Kebo Iwa, the legendary strongman and minister to the last king of the Bedulu kingdom. A massive statue depicting him in full warrior mode adorns a roundabout on the main road between Blahbatuh and Gianyar. An 11th-century carved head of Iwa can be admired in the village's major temple, **Pura Puseh Desa Blahbatuh**. Just north, **Pura Kahyangan Jagat** has Bukit Dharma (Dharma Hill) as a backdrop. Climb the hill to reach a shrine featuring a stone statue of the six-armed goddess of death and destruction, Durga, killing a demon-possessed water buffalo.

Learn about traditional textile art

A symphony of click-clacking looms greets visitors to **Pertenunan Putri Ayu**, which produces colourful batik and ikat fabrics (including Bali's much-prized *endek* style) using ages-old methods. Staff will show you through the workshop and explain the process. Fabric and clothes are for sale.

Witness rushing waters

Community-driven development of waterfall tourism is sweeping Bali. Dozens of sites across the island now have trails, amenities and admission fees. Near Blahbatuh, in the tiny village of **Kemenuh**, residents lead visitors on a five-minute walk shaded by bamboo down a steep set of steps into a gorge misted by the pounding water of **Air Uma Anyar**. There's swimming and sun loungers.

Batuan

Thousand-year-old temples

Batuan's recorded history goes back 1000 years; in the 17th century, its royal family controlled most of southern Bali. The decline of its power is attributed to a priest's curse, which scattered the royal family to different parts of the island. The twin temples of **Pura Puseh Batuan** and **Pura Dasar Batuan** are among Bali's oldest. They're accessible studies in classic Balinese temple architecture. The former is renowned for the quality of its sculptures and its Javanese-influenced water garden.

Sukawati

Some arts and crafts

Once a royal capital, **Sukawati** is now known for its modern market and specialised artisans, who busily work in small workshops lining the roads. Look for ones marked *tukang prada*, where you'll find temple umbrellas that are beautifully decorated with stencilled gold paint.

To the west, artisans in the villages of **Puaya** and **Singapadu** specialise in high-quality leather shadow puppets and

SHOPPING FOR WOODCARVINGS

Woodcarving was a traditional art of the priestly Brahmana caste, with the skills said to be a gift from the gods. Historically, carving was limited to temple decorations, dance masks and musical instruments, but in the 1930s carvers began depicting people and animals. Today, Bali's woodcarvers also turn their skills to furniture making and traditional handicrafts. And many moonlight carving the island's top-selling souvenir, the penis-shaped bottle opener.

You'll find carvers plying their trade across the Ubud region. Mas is a big player in Bali's furniture industry, producing chairs, tables and antiques ('made to order!'), mainly from teak imported from other Indonesian islands. Be sure to check the wood's authenticity if you're purchasing something in sandalwood.

A FAMILY'S BAMBOO REVOLUTION

Opened in 2008, **Green School Bali** in Abiansemal enjoyed immediate hype for both its unorthodox curriculum and its flamboyant bamboo architecture. A passion project of expat John Hardy (of the namesake international jewelry mega-brand) and his wife Cynthia, the school's sinuous and soaring bamboo trusses were soon repeated by Hardy in his own home. From there, the look spread across Bali, from beach clubs in Canggu to upscale restaurants amidst Ubud's rice fields to housing projects in Denpasar.

Intrigued by the look and its sustainable promise? **Bamboo U**, a project that includes Hardy's son Orin, offers online training in bamboo design and construction. Hardy's daughter Elora's architecture firm Ibuku creates bamboo structures worldwide.

LITO_LAKWATSERO/SHUTTERSTOCK ©

Stone carvers, Batubulan

masks for Topeng and Barong dances. On the main street, look for workshops where local artisans both make and sell ceremonial items for dance performances. **Nyoman Ruka** runs a studio famous for its Barong masks.

Batubulan

TIME FROM UBUD: **75 MINS** 🚗

Enjoy a village of stone carvers

Stone carving is the main craft of **Batubulan**. Workshops are found right along the road to Tegaltamu, with another batch further north around Silakarang. The village is the source of the stunning temple-gate guardians seen all over Bali. The stone used for these sculptures is a porous grey volcanic rock called *paras*, which resembles pumice; it's soft and surprisingly light. It also ages quickly, so that 'ancient' work may be years rather than centuries old. By night, the village is a hub of Balinese dance, which makes it an attractive option for visitors from the south who don't want to go all the way north to Ubud. Depending on the night, Kecak, Barong and fire dances are performed in the village's **Sahadewa**, a large venue.

Family fun with birds and reptiles

More than 1000 birds from 250 species and seven regions of the world flit about **Bali Bird Park**, including rare cendrawasih (bird of paradise) from Papua and the iconic Bali starling. Daily free-flight bird shows are staged. The park is popular with kids; allow at least two hours. **Bali Reptile Park** has snakes and lizards galore. Try to time your visit with the daily feedings of the park's huge prehistoric Komodo dragons (11am and 2.30pm).

Places We Love to Stay

$ Cheap $$ Moderate $$$ Pricey

Ubud
p122

Suryadina Guest House $
Tucked away down a small
gang (narrow lane) in a central
location. Family run.

Three Win Homestay $ Off Jl
Hanoman, the family here offers
five modern guest rooms in
their compound. Get one with a
spacious balcony.

**Batik Sekar Bali Guest House
$** On Jl Sugriwa, this family
homestay offers the timeless
Ubud experience. Come and go
as the family makes offerings.

Aji Lodge $ Off Jl Sukma and
run by local painter Aji, a quiet
homestay next to a river with
rooms with terraces.

Eka's Homestay $ The home of
Wayan Pasek Sucipta, a teacher
of Balinese music.

Biangs Homestay $ In a little
garden, these rooms overlook
the forest. Three generations
live here.

Hotel Tjampuhan $$
Overlooks two rivers. The artist
Walter Spies lived here in the
1930s, and his former home is
part of the hotel.

Sama's Cottages $$ Terraced
down a hill, this lovely hideaway
has a mix of rooms, cottages
and pool villas, all with Balinese
style.

**Puri Saraswati Bungalows
$$** Centrally located, with
lovely gardens that open onto
beautiful Pura Taman Saraswati
and attractive bungalow-style
rooms.

Villa Nirvana $$ Designed by
local architect Awan Sukhro
Edhi, a serene retreat by a river
in Penestanan. Modern villas
set in garden surrounds, many
with pools.

Capung Cottages $$
Comfortable compound just
north of the centre on a quiet
street. A variety of appealing
rooms around a large pool.

Swasti Eco Cottages $$ A
five-minute walk south of the
Monkey Forest, featuring an
organic garden, pool, yoga
shala and traditional houses.

Oka Wati Hotel $$ Rooms
have terraces or balconies and
there's always a thermos of tea
available; older bungalows are
the most atmospheric.

**Komaneka at Monkey Forest
$$** Hidden in lush gardens
overlooking a rice field
and remarkably tranquil.
Comfortable suites and villas
have elegant decor.

Alam Indah Ubud $$ South
of the Monkey Forest, this
spacious and tranquil resort has
traditionally designed rooms
with views.

Kertiyasa Bungalows $$ In
a quiet Nyuhkuning location,
expect well-sized rooms with
a large pool, set in a spacious
grounds.

Tegal Sari $$ Amidst rice
fields, the huge rooms and
suites with a chic contemporary
decor are set in modern brick
buildings. Well-located south of
the centre.

Amandari $$$ Luxurious
resort does everything with the
charm and grace of a classical
Balinese dancer. Superb views
over the green Sungai Valley.

Mandapa $$$ Set in the
spectacular Sungai Valley and
enclosed by rice fields, the
stunning Ritz-Carlton resort
is the size of a small village.
Myriad facilities and activities.

Bambu Indah Resort $$$ From
famed entrepreneurs John and
Cynthia Hardy, this ecoresort
near the Ayung Valley has
100-year-old Javanese wooden
houses and extraordinary
bamboo structures.

Four Seasons Resort $$$ Set
below the Sungai Valley rim, the
curved open-air reception area
looks like a Cinerama screen of
Sayan beauty.

Ibah $$$ (Map p124–5)
Overlooking rushing
waters and rice-clad hills in
Campuhan, these suites and
villas combine ancient and
modern details. All could
feature in an interior-design
magazine.

Maya Ubud $$$ East of the
centre in a river valley amidst
rice fields in Peliatan, the
riverside spa and swimming
pool are major draws.

East Bali

SACRED TEMPLES, VERDANT HIKES, HISTORICAL ADVENTURE

Ringed on three sides by beaches and beautiful coastline, east Bali rises to the island's highest point on Gunung Agung.

Wandering the roads of east Bali is one of the island's great pleasures. Rice terraces spill down hillsides under swaying palms, wild volcanic beaches are washed by pounding surf and age-old villages soldier on with barely a trace of modernity. Watching over it all is Gunung Agung, the 3142m active volcano known as the navel of the world, which has a perfect conical shape that you might glimpse on hikes from Tirta Gangga. Waterfalls, temples, palaces and water gardens are dotted throughout the landscape. Two of the temples – Pura Besakih and Pura Lempuyang – are among Bali's most important pilgrimage sites.

You can find Bali's past amid evocative ruins in the former royal city of

Klungkung. Follow the rivers coursing down the slopes around Sidemen to find rice terrace vistas and valleys that could have inspired Shangri-la. Down along the coast, a string of easily accessible black-sand beaches offer surfing, seclusion and seaside temples. Further east is the slow-paced ferry hub of Padang Bai and relaxed Candidasa.

Resorts and hidden beaches dot the seashore and cluster on the Amed Coast. Just north of there, Tulamben is all about external exploration: the entire town is geared for diving, especially at the iconic local shipwreck. On the northeast coast, surprises await in an evocative region of Bali where tourism is barely known.

GEKKO GALLERY/SHUTTERSTOCK ©

THE MAIN AREAS

KLUNGKUNG	**PADANG BAI**	**AMLAPURA**
Centre of historic and scenic Bali.	Port town on the varied coast.	Royal city amidst temples, coast and beauty.
p158	**p170**	**p174**

Above: *Liberty* wreck (p181); Left: Gunung Agung (p168)

Find Your Way

Shaped like a reverse crescent, east Bali's coastline is backed by mountains. Soaring Gunung Agung dominates the centre, and much of the region is on its sloping hillsides, cleaved by rivers and punctuated by waterfalls.

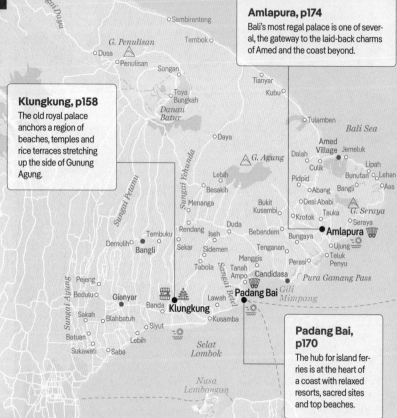

Amlapura, p174
Bali's most regal palace is one of several, the gateway to the laid-back charms of Amed and the coast beyond.

Klungkung, p158
The old royal palace anchors a region of beaches, temples and rice terraces stretching up the side of Gunung Agung.

Padang Bai, p170
The hub for island ferries is at the heart of a coast with relaxed resorts, sacred sites and top beaches.

MOTORBIKE OR CAR
East Bali is all about exploring. Having your own wheels is essential in order to give you the freedom to discover untrod beaches, pristine waterfalls, remote sacred temples and timeless villages.

WALKING
Walkers and hikers are spoiled for choice, from beachside strolls to rice-field jaunts to the formidable climb up Gunung Agung. From trekking hubs like Sidemen and Tirta Gangga, you can explore the virescent countryside.

Pura Besakih (p167)

Plan Your Time

Much of east Bali can be explored on looping day trips from Ubud and the south, but staying in the region lets you get into the groove of its relaxed rhythms.

Pressed for Time

Pick your theme for east Bali and stick to it. For **beaches** (p163), stroll the black sands stretching northeast of Sanur to Kusamba. For Balinese culture, visit **Klungkung** (p158), **Bangli** (p164) and **Gianyar** (p161). For sacred Hindu temples, visit the mother temple of **Besakih** (p167). For Balinese life, journey to the **Samsara Living Museum** (p169). For a window into royal life, see the palaces of **Amlapura** (p174).

Five Days or More

With the luxury of more time, combine some Pressed for Time day trips together. Pause along the coast, whether it's an **East Coast beach** (p163), the low-key resorts of **Padang Bai** (p170) or **Candidasa** (p173), or the dozens of choices in the far east at **Amed** (p178). Get a room with a rice terrace view in **Sidemen** (p165). Mosey up the northeast coast, diving at **Tulamben** (p181) and stopping at **Les** (p182).

SEASONAL HIGHLIGHTS

MAR–MAY
The best time to visit is during the dry season beginning in April. Along the coast, there's little reason to pick one month over another.

JUNE–AUGUST
Top-end resorts and coastal accommodation get crowded in July and August, but the region remains more mellow than south Bali and Ubud.

SEPTEMBER–NOVEMBER
The dry season ends in September, which is also the end of the best walking weather. The best surfing begins in October.

DECEMBER–FEBRUARY
Great surfing continues to March even as rains fall across the region. Expect resorts to book up for Christmas and New Year's.

157

Klungkung

HISTORY | ARCHITECTURE | MARKETS

GETTING AROUND

Klungkung is best reached with your own wheels. The main road along the east coast runs only 4km south of the centre, so it's an easy detour. It's also convenient to Gianyar, Bangli, Pura Besakih and Sidemen. Klungkung is compact, so it's easy to walk everywhere. Stashing a car or motorbike is not hard; street attendants will collect a small fee. The town can be reached in an hour or less from both Ubud (via Gianyar) and Sanur (via the coast road).

Officially called Semarapura but commonly known by its traditional name Klungkung, this district capital is home to the historically significant Puri Agung Semarapura (Klungkung Palace), a relic of the days of Klungkung's rajas (lords or princes), the Dewa Agungs. Once the centre of Bali's most important kingdom, the town retains the palace compound from its royal past and has a busy market opposite the centrally located palace compound. The town is busy through the day and the streets are lined with popular shops. Just east, the main road crosses one of Bali's largest rivers, Sungai Unda. Throughout the area there are both large temples and mosques.

It's easy to spend a couple of hours here exploring the remains of the palace and the market. Klungkung is a hub of roads, so it's easy to visit other areas of the south from here, or stop off as part of a larger itinerary.

Bali's Most Historic Palace
Evocative architecture and museum

Built when the Dewa Agung dynasty moved here in 1710, the **Puri Agung Semarapura** compound (often called Klungkung Palace) was laid out as a large square, believed to be in the form of a mandala, with courtyards, gardens, pavilions and moats. Most of the original palace and grounds were destroyed by the 1908 Dutch attacks; all that remains are the carved **Pemedal Agung**, the gateway on the south side of the square, the **Kertha Gosa** and the **Bale Kambang**.

Located within the palace compound, the ceiling of the beautiful water-surrounded *bale* (open-sided pavilion) showcases rows of paintings dealing with various subjects. The first row is based on the astrological calendar, the second on the folktale of Pan and Men Brayut and their 18 children, and the upper rows on the adventures of the hero Sutasona.

☑ TOP TIP

Despite the sights, Klungkung is not a tourist town so don't expect to find many options for eating and drinking. However, the market is great for fruit, especially before noon. Just east on Jl Nakula, you can get a simple meal at Bali Indah, a 1930s storefront cafe.

The open-sided **Kertha Gosa** pavilion in the northeastern corner of the complex was effectively the supreme court of the Klungkung kingdom, where disputes and cases that could not be settled at the village level were eventually brought. A superb example of Klungkung architecture, it features a ceiling covered with fine 20th-century paintings in Kamasan (aka *wayang*, or shadow-puppet) style. These replaced the original 19th-century cloth paintings, which deteriorated over time, and depict the Garuda story among scenes related to karma.

Much improved in recent years, the **Museum Semarajaya** is housed in a colonial-era building on the western side of the complex. Among the highlights is a moving painting with a detailed depiction of the 1908 *puputan* (mass ritual suicide) courtesy of the Dutch troops. Displays include traditional weapons, costumes and cherished ceremonial items alongside some interesting old photos of the royal court, including a portrait of Dewa Agung Gede Jambe, the five-year-old crown prince who died in the *puputan*. Displays include English descriptions and QR codes.

The Puri Agung Semarapura ticket office is on the opposite side of Jl Untung Surapati, next to the Puputan Monument.

Monument to Sacrifice

Honouring ritual suicide

Klungkung was the last Balinese kingdom to succumb to the Dutch (1908) and the sacrifice of its royal family, who committed *puputan* rather than surrender, is commemorated in the towering **Puputan Monument**, just across Jl Serapati from

KLUNGKUNG'S BLOODY HISTORY

In 1849 the rulers of Klungkung and Gianyar defeated a Dutch invasion force at Kusamba. Before the Dutch could launch a counterattack, a peace settlement was brokered. For the next 50 years, the south Bali kingdoms jostled for supremacy until the raja of Gianyar petitioned the Dutch for support.

When the Dutch finally invaded, the king of Klungkung had to choose between a *puputan* (ritual suicide) or an ignominious surrender, such as that made by Tabanan's raja. He chose the first option. On April 28, 1908, as the Dutch surrounded his palace, the king led hundreds out to certain death from Dutch gunfire or the blades of their own kris (traditional daggers).

Kertha Gosa (p159)

Puri Agung Semarapura. It's on a large square with water features. It serves as a modern counterpoint to the old royal palace across the road and makes for a lovely, frangipani-scented park where you can take a pause from the day's adventures.

East Bali's Best Market

From fresh fruit to textiles

Klungkung's **market** is a vibrant hub of commerce and a meeting place for people of the region. You can easily spend an hour wandering about the warren of stalls crammed into a series of buildings on three levels and in the surrounding streets. It's chaotic, yes, but also fascinating, and has not been replaced by the huge antiseptic market buildings such as those in Gianyar and Sukawati. Straw baskets of fresh produce are islands of colour amid the hubbub, and there's plenty of jewellery and ikat (the latter sells for a fraction of what you'll pay elsewhere). It's best visited before noon.

Beyond
Klungkung

From wild beaches to the top of Bali's highest peak, the lands around Klungkung combine beauty, sacred meaning and cultural interest.

You'll be spoiled for day trips and adventures in the region outside Klungkung. Look for surprises along the lovely roads linking towns and cities like Bangli and Gianyar. The coast is lined with black-sand beaches, noted for pounding surf and few crowds. Some of Bali's lushest scenery is found at the Sidemen rice terraces. In the surrounding hills, dozens of waterfalls are the essence of tropical beauty. The island's mother temple, Pura Besakih, is far up the side of its father volcano, Gunung Agung. The latter is one of Indonesia's iconic climbs, although you can also enjoy it from a temple far up its slope. Lose yourself in Balinese culture at the island's best museum.

Places

Gianyar
TIME FROM KLUNGKUNG: **20 MINS** 🚗

Artisanal shops and the temple of the dead

This is the affluent administrative capital and main market town of the Gianyar district, which also includes Ubud. The town has workshops producing batik and ikat fabrics, and a tidy centre with some excellent food, especially at the famous night market. Note that Gianyar's traditional market was destroyed by fire and replaced by a hulking structure that looks more like the Ministry of Markets than an actual commercial centre. However, the surrounding streets are still interesting; look for shops selling traditional sweets.

The temple of the dead, **Pura Dalem Sidan**, has fine stone carvings, including a sculpture of Durga with children by the entrance gate. Also notable is the separate enclosure in one corner of the temple dedicated to Merajapati, the guardian spirit of the dead. The temple is northeast of Gianyar on the road to Bangli.

Bali's best night market

The sound of scores of cooking pots and the glare of bright lights add a frenetic and festive clamour to Gianyar's delicious and wonderfully aromatic **night market** (*pasar malam*), where some of the best street food in Bali is on offer. Scores

GETTING AROUND

Whether you drive yourself or allow someone else the honour, you will need your own wheels to explore the close-in east. The region is ideal for random adventures as you can never get too lost and there's always another surprise – be it a waterfall, view, temple or village. If you're staying in Ubud or south Bali, you might consider using a taxi for a one-way ride to Gianyar or the beaches.

LITTLE OFFERINGS EVERYWHERE

Bali's gods, ancestors, spirits and demons are presented with offerings throughout the day to show respect and gratitude. These gifts to higher beings must look attractive, so each offering is a tiny work of art. The most common is a banana-leaf tray little bigger than a saucer, artfully topped with flowers, food and more. Once presented to the gods, an offering cannot be used again, so new ones are made each day, usually by women.

You'll see the components for sale in village and town markets across Bali, such as those in Gianyar and Ubud's produce market. Dogs hover around fresh offerings, but given that gods instantly enjoy an offering's essence, the critters are just getting leftovers.

Night market, Gianyar (p161)

of stalls set up each night near the town's main street and cook up a mouthwatering and jaw-dropping range of dishes, including delectable *babi guling* (spit-roast pig stuffed with chilli, turmeric, garlic and ginger; p39).

Much of the fun here is just strolling, browsing and choosing. Street chefs serve everything from fragrant *bakso* (meatball) soup to *sate* (satay), and coconut sweets to *pisang goreng* (fried banana). With a group you can sample a lot and be happier for it. Peak time is during the two hours after sunset. Best of all, the night market is only a 20-minute drive from Ubud.

Savouring babi guling

There's no need to wait for nightfall to enjoy Bali's iconic *babi guling*. There are numerous outlets for the traditional meals of roast pork near Gianyar. Two of the best are **Babi Guling Ibu Desak**, which is a busy roadside place on the route to Ubud, and **Warung Babi Guling Pande Egi**, a lovely open-air outlet overlooking rice fields in a somewhat rural area northwest of the centre.

Bali's unique endek fabric

Gianyar was once known for its factories producing the vibrantly patterned weft ikat, which is called *endek* in Bali. Although many have closed in recent years, two notable holdouts remain. **Pertenunan Setia Cap Cili** is a textile factory dating to 1948. There's a large showroom where you can buy material by the metre. Weavers operate dozens of clacking wooden looms and you can see how the entire *endek* production process works, beginning with the dying of the thread. You can have a similar experience about 500m west at **Cap Togog**.

CONSTANTIN STANCIU/SHUTTERSTOCK ©

East Coast Beaches

TIME FROM KLUNGKUNG: **20–40 MINS** 🚗

Enjoy over 20km of sand

The coastal highway between Sanur and Kusamba runs alongside a swathe of **black-sand beaches** for over 20km. Pretty much any road or lane heading towards the water will end up at a beach. The shoreline is striking, with beaches in volcanic shades of grey pounded by waves. The entire coast has great religious significance and there are oodles of temples scattered along it. At the many small coastal village beaches, cremation formalities reach their conclusion when the ashes are consigned to the sea.

Some beaches have places for food and drink; others have nothing at all. Few will be crowded. Two of the island's best **surf breaks** are at Keramas and Ketewel. The beaches here are listed from west to east.

Pantai Ketewel is known for surfing, which demands advanced skills; it's a tricky reef-rocky right. For a more transcendent experience, **Pantai Purnama** is a small beach that reflects billions of sparkles in the sunlight. Religion is big here: the temple close to the coastal highway, **Pura Erjeruk**, hosts elaborate full-moon purification ceremonies. There are small temples and shrines on the beach.

Pantai Keramas has consistent surf that's world-class. There are many rental villas along this swath of coast. Just up the coast, **Pantai Selukat** is a centre of tourism development with guesthouses, villas and upscale hotels. The beach is wide and dark; at low tide, algae-covered rocks are exposed at the shore. Views to Nusa Lembongan are sweeping. There are various cafes here, including **Locas Waroeng**, which is right on the sand and a good place to let a day slip away as you enjoy the sound of the surf.

Pantai Masceti is a study in contrasts. It has a few drinks vendors and one of Bali's sacred directional temples, Pura Masceti. Right on the beach, the temple is built in the shape of a *garuda* (a large mythical bird) and enlivened with flamboyant statuary. There's a certain irony to the bird shape as both the temple grounds and a huge *wantilan* (traditional meeting building) nearby are used for cockfights. Nearby **Pantai Lebih** is just off the coastal highway and has glittering mica-infused sand. Fishing boats line the shore and the air is redolent with the smell of BBQ fish emanating from a cluster of **beachside seafood warungs**; this is an excellent stop for lunch.

Pantai Lepang is worth visiting just for the little slice of rural Bali you pass through on the 600m drive from the main road. Down at the carbon-coloured sand you'll find small dunes, no shade, a couple of vendors and a sea turtle sanctuary. **Pantai Klotok** is where sacred statues from Pura Besakih are brought for ritual cleansing. Workers toil in the sun, sorting stones for use in ornamental gardens.

TIPS FOR EAST BALI'S BEACHES

Swimming in the pounding surf is dangerous. There are no lifeguards and emergency services are not readily available. Also be aware that many beaches have no shade and the dark sand can get very hot. Some beaches have tree-shaded areas behind the sand.

There is usually a food or drink vendor or two, although these may only be open on weekends. When in doubt, bring plenty of water (there are plenty of convenience stores along the coastal highway). You'll need your own transport to reach these beaches, though the number of places to stay is rapidly increasing. Residents will sometimes charge you a small access or parking fee.

Rubbish is a depressing fact at many of the beaches, but colourful ceremonies are common.

GAMELAN & CRAFT VILLAGES

Several workshops in **Tihingan**, a village between Klungkung and Gianyar, are dedicated to producing gamelan instruments. Small foundries make the resonating bronze bars and bowl-shaped gongs, which are then carefully tuned by the craftsperson, the Pande Gong, until they produce the correct tone. Many workshops with signs out front are open for visits.

As in other places devoted to crafts production around Ubud and east Bali, you'll find workshops scattered throughout the village. Look for 'gamelan' and 'gong' on signs. Workshops are most active in the morning before the heat of the day. Later, as is normal at many craft workshops, you may only find a genial Pande Gong happy to explain their work, or no one at all.

Textiles, seaside meals and live music

Fine Indonesian ikat and batik textiles are displayed at **Masa Masa**, which has shops with beautifully curated collections of fabrics, clothes, historic prints, antiques and more. Superbly curated and lavish shows detailing aspects of local culture are mounted in the Galerie Wastraku. Casual lunches and elegant dinners are served in the cafe, which is cooled by sea breezes. On some nights there is live music, from jazz to acoustic.

Wine-tasting stopover

Right off the coast highway, **Sababay Winery** is home to wine that hits above its weight, given that many consider wine-making and tropical climates mutually exclusive. Set amidst shady gardens, the complex has an upscale outdoor cafe, shop and production facility where you can learn how grapes grown in north Bali are turned into Sababay's 14 varieties of wine, including the excellent Reserve Red from 2020.

Bangli
TIME FROM KLUNGKUNG: **45 MINS**

Depictions of the afterlife

Moving up the mountainside, Bangli is a once-humble market town that is enjoying a facelift, thanks to the region's growing tourism. It's a verdant area with beautiful drives on jungle roads that run east past rice terraces; it connects at Sekar with roads to Rendang and Sidemen.

Worth a stop, the fascinating temple **Pura Dalem Penunggekan** has an exterior wall featuring vivid relief carvings of evil-doers getting their just desserts in the afterlife. One panel addresses the lurid fate of adulterers (note the godlike creature wielding a saw on a wayward man's privates). Other panels portray sinners as monkeys, while another is a good representation of those begging to be spared the fires of hell.

Temple of the treasures

The state temple of the Bangli kingdom, **Pura Kehen**, is a miniature version of Pura Besakih (p167), Bali's most important temple. It's terraced up the hillside, with a flight of steps leading to the beautifully decorated entrance. The first courtyard has a huge banyan tree with a *kulkul* (hollow tree-trunk drum used to sound warnings) entwined in its branches; the inner courtyard has an 11-roof *meru* (multi-tiered shrine). Other shrines have thrones for the Hindu trinity: Brahma, Shiva and Vishnu. See if you can count all 43 altars. The name means 'treasures', but they are hidden away in shrines and are reputed to be ancient copper sheets with sacred engravings. Take heart in the legend that any who enter the temple with pure hearts will be protected from evil.

MICHAELBALLERONI/SHUTTERSTOCK ©

Pura Kehen

BANGLI'S HISTORY

The hillside town of Bangli dates from the early 13th century. In the Majapahit era, it broke away from Gelgel (the forerunner of Klungkung) to become a separate kingdom, even though it was landlocked, poor and involved in long-running conflicts with neighbouring states.

In 1849, Bangli agreed to a treaty with the Dutch that gave it control over the defeated north-coast kingdom of Buleleng (where today's Singaraja is the capital), but Buleleng then rebelled and the Dutch imposed direct rule there. In 1909 the raja of Bangli chose to sell out and become a Dutch protectorate rather than commit a *puputan* (ritual suicide) like its former rival Klungkung.

Penglipuran tourist village

One of Bali's most popular attractions – especially with tourists from other parts of Indonesia – is the traditional village of **Penglipuran**. Organised around a gently descending, grass-lined, 400m-long pedestrian avenue, several dozen old Balinese family compounds have been turned into a combination of snack stands and souvenir shops. It gets very crowded with day trippers; clever visitors get dropped off at the north end of the village amidst a bamboo forest and then enjoy a 20-minute stroll to the south end to be picked up.

Sidemen

TIME FROM KLUNGKUNG: **25 MINS** 🚗

Hilltop village idyll

In **Sidemen** (pronounced si-da-men), a walk in any direction is a communion with nature. Winding through one of Bali's most beautiful river valleys, the road to this hilltop village offers marvellous rice-terrace scenery, a delightful

EAST BALI'S BEST WATERFALLS

Air Terjun Jagasatru Narrow stream plunging down into a hidden pool; reached by a steep set of concrete stairs.

Air Goa Giri Campuhan Walk through a rice field, then down through caves to a series of waterfalls burbling over huge rocks.

Air Tukad Cepung A forest walk leads to steep steps descending to a narrow stone canyon that opens onto a wide waterfall.

Air Goa Raja Lush scenery shades a walk over bridges and down steps to tall falls.

Air Gembleng Climb up to platforms offering sweeping views of the Sidemen area and the lovely top of the falls.

PHRAISOHN SIRIPOOL/SHUTTERSTOCK ©

Pura Besakih

rural character and extraordinary views of Gunung Agung, which looms large to the northeast.

German artist Walter Spies (p129) lived in a villa in the village of **Iseh** near Sidemen after 1932 in order to paint the sublime scenery and escape the perpetual party of his own making in Ubud. These days, people flock here to revel in the lush, luxuriant countryside while relaxing in low-key guesthouses and hotels (almost all of which have places to eat). It can get cool and misty at night.

Walking Sidemen

Although simply soaking up the views is temptation enough, there are many **walks** through the rice and chilli fields in the multihued green valley, which is laced with gushing *subak* irrigation channels. One involves a spectacular three-hour,

EATING IN SIDEMEN: OUR PICKS

Warung Melita Riverside *bale* (open-air pavilion) in the Darmada Eco Resort with Balinese and Western dishes; grows its own organic veggies. **$$**

Warung Dapur Kapulaga Organic menu of Western and Balinese staples, in front of the Alamdhari Villa. Great *pisang goreng*. **$$**

Joglo D'Uma Pavilion restaurant with a sensational view of rice terraces; food is tourist-friendly with gentle seasoning; excellent peanuts. **$$**

9am Coffee Name says it all at the best Sidemen spot for a morning coffee and snack before a day walking the rice terraces. **$**

round-trip climb up to **Pura Bukit Tageh**, a small temple with big views. To the east, follow the aroma of fermentation to the tiny village of **Tri Eka Buana**, a centre of the traditional distillation of *arak*, Bali's own liquor made from palm sap.

No matter where you stay, you can either arrange guides for day hikes or simply set out on your own. Among many good choices, **Nyoman Subrata** (0852 3999 5789; nyomansidemen@gmail.com) can guide you through the area.

All that glitters is woven

Sidemen is a centre for culture and arts, particularly *endek* cloth (vibrantly patterned weft ikat) and *songket* (silver- or gold-threaded cloth). Learn about these textiles and watch them being made at **Pelangi Traditional Weaving**.

Scenic drives through timeless Bali

The hilly road through Sidemen can be a beautiful part of any day trip from south Bali or Ubud. It connects in the north with the Rendang–Amlapura road just west of Duda. Sidemen can be combined with scenic drives that include Pura Besakih, Bangli and Klungkung. Signs for waterfalls abound throughout the region.

One of the best routes includes the road that begins about 5km east of Gianyar on the main road to Klungkung. It runs north for about 12km to the village of Tembuku and passes through a score of tiny traditional villages. There are **rice terrace and river valley views** along its length. You'll see huge beams of yellow wood on the roadside that are used in temple construction. These are from jackfruit trees and are prized for their long-lasting quality. This road links up to the Rendang–Amlapura road, which leads to the turn for Sidemen.

Pura Besakih

TIME FROM KLUNKUNG: **45 MINS** 🚗

Bali's holiest temple

Perched nearly 1000m up the side of Gunung Agung is Bali's most important temple, **Pura Besakih**. It is a vast complex of 23 separate but related temples that together form a landing complex for the gods on Bali (*besakih* is derived from the Sanskrit word for 'sanctuary'). Constant processions of village groups arrive for ceremonies, blessings and to take holy water back to their own temples. On a misty day, the scores of jet-black *meru* soaring towards the sky are a moving and dramatic sight.

The oldest temple, **Pura Penataran Agung**, is dedicated to Shiva. Like many of the other temples at this hillside site, it is not always open to visitors, although you can usually walk amidst the various holy sites. An enormous new parking garage that seems suited for an airport was completed in 2022. It comes with new procedures for visits that are meant to limit the myriad hassles that have bedevilled

TIPS FOR VISITING BESAKIH

Services of a guide are included in the ticket price. However, the services rendered vary greatly in quality and you can forgo a guide. Tip only if you're pleased with your guide.

Inside the complex, you may receive offers to 'come pray with me'. Visitors who seize on this chance to enter a closed temple may face extortionate demands. People may try to give you offerings – if you accept them, they will then demand payment. Offerings are not necessary in temples. Sarong and sash hire is included in the ticket price.

To avoid the 600m walk back to the entrance past the souvenir shops, simply board a cart heading downhill.

AGUNG DOS & DON'TS

Gunung Agung is a hard climb. Always check official warnings before setting out and use a guide. While hiking, respect your guide's pauses at shrines for prayers on the sacred mountain. Aim on getting to the top before 8am – the clouds that often obscure Agung also obscure the view from the summit. Take a strong torch (headlamp), extra batteries, plenty of water (2L per person), snacks, waterproof clothing, a warm layer and appropriate shoes or boots.

Be aware that the trails are steep. The descent is difficult as the trails have a lot of loose rocks, which makes footing very difficult. Take frequent rests and don't be afraid to ask your guide to slow down.

tourists here for years. Unfortunately, hassles remain. On the plus side, you now get a ride up the long hill to the temple complex in an electric cart.

Of the dozens of stalls selling snacks around the complex, none rise above the level of boiling water for noodle cups. However, you can get good Balinese food from warungs selling *babi guling* and other treats along the roads to Besakih and at the market in the village of **Menanga**.

Gunung Agung
TIME FROM KLUNGKUNG: **45–75 MINS**

Climb to the centre of everything

Bali's highest and most revered mountain, **Gunung Agung** (Mt Agung) – known as the 'Navel of the World' and 'Mother Mountain' – is an imposing volcano that can be seen from most of south and east Bali when clear of clouds and mist. Most sources say it's 3142m high. The summit is an oval crater about 700m across. As it's the spiritual centre of Bali, traditional houses across the island are laid out on an axis in line with Agung and many Balinese always know where they are in relation to the peak, which is thought to house ancestral spirits.

Scaling Gunung Agung is one of Bali's most challenging adventures. However, climbing is not permitted when major religious events are being held at Pura Besakih, and there has been talk of closing Gunung Agung to climbers due to inappropriate behaviour by tourists, so confirm it remains open. The climb takes you through a verdant forest in the clouds and rewards with sweeping dawn views. It's best to trek during the dry season (April to September); July to September are the most reliable months. At other times the paths can be slippery and dangerous and the views are clouded over.

The two most popular climbing routes are via Pura Pasar Agung Sebudi and Pura Besakih. The Pura Pasar Agung Sebudi (on the southern slopes; about four hours to ascend) route is the shortest and most direct because the temple is high on the southern slopes of the mountain (around 1550m). The Pura Besakih (on the southwest side of the mountain; about six hours to ascend) climb is much tougher than the already demanding southern approach and is only for the physically very fit. It starts at 900m.

Most of the places to stay in the region, including those at Selat, along the Sidemen road and at Tirta Gangga, can recommend climbing guides. Two recommended guides are **Wayan Tegteg** (0813 3852 5677; facebook.com/wayan. tegteg.7) and **I Ketut Uriada** (0812 364 6426; ketut.uriada@ gmail.com).

Ascending to Agung's holy temple

Far up on the south face of Agung, **Pura Pasar Agung Sebudi** is the mountain's holy temple. It's perched on a rocky outcrop and has sweeping views up to the volcano's jagged crater as well as out across Bali and onto Lombok. On overcast days, you'll likely be above the clouds and looking out over a fluffy, white blanket. It's a 9.5km drive up the side of

Gunung Agung

READY TO BLOW?

In November 2017, Gunung Agung erupted spectacularly, prompting thousands to evacuate, causing ash damage to the region and shutting down Bali's airport. Lesser eruptions continued through 2018 and into 2019. While disruptive, the activity was also a valuable reminder that the island's spiritual center is not just a placid peak but rather an active volcano that can turn dangerous at any time.

Older Balinese recall with horror the catastrophic 1963 eruption that killed from 1000 to 2000 people and destroyed scores of villages – 100,000 people in all lost their homes. Streams of lava poured down to the sea, isolating east Bali for some time. Ash landed as far as the capital Jakarta.

Agung from Selat. Scenery along the road is stark, a legacy of the 1963 eruption that devastated all the local villages. At the top, there is a parking area with stalls selling snacks and offerings. From here it's a climb of 300 steep steps up to the temple.

Bali's best museum

Run by the local community, **Samsara Living Museum** in the rural village of Jungutan offers an engaging and well-curated window into Balinese culture and daily life. Volunteers take visitors through the 14 important ceremonial events in Balinese life and then offer hands-on demonstrations of topics as diverse as gamelan instruments, *arak* distillation, coffee, offerings and much more. Optional extras include cooking lessons, a water blessing ceremony and a dance class. The museum grounds are a green idyll. It's easy to have a two-hour visit turn into three or more hours. Sitting at the knees of village women while they fluidly make different types of offerings is captivating. The museum is about an hour's drive from Klungkung and about 30 minutes from Amlapura.

You can experience more community-based tourism on the excellent tours of the nearby village of **Sibetan** run by the non-profit JED (jed.or.id).

Padang Bai

BEACH TOWN | UNDERWATER ADVENTURES | TRANSPORT HUB

GETTING AROUND

Padang Bai is a hub for ferries, fast, slow and otherwise. Lombok can be reached by slow car ferries. Fast boats to Lombok and the Gilis depart from a separate and crowded dock to the east. The large ferry serving Nusa Penida also leaves from Padang Bai; this is the boat for people who want to take their motorbikes. Ground transport choices are limited; many fast-boat tickets include transfers. Otherwise, people tend to arrive with their own wheels.

☑ TOP TIP

If you're waiting for a boat, the further you walk away from the piers, the better your eating and drinking choices will be. This also applies at night for people staying in town.

Transport overshadows this beach town: Padang Bai is the busy commercial port for the public car ferries connecting Bali with Lombok, and it's also the tourist-thronged port for the fast boats to Lombok, the Gilis and Nusa Penida. Late in the day when the boat traffic diminishes, Padang Bai takes on a more mellow mood, with visitors wandering the waterfront and hanging out at backpacker cafes and simple restaurants. When the moon reflects off the bay, it's almost romantic. Accommodation ranges from appealing hostels to tired guesthouses to a couple of decent resorts.

By day, avoid the transiting mobs and hit nearby beaches, or go diving or snorkelling. Take a short walk around the headland to Pura Silayukti, the place where Empu Kuturan – who introduced the caste system to Bali in the 11th century – is said to have lived.

Hit the Beach

Walk to top choices

The dive shops and guesthouses at the east end of town along Jl Silayukti are fronted by a long strip of **beach**, which would be more appealing if it weren't for all those ferries groaning about offshore. Still, it's a good place to relax and read a book.

On the far side of Padang Bai's eastern headland, about a 500m walk from the town centre, is **Blue Lagoon Beach**. It has a couple of warungs and gentle, family-friendly surf. The water quality is very good. Walk southwest from the ferry terminal and follow the trail up the hill for about 1.3km to **Bias Tugal**, also known as Pantai Kecil (Little Beach), on the exposed coast outside the bay. Be careful in the water as it's subject to strong currents. There are a couple of day-time warungs here.

Diving & Snorkelling

Accessible underwater adventures

Padang Bai is one of Bali's main centres for **diving** and **snorkelling**; there are a number of dive centres and shops on Jl Silayukti, opposite the beach. There is good diving on the

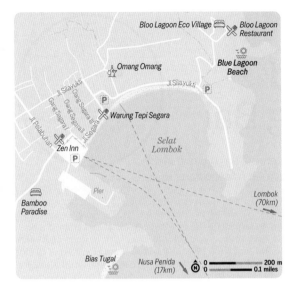

TIPS FOR PADANG BAI PORT

Buy fast boat tickets online in advance, and only buy public car ferry tickets from the official window in the ferry building. Watch out for scams where someone may try to sell you a ticket you've already bought.

Touts on motorcycles intercept arriving cars with offers of tickets, snorkelling trips and oceanfront land. Ignore them and those who meet all arriving boats with overpriced transport offers. Use rides included with boat tickets, arrange transport in advance or use a ride app.

Anyone who carries your luggage on or off the car ferries or fast boats will expect to be paid; agree on the price first or carry your own stuff. The docks can get quite manic, so try to travel light.

coral reefs around Padang Bai, but the water can be a bit cold and visibility is not always ideal. The most popular local dives are **Blue Lagoon** and **Teluk Jepun** (Jepun Bay), both in Teluk Amuk, the bay immediately east of Padang Bai. There's a good range of soft and hard corals and varied marine life, including sharks, turtles and wrasse. Blue Lagoon boasts a 23m wall.

Many local outfits offer diving trips in the area, including to nearby **Gili Tepekong** and **Gili Biaha**, two islets just off Teluk Amuk. The dive shops also sell trips to Tulamben and Nusa Penida. Realistically, any place further away, such as Pulau Menjangan, is too distant to be worth visiting from Padang Bai.

Near Padang Bai, **Blue Lagoon Beach** is an excellent and accessible walk-in snorkel site. Note that it is subject to strong currents when the tide is out. Other sites such as the waters off Teluk Jepun can be reached by local boat. A steady stream of former fishing boats buzz away from Padang Bai's beach all day long with tourists going to snorkelling sites. You can also check with the dive operators to see if they have room for snorkellers on their boats.

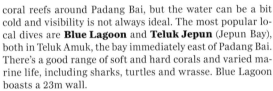

EATING & DRINKING IN PADANG BAI

Bloo Lagoon Restaurant Worth the walk to the modest resort; enjoy well-made seafood, pizza and local dishes alongside sweeping views. $$

Zen Inn Hidden by the car ferry port, Western mains are served in this sparkling cafe that stays open late by local standards. $

Warung Tepi Segara The sole dining option on the water has garlicky Balinese seafood dishes, a full-on bamboo vibe and atmospheric ferry lights. $$

Omang Omang Cafe and live-music venue back from the beach with a loyal crew of regulars; the house blues band has a cult following. $

Beyond
Padang Bai

A famous beach and temple are the two main sights along the coast road near Padang Bai.

Places

Kusamba p172

Candidasa p173

Pantai Pasir Putih p173

GETTING AROUND

The main coast road east and west of Padang Bai is busy with traffic. Any nearby lodging will be noisy around the clock. It's also narrow, making cycling a chore rather than a delight. Your own wheels are the main transport option. Near Manggis, west of Candidasa, a narrow paved road climbs the hillside through appealing scenery and meets the main road, which links the sights at the base of Gunung Agung.

The nearly 30km of coastline around Padang Bai is a green, rocky ribbon backed by steep hills. The road is busy with traffic, especially large trucks going to and from the port. Kusamba is the last of the flatlands to the west and mixes traditional work with the sacred. Pura Goa Lawah blends mystical lore with its namesake bats. Further on, Candidasa is a quiet strip of hotels; those removed from the roadside offer mellow, waterfront stays. The beach at Pantai Pasir Putih makes up for the lack of sand elsewhere in the area with a long brilliant white strand that's the envy of other Balinese beaches. It's popular with day trippers from across the island.

Kusamba

TIME FROM PADANG BAI: **20 MINS**

Fishing village

At the fishing and salt-making village of **Kusamba** (a port for Nusa Penida fast boats) you'll see rows of colourful fishing boats lined up along the beach. The 'eyes' on the front of the boats help navigate at night. Stop into waterfront **Uyah Kusamba** to learn about the back-breaking work of salt production (p182), which turns seawater into sodium chloride via long wooden troughs. The mineral-packed results are on sale.

Discover the bat cave

One of Bali's directional temples, the small **Pura Goa Lawah** (Bat Cave Temple) is in a cliff face full of both fruit bats and tour groups. An unconfirmed legend says the cave leads all the way to Pura Besakih (p167), some 19km away. The bats provide sustenance for the legendary giant snake, the deity Naga Basuki, which is also believed to live in the cave. Ignore touts offering unnecessary guiding services. Stop for a fine lunch at the nearby **Warung Lesehan Sari Baruna**, where the sole meal option consists of spicy fish satay, fishball broth, steamed fish, rice, snake beans and a fiery red sambal. The cave is 3km east of Kusamba.

GEDE SUYOGA/SHUTTERSTOCK ©

Perang pandan **contest, Tenganan**

Candidasa

TIME FROM PADANG BAI: **25 MINS** 🚗

A low-key pause

Officially known as Segkidu Village but called **Candidasa** for tourism purposes, this coastal settlement is mostly a long stretch of hotels. The beach here was destroyed in the 1980s, when the offshore reef was mined for lime to make cement to build hotels. Those seeking a beachy stay should steer clear. However, modest waterfront hotels east and west of the noisy main drag in the centre offer unpretentious and restful stays. Away from the water, **Trekking Candidasa** (trekking candidasa.com) offers walks through the verdant rice fields and hills behind town.

Centuries-old settlement

The walled village of **Tenganan** is home to Bali Aga people – the descendants of the original Balinese who inhabited the island before the Majapahit arrival in the 11th century. An hour-long visit today takes in traditional homes in a car-free setting that's only 500m by 250m. You may be greeted by a guide who will take you on a tour. Look for the cloth known as *kamben gringsing*, which has traditionally been woven in Tenganan, and traditional Balinese calligraphy, with the script inscribed onto *lontar* (a palm-leaf manuscript). Most homes double as shops. It's 16km from Candidasa.

Pantai Pasir Putih

TIME FROM PADANG BAI: **45 MINS** 🚗

A sandy rarity

A white-sand beach on an island where almost all beaches are tan, brown or charcoal, **Pantai Pasir Putih** (aka Virgin Beach) is wildly popular. The long crescent backed by coconut palms makes for a fine day out if you can avoid the crowds. Cafes rent loungers and the surf is swimmable. There are two access routes from the main coast road: the traditional one near **Perasi** in the east ends at a parking lot with a long steep walk down to the sand. A newer western route starts at **Bugbug** village and meanders scenically right down to the beach and parking.

Tenganan is one of many Bali Aga villages in mostly remote parts of east Bali. Though the Bali Aga have a reputation as being conservative and resistant to change, this is more out of poverty than preference. Fueled by tourist money, the residents of Tenganan have TVs and other modern conveniences hidden away in their traditional houses and most carry phones.

Ancient customs include an unusual, old-fashioned version of the gamelan known as the *gamelan selunding*. Girls dance an equally ancient dance known as the Rejang; a good time to see this is during the **Usaba Sambah Festival**, which honours gods and ancestors. It's famous for its contest of *perang pandan* (ritual combat using thorny stalks made of pandan leaves), which is usually held in June or July.

173

Amlapura

WATER PALACES | BALINESE CUISINE | SPLENDID HIKING

GETTING AROUND

Amlapura's sights are scattered far and wide and as there is no public transport, you'll need a car to get between them. Most offer good walking – particularly at Tirta Gangga – but only Taman Ujung and Pura Lingga Yoni can be linked on foot. Fortunately, traffic here is pretty fluid. A popular – and very long – day trip from south Bali and Ubud includes a quick bit of snorkelling at Tulamben followed by flying visits to Tirta Gangga and Taman Ujung.

☑ TOP TIP

For lunch, the centre of Amlapura has a few simple warungs around the *pasar* (market). Warungs and cafes geared towards tourist tastes ring the Tirta Gangga parking areas.

Amlapura is the tidy capital of Karangasem district and the main city at the east end of Bali. The smallest of Bali's district capitals, it's a multicultural place with both Muslim and Chinese residents. The former royal family built palaces across the region during their reign and three can be visited today: the principal royal palace in the city and two nearby water palaces. All are reminders of Karangasem's grand period as a kingdom supported by Dutch colonial power in the late 19th and early 20th centuries.

Tirta Gangga has a holy temple, some great water features and some of the best views of rice fields and the sea beyond. It's an area laced by splendid walks and there's even a world-class restaurant, Bali Asli.

Down at the coast is the other water palace, Taman Ujung, as well as relaxed Jasri Bay with its beaches and chocolate factory.

Bali's Most Lavish Palace

Beauty in the heart of Amlapura

Enter the appealing 19th-century **Puri Agung Karangasem** past beautifully sculpted panels and an impressive multi-tiered gate (all entrances point you towards the rising sun in the east). The main building of the rambling palace complex is the **Maskerdam** (Amsterdam), built as a gift by the Dutch as a reward for the Karangasem kingdom's acquiescence to Dutch rule. On a half-hour visit, don't miss the vintage photos. A highlight of the lovely, manicured grounds is the **Bale Kambang**, an ornate floating pavilion surrounded by a large pond.

A Popular Water Palace

Strolling Taman Ujung

A popular location for wedding photographs and romantic saunters, the **Taman Ujung** complex south of Amlapura city dates to 1921, when the last king of Karangasem completed the

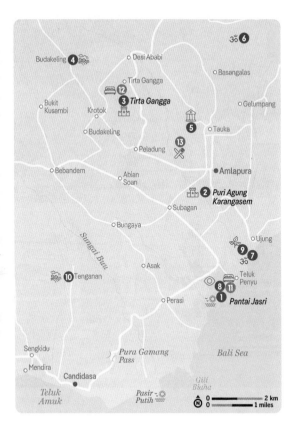

construction of a grand water palace here. Largely destroyed by a 1979 earthquake, it has been somewhat blandly restored over the years. Manicured **gardens** surround large pools, bridges and pavilions, which can be covered in half an hour.

The name, Taman Ujung, means 'Garden at the Edge' and it was built around an old ceremonial pool where people thought to be in the thrall of black magic could be purified.

Fertility by the Sea

Lingga and yoni in stone

A short walk from Taman Ujung is a rocky waterfront home to **Pura Lingga Yoni**, one of the more unusual sights in east Bali – a 2m-long penis-shaped rock (*lingga*). Balinese attribute great power to the rock and it's now the scene of regular ceremonies. Experts speculate that the stone is an ancient fertility symbol, especially given its companion, a large stone that somewhat resembles a *yoni* (the female counterpart of a *lingga*).

PALM-FROND BOOKS

Lontar is made from the fan-shaped leaves of the *lontar* (or *rontal*) palm. The process is complex: the leaf is dried, soaked in water, cleaned, steamed, dried again, then flattened and cut into strips. Words and pictures are inscribed onto the strips using a very sharp blade or point, then coated with a black stain that highlights the inscribed surface.

Holes in the *lontar* strips are threaded onto a string, with a carved bamboo 'cover' at each end. *Lontar* palms are easily spotted by their shorn tops, as the fronds are harvested as fast as they grow to satisfy the demand for *lontar* books and *arak* (the fronds are part of the distillation process).

SUN_SHINE/SHUTTERSTOCK ©

Tirta Gangga

The Joys of Jasri Bay
Turtles, beaches and chocolate

Just south of Amlapura, **Jasri Bay** has earned the nickname Teluk Penyu, or Turtle Bay. The shelled critters come here to nest and there have been some efforts made to protect them. The curving **Pantai Jasri** is a quiet black-sand beach with good views and a couple of tiny cafes. The area is rife with posh rental villas. Down a rough track, the **Sorga Chocolate Factory** offers one-hour tours with tastings, as well as chocolate-making workshops using cocoa beans grown in west Bali.

Bali's Ancient Manuscripts
Learn how palms become books

Set on a bamboo-covered hillside, the open-air **Museum Pustaka Lontar** is a simple place that honours Bali's centuries-old form of publishing: *lontar* books. On a brief visit, villagers show how fronds from indigenous *lontar* palms are prepared for written engravings and then woven together into a 'book'. It's a good companion to the Gedong Kirtya Library (p203) in Singaraja.

A Captivating Water Palace
Frolic at Tirta Gangga

Northwest of Amlapura, **Tirta Gangga** (Water of the Ganges) is the site of a *taman* (garden) built for the enjoyment of the last raja of Karangasem in 1946; it has some of the best rice-terrace vistas in east Bali. This 1.2-hectare water palace serves as a fascinating reminder of old Bali and is a companion of Taman Ujung (p174). On a one-hour visit, admire the 11-tiered **Nawa Sanga fountain**, which bears traces of the influence of the Chinese architects who helped design the garden. **Ponds** are filled with huge koi and lotus blossoms; jump between the stepping stones in the water. You can swim in the two stone spring-water pools. Almost fully destroyed by the eruption of nearby Gunung Agung in 1963, the complex was subsequently rebuilt.

Hiking around Tirta Gangga
Spectacular scenery and views

Hiking in the surrounding hills above Amlapura and Tirta Gangga transports you far from frenetic south Bali. This eastern corner of the island is alive with streams coursing through rice fields and tropical forests that suddenly open to reveal vistas taking in Lombok, Nusa Penida and the lush green rice terraces stretching down to the sea. It's a majestic vision of emerald steps receding into the distance.

Back roads and walking paths take you to traditional villages such as **Budakeling**, home to a Shiva-Buddhist community that dates back to the 15th century. A six-hour loop visits **Tenganan** (p173) village.

Hiring a guide is a good idea as they can help you plan routes and see things you simply would never find otherwise. Ask at any of the various accommodation options. **Komang Gede Sutama** (0813 3877 0893) has a good reputation. **I Wayan July** (0813 3775 3297) leads thrilling three-hour bike tours.

The small village around Tirta Gangga is an excellent place to stay or get a meal if you're hiking the surrounding countryside, which is dotted with temples, including the magnificent Pura Lempuyang (p181).

A Gourmet Feast
The Bali Asli restaurant and culinary school

Located in the green foothills of Gunung Agung near Amlapura, the farming village of Gelumpang is where famed Australian chef Penelope Williams runs **Bali Asli**, a world-class culinary experience. *Asli* is the Balinese term used for something created in the traditional way, and there is much that is traditional here – the Balinese menu changes daily, dictated by what's fresh at the local *pasar* or has been harvested in the restaurant's garden. By day, there are **cooking classes** and **hikes** across the rice terraces.

THE ROYALTY OF KARANGASEM

Amlapura's royal family ruled their regency of Karangasem with savvy and guile. In the 19th century, they led the domination of Lombok just across the channel, which brought them great wealth.

As the 1890s wore on and the colonial Dutch consolidated their grip on Bali and the region, the royal family cut deals with the Dutch that saw the Europeans treat the region as a protectorate (they even built the palace, Puri Agung Karangasem, as a gift) instead of a conquered foe. Before the royals were replaced by a republic, the last king of Karangasem – I Gusti Bagus Jelantik – used his riches to build the lavish water palaces during his rule from 1908 to 1950.

Beyond Amlapura

The relaxed joys of Amed contrast with the underwater pleasures of Tulamben and the undiscovered country of the northeast.

The coast north and east of Amlapura is a study in contrasts. The collection of hotel-packed villages known as Amed is a popular escape for long days of sunny relaxation. Nearby Tulamben is also popular, but in this case it's for active pursuits below the water. The entire village is given over to diving and snorkelling, anchored by a famous shipwreck right offshore. From here the scenery becomes more sparse and the dry hillsides are home to poor villages. Some, like Muntigunung, are finding ways to a better and sustainable future through tourism. Finally, in the far northeast, the community of Les offers intriguing activities on and off the coast in a low-key village setting.

GETTING AROUND

There are two routes to reach Amed, the well-known way via Amlapura and Tirta Gangga and the less-known but more rewarding coastal route from the south (p181). Within the Amed region, road-building is rapidly improving the once bumpy road and adding sidewalks to ease getting between villages on foot. North of Amed, everything is reached by the main coast road that stays near the water as it arcs around to northwest and north Bali.

Amed & the Far East Coast

TIME FROM AMLAPURA: **45 MINS**

A relaxing escape

Stretching from Amed village to Bali's easternmost tip near Kusambi, the semi-arid coast generically called 'Amed' draws visitors with its succession of small scalloped bays, where fishing boats are lined up like a riot of multi-hued sardines on the grey-sand beaches. The area revels in its relaxed atmosphere, boho vibe and enjoyable diving and snorkelling.

The 15km coastline is dotted with resorts, flush with yoga shalas, infinity pools and open-air restaurants; overnight options cover most price points and wide-ranging tastes and interests. There are dive resorts, health and meditation retreats, and dozens of hotels and guesthouses.

Most places to stay have a restaurant or cafe. Amed village and Jemeluk are dining hotspots and vegetarian and vegan options are as common as space to stash your yoga mat. Many people come to Amed for a day or two and end up staying for much longer.

PURWANTO NUGROHO/SHUTTERSTOCK ©

Sea fans, Amed

Snorkel and dive

Snorkelling is excellent along the coast. Jemeluk is a protected area where you can admire live coral and plentiful fish within 100m of the beach. The coral gardens and colourful marine life at Selang are highlights. The much-hyped **sunken Japanese fishing boat** at Banyuning is little more than a few bits of wooden debris.

Diving is also good, with dive sites off Jemeluk, Lipah and Selang featuring slopes and drop-offs with soft and hard corals and abundant fish. Some are accessible from the beach, while others require a short boat ride. The *Liberty* wreck at Tulamben (p181) is only a 20-minute drive away.

Amed is a centre for the daring sport of **freediving**. At **Ocean Prana**, champion freediver Yoram Zekri has created a 'freediving village' in Jemeluk with a practice pool. Nearby, **Apneista** offers freediving classes and workshops; its freediving techniques use skills from yoga and meditation.

DECODING AMED

Called 'Amed' by both tourists and marketing-minded residents, tourist development here began at **Amed village**. It soon spread to three nearby bays with fishing villages: **Jemeluk**, which has a buzzy travellers strip; **Banutan**, with both a beach and headlands; and **Lipah**, which has a lively mix of cafes. Development has marched onward through **Lehan**, **Selang**, **Banyuning**, **Aas** and on to **Kusambi**, each a minor oasis at the base of the arid hills.

For accommodation, you'll need to choose between the villages and the sunny headlands in between. The former puts you right on the sand and offers a small amount of community life, while the latter gives you sweeping vistas and isolation.

EATING IN AMED: OUR PICKS

Warung Amsha In Amed village, this popular beach warung has tables on the sand, fresh-caught seafood and local veggies and herbs. **$**

Warung Enak In Amed village, serving food sourced from its own organic garden. Try the tasty *ikan kare* (fish curry) and black-rice pudding. **$$**

Green Leaf Cafe In Jemeluk, this chilled cafe on the beach serves vegetarian, vegan and gluten-free delicacies, plus medicinal juices. **$**

Joli Beast View Cafe In Jemeluk, on a hillside with a grand view to the north. Beautiful snacks, seafood and Indonesian dishes are the stars. **$$**

179

AMED'S BEST YOGA STUDIOS

Blue Earth Village In Jemeluk; gorgeous views from an elevated bamboo shala, with daily hatha yoga classes.

Ocean Prana (p179) In Jemeluk; offers daily yoga classes popular with freedivers who use the disciplines to regulate their breathing.

Life in Amed In Lehan; new-age hotel with a yoga shala and regular sessions that are open to non-guests.

Buddha Sunset Yoga In Aas at the Meditasi resort; daily meditation, healing and yoga classes are held in an east-facing venue.

Green Leaf Cafe (p179) In Jemeluk; a yoga hub with a freediving accent. Offers a wide range of styles and classes.

NOKURO/SHUTTERSTOCK ©

Pura Lempuyang Luhur

Climbing Gunung Seraya

Trekking up the slopes of **Gunung Seraya** (1175m) is both a good workout and a fascinating look at this side of Bali. It takes three hours to reach the summit; note that there is sparse vegetation and it gets hot. Most trails are well-defined, so guides aren't required. Start from the rocky ridge just east of Jemeluk. Sunrises are spectacular but will require hiking in the dark, so you will need a guide for this. Inquire at your lodging.

Yoga mats and sun salutations

Yoga devotees love Amed because it bends over backwards with a plethora of studios and shalas. Classes, lessons and workshops are widely offered at hotels, cafes and even dive shops. It's easy to find sessions in even the most esoteric styles.

 EATING IN AMED: OUR PICKS

Gusto In Banutan, come for an eclectic mix of Indonesian, Italian and Hungarian dishes. Fine sea views; book ahead for dinner. $$

Green Coco Warung In Lipah, a traveller-friendly menu of banana pancakes in the morning and Balinese fare, curries and seafood later in the day. $$

Wawa-Wewe I In Lipah, this old-fashioned backpackers dive and lively cafe is open late. Live music some nights. $

Smiling Buddha In Aas at the Meditasi hotel, specialising in organic fare sourced from its garden. Balinese and Western dishes in a beach pavilion. $$

Amed, the long way

Typically, travellers bound for the coast of Amed travel the inland route through Tirta Gangga. However, there is a longer, twistier and less-travelled route that runs from **Ujung** near Amlapura to the Amed region, following the coastline. The road twists and turns along the sides of the twin peaks of Seraya and Lempuyang; the views out to sea are often breathtaking. After the lush east, it's noticeably drier here and the people's existence thinner; corn replaces rice as the staple. Look for tiny roads that allow motorbike access down to hidden pocket beaches. Covering the 30km to **Kusambi** and Bali's easternmost point will take about one hour without stops. Combine this with the inland road through Tirta Gangga for an enjoyable circular visit to Amed from the west.

Pura Lempuyang   TIME FROM AMLAPURA: **30 MINS** 🚗
Ascend to the heavens

One of Bali's important directional temples, **Pura Lempuyang** is a complex of seven temples. It's perched on the steep slopes of **Gunung Lempuyang** (1058m), a twin of neighbouring Gunung Seraya. Together, the pair form the distinctive double peaks of basalt that loom over Amlapura to the south and Amed to the north. From the temples, the mottled green patchwork of east Bali unfolds before you.

The largest and most easily accessed temple is **Pura Penataran Lempuyang**; it's a five-minute walk from the parking area or a 30-minute trek from Tirta Gangga. Many visitors queue for hours to be photographed in front of the iconic *candi bentar* (split temple gateway). From here, the second temple is 2km uphill and after that the calf-punishing stair climb begins: it's 1700 steps from the second temple to the highest, **Pura Lempuyang Luhur**. Visiting all seven temples takes at least four hours and involves a breathtaking 2900 steps.

Tulamben   TIME FROM AMLAPURA: **50 MINS** 🚗
Bali's best wreck ddive

Tulamben's big attraction sunk over 80 years ago. The **wreck** of the US cargo ship **Liberty** is among the most popular **dive sites** in Bali and has transformed what was once a simple fishing village into an entire resort town based on diving. Even **snorkellers** can easily swim the 50m out and explore the wreck. You'll see the stern rearing up from the depths, 5m below the surface. It's heavily encrusted with coral and swarming with dozens of species of colourful fish – and with **scuba divers** most days. The ship's hull is broken into sections – the most interesting parts are between 15m and 30m deep. The **coral reefs** lining this coast are also a draw.

THE WRECK OF THE LIBERTY

In January 1942, the US military cargo ship USAT *Liberty* was torpedoed by a Japanese submarine near Lombok, while sailing from Australia to the Philippines. It was beached at Tulamben so that its cargo of rubber and railway parts could be saved. The Japanese invasion prevented this and the ship sat on the beach until the 1963 eruption of Gunung Agung broke it in two and left it sunk just off the shoreline, much to the delight of divers and snorkellers.

The *Liberty* was built in 1918 for service during WWI. Over 125m long, it had a globe-spanning career before WWII. (And for the record, it was not a WWII Liberty-class freighter.)

MAKE SALT WHEN THE SUN SHINES

Around Bali's coast you can see the hard work of traditional salt production in scattered locations. The process is labour-intensive: sand is saturated with seawater, dried in the sun and then rinsed with more seawater, which is collected. The resulting very salty water is poured into a shallow trough *(palungan)*, made of palm tree trunks split in half. Hundreds of these troughs are lined up along beaches and as the hot sun evaporates the water, the almost-dry salt is scraped out for processing dried fish – although some is now sold to tourists. You can learn more about the process at Kusamba (p172), in Amed at the Hotel Uyah Amed and on the waterfront in Les.

Muntigunung

TIME FROM AMLAPURA: **70 MINS** 🚗

Tours of untouched Bali

Northeast Bali remains one of the poorest regions of the island. It's common for people in the scattered villages to walk four or more hours each day just to retrieve drinking water from springs. In one village, **Muntigunung**, community initiatives are working to improve lives through activities aimed at tourists (muntigunung.com). **Food production** (cashews, rosella, palm sugar) and **handicrafts** (batik, *lontar* baskets, hammocks) are part of tours and demonstrations. You can also go **trekking** through the untouched countryside.

Les

TIME FROM AMLAPURA: **90 MINS** 🚗

Bali's secret northeast coast

The village of **Les** is at the heart of Bali's lush northeast coast, an area mostly undiscovered by tourists. This is small-town Bali at its best: fishing boats line the rocky shore, residents wave to visitors as they stroll by and palms arch thickly overhead. **Activities** include waterfalls, treks, boat tours, snorkelling, lessons in salt production, visits with craftspeople and more. All can be arranged through your local accommodation or at **Dapur Bali Mula**. There's a variety of good places to stay along the coast.

High falls and natural baths

One of Bali's tallest waterfalls, **Air Terjun Yeh Mampeh** (aka Les Waterfall) is 40m high and 2.5km off the coast road. Look for the 'Welcome to Waterfalls' sign. The spectacle is at its dramatic best between December and February, during the peak rainy season. It's a 20-minute walk from the parking area; on-site guides can lead you on longer **treks** along the lush hillside.

About 4km northwest in the village of **Tejakula** you can see more evidence of the region's watery blessings at the **Kayoan Tejakula** (Tejakula bath). The bathing areas are behind walls topped by rows of flamboyant statues and decorations. It's 100m inland from the coast road.

Exquisite meals and more

Les native Jero Mangku Yudi loves to cook. After leaving home, he opened a hugely popular restaurant in south Bali and became a top chef on Indonesian TV. But he missed Les and a few years ago moved back to his family compound, which he transformed into a restaurant and cultural centre: **Dapur Bali Mula** (@dapurbalimula). Extraordinary Balinese lunches and dinners are available by prebooking. Chef Yudi is also a wizard at traditional *arak* fermentation and offers **cooking classes**. There will soon be guestrooms here and you can book myriad **activities** in the area.

Places We Love to Stay

$ Cheap $$ Moderate $$$ Pricey

East Coast Beaches p163

Blue Coco Guesthouse $ In the Keramas area just up from Pantai Selukat. It's close to the beach and caters to surfers with great rates.

Hotel Komune $$$ The surf at Pantai Selukat is among Bali's best. Perfect for a luxe resort with a surfing theme and nighttime waves.

Sidemen p165

Darmada Eco Resort $$ Set in a lush river valley, rooms here are simple, with a spring-water swimming pool and other activities (meditation, yoga, trekking).

Alamdhari Villa $$ Comfy boutique choice with light and airy rooms, beautiful pool, spa and spectacular views. Revel in ultimate relaxation.

Uma Agung Teras $$ Great value hotel with bungalow-style rooms set around a lush pool area. Everything's green but the water (it's blue).

Villa Iseh $$$ In the village of Iseh north of Sidemen, this was the villa of Walter Spies (p129) and later hosted rockers Mick Jagger and David Bowie.

Padang Bai p170 (Map p171)

Bamboo Paradise $ Top budget accommodation close to the port. Has a laid-back vibe, bar, lounge, dorm accommodation and private rooms.

Bloo Lagoon Eco Village $$$ Crowning a clifftop, splurge for a sea-facing yoga deck, kid-friendly pool and bungalows overlooking Blue Lagoon Beach.

Candidasa p173

Amarta Beach Cottages $$ A variety of rooms in a garden compound on a waterfront plot. Great views and a quiet location west of Candidasa.

Amankila $$$ Perched on jutting cliffs, this luxury resort has three infinity pools that step down to the sea and free-standing bungalow-style suites. In Manggis.

Amlapura p174 (Map p175)

Pondok Batur Indah $ Jaw-dropping rice-terrace views from the terrace of this family-run homestay on the ridge above Tirta Gangga. Simple rooms; on-site restaurant.

Jasri Bay Hideaway $$ Three wooden tribal houses beautifully restored and kitted out, one with its own pool. In a quiet, secluded spot south of Amlapura.

Amed p178

Narayana Homestay $ Family compound on the mountainside in Amed Village; rooms are set around a pool and have contemporary all-white decor.

Ocean Prana Hostel $ In Jemeluk; these shared bungalows are attached to the freediving school. Has a pool (often used for freediving training).

Hotel Uyah Amed $$ In Amed Village, the rooms here have small terraces and are decorated with attractive local textiles; cultural activities on offer.

Apa Kabar Villas $$ Villas in Banutan come in many sizes; all have kitchens and some have sea views. There's a pool on the rocky shore.

Meditasi $$ In Aas, this off-the-grid, chilled-out hideaway has meditation, healing and yoga classes. Rooms are well situated for swimming and snorkelling.

Stairway To Heaven Bungalows $$ Romantic wooden cottages on a hillside in Banyuning with grand ocean views and great staff.

Tulamben p181

Matahari Tulamben Resort $$ Modest digs with varying room styles. It's popular with divers and many stay long-term.

Siddhartha Oceanfront Resort & Spa $$$ Oceanside pool and yoga pavilion at a swish resort. Well-spaced rooms and villas.

Les p182

Segara Lestari Villa $ Associated with the Sea Communities NGO (seacommunities.com), this oceanside guesthouse has simple garden bungalows and dorm rooms.

Spa Village Resort Tembok $$$ In Tembok, southeast of Les, is this tranquil oceanfront resort with all-inclusive healthy meals, spa treatments and activities.

Above: Rice terraces, Jatiluwih (p192); Right: orchids

Central Mountains

VOLCANOES, FORESTS AND BEAUTIFUL MOUNTAIN VIEWS

The Central Highlands, lush with forests and sculpted by volcanoes, feel a world away from the island's tropical coastline.

Hikers, birdwatchers, mountaineers and nature lovers are drawn to Bali's Central Highlands, where tangled forests, towering plantations and stark volcanic landscapes form the backdrop for a diversity of adventures. The old town of Munduk – rich in Dutch colonial history – is the ideal base from which hikers and waterfall seekers can explore terraced hillside paddies and spice-scented plantations, while the sacred crater-lakes of Danau Tamblingan and Danau Buyan shimmer amid steaming virgin forests. The Bali Botanical Garden offers an accessible way to experience the floral wealth of the world's second-most biodiverse country, and winding mountain roads make for beautiful journeys where, it seems, every corner reveals a different view.

This is a land of water and fire, and from the rim of a caldera you can look down on, or hike to, both the sacred Danau Batur (with the open-air cemetery of the 'Hindus of the Wind' beside the lake) and to the 1717m peak of Gunung Batur. Every morning this active volcano draws hundreds of trekkers seeking unforgettable sunrise views.

The Central Mountains are rich in culture and it's here that you'll find astounding temples like Pura Ulun Danu Bratan and Pura Luhur Batukau. In the lower region, hillside slopes have been carved into the picturesque terraces that form Jatiluwih, a traditional rice-growing area where water distribution is governed by the ancient *subak* system and protected by UNESCO.

MARDIVA/SHUTTERSTOCK ©

THE MAIN AREAS

MUNDUK
Search for waterfalls and hike through forests.
p188

BEYOND MUNDUK
Gunung Batur: a geological marvel.
p193

Find Your Way

Stay close to Munduk town and you'll find (with the help of local guides) enough trails to keep you inspired for a week without even needing transport. To explore more widely around the highlands, you'll need private transport or an arranged tour.

PRIVATE CAR

Self-driving is the ideal way to get around if you are confident on tightly winding mountain roads that are frequented by heavy trucks. For guests who prefer to hire a car with a driver, many hotels have separate (basic) driver accommodation.

MOTORBIKE

While the highland traffic is a breeze compared to the coastal towns, motorcycling up here comes with its own complications as roads are steep and frequently potholed. If you're travelling as a pair, rent a more powerful scooter.

Munduk, p188

This enchanting town surrounded by plantations is the heart of Bali's best hiking area, and an ideal base from which to explore the highlands.

HAPPY AUER/SHUTTERSTOCK ©

Waterfall (p192), Munduk

Plan Your Time

Distances are small; less than 40km separates Munduk town (in the west of the Central Highlands) from Gunung Batur (to the east). Due to the winding roads the incredibly scenic drive takes two hours.

Pressed For Time

For blissful mountain solitude head to **Munduk** (p188). Spend the morning hiking to the spectacular **waterfalls near town** (p192) and an afternoon exploring the **nutmeg and clove forests** (p190) with one of Munduk's excellent guides. If time allows, head to **Danau Tamblingan** (p191) for a walk through the protected primary jungle and a boat ride across the crater lake.

Five Days in the Highlands

Stop at the rarely visited **Pura Luhur Batukau** (p191) and the well-known **Jatiluwih** (p192) rice terraces on your way to **Munduk** (p188). Then drive east, stopping to explore the **Bali Botanic Garden** (p191). Visit the **Batur Geopark Museum** (p193) in the afternoon, and watch the sunset from a cafe on the **crater rim** (p194). See the sunrise the following day from **Gunung Abang** (p194).

SEASONAL HIGHLIGHTS

JANUARY	APRIL	JULY	AUGUST
Nights during the wettest month can be very cold, so pack warm layers for sunrise treks and cozy evenings.	The end of the rains is a great time to see flowers and birds in the forests around Munduk.	Clove-harvesting season is a fascinating time to be in the highlands; the work is done on 10m-long bamboo ladders.	Roll down the windows as you drive through the highlands; the scent of the harvested cloves fills the air.

187

Munduk

SPECTACULAR WATERFALLS | SCENIC HIKING | EXCEPTIONAL VIEWS

GETTING AROUND

Munduk town and the surrounding hillsides are best explored on foot. Motorbikes are available for rent if you want to explore further afield (you can get to the north coast from here in a little over half an hour). Cars with drivers are easily organised through any hotel, and (as with hiking guides) the best drivers will also serve as informative guides.

☑ TOP TIP

This might be Bali but don't be fooled – night-time temperatures regularly drop below 20 degrees Celsius. Pack warm layers, especially if you plan on getting up for a sunrise hike. August is the coldest month up here.

Long before the Dutch took advantage of Munduk's blissful climate to establish a hill station here around 130 years ago, these pretty highlands had been settled by the early Balinese (some say the Bali Aga) who, according to legend, were escaping a plague of ants. Whatever the case, Munduk and the exquisite surrounding highlands make for an idyllic escape, even today.

The views across hillsides of plantations of clove, nutmeg, coffee and cacao trees – all the way to the ocean – are astounding, and there are some special lodges and homestays tucked in between the trees. The hills and UNESCO-protected terraces of this quiet region are laced with tracks and walking trails, and while it's possible to explore some solo, Munduk has an established network of experienced guides who share anecdotes, legends, and the enthralling culinary and medicinal traditions that are still an integral part of life in these lush highlands.

The Road Least Travelled

Take a scenic route to Munduk

The journey up to Munduk can be just as spectacular as time spent hiking in the Central Highlands. A stunning entry to the area is to take the **Antosari road**, which leads from Pantai Soka on the coast of west Bali up to Pupuan, and will take you past pretty rice terraces, palm trees and tumbling bougainvilleas. If you're happy to explore a bit, then turn right onto the Jl Gunung Batukaru in the village of Punjungan, and set Google Maps to take you to Munduk. It's a magnificent journey along small rural roads that will have you ogling fields of hydrangeas, plantations of cloves and fruit trees, and hedges of hibiscus.

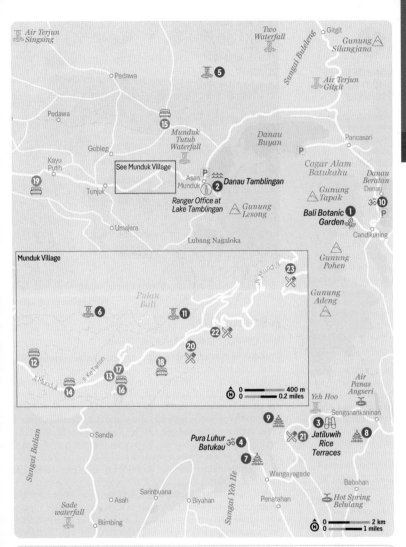

HIGHLIGHTS

1. Bali Botanic Garden
2. Danau Tamblingan
3. Jatiluwih Rice Terraces
4. Pura Luhur Batukau

SIGHTS

5. Banyumala Twin Waterfalls
6. Melanting
7. Pura Jero Taksu
8. Pura Luhur Besikalung
9. Pura Luhur Pucak Petali
10. Pura Ulun Danu Bratan
11. Red Coral

SLEEPING

12. Bali Rahayu Homestay
13. Made Oka Homestay
14. Meme Surung Homestay
15. Munduk Moding Plantation
16. Nadya Homestay
17. Puri Lumbung Cottages
18. Puri Sunny Guesthouse
19. Sri Lestari Banyuatis

EATING

20. Eco Café 2
21. Jatiluwih Resto
22. Made's Munduk
23. Ngiring Ngewedang

ONE OF BALI'S MOST ICONIC TEMPLES

Beautiful lakeside **Pura Ulun Danu Bratan**, which was built around 1634 CE, is an important place of worship for Balinese Hindus. It honours Dewi Danu, the goddess of water, and ceremonies are held here to ensure that there is a sufficient supply of water in the *subak* system for the island's rice farmers.

Images of the temple – with its striking *merus* (multi-roofed shrines), formally landscaped garden and stunning backdrop mountain reflected in the still water of the lake – have become iconic of Bali, and the temple attracts busloads of tourists every day. While it remains a functioning temple, tourism here is big business, so expect souvenir stalls lining the parking area, a children's playground, and some restaurants on the lakeside property.

JEROBEAM/SHUTTERSTOCK ©

Puri Lumbung Cottages

A Scented Trail

Hike through Munduk's spice plantations

Munduk is surrounded by hills, forests, paddies and plantations, and travellers who are seeking to connect with nature gravitate to the small town in order to hike to waterfalls and through the hills of this densely forested region. While there are virgin forests in the area, the majority of trees form working plantations of cloves, nutmeg, coffee and cacao, and a network of trails connects them with villages, markets and homesteads.

It's possible to walk some trails independently from Munduk – around town you'll see signs indicating paths to some of the area's waterfalls – but for fascinating insight into local history and lifestyles, consider hiring a guide (easily organised through **Puri Lumbung Cottages**). To an uninitiated observer, the wooded valleys might appear as pristine jungle, but almost everything seems to be either edible or medicinal, and a guide can add interesting layers to your walk by telling you about the intricacies of ancient spice crops, as well as the complicated methods of preparing staples like cassava, taro, palm sugar and *arak* (colourless, distilled palm wine). More recent arrivals from other regions are also dispersed throughout the plantations, and you can learn about the cultivation of coffee, cacao and vanilla (which is pollinated entirely by hand). There are set routes you can walk, and guides can also tailor treks to your requirements. The blissful highland temperatures – typically around 20 to 25 degrees Celsius – make this idyllic hiking country.

Explore a Sacred Forest

Trek around Danau Tamblingan

Shrouding the rim of the caldera that forms **Danau Tamblingan** is an ancient, sacred rainforest that for centuries has been a source of plants for traditional medicine. It's an enchanting place, with towering nettle trees and magnificently tangled ficus trees (some older than 600 years) growing as pillars of a lush ecosystem entangled with ferns, orchids and vines. The forest is home to birds like woodpeckers, hummingbirds, parrots and kingfishers, and mammals include porcupine, mongoose, civets and squirrels. Walking trails here vary from a short 1.5-hour stroll to an invigorating six-hour hike through the forest up **Gunung Lesong** and down into **Jatiluwih** (p192). Most walks end with a peaceful canoe trip across the lake. You must have a guide, and will be assigned one when you arrive at the **ranger office** at Lake Tamblingan. Entrance to the protected forest is 100,000Rp per person, plus the rate for the walk (which varies depending on the length of the trail you do). The **Getaway Camp Bali** and **Bali Jungle Trekking** offer overnight camping experiences.

Discover Indonesia's Botanical Riches

Visit Bali's beautiful botanical garden

After Brazil, Indonesia is the world's most biodiverse country, and the **Bali Botanic Garden** – known locally as Kebun Raya Bali (kebunraya.id/bali) – showcases some of its floral riches. You could spend almost an entire day slowly wandering around the collection of themed gardens, but if time is short, hire an e-scooter, electric moped, e-bike or bicycle to zip around on. These vehicles are rented out in half-hour blocks, but to do justice to these extensive gardens you will need a minimum of an hour (and that's just to scratch the surface). At almost 160 hectares, Indonesia's largest botanic garden boasts 2400 species of plants. The **Cactus Greenhouse** features a collection of 68 species and the **Rhododendron Garden** has more than 100; both are interesting to visit. The **Orchid Garden** – at its most colourful when many specimens are flowering around mid-year – is extensive, and **Taman Usada**, which has more than 300 plants used by traditional healers, is particularly worth exploring. Birdwatchers are also drawn here by an estimated 79 resident and migrant bird species, and **Bali Birding Tour** offers full-day tours in the garden.

THE MYSTERIOUS TEMPLES OF BATUKARU

Established in the 11th century, **Pura Luhur Batukau** (often written Batukaru) stands at the end of a lonely road on the slopes of Gunung Batukaru. Hindu worshippers will invariably stop first at **Pura Jero Taksu**, which serves as a spiritual and literal gateway to Batukau – it's believed that only if you pray there first will your Batukau prayers reach the gods.

Batukau was historically said to be a lair for bandits, and 2km from the old temple is the almost-forgotten **Pura Luhur Pucak Petali**. Dedicated to Sang Hyang Maling ('God of Thieves'), this temple, along with **Pura Luhur Besikalung** nearby, is said to have been the place to pray at if you wanted to become adept at the thieving trade.

EATING AROUND MUNDUK: RESTAURANTS WITH VIEWS ——— MAP p189

Made's Munduk
Made's has a selection of delicious Balinese meals. It also has a view across Munduk's clove plantations. $

Eco Café 2 With a lovely outlook over Bali's hills, this cafe serves Balinese food. The *lumpia* (similar to spring rolls) are superb. $

Ngiring Ngewedang This restaurant, perched at the very top of Munduk's hills, has an outstanding view across the north of the island. $$

Munduk Moding Plantation Book a table at the resort's restaurant for sunset views, and look across an infinity pool all the way to Java. $$

191

MUNDUK'S WONDERFUL WATERFALLS

Ketut Darma, a senior trekking guide in Munduk, on some of the best waterfalls in the area. (purilumbung.com)

Red Coral waterfall is very easy to access, so it's a good one to visit for older people and those travelling with small children. You'll walk through plantations of coffee, cloves, avocados and vanilla to get there. **Melanting** is a waterfall that not many people go to; it's one of Bali's tallest and is really pretty. There are about 500 steps that you'll need to go down, which can be slippery in the wet season. If you want to swim, then **Banyumala** – the twin waterfall – is a good option; there is a wonderful clear pool at the bottom.

ARRIAND/GETTY IMAGES ©

Rice terraces, Jatiluwih

Fingerprints of the Gods

Walk among terraced rice fields

With elegantly stepped terraces shaped like enormous finger-prints, the sweeping rice terraces of **Jatiluwih** offer those stunning postcard views of Bali. This 195-sq-km area is protected by UNESCO, and it's here that the island's *sub-ak* – a complex agricultural (and religious) tradition that dates back to the 9th century – remains deeply rooted. It's easy to explore the area on your own, and a good starting point is **Jatiluwih Resto**, opposite which is a paved track marked on Google Maps as 'Jl Bikes Only'. Walk this wind-ing trail and you'll soon find yourself surrounded by iconic terraces peppered with intricately sculpted shrines. Accord-ing to Balinese farmers, water and the fertile volcanic soil are only two of the facets that make up this agricultural system – without the all-important offerings to Dewi Sri, the goddess of fertility, the harvest will ultimately fail. Bali can achieve two or three rice harvests a year and, since the paddies are in a constant state of transition, you could visit Jatiluwih many times over and always be presented with a radically different landscape.

Beyond
Munduk

With its lake, smouldering peak and extensive black lava fields, Gunung Batur is one of Indonesia's geological marvels.

The Gunung Batur area is a geological marvel, and the volcano you see today rises from within a caldera formed during an eruption 30,000 years ago. The town of Kintamani spreads around the southern rim, overlooking a crater lake and barren black lava fields, and onto the peak of the 'new' (still active) volcano. It's here that hundreds of visitors arrive in the early hours of every morning, eager to climb its slopes and catch a view of the sunrise with mighty Gunung Agung in the distance. This area is as captivatingly stark as Munduk is lush, and the atmosphere here – possibly fuelled by the Earth's fiery forces – is filled with a rugged sense of adventure.

Places

Gunung Batur p193

GETTING AROUND

To trek Gunung Batur you'll need a guide, and every hotel and homestay around Kintamani will be able to set one up for you, and arrange your return transport to the starting point of the hike. Most people come here for the sunrise walk only, and tour companies include in their price an exceptionally early-morning accommodation pickup from almost anywhere on the island. If you're staying longer, explore the surrounding area by renting a scooter, which is easily arranged via your accommodation.

Gunung Batur

TIME FROM MUNDUK: **2 HR 20 MINS**

Witness extraordinary geology

Gunung Batur stands as the centrepiece of the **Batur UNESCO Global Geopark**, a 370-sq-km area renowned for its unique geological and cultural significance. It is encircled by a vast caldera, the remains of a 3000m-high volcano that erupted 30,000 years ago, and within it the rugged lava fields from various eruptions are flanked by a lake, clustered with houses, and tamed pockets of farmlands. Just off the southern rim of the caldera is the imposing **Batur Geopark Museum**, which serves as a portal to the geological and cultural heritage of the area. Its exhibits showcase the fascinating history of volcanic eruptions, the evolution of the landscape and, in the upstairs section, the deep-rooted relationship between the people of this region and their surroundings. An hour here will add a rich layer of understanding to the time you spend around this dramatic landscape.

A volcano sunrise trek

A sunrise trek up Gunung Batur has long been one of Bali's most popular excursions, with hundreds of people setting off in the darkness every morning for a dawn rendezvous. Spectacular as the view might be, with so many hikers it is hardly a spiritual experience, and daily erosion on the mountain trail caused by hundreds of hiking boots is barely

THE SKY BURIALS OF TRUNYAN VILLAGE

Isolated and tucked up against the shore of Danau Batur is **Trunyan**, a village that is unique in Bali when it comes to burial practices. Instead of cremating their dead, the people of Trunyan use an open-air cemetery where bodies are laid to rest under a sacred tree, which is believed to neutralise the odour of decomposing bodies.

To protect them from animals, the deceased are covered with a triangle of bamboo (called *ancak-saji*). The people of Trunyan are Bali Aga (descendants of the island's original inhabitants) and sometimes call themselves Hindus of the Wind. There are 38 Bali Aga villages, and Trunyan is the only one to use what some researchers call a sky burial.

sustainable (and potentially dangerous). Neighbouring **Gunung Abang** is only 7.5km closer to the rising sun, but at 2151m it is Bali's third-highest mountain, reaching just below the level of Gunung Batukaru and almost 1000m below mighty Gunung Agung. More importantly, Abang offers an exceptional sunrise view all of its own, and a poignant solitude that reflects the natural majesty of the Island of the Gods.

The hike to Abang's summit typically starts at 3am and you must arrange the hike through a local hiking company – **Bali Sunrise Trekking and Tour** is highly recommended – since, apart from providing crucial revenue for guides from the local communities, the challenging trail passes through thick forest. Even relatively fit hikers will take up to three hours to reach the summit. Once on the peak you'll have unspoiled sunrise views to the summit of Agung to the east, and to the west a view of Batur across the mirror-like expanse of the crater lake.

Watch the sunrise from the roof of a 4WD

Every morning hundreds of travellers converge on the slopes of Gunung Batur to watch the sun rise and shoot selfies as it does. While most walk to the summit, a more accessible option is a 4WD 'tour', and the photographs you can get – with the rugged 4WD playing a star role and Gunung Abang and Gunung Agung (p168) in the background – will tell tales of fun, freedom and adventure. This is not an experience wrapped in wild solitude, however. In low season about 100 colourful 4WDs park bumper to bumper on a terraced section of Batur's lower slopes, and some drivers estimate there are 300 here during July and August. The 4WDs are modified short-wheel-base Suzukis with two open seats in the back and a roof rack that's sturdy enough to hold the weight of three people (important for those photos). The drive is only 1.3km up a rough road, but you'll need to reach the viewpoint at least an hour before sunrise to secure a good parking space; buy a coffee or hot chocolate while you wait for the sun to rise. Some companies like **Sunrise Jeep Adventure** offer the option to visit the black lava fields afterwards. This is an opportunity to get more photographs, or to walk through the lava from Batur's 1963 eruption.

EATING IN KINTAMANI: RESTAURANTS WITH VIEWS

Ritatkala Cafe A chic cafe with a striking view of Gunung Batur, the lake and caldera. **$$**

Oculus This restaurant serves Western and Indonesian food, and has a rooftop terrace with views of Batur, the lake and lava fields. **$$**

Caldera A wide menu of affordable food – from nasi goreng (fried rice) and crispy duck to burgers and pizzas – and a view framed by arched windows. **$$**

Okuta This stylish restaurant serves contemporary Asian cuisine. The food is delicious and the view is brilliant. **$$**

Places We Love to Stay

$ Cheap $$ Moderate $$$ Pricey

Munduk
p188 (Map p189)

Meme Surung Homestay $ An atmospheric guesthouse with a long veranda, two old Dutch houses and a gorgeous garden (and views).

Made Oka Homestay $ A million-dollar view for a budget-friendly price and a great little restaurant make this homestay a very affordable base for exploring the Munduk area.

Puri Sunny Guesthouse $$ This cozy guesthouse, packed with charm, is right in Munduk village. The rooms are large and enjoy beautiful mountain views.

Nadya Homestay $$ The view over north Bali from this comfortable homestay is worth paying triple for. Enjoy rooftop breakfasts and lazy afternoons in the infinity pool.

Bali Rahayu Homestay $$ This comfy, cozy homestay has outstanding views over the plantations from all the rooms. There's an infinity pool and a good restaurant, too.

Puri Lumbung Cottages (p190) **$$** A very comfortable mountaintop resort with a variety of rooms. All sorts of experiences can be arranged, from hiking to medicinal plant workshops and dance classes. If you're looking for a hiking guide in the Munduk area, come here.

Sri Lestari Banyuatis $$ Situated on the northern slopes below Munduk, this peaceful, intimate six-bungalow property is surrounded by rice fields. There's also a lovely pool, a good restaurant and a spa.

Munduk Moding Plantation (p191) **$$$** A luxury property with good eco-credentials set on an organic coffee plantation. It has brilliant views of north Bali. If you've seen photos of an infinity pool that looks like it's situated at the edge of the world, it was probably taken here.

Kintamani
p193

Bali Cottages Lake View $ This small guesthouse – a collection of four *lumbung* (rice barn)-style rooms –has a fantastic view of the lake, with Gunung Abang and Gunung Agung in the distance. It's well worth staying here for sunrise, instead of hiking up Agung.

Geopark Village & Spa $ This small hotel is good value for money. The bungalows are surrounded by trees and bamboo, and the space feels quite nurturing, which is unusual for this harsh-looking area.

Caldera $$ The restaurant decor at the road level is alluring, but the rooms are very plain; they have good views of Gunung Batur, though. The hotel corridors have a weird basement sort of feel (due to its caldera-side location).

Lakeview Hotel $$ This solid old hotel has a range of rooms. The standard ones are very basic, while the deluxe and 'new deluxe' feel more luxurious; all have a view of Gunung Batur and the lake.

Oculus $$$ A Brutalist-style concrete structure that protrudes from the side of the caldera, this modern hotel is one of the few high-end properties in the Kintamani area. The view makes up for the maintenance, which could be improved.

North Bali

ADVENTURE AND NATURE ALONG THE COAST

Diving, trekking, waterfall-spotting and doing as little as possible are the best ways to fill your north Bali days.

The land on the other side, that's north Bali. Although one-sixth of the island's population lives here, this vast region is overlooked by many visitors who stay trapped in the south Bali–Ubud axis.

The big draw is the incredible diving and snorkelling at Pulau Menjangan, which is in West Bali National Park – a nature wonderland, with surprisingly good animal spotting. Arcing around a nearby bay, Pemuteran may be Bali's best beach town: a relaxed oasis where residents and tourists mix in a convivial stew. To the east is Lovina, a sleepy beach strip with cheap hotels and even cheaper sunset beer specials. All along the north coast are outcrops of quiet hotels and villas, set on the reef-protected shore with its gentle surf.

Inland, north Bali thrums to the roar of dozens of waterfalls cascading down from impossibly green hillsides thick with wild fruit trees and laced with hiking trails. Museums and history await in Bali's second city, Singaraja, which was once the gateway to the entire island.

Getting to north Bali for once lives up to the cliché: it's half the fun. Routes follow the thinly populated coastlines east and west, or you can go up and over the mountains by any number of routes, marvelling at crater lakes and maybe stopping for a misty trek on the way.

JHON IMAGES/SHUTTERSTOCK ©

THE MAIN AREAS

Above: Sekumpul Waterfalls (p204); Left: clownfish, Pulau Menjangan (p210)

Find Your Way

North Bali is just that, the island-spanning swath that starts in the chain of central mountains and flows down to the minimal surf at the shore. Explore it via its traffic-free main road.

WALKING

Hiking in waterfall-punctuated hillsides or across the wildlife-filled expanses of West Bali National Park are highlights, but you can also explore Lovina, Singaraja and Pemuteran on foot.

MOTORBIKE OR CAR

You don't need your own wheels in north Bali, but as always they aid your freedom to explore. Get a car and driver from the south and then arrange rides. Rent wheels for just a day.

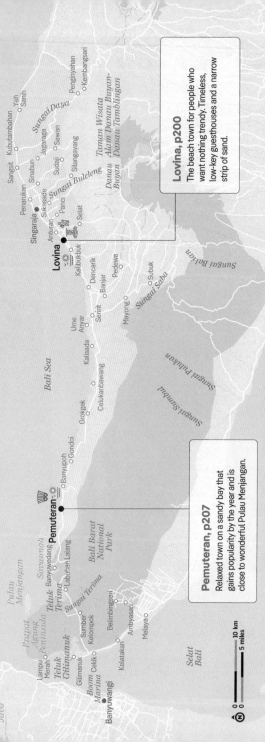

Lovina, p200

The beach town for people who want nothing trendy. Timeless, low-key guesthouses and a narrow strip of sand.

Pemuteran, p207

Relaxed town on a sandy bay that gains popularity by the year and is close to wonderful Pulau Menjangan.

EDMUND LOWE PHOTOGRAPHY/SHUTTERSTOCK ©

Pulau Menjangan (p210)

Plan Your Time

In general, north Bali is a brilliant antidote to the throngs of the south and Ubud. During rainy season its beauty is at its most lush.

Pressed for Time

With only a day or two, choose your delight. Getting to the north from south Bali takes a few hours, so make your time count. There is world-class diving and snorkelling at **Pulau Menjangan** (p210), which can include an overnight in nearby **Pemuteran** (p207). Or you can opt for the workaday charms of **Lovina** (p200) and its proximity to scores of **waterfalls** (p204).

Five Days to See It All

Start in the east, coming north on the coast from Les and Amed. See the temples at **Yeh Sanih** (p203) and then delve into **Singaraja** (p202), Bali's historic second city. Stop at **Lovina** (p200) and check out the many nearby temples and waterfalls like **Air Terjun Singsing** (p205). Continue west, stopping for some boutique rest near **Seririt** (p206). Stop at **Pemuteran** (p207) for diving and **trekking** (p209).

SEASONAL HIGHLIGHTS

MARCH–MAY	JUNE–AUGUST	SEPTEMBER–NOVEMBER	DECEMBER–FEBRUARY
Waterfalls in the lush hills are at their thundering best as the rainy season nears its end.	Pemuteran and Pulau Menjangan get busy as holidaymakers flock to Bali from around the world.	West Bali National Park is at its driest and the sparse vegetation makes for easier wildlife spotting.	Christmas is busy at Pemuteran. Rain brings lush beauty to the hills and rice terraces.

Lovina

QUIET DAYS | QUIET NIGHTS | MELLOW BEACHES

GETTING AROUND

The trip to Lovina can take three to five hours over the Central Mountains from south Bali. Descending the fertile hillsides brings alluring scenery and opportunities to stop at waterfalls. Most people use their own wheels or line up a ride through their accommodation at either end of the trip. Alternatively, you can reach Lovina from the coasts to the east or west, which takes longer than from the south but also allows for many stops along the way. There are also a few tourist shuttles from the south.

☑TOP TIP

Avoid hotels near the main road due to traffic noise. During slow periods, room prices are negotiable. Beware of touts who'll quote prices that include a large kickback. Always ask to see a few rooms as some properties are rather dated.

Lovina is at its best when the setting sun nears the horizon, setting off a brilliant display of fiery colours. Otherwise, 'relaxed' is how most people describe this strip of beachside development and fishing villages, aside from the pushy touts. Low-key, low-rise, low-priced Lovina is the antithesis of Canggu. The waves are calm, the beach is thin and there are no Insta-ready poseurs.

A highlight every afternoon at fishing villages such as Anturan is watching *prahu* (traditional outrigger canoes) being prepared for night fishing. When sunset reddens the sky, the boats flicker to life as dozens of points of light moving across the horizon.

Lovina is not overstocked with sights, but it's close to various temples, good hikes, soaring waterfalls and the urban charms of Singaraja about 10km to the east.

Hit the Beaches
Grey sand and gentle surf

The beaches are made up of washed-out grey and black volcanic sand, and while they're mostly clean near the hotel areas, they're not spectacular. Reefs protect the shore, reducing the waves to ripples most of the time.

A paved **beach footpath** runs along the sand in **Kalibukbuk** and extends in a circuitous route along the seashore, and is possibly Lovina's best feature. Enjoy the postcard view to the west of the mountainous north Bali coast.

The best beach areas include the main beach east of Kalibukbuk's elaborate **Dolphin Monument**, as well as the curving stretch a bit west. Look for pickup volleyball games on the sand; they get heated.

Spectacular Sunsets
Lovina's free show

Don't miss **sunsets** from the waterfront when the western sky becomes a beautiful show of orange and crimson. The best place for viewing is the **drinks vendors zone** about 150m northeast of the Dolphin Monument. Shaded by trees, there is a mixed bag of chairs, loungers and reclining pillows on

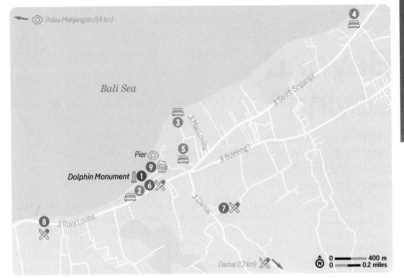

the sand where you can enjoy cheap beer and drinks sold by charming vendors. Nearby, there's a crumbling **pier** popular with residents for sunset-watching at the end of Jl Mawar.

Dolphin Watching

Early-morning aquatic adventure

Sunrise boat trips to see **dolphins** are Lovina's much-hyped tourist attraction. Most of the time at least a few surface. Expect pressure to join a tour from your hotel and touts. Prices are fixed by the boat owners' cartel. Trips start at a non-holiday-like 5.30am and last about two hours.

The ocean can get pretty crowded with roaring powerboats. There's debate about what all this means for the dolphins. Do they like being chased by boats? If not, why do they keep coming back? Maybe it's the fish, of which there are plenty.

Diving & Snorkelling

Explore Lovina's reefs

Diving on the local reef is best at lower depths and night diving is popular. Many people stay here and dive Pulau Menjangan (p210), a 1½ hours west. Generally, the water is clear and parts of the reef are good for **snorkelling**, though the coral has been damaged by bleaching and dynamite fishing. The best spot is 1.3km west, a few hundred metres offshore.

HIGHLIGHTS
1 Dolphin Monument

SLEEPING
2 Funky Place
3 Lovina Beachhouse Villas
4 Mandhara Chico Bungalow
5 Villa Taman Ganesha

EATING
6 Akar
7 Buda Bakery
8 Tanjung Alam

DRINKING & NIGHTLIFE
9 Drinks Vendors Zone

✖ EATING IN LOVINA: OUR PICKS

Tanjung Alam An open-air waterfront restaurant in Kaliasem where grilled seafood is king. $

Akar Vegetarian cafe with earth-friendly ethics; savor organic smoothies and house-made gelato. $

Buda Bakery A great bakery behind Kalibukbuk. The upstairs cafe serves superlative Indonesian and Western fare. $$

Damai Renowned restaurant on the hill near Lovina. Great views, organic fare and fine seafood. $$$

201

Beyond Lovina

Trek through luxuriant landscapes where water flows year-round and discover urban culture in Singaraja, intriguing temples and beachside retreats.

Places

GETTING AROUND

Singaraja is served by long-distance buses from Java via Gilimanuk as well as occasional large buses from Denpasar. Generally, it's best to have your own wheels as the lands around Lovina reward free exploration. Taxis are not common, but you can arrange riders through accommodation. Guides usually provide transport for days out. You can often get a ride on the back of a motorbike *(ojek)* near waterfalls and other places where there are steep climbs.

Waterfalls, waterfalls, everywhere! That's the glorious truth about the lands south of Lovina. Impossibly green mountainsides are cleaved by gorges and sprayed by pounding cascades of water. Hiking here is a delight, with evocative scents in the air, ripe fruit hanging from trees and magical vistas in every direction.

The city of Singaraja embodies Balinese history in its museums and architecture – in particular at the old port. Throughout the region there are temples that are core to Balinese beliefs, and many have surprising features in their ornamentations.

The Bali Sea laps this reef-protected coast. The junction town of Seririt is both the gateway to relaxed seaside resorts and spectacular rice-terrace scenery inland.

Singaraja

TIME FROM LOVINA: **20 MINS**

Historic waterfront

Singaraja (which – Disney licensing aside – means 'lion king') is Bali's second-largest city and the capital of Buleleng Regency, which covers much of the north. It's worth exploring the tree-lined streets for a couple of hours; most people stay in nearby Lovina.

At the charmingly sleepy **waterfront** north of Jl Erlangga, you'll find the atmospheric old harbour, once Bali's main port before WWII. A modern **pier** juts out over the water with a couple of simple cafes.

Across the car park, look for some old Dutch shipping company buildings. One has been restored and now houses the small but interesting **Museum Soenda Ketjil**. It covers the colonial era of Buleleng with displays in English. Other exhibits include early European contact, the role of the royal family and the multicultural mix (Balinese, ethnic groups from across the archipelago, Chinese, Indians, Arabs and Europeans).

Nearby is the vibrantly red Chinese temple **Ling Gwan Kiong**, which dates to 1873, and a few old canals. Walk up Jl Erlangga to see the art deco lines of late-colonial Dutch buildings. A bit south, **Jl A Yani** is Singaraja's main commercial strip. Two neighbouring bakeries offer appealing Indonesian treats: **Istana Cake & Bakery** and **Valencia Bakery**.

Ling Gwan Kiong

THE HISTORIC GATEWAY TO BALI

In the 18th century, the colonial Dutch became the main purchasers of enslaved Balinese people. In the 1840s, the Dutch tried to make treaties with Balinese rajahs to get ahead of other colonial powers. But ultimately the Dutch resorted to force and seized control of much of the island in 1849. Singaraja became the centre of Dutch power in Bali and remained the administrative centre for the Lesser Sunda Islands (Bali through to Timor) until 1953.

Until the airport in south Bali became the main means of arrival after World War II, most visitors arrived on steamships at Singaraja. Some travel writers complained it was too commercial and preferred south Bali because it was less developed.

Royal Museums

Singaraja's royal family maintains a compound with two worthwhile museums. Most compelling is the **Gedong Kirtya Library**, a historical centre established in 1928 by Dutch colonialists and named after the Sanskrit for 'to try'. It has a superb collection of over 2000 *lontar* (dried palm-leaf) books, the traditional form of printed text on Bali going back for many centuries. Curators give intriguing demonstrations of how *lontar* books are created. Displays cover some of the more notable works preserved here, including manuscripts written on copper plates *(prasasti)*.

Nearby, the **Museum Buleleng** recalls the life of the last *radja* (rajah or prince) of Buleleng, Pandji Tisna, who is credited with developing tourism in Lovina in the 1970s. It's a bit like an uncurated attic of artefacts.

Yeh Sanih

TIME FROM LOVINA: **45 MINS** 🚗

A pool and a temple

The Yeh Sanih area sits along a secluded stretch of the main coast road that runs to east Bali. The freshwater springs of **Air Sanih** are channelled into large swimming pools before flowing into the sea. The pools are alive with frolicking kids; it's about 15km east of Singaraja.

Also worth a pause is **Pura Maduwe Karang** (Temple of the Land Owner), one of the most intriguing temples in the region. Its walls are decorated with detailed panels, including a famous **bicycle relief** that depicts a man in Balinese clothes riding a bicycle with a lotus flower serving as the back

HIKING TIPS NEAR LOVINA

Komang Dodik, hiking guide in Lovina, shares his favorite hiking tips. lovina. tracking@gmail.com

After a three-hour hike in the rainforest, I love cooling off in the pools at **Air Terjun Aling-Aling** (Aling-Aling Waterfall). Many people know of the 30m waterfall here, but few people know about the seven more up the gorge near the village of Sambangan. You can slide down rocks into the water or do a high dive.

On our walks in the forest, I like picking ripe fruit like papayas. You can see and smell everything: vanilla, cacao, mangosteen, breadfruit and even durian. We drink from fresh coconuts. Farmers give us coffee from beans they've grown and roasted. My favourite hike takes six hours and goes to Munduk.

wheel. The cyclist may be WOJ Nieuwenkamp, a Dutch artist who, in 1904, brought what was probably the first bicycle to Bali. Outside the walls are 34 carved figures from the Ramayana. The frangipani-scented temple is dedicated to agricultural spirits looking after non-irrigated land. It's in Kubutambahan, 4km west of Yeh Sanih.

Sekumpul

TIME FROM LOVINA: **1 HR**

Sublime hikes to the Sekumpul cascades

Half a dozen waterfalls pour over cliffs in a verdant bamboo-forested valley. Collectively known as the **Sekumpul Waterfalls**, the cascades are up to 80m high and accent a green gorge that's almost mystical in its beauty. Trees including clove, cacao, jackfruit and mangosteen scent the air.

Trails wind through the valley from one cascade to another and it's easy to spend a day here revelling in the splendour. There are several approaches to the falls. From the north, there is parking at **Spice Warung**. From here it's a gorgeous but steep and winding 10-minute walk along coursing channels of water to an entrance gate. Here, as is the case elsewhere at Sekumpul, there are potential hassles. There's a modest admission charge to the trails (about 20,000Rp), which includes the spectacular **lookout point** just a three-minute walk from the ticket booth. However, guides may try to convince you that you need their pricey services to access the lookout area. This is *not* the case and guides may only be useful for complex trekking. There's another route to the falls from the south, with parking near the **Ananda Homestay** (p213). The same caveats about guides apply here.

Once in the waterfall zone, trails – often steep and muddy – climb all around the gorge and dense jungle. Around the rim and access points are hotels, guesthouses and cafes offering hot drinks, which are much appreciated on cool, misty days.

Back towards Singaraja, the village of **Sawan** is a centre for manufacturing gamelan instruments. You can see the gongs being cast and the intricately carved gamelan frames being fashioned at **Pande Gong**, a foundry that welcomes visitors. Watching the intricate process of tuning new gongs is fascinating.

Air Terjun Gitgit

TIME FROM LOVINA: **40 MINS**

Popular roadside waterfall

Although touristy and populated with vendors and dubious guides to nowhere, **Air Terjun Gitgit** is the best waterfall for visitors short on time. It's right on the main road to south Bali, around 11km south of Singaraja. An 800m path from the parking area leads to impressive 40m-high falls that pound away, producing welcome and refreshing mists. With more time, you can lose the crowds 2km further up the hill where there's a multitiered waterfall about 600m off the western side of the main road.

Sekumpul Waterfalls

Air Terjun Singsing
TIME FROM LOVINA: **15 MINS**

Daybreak falls

Air Terjun Singsing (Daybreak Waterfalls) is appealing for its proximity to Lovina, which is 5km southwest. You can cycle or even walk there. A 200m path leads to the lower of two sets of falls, which is near a hotel. A short but steep climb leads to another set of falls. Though not very high, the waterfalls flow into large pools that are good for swimming, and the surrounding scenery is lush and green. Note that the falls may stop flowing during the dry season, which runs from April to October.

Brahma Vihara Arama
TIME FROM LOVINA: **20 MINS**

Sylvan Buddhist temple

Bali's only Buddhist monastery, **Brahma Vihara Arama** is a fascinating place to explore, with a lofty location that affords great views down across the rice fields to the north coast. The sprawling site's manicured gardens have a profusion of hibiscus flowers. Highlights include a miniature version of Borobudur, the famous Buddhist temple and UNESCO site in Java. Statues of Buddha and lotus ponds abound. There are daily meditation programmes in prayer pavilions. The site is southwest of Lovina in the foothills.

LESSER-KNOWN TEMPLES

Pura Ponjok Batu
Legend holds that it was built to provide spiritual balance to all the temples in the south; it's 7km east of Yeh Sanih.

Pura Beji Temple for the *subak* (association of rice growers), dedicated to the goddess Dewi Sri. Sculptured panels feature demons; in Sangsit.

Pura Dalem Sangsit
This temple of the dead 500m from Pura Beji shows scenes of punishment in the afterlife.

Pura Dalem Jagaraga Small temple with delightful sculptured panels. Look for a vintage car, a steamer at sea and an aerial dogfight; in Jagaraga.

Pura Melanting
Dedicated to good fortune in business. Look for the dragon statue bearing a lotus blossom; 2km inland from **Pura Pulaki** (p208).

FRUITS OF THE FOREST

On hikes in the lush hills of the north, look for the following fruits growing both wild and on farms.

Jackfruit (*nangka*) Can be huge, with a spiky green exterior. The fruit forms into sweet bite-sized nodules that combine many tropical flavours.

Mangosteen (*manggis*) Despite its name, it's not related to the mango. Its white centre has a peach-like flavour and texture; it's often called 'queen of fruit'.

Passionfruit (*markisa*) Popular whether eaten raw or used as the base of a drink or dessert; have a spoon ready to scoop out the jelly-like interior.

Snake fruit (*salak*) Named after its brown scaly skin, has firm orbs inside that are like a cross between segments of apple and pear.

Air Panas Banjar

TIME FROM LOVINA: **20 MINS** 🚗

Soak in hot springs

Hot springs percolate amid lush tropical plants at **Air Panas Banjar**. Eight fierce-faced carved stone *naga* (dragons) pour water from a natural hot spring into the first bath, which then overflows (via the mouths of five more *naga*), into a larger pool. In a third pool, water pours from 3m-high spouts to give you a pummelling massage. The water is slightly sulphurous and pleasantly steamy (about 38°C).

You must wear a swimsuit. You can relax here for a few hours and have lunch at the cafe, or even stay the night at a nearby modest guesthouse, **Pondok Wisata Grya Sari**. It's 10km southwest of Lovina.

Seririt

TIME FROM LOVINA: **20–45 MINS** 🚗

Spectacular views from an important crossroads

Seririt is located at an important junction. From here, one road runs south and on to Munduk (p188) and beyond; another leads to west Bali near Balian Beach (p223), via the beautiful Antosari Road (p188) and the equally scenic road via Pulukan to Medewi (p223). The market in the centre of Seririt is renowned for its many stalls selling supplies for offerings; it makes a good stop for refreshments.

The road south soon plunges you into the natural bounty of north Bali as you head up the hill. From November to March, you'll catch the scent of the odoriferous durian fruit as it reaches its peak ripeness at plantations found down small farm roads. Other plantations grow coffee, cloves and a huge variety of fruits.

South of the junction with the Munduk road, the route passes through some of Bali's most spectacular **rice terrace views** after the village of Kekeran.

Quiet beach escapes

Some 2km west of Seririt on Jl Singaraja-Gilimanuk, the small road Jl Umeanyar leads north to one of Bali's newest swaths of beach development. **Pantai Umeanyar** and **Pantai Nalika** are adjoining beaches with slate-coloured sand. Secluded boutique hotels, guesthouses and low-key resorts are popping up along the coast, amidst the rice fields and up on the low headlands. The area offers a real escape. Right on the water, **Warung Segara Mas** offers upscale seafood and sweeping views. Fortunately, you can't see or smell the huge power plant 8km west at Celukanbawang.

Pemuteran

BEACH PLEASURES | RELAXATION | UNDERWATER ADVENTURES

One of Bali's most delightful beach towns, Pemuteran is a popular oasis in Bali's northwest. Artful resorts mix with welcoming homestays, all set back from a dog-bone-shaped bay. The beach is calm, thanks to its location within an extinct volcano crater protected by flourishing coral reefs. You can delight in days of relaxation on a sun lounger under a shady tree. Most people spend at least some time viewing the undersea wonders at nearby Pulau Menjangan (p210).

The busy Singaraja–Gilimanuk road is the town's spine and many businesses aimed at visitors can be found along it. While noise can be distracting along the main road, there are numerous good cafes and restaurants scattered throughout the area. Despite its popularity, Pemuteran's community and tourism businesses have forged a sustainable vision for development that should be a model for the rest of Bali.

Pemuteran's Sandy Idyll

Life's a beach

Strolling Pemuteran's **beach** is popular, especially at sunset. It's a fun scene, with village children playing football amidst smiling visitors and couples strolling the hard-packed grey sand. You can walk the isolated beach for over 4km from its western end east to **Pura Pulaki** (p208). At the west end where the hotels are concentrated, you can rent sun loungers and get refreshments. Waves in the reef-protected waters are gentle.

Under the Sea

Reefs and man-made surprises

Extensive coral reefs are about 3km offshore and closer coral is being restored as part of the **BioRock** project (biorock-indonesia.com; there's an info booth on the beach). **Diving** and **snorkelling** are popular. Closer to shore, the bay is less than 15m deep, so shore diving is popular, especially at night. You can make like Indiana Jones at the intriguing **Garden of the Gods dive site**, where over 30 statues and sculptures have been erected on the seafloor about 400m offshore.

GETTING AROUND

Pemuteran is a three- to five-hour drive from south Bali, either over the Central Mountains or around the west coast. Hotels at either end of the journey can arrange a car and driver. With your own car, consider taking more than a day to reach Pemuteran from south Bali or Ubud. Lovina is about an hour's drive to the east. Pemuteran is on the Gilimanuk–Lovina–Singaraja public bus run. Just flag down a bus. Tourist buses generally do not serve the area. You can get around all of Pemuteran by walking.

☑TOP TIP

It pays to check the location of places to stay. It's possible to stay close to the beach, even at budget level. Some options are far from Pemuteran's waterfront and tourist businesses. The main road is noisy 24/7.

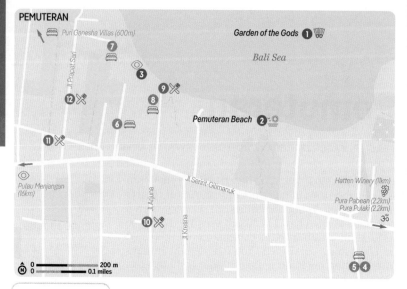

PEMUTERAN

Puri Ganesha Villas (600m)

Garden of the Gods ①

Bali Sea

⑦

③

⑨ ⑫ ⑧

⑥

Pemuteran Beach ②

⑪

Pulau Menjangan (16km)

Jl Seririt-Gilimanuk

Hatten Winery (11km)

Pura Pabean (2.2km)
Pura Pulaki (2.2km)

③

Jl Prabat Sari

Jl Arjuna

Jl Kresha

⑩

⑤ ④

0   200 m
0   0.1 miles

HIGHLIGHTS
① Garden of the Gods
② Pemuteran Beach

SIGHTS
③ BioRock Indonesia Info Booth

SLEEPING
④ Double You Homestay
⑤ Kubuku Eco Divelodge
⑥ Pondok Shindu Guest House
⑦ Taman Sari Bali Resort
⑧ Taman Selini Beach Bungalows

EATING
⑨ Dimpil Beachbar & Resto
⑩ Warung Bukit
⑪ Warung D'Bucu
⑫ Warung Santai

A Vital Temple

Sacred sites

Pura Pulaki at the east end of the beach is home to a large troop of monkeys. Dating to at least the 16th century, this is one of Bali's auspicious sea temples, part of a chain of sacred places that protect the island from waterborne evil spirits. About 150m across the busy road, a subsidiary temple, **Pura Pabean**, has a lovely location on a waterfront knoll. By tipping the attendant, you can tour its unusual Chinese-accented architecture, a legacy of traders who once lived here.

Taste Bali Wine

Local terroir

You can't miss the grapevines east of Pemuteran, a surprise for those lulled by the rice fields that cover so much of Bali. Yet the island has a burgeoning wine scene that has been developing for two decades. One of the pioneering vineyards is **Hatten Winery**, which like east Bali's Sababay Winery (p164) creates very drinkable white, rosé, red and sparkling wines.

 EATING IN PEMUTERAN: OUR PICKS

Dimpil Beachbar & Resto Delightful open-air beach joint. Excellent mixed drinks and a fun vibe complement tasty seafood and Indo mains. **$**

Warung D'Bucu A talented family runs this excellent warung in a good restaurant area between the beach and main road. Great seafood. **$**

Warung Bukit South of the main road on a narrow lane, creative cooks prepare Asian mains such as pad thai and Balinese seafood. **$**

Warung Santai Well off the main road, this atmospheric Indonesian restaurant serves spicy, authentic dishes – with many vegetarian options. Cooking classes too. **$$**

Beyond Pemuteran

Bali's best snorkelling and diving draw visitors to the island's only national park, which also offers wildlife spotting and hiking.

Most visitors to West Bali National Park (Taman Nasional Bali Barat) are struck by the sounds emanating from the birds darting among the rustling trees. The park covers 190 sq km of the western tip of Bali, including almost 70 sq km of coral reef and coastal waters. Together, this is a significant commitment to conservation on a densely populated island. It's a place where you can enjoy Bali's best diving at Pulau Menjangan, hike through forests, explore coastal mangroves and discover untrodden white-sand beaches. Staying in Tulamben gives you a wide range of hotel choices and puts you close to everything the park has to offer.

West Bali National Park

TIME FROM PEMUTERAN: **30–60 MINS** 🚗

Hiking in a natural wonderland

From a trail west of Labuhan Lalang, a three-hour hike exploring **Teluk Terima** (Terima Bay) begins at the **mangroves** and visits **beaches**. A three- to four-hour hike will allow you to explore the **savannah** area at the heart of the park. There are many more hiking options, including a longer hike up **Gunung Kelatakan** (Mt Kelatakan; 698m). Note seasonal variations: in the dry season vegetation is brown and sparse, which aids animal-spotting. In the wet season, the park gets green and lush, but animals also have plenty of cover.

Guides, who can be found at the various park gates and who are required for tours, are of variable quality. Good ones will offer a range of customisable hiking routes as well as cycling tours or camping. Three who are recommended: **Parianto** (WhatsApp: +62 8810 3730 6510), **Idris** (WhatsApp: +62 8234 018 5768) and **Iwan Melali** (iwan.melali@gmail.com).

Visit the Bali starling centre

Previously tightly guarded, the **Bali Starling Centre**, a facility deep within the park, is home to scores of the once rare **Bali starling**, a brilliant white bird with cobalt highlights around the eyes. It once collected to the point of extinction,

Continues on p212

Places

West Bali National Park
p209

Banyuwedang p212

GETTING AROUND

West Bali National Park can be reached from north Bali or via the busy road to the Java ferries in Gilimanuk, which runs west from south Bali. The closest tourist centre is Pemuteran. You can either arrange rides with your accommodation or use your own wheels. Walking and trekking are major reasons to visit the park, but be aware that most excursions require the services of a park guide.

209

DUDAREV MIKHAIL/SHUTTERSTOCK ©

TOP EXPERIENCE

Pulau Menjangan

Bali's best-known underwater attraction is ringed by over a dozen superb dive sites. The experience is excellent – iconic tropical fish, soft corals, great visibility, caves and spectacular drop-offs.

DON'T MISS

Southwest Drift from the Jetty

Jetty Wall

Mangrove Point

Coral Gardens

Anker Wreck

Eels Garden

Pura Gili Kencana

Beaches

The Jetty Area

A small **jetty** on the southeast side of the island is the focus of day trips, especially for snorkellers. The **wall** here – which rewards divers *and* snorkellers – is directly out from the shore. The gentle currents allow for a **southwest drift** so you can just go with the flow and enjoy the underwater spectacle. The area close to shore is suitable for novices. You can also venture out to where the shallows drop off in dramatic cliffs, a magnet for experienced divers, who can choose from eight walls here. Try to hover over the divers along the walls. Watching their bubbles sinuously rise in all their multihued silvery glory from the inky depths is a remarkable spectacle.

South of the Jetty

The **coral wall** extends far to the southwest from the jetty and gets more pristine and awe-inspiring as you go. For jetty stops, your guide may try to get you to swim back to the boat along the less-interesting bleached coral near the shore; this turns out to be for their convenience. Instead, suggest that the boat come down and pick you up when you're ready, thus avoiding the swim against the current followed by downtime at the jetty.

Pura Gili Kencana

North of the Jetty

North of the jetty, you can snorkel from shore and cover the sites in a big circle. It's a stunning area and is the best place to go midday. The coral is more varied here and there are turtles. **Mangrove Point** is an excellent snorkelling area.

Elsewhere

In the north, **Coral Gardens** is a fine spot. In the west, the **Anker Wreck**, a mysterious 19th-century wooden boat, challenges even experts. Nearby, **Eels Garden** offers a stunning mix of coral and fish from 20m and below.

Exploring the Island

Uninhabited Pulau Menjangan has what is thought to be Bali's oldest temple, **Pura Gili Kencana**, dating from the 14th century and about 300m from the pier. It has a huge Ganesha (the elephant-headed Hindu deity) carved from brilliant white stone at the soaring arched entrance.

An easy 6km trail that circles the island takes about 90 minutes. On the way you'll pass **small temples**, **mangroves** and some thin but lovely **beaches** on the northwest side. Having a **picnic** lunch here is one of the good reasons to arrange for your own boat with a skipper amenable to a flexible schedule.

Getting There & Away

The closest and most convenient dive operators are found at Pemuteran, where the hotels also arrange diving and snorkelling trips. Try to get a trip that leaves from the Pemuteran's beach as it saves the hassles of going via chaotic Banyuwedang. Independent snorkellers can arrange trips from Banyuwedang (p212) and Labuhan Lalang (p212); the latter offers the shortest boat trip to Menjangan. If you are daytripping from elsewhere on Bali, find out how much time you'll be travelling each way. From Seminyak, congestion woes can make for four or more hours on the road one-way.

UNDERWATER SPECIES

These waters are tops for spotting underwater sea life. Fields of coral include soft coral, fan coral, hard coral, whip coral and Gorgonian sea fans. Smaller fish include reef fish, anemone shrimps, moorish idols and pygmy seahorses. Larger species include turtles, barracudas, various sharks and the odd whale shark.

TOP TIPS

- Although the jetty is justifiably popular, most boat operators take you there because it's close to the harbours and saves fuel.
- Menjangan is part of West Bali National Park, so entrance fees apply.
- Arranging your trip ad hoc can be costly. There's boat rental (for one to 10 people), mandatory guide, snorkel-set rental, diving and snorkelling fees, and insurance.
- Typical snorkelling trips take three to four hours, with one hour of that transit time.
- If your guide adds to your experience, tip accordingly.
- Friends of Menjangan has info on efforts to keep the island clean; see its Facebook page.

LOUISE HEUSINKVELD/ALAMY STOCK PHOTO ©

FLORA & FAUNA IN THE PARK

Most of the natural vegetation in Bali Barat National Park is not tropical rainforest, which requires year-round rain, but coastal savannah, with deciduous trees that become bare in the dry season. The southern slopes receive more rainfall, and so have more tropical vegetation, while the coastal lowlands have extensive mangroves.

There are more than 200 species of plants growing in the park. Local fauna includes leaf monkeys and macaques; rusa and barking deer; and wild pigs, squirrels, buffalo, iguanas, pythons and green snakes. There were once tigers, but the last confirmed sighting was in 1937 – and that one was shot. The birdlife is prolific, with many of Bali's 300 species found here.

AULIA ANANTA/SHUTTERSTOCK ©

Bali starlings (p209)

Continued from p209

but breeding programmes here and elsewhere have reintroduced the starling into the park and Nusa Penida. On a half-hour visit, staff explain the facility and talk about the birds. It's only 200m from a park entry gate near Sumber Kelompok, but you will have to pay the pricey park admission. You don't need a guide.

Book a boat trip at Labuhan Lalang

To catch a boat to visit or snorkel around Pulau Menjangan (p210), book a trip at this **boat dock**. It's also a good place to get a boat to one of the white-sand beaches within the park and meet guides. All prices are negotiable. There are warungs and a pleasant beach 200m east.

A temple to Bali's Romeo

Jayaprana, the foster son of a 17th-century king, planned to marry Leyonsari, a girl of humble origins. The king, however, also fell in love with Leyonsari and had Jayaprana killed. Leyonsari learned the truth of Jayaprana's death in a dream and killed herself rather than marry the king. This Romeo and Juliet story is a common theme in Balinese folklore, and the grave is regarded as sacred. A 20-minute walk up stone stairs will bring you to the monkey-filled temple with Jayaprana's grave, **Pura Jayaprana**. There are fine views to Pulau Menjangan. It's just southwest of Labuhan Lalang.

Banyuwedang

TIME FROM PEMUTERAN: **20 MINS**

Boats and hotels

This **mangrove-fringed cove** east of the West Bali National Park is the main hub for pre-booked boat trips to Pulau Menjangan. If you are visiting Menjangan to dive or snorkel as part of a group, it's likely that you'll catch your boat at this bustling little **harbour**. Scattered beach clubs are aimed at daytrippers, and many resorts are scattered around the uneven shoreline. It's all reached over astonishingly bad roads.

Places We Love to Stay

$ Cheap $$ Moderate $$$ Pricey

Lovina   p200 (Map p201)

Funky Place $ In Kalibukbuk; a rollicking hostel that has dorms, a treehouse and proximity to the beach. It's famous for beer pong.

Mandhara Chico Bungalow $ In Anturan; family-run guesthouse on a small strip of charcoal-sand beach lined with fishing boats. Rooms are basic but tidy.

Lovina Beachhouse Villas $$ In Anturan; close to the waterfront, villas here are historic wooden structures brought from Java and have private pools.

Villa Taman Ganesha $$ In Anturan; lovely guesthouse on a quiet lane, which has lush grounds with frangipani, and private and comfortable villas.

Damai $$$ Set on a hillside behind Lovina; expect sweeping views from luxury villas that mix antiques and a modern style. Great infinity pool and restaurant.

Sekumpul   p204

Ananda Homestay $ Basic homestay with simple rooms close to the Sekumpul Waterfalls. Lovely family owners and many opportunities for hiking in the surrounding rainforest.

Villa Manuk $$ In the hills near the Sekumpul Waterfalls is this small villa complex with rice-field views. It has its own natural-spring-fed pool.

Yeh Sanih   p203

Cilik's Beach Garden $$ Three kilometres east of Yeh Sanih, staying here is like visiting rich friends with good taste. Large oceanfront villas and extensive private gardens.

Air Sanih Beach Villa $$$ Amidst modest choices, luxury villas stand out. This one is large with waterfront frontage, gardens and a pool behind a seawall.

Seririt   p206

Nalika Beach Resort $$ Great-value small hotel right on the narrow beach. Large, comfortable rooms at the end of a quiet road.

Bali Nibbana Resort $$ On the road to Nalika Beach, a low-key hotel with views to the ocean from its tree-shaded hillside setting.

Mayo Resort $$ At Pantai Umeanyar is this small waterfront resort with large units; each has a big terrace. Right on the beach near seafood warungs.

Zen Resort Bali $$$ The name says it all. Yoga and a lavish spa define this resort on a hillside 200m back from Nalika Beach.

Pemuteran   p207 (Map p208)

Pondok Shindu Guest House $ Ideal family-run guesthouse a brief walk from the beach. Rooms have trad-style open-air bathrooms. Good breakfasts.

Double You Homestay $ On a lane south of the main road, a stylish guesthouse with immaculate units set in a flower-filled garden.

Kubuku Eco Divelodge $$ Modern rooms and pool in a mountainside compound off the main road. Yoga and diving.

Taman Sari Bali Resort $$ Off a small lane, traditional-style bungalows with intricate carvings and traditional artwork. Located on a long stretch of quiet beach.

Taman Selini Beach Bungalows $$$ Bungalows recall an older Bali, from the thatched roofs down to the antique carved doors. It's on a beachfront garden.

Puri Ganesha Villas $$$ Two-storey villas on sweeping waterfront grounds, each with a unique style that mixes antiques with relaxed comfort and a pool.

Banyuwedang   p212

NusaBay Menjangan by WHM $$ Secluded deep in West Bali National Park on a beautiful white-sand beach reached by private boat. Comfortable rooms, glamping.

Plataran Menjangan Resort $$$ In West Bali National Park is this luxe resort set on 382 hectares. There's an outback bush section and beach villas.

Above: Pura Taman Ayun (p218); Right : boats, Jembrana Coast (p223)

West Bali

BEACHES, NATURE AND TEMPLES

Go west, happy traveller! Bali's tourist buzz fades away on this coast of delights, abetted by traditional culture and the odd surf break.

Even as development from south Bali sprawls outward, Bali's true west, which is split by the busy main road from Denpasar to Gilimanuk, remains dotted with corners where solitude is the norm, not an option. It's easy to find serenity amid its wild charcoal-coloured beaches, jungle and rice fields.

And if you want a more developed vibe, the lands east of the improbable-looking Pura Tanah Lot are alive with new projects and beachside cafes. Besides this temple, some of Bali's most sacred sites are here, including the accessible splendour of Pura Taman Ayun and the wonderful isolation of Pura Rambut Siwi.

The tidy town of Tabanan is at the hub of Bali's UNESCO-listed *subak*, the system of irrigation that ensures everybody gets a fair share of the water. On narrow back roads you can cruise beside rushing streams with bamboo arching overhead and fruit piling up below.

On the coast, surfers hit the breaks at funky beachside communities that some people never manage to leave. The waves at Balian Beach have a following, and a small surfer community has sprung up with simple guesthouses and somewhat posher retreats. Hang out with locals who know the waters well. Further west, Medewi is even more remote. A burgeoning collection of guesthouses, resorts and some superb places to eat offer comfort, pleasure and relaxation.

SONY HERDIANA/SHUTTERSTOCK ©

THE MAIN AREAS

Find Your Way

West Bali is a long strip of lands, shadowed by mountains to the north and ending in dark sands in the south. You can spend a week here, or pass through in half a day.

WALKING

All those beaches are made for walking, and you don't need boots – bare feet will do. Elsewhere, following a small lane through rice fields can be sublime.

MOTORBIKE OR CAR

Your own wheels are the secret to west Bali adventure, where tiny roads off the main highway beckon with adventure and rewards. Near Canggu, a motorbike is best because of traffic.

Tabanan, p218

Thirty minutes from extraordinary temples, crafts and wild coast.

Denpasar

Teluk Benoa

Sungai Wos

Sungai Ayung

Muncan

Sangeh

Sembung

Wanasari

Jegu

Mengwi

Beraban

Seseh

Tabanan

Dukuh

Pucuk

Pejeten

Sungai Yeh He

Wangayagede

Byahan

Kerambitan

Yeh Gangga

Antosari

Tibubiyu

Batungsei

Sanda

Blimbing

Sungai Balian

Kutuh

Bali Sea

Mangassari

Pulukan

G. Patas

Sungai Pulukan

Air Satang

Sungai Sumbul

Yeh Embang

G. Mesehe

Sungai Bilukpoh

Jembrana

Mendoyo

G. Merbuk

Sungai Daya

Negara

Loloan Timur

Perancak

Bali Barat National Park

Pengambengan

Prapat Agung Peninsula

Teluk Terima

Sungai Terima

Palasari

Candikesuma

Sungai Melaya

Belimbingan

Melaya

Selat Bali

Teluk Gilimanuk

Cekik

Boom Marina

Banyuwangi

0   20 km
0   10 miles

Pura Tanah Lot (p222)

Plan Your Time

With just a few days, you can savour all the west has to offer and still have the freedom to make decisions on the fly.

Pressed for Time

Zipping through west Bali – maybe on the way to dive in Pemuteran? – doesn't mean you need to miss the highlights, as so much is easy to reach. From the south or Ubud, stop first at **Pura Taman Ayun** (p218), one of Bali's most rewarding temples. Next, cruise to the waterfront at **Balian Beach** (p223) for lunch. Then see the diverse sights of **Perancak** (p224).

Five Days to Explore

With more time, you can shred your itinerary at will. Besides the one-day highlights, take a morning at **Pura Tanah Lot** (p222) before cruising for the perfect villa in the nearby beach villages like **Cemagi** (p221). Head west, stopping at beaches like **Yeh Gangga** (p224) before considering a longer pause at **Balian Beach** (p223). Settle in at delightful **Medewi** (p223), where you can explore **Pura Rambut Siwi** (p224).

SEASONAL HIGHLIGHTS

MARCH–MAY	JUNE–AUGUST	SEPTEMBER–NOVEMBER	DECEMBER–FEBRUARY
The dry season offers the best weather for lounging on the beaches or by the pool.	Even when south Bali is overrun during the peak months of July and August, west Bali remains quiet.	Rainy season; good for watching storms in beach towns and waterfront resorts.	Cemagi villas and towns such as Balian Beach and Medewi can book up.

Tabanan

RICE FIELDS | VERDANT VISTAS | UNMISSABLE TEMPLE

GETTING AROUND

Much of the joy of the Tabanan area comes from exploration: driving the backroads and discovering views, workshops, temples and more. You can explore the heart of the town on foot, but otherwise, you'll want your own wheels to head north and south of the traffic-choked main road linking the ferry port of Gilimanuk with Denpasar. Useful public transit is non-existent. For stays in the scattered guesthouses, hotels, retreats and resorts, either make arrangements through your lodging or use a ride app. From Seminyak, it can take 90 minutes or more to drive here.

☑**TOP TIP**

When exploring the area, avoid the main Gilimanuk–Denpasar road as much as possible. Secondary roads will always be more scenic and less jammed up.

Tabanan, like most regional capitals in Bali, is a large, well-organised place with a central temple next to a huge banyan tree. The verdant surrounding fields are emblematic of Bali's rice-growing traditions and are part of its UNESCO recognition of the *subak* system of irrigation. The magnificent temple Pura Taman Ayun celebrates this. Also check to see if Tabanan's Mandala Mathika Subak (Subak Museum) has reopened after its long reconstruction.

The area north of Tabanan is a good spot to travel around with your own transport. Driving the fecund back roads, you'll pass rice-field vistas around almost every turn while bamboo arches temple-like above you. There are plenty of idiosyncratic and interesting places to stay here.

The southern part of Tabanan district takes you through charming villages, past vigorously growing rice shoots and villas. The fields are revered by many as the most productive in Bali. Pejaten and Kediri villages are centres of ceramic production.

Beautiful Pura Taman Ayun

One of Bali's most alluring temples

One of the most rewarding temples on Bali to visit, **Pura Taman Ayun** is a beautiful place of enveloping calm. This huge royal water temple northeast of Tabanan in Mengwi is surrounded by a wide, elegant moat. It was the main temple of the Mengwi kingdom, which survived until 1891, when it was conquered by neighbouring kingdoms. The complex was built in 1634 and extensively renovated in 1937.

The first courtyard is an open grassy expanse. The inner courtyard (*jeroan*) is screened by a low wall, which unusually for Bali allows easy viewing of the thicket of evocative *meru* (multi-tiered shrines) within. The canal-bordered walk around the perimeter of the *jeroan* is a sublime treat.

Lotus blossoms fill the temple's frangipani-shaded pools; the temple is part of the *subak* system (rice-field irrigation) recognised by UNESCO. Fittingly, canals and water features

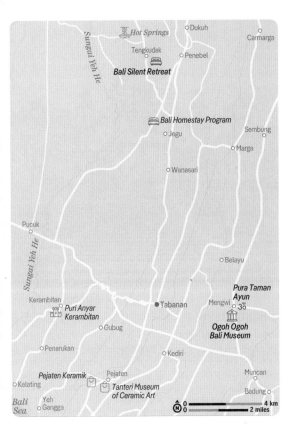

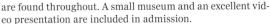

MONSTROUS OGOH-OGOH

In the weeks prior to Nyepi (usually in March), huge and elaborate papier-mâché monsters called *ogoh-ogoh* are built in villages across the island, involving everybody in the community. Construction sites buzz with fevered activity around the clock. It's a recent tradition, beloved by village youth.

On Nyepi eve, large ceremonies across Bali lure out the demons. The whole island erupts in mock 'anarchy', with people banging drums, setting off firecrackers and yelling '*megedi megedi!*' (get out!) to expel the demons. For the grand finale, the *ogoh-ogoh* all go up in flames. Any demons that survive this wild scene are believed to evacuate the village when confronted with the boring silence on the morrow.

are found throughout. A small museum and an excellent video presentation are included in admission.

Just west of the temple complex, the **Ogoh Ogoh Bali Museum** celebrates the huge and outlandish papier-mâché monsters that have become a part of Nyepi celebrations. The market area immediately east of the temple has good warungs for lunch.

South to the Coast

Ceramics, workshops and a timeless palace

Pejaten and Kediri villages, 10km south of Tabanan, are centres for the production of traditional pottery, including elaborate ornamental roof tiles. The **Tanteri Museum of Ceramic Art** is part showroom and part factory; nearby, **Pejaten Keramik** manufactures trademark pale-green pieces.

Closer to the main road to Gilimanuk, Kerambitan village is noted for its dance troupe and musicians who perform in Ubud. Banyan trees shade the 17th-century palace **Puri Anyar Kerambitan**, which quietly moulders away. On a visit, you can get a sense of Balinese royal life in days gone by.

CHRISTIAN BALI

Discouraged by the secular Dutch, Christian evangelism via sporadic missionary activity in Bali resulted in few converts, many of whom were subsequently rejected by their own communities. In 1939 they were encouraged to resettle here in the wilds of west Bali. The two communities they established are examples of the hidden multiculturalism of the island.

Palasari boasts the huge **Sacred Heart Catholic Church**, largely made from white stone and set on a large town square. It's a peaceful, off-the-beaten-path spot with gently waving palms. Nearby Belimbingsari was established as a Protestant community, and now has the largest Protestant church, **Pura Gereja**, on the island. It has Balinese details such as a *kulkul* (hollow tree-trunk drum) instead of a bell.

DANIEL_FERRYANTO/SHUTTERSTOCK ©

Sacred Heart Catholic Church

Unique Stays

Silence and local life

Set amid gorgeous scenery, **Bali Silent Retreat** is just what its name says: somewhere to meditate, practise yoga, go on nature walks and more – all in total silence. The minimalist ethos stops at the food, however, which is organic and fabulous. It's 18km northwest of Tabanan.

You can experience village life as part of the innovative **Bali Homestay Program** (bali-homestay.com) that places travellers in the homes of residents of the rice-growing village of **Jegu**, 9km north of Tabanan. The recommended full two-night package includes activities such as making offerings, village visits and cultural tours, plus all meals.

MORE ON SUBAK

Rice cultivation and irrigation is central to Bali's culture. The intricate social systems that govern rice cultivation (and village life) are part of the *subak* system. Pura Taman Ayun is central to *subak*; west Bali is the heart. Read **Bali's Subak System** (p351) for more.

Beyond Tabanan

Beaches, sacred places and surprises are never far from the vital Gilimanuk–Denpasar main road that spans west Bali.

Conga lines of tourists descend on the sacred temple Tanah Lot for sunset, but at other times of day it's possible to enjoy this lovely place with less hassle. To the west, the Cemagi area is alive with development but still has some quieter corners to appreciate the seaside vistas.

Going west, crowds thin out quickly. Balian Beach remains a low-key spot for surfing and hanging out. The Jembrana Coast, Bali's most sparsely populated district, offers beautiful scenery and lots of long dark-sand beaches. Medewi is the most developed area and offers surfing, funky accommodation and fine food. The main road ends at Gilimanuk, where you can catch a ferry to Java and have a good lunch.

Places

GETTING AROUND

Whether transiting to Java or taking the coast route to north Bali and West Bali National Park, the main road with its impatient strings of jockeying cars and trucks will figure in your drive. You can get a bus from the ferry port of Gilimanuk to Denpasar; otherwise, you will either be travelling the region with your own wheels or leaving the driving to someone else. Distances are far; don't expect to walk much.

Cemagi Area

TIME FROM TABANAN: **30–45 MINS**

Beaches and development

Bali's frenetic tourism development now stretches from the overwrought Canggu (p52) west to Pura Tanah Lot and beyond. The entire area has generically picked up the name Cemagi, which encompasses several named beaches. You can easily spend a day relaxing on the beaches and visiting a waterfront temple.

Closest to Canggu, **Pantai Seseh** is a wide grey-sand beach with a lot of villas and waterfront cafes that are good for watching the surf and sunsets. Beach loungers are easily rented. The enormous Yaryan Dragon Resort has sparked much community opposition over its size and gaudy architecture, but to no avail.

Within the core of Cemagi, **Pura Gede Luhur Batu Ngaus** sits atop a dramatic outcrop of black lava rock jutting out into the pounding waves. It has all the classic elements of a Balinese temple and looks like a mini version of Tanah Lot, which is a further 3km northwest. To the immediate southeast, there are a long series of simple warungs that serve drinks and snacks at cliffside tables. The views of the striking coastline are sweeping and – traffic aside – it's a great place at sunset, especially along the relaxed and traffic-free **cliff path** beyond the turn in the road. Just north of the temple is the black-sand **Pantai Mengening**, a fine place to while away an afternoon.

SEEING SEA TEMPLES

The legendary 16th-century priest Nirartha is credited with introducing many of the complexities of Balinese religion to the island, as well as establishing the chain of 'sea temples' (*pura segara*). These coastal sacred spots both honour the sea gods and protect Bali from sea demons. Each was intended to be within sight of the next, and several have dramatic locations.

In addition to the famous – Pura Luhur Ulu Watu (p99) on the island's southwest tip – and the lesser-known – Pura Pulaki (p208) near Pemuteran on the north coast – the sea temples are most heavily concentrated in west Bali. Notable examples include Pura Tanah Lot, Pura Rambut Siwi (p224) and Pura Gede Perancak (p224).

GEKKO GALLERY/SHUTTERSTOCK ©

Pantai Seseh (p221)

Development is in full swing north of Sungai Jeh Poh (Jeh Poh River). The adjoining beaches of **Pantai Nyani** and **Pantai Sanja** are wide open and flat expanses of dark sand. Just behind the shore, a number of developments are bringing resorts and Canggu-style beach clubs. Some seem much higher than the local rule that no structure should be taller than a palm tree.

Like the earlier hotspots to the southeast, transportation is already a problem in the Cemagi area, with traffic chokepoints and narrow roads that peter off near the ocean, with no easy way for a car to turn around. Motorbikes are the best way to get around the area.

Pura Tanah Lot

TIME FROM TABANAN: **30 MINS** 🚗

Beating the crowds

A hugely popular tourist destination, **Pura Tanah Lot** has great spiritual significance to the Balinese. However, this can be hard to discern amid the crowds, clamour and chaos – especially for the overhyped sunsets. It's the most visited and photographed temple in Bali, but it has all the authenticity of a stage set – even the tower of rock that the photogenic temple sits upon is an artful reconstruction, and more than one-third of the rock

EATING BEYOND TABANAN: OUR PICKS

Organic Ocean Excellent seafood, vegetarian and vegan meals in Seseh come with a dose of sustainable philosophy. Produce is sourced from the house farm. $$

Casa Balian Cafe Back away from the cliffs in Balian Beach, this is the spot to get fine coffee drinks along the coast, plus good meals throughout the day. $

Dewi and Rasta Cafe The best meals in the west are in Medewi, in this beloved cafe that's the passion project of its namesake owners. $

Holy Tree Kitchen Right on the beach in Medewi at Pantai Yeh Sumbul, with good coffee, healthy breakfasts, tasty lunches and addictive views. $

is artificial. The ferocious tourism development to the east is controversial because many Balinese feel that the heights of some of the new resorts are disrespectful of Pura Tanah Lot.

For the Balinese, Pura Tanah Lot is one of the most important and venerated sea temples. It is closely associated with the Majapahit priest Nirartha. You can walk over to the temple at low tide, but non-Balinese people are not allowed to enter. Two sacred snakes are said to live in the innermost sanctum. Follow the pathways in the gardens along the overlooking clifftop to escape the crowds and enjoy a somewhat more contemplative atmosphere. **Pura Batu Bolong** is connected to land by a natural bridge of stone over the surf.

To reach Tanah Lot, you normally follow walkways that run from the vast car parks through a mind-boggling sideshow of tatty souvenir shops, animal attractions and other schlock down to the sea. Clamorous announcements screech from loudspeakers. Try to get dropped off and picked up just north at the small Pura Batu Mejan to avoid the worst of the scrum.

Note that during the pre- and post-sunset rush, traffic is awful, with backups stretching for many kilometres. So why not just skip Tanah Lot? Mainly because it is an important spiritual place and the temple and its site have an innate beauty. The secret is to arrive before noon: you'll beat the crowds and the vendors will still be asleep. You'll hear birds chirping rather than buses idling. Besides, you can always enjoy the sunset from plenty of other less-crowded spots in south and west Bali.

Balian Beach
Surfing and crocodiles
TIME FROM TABANAN: **50 MINS** 🚗

Ever more popular, **Balian Beach** is a rolling area of dunes and knolls that overlooks pounding surf. It attracts both surfers and those looking to escape the bustle of south Bali. The sand is right at the mouth of the wide Sungai Balian (Balian River); it's 800m south of the town of Lalang-Linggah.

Wander between cafes and join other travellers for a drink, to talk surf or watch the sunset. The surf break is a reliable walled-up clean left shoulder; other activities include yoga and bodysurfing. Many try to snag photos of the crocodiles that inhabit the river. Tourist businesses stretch in an unbroken strip from the main road to the beach.

Jembrana Coast
Surfing Medewi
TIME FROM TABANAN: **90–120 MINS** 🚗

A top surf break, **Medewi Point** has a much-vaunted long left-hand wave. Rides of 200m to 500m are common. The immediate beach, **Pantai Medewi**, is a stretch of huge, smooth grey rocks interspersed among round black pebbles – think of it as free reflexology. Just west, **Pantai Yeh Sumbul** is a long swath of grey-sand beach with an embryonic tourism scene.

Spectators view Medewi's action out on the water from the point. There are guesthouses, hotels, cafes and surf shops in the area. Medewi proper is a classic market town with shops selling all the essentials of west Bali life.

THE OTHER ROAD TO PUPUAN

You can reach the mountain village of **Pupuan** on the wonderfully scenic route to north Bali via the Antosari Road (p188), which breaks off from the Gilimanuk–Denpasar road and heads through its namesake village and then up and over via spectacular rice terrace scenery.

There's another lesser known route to Papuan that heads uphill near Medewi. This narrow road climbs steeply from the coast, providing fine views back to the sea. It runs through spice-growing country – you'll see (and smell) spices laid out to dry by the road. After about 10km and just before Manggissari, the winding road runs right through **Bunut Bolong** – a tunnel formed by two enormous trees (*bunut* is a type of ficus and *bolong* means 'hole').

LESSER-KNOWN BEACHES IN WEST BALI

Pantai Yeh Gangga
West of Tanah Lot, the coast here is still secluded and has some luxe lodging options and dramatic rock formations.

Pantai Rahasya
Aka 'Hidden Beach'. Enjoy a sandy escape less than an hour from Canggu before it becomes too unhidden.

Pantai Tibubiyu
About 5km from southern Kerambitan is this small beachside village. The sand is hard-packed and at low tide you can cycle for great distances.

Pantai Bonian Vast tidal flats of black sand bookended by rivers make this beach a moody stop.

Pantai Melaya In the far west, a beach with natural shade and no development. A few fishing boats and stunning sunsets.

Holy Pura Rambut Siwi

Picturesquely situated on a clifftop overlooking a wide stretch of grey-sand beach, **Pura Rambut Siwi** is a superb temple shaded by flowering frangipani trees and is one of the important sea temples of west Bali. Like Pura Tanah Lot (p222) and Pura Luhur Ulu Watu (p99), Pura Rambut Siwi was established in the 16th century by the priest Nirartha, who had a good eye for ocean scenery. Unlike Tanah Lot, it remains a peaceful and little-visited place.

Legend has it that when Nirartha first came here, he donated some of his hair to the local villagers. The hair is now kept in a box buried in a three-tiered *meru* (multi-tiered shrine), whose name means 'Worship of the Hair'. A path along the cliff leads to a staircase down to a small and even older temple, Pura Penataran. There are another five small temples in the immediate area. The main temple is located 7km west of Medewi.

Turtles and temples in Perancak

Some 10km south of the regional centre of Negara, the fishing village of **Perancak** is the site of Nirartha's arrival in Bali in 1546, commemorated by the limestone sea temple **Pura Gede Perancak**. It's on a wide river inlet, between mangroves and the ocean. Look for the multi-hued, elaborate fishing boats called *perahu selerek*. A string of humble cafes near the oceanfront point have sunset drinks and fresh seafood.

The beach to the east is gaining a long paved path. Midway along, **Kurma Asih Sea Turtle Conservation Center** has been buying and incubating turtle eggs for over 25 years. They have released thousands of turtles back into the sea; learn about their work and the turtles on a 30-minute tour.

Gilimanuk

TIME FROM TABANAN: **3 HRS**

Ferries, mangroves and tasty chicken

Gilimanuk is the terminus for ferries that shuttle back and forth across the narrow strait to Java. Most travellers to/from Java can get an onward ferry or bus straightaway, although the views of the scruffy ferries groaning across the water and the volcanoes of Java just across the strait are worthwhile.

With a little extra time, you can discover traces of prehistoric Bali 500m east of the ferry port at the **Museum Manusia Purba**. Archaeological excavations here during the 1960s yielded the oldest evidence of human life on the island. Finds include burial mounds with funerary offerings, bronze jewellery and earthenware vessels from around 1000 BCE, give or take a few centuries. Nearby, there's an entrance to West Bali National Park (p209) where you can arrange tours of the mangroves. Note that the park headquarters just south in Cecik has little useful info for visitors.

Even if not catching a ferry, Gilimanuk is worth the short detour for its famous local speciality, *betutu* chicken, a spicy form of steamed chicken that is redolent with herbs. The favoured – and original – outlet is **Warung Men Tempeh**. It's surrounded by many copycats.

Places We Love to Stay

$ Cheap $$ Moderate $$$ Pricey

Cemagi Area   p221

KD Suites $$ Big balconies with rice-field views are the top feature of this newish hotel with a pool; not far from beaches.

Udara Bali $$$ Yoga classes with sea views and many more new-agey programmes, like sonic baths, feature here. It's right near the waterfront; opt for an all-inclusive healthy package.

Yeh Gangga   p224

WakaGangga $$$ On a black-sand beach, a small villa compound with multiple private pools amidst rice terraces. It's a quiet area.

Soori Villas $$$ A luxury villa compound in Kelating, on a quiet stretch of Bali's west coast. Each villa has its own plunge pool. Expect modern minimalism in a secluded setting.

Tibubiyu   p224

Amarta Beach Retreat $$ Modest hotel on the beach away from massive development. It's good value, with a pool and unfussy vibe.

Villa Leona by Nakula $$$ Northwest of Tibubiyu, this is the place to come if you want your own vast estate on a secluded stretch of beach. Staff win plaudits for providing luxury.

Balian Beach   p223

Surya Homestay $ One of a dozen excellent homestays at Balian Beach. Owners are charmers; the basic rooms are close to the surf break.

Gajah Mina $$ This small boutique hotel is close to the ocean and was designed by the French architect-owner. The private walled bungalows are on an outcrop surrounded by surf.

Medewi   p223

Asri Villas $ A comfy, welcoming budget guesthouse that you won't want to leave. Features large bungalow-style rooms, a shared kitchen and a pool. It's southeast of the surf break.

Anara Surf Camp $ A surf camp and modern guesthouse near the sea and rice fields, at Pantai Yeh Sumbul. Attractive hardwood motifs.

Wide Sands Beach Retreat $$ A small beach resort at Pantai Yeh Sumbul that spans a quiet lane with loungers and cafe on the sand.

Puri Dajuma Cottages $$ Suites, cottages and villas have private gardens, hammocks and walled outdoor baths. Most have ocean views too.

Lombok

BALI'S LESSER-TRAVELLED NEIGHBOUR

With sweeping coastlines, lust-worthy surf and one of Indonesia's most sought-after mountain treks, calling Lombok diverse would be an understatement.

It's hard to play favourites when it comes to islands in Indonesia, but Lombok's fan base of travellers just keeps growing. Equipped with impressive bays, the archipelago's second-highest peak and an ever-increasing number of enticing places to stay and dine, this island continues to attract the masses. Surfers flock to the southern half of the island for highly lauded waves, while trekking enthusiasts traverse the north-central region to Gunung Rinjani, an active volcano clocking in at 3726m high. Those with less intensive hobbies find themselves somewhere in between, typically with their toes in powdery-soft sand.

Unlike Bali, Lombok's indigenous community – the Sasak – are predominantly Muslim. Across the varied landscape, you'll see ornately designed mosques and hear the call to prayer five times a day. The island's cultural makeup remains diverse, however, with lasting remnants of Balinese rule during the 1800s, when the Dutch and Balinese entered into a joint power-sharing agreement. By 1894, the Dutch eliminated Balinese rule, fully colonising the island on their own. This continued until the Indonesian National Revolution in 1945, marking the end of three centuries of Dutch colonial rule. Well-paved main roads make it easy to get around the island, whether you opt to rent a motorbike or take private or public transport. Thankfully, traffic is seldom a gripe in Lombok, compared to the often choked streets of southern Bali.

JORGE/DIRKKEN/CC BY-SA 3.0/WIKIMEDIA COMMONS ©

THE MAIN AREAS

Above: Hiking Gunung Rinjani (p246); Left: Masjid Kuno Bayan Beleq (p244)

Find Your Way

Lombok's 4739 sq km encompass a variety of terrain: mountains, seaside cliffs, tobacco and rice fields, plus shimmering shoreline in all directions. When hopping from one destination to the next, expect the journey to last between 1 and 3 hours.

CAR

Private car rides start at around 200,000Rp for a 30-minute ride, such as from **Lombok International Airport** (p242) to Kuta. Car rentals start at around 400,000Rp per day.

SCOOTER

Scooter rentals start at around 80,000Rp per day. Longer rentals often have cheaper rates. You can hop on a bemo (minibus) for a fraction of the price.

Senaru, p243

Gear up for Gunung Rinjani trekking, swim in a waterfall, and learn about traditional Sasak practices in this nature-shrouded town.

Senggigi, p237

Lombok's original resort town is quieter these days, but the palm-fringed beaches along the entire western coast maintain their allure.

Southwestern Peninsula & The Secret Gilis, p249

Far from any noise, Lombok's Southwestern Peninsula is a prime pick when it comes to surfing, snorkelling and diving.

Mataram, p240

The island's biggest (and really, only) city is an amalgam of traditional Indonesian culture, with both Balinese Hindu and Muslim influences.

Kuta, p230

This fast-growing town is popular among travellers and expats, just a half hour's drive from some of Lombok's most loved beaches.

Rice fields, Tetebatu (p234)

Plan Your Time

You can meander Lombok's finest beaches in a weekend, but the island is not one to be underestimated. It's easy to spend an entire week (or longer) checking out all the best spots.

One-Week Sampler

With one week, you can experience the duality of Lombok's stunning coastlines and impressive mountainous region. Using **Kuta** (p230) as your base for the first four days, you can surf, swim and snorkel the surrounding beaches – including the **Southwestern Peninsula** (p249) if you're feeling adventurous. Head up to the mountains for **Gunung Rinjani** (p246) and the **Sembalun Valley** (p245) when you're ready for something different.

The Big Loop

Bask in the satisfaction of completing a giant loop in two weeks. Start by travelling from **Senggigi** (p237) to **Mataram** (p240), the capital city. Base up in **Kuta** (p230) for several days to explore the beaches and the **Southwestern Peninsula** (p249). Spend your remaining time taking in the beauty of the rice fields in **Tetebatu** (p234) and the lofty heights of **Gunung Rinjani** (p246) before concluding in **Senaru** (p243).

SEASONAL HIGHLIGHTS

JANUARY–MARCH

Bring a raincoat and don't plan treks. Gunung Rinjani is closed January to March. Ramadan begins early March.

APRIL–JUNE

The occasional shower lingers. High season begins late June, and trekking starts up again as the seasons shift.

JULY–SEPTEMBER

Dry season begins. The land is considerably less green, but dazzling against the ocean nonetheless.

OCTOBER–DECEMBER

There's still plenty of sun in October. Be aware of downpours mid-November to December.

Kuta

STUNNING BEACHES | FAMOUS SURF | CAFES & SHOPS

GETTING AROUND

Kuta itself is walkable. It takes 15 minutes to stroll the main strip, Jl Raya Kuta. The main streets have footpaths. As the best natural sights are just outside of Kuta, it makes sense to rent a car or scooter for the duration of your stay. If you don't drive, you'll have no trouble finding a driver – signs with ride rates for frequented destinations can be found around town, or arranged with most accommodations. The coast makes for a beautiful journey.

☑TOP TIP

Since Kuta is a popular weekend getaway, accommodations can get booked up on the weekend. If swinging by Friday to Sunday, consider booking in advance if you want the full gamut of places to choose from, especially during July and August.

Fast-growing and increasingly popular, Lombok's Kuta is often confused with Bali's Kuta, despite vast differences. With close proximity to many of Lombok's most acclaimed beaches, Kuta has become a hotspot for surfers and beachgoers. The most fantastic sandy stretches are within just a half hour's drive of the town's centre. Development has boomed in recent years, from the large-scale Mandalika resort area to the outcrop of trendy restaurants catered towards visitors. Regardless of the seemingly constant stream of new business, crowds and traffic aren't really a thing here.

You'll see surf shops up and down the town's main streets, with Jl Raya Kuta running from north to south, and Jl Mawun running west to east. While there's no shortage of places to grab a beer on an evening out, the nightlife is far more relaxed here – with most people waking up early to head out for explorations rather than partying the night away.

Get the Lay of the Land

Swims and sunsets

Drive 20 minutes to the east of Kuta to **Tanjung Aan**: a horseshoe-shaped bay that definitely deserves to be your first beach experience in Lombok. Set up shop for the afternoon, grab a coconut and say hello to our friends at **Warung Turtle Resto Cafe**.

When the sun starts to hang low in the sky, hop a few minutes over to **Bukit Merese**: a hill just above Tanjung Aan, locally known for being one of the best places to watch the sunset. Roughly a 15-minute ride from the centre of Kuta, it's a prime spot for views of the south coast in both directions, giving you a taste of what to expect as you plan adventures to more far-flung beaches. You'll have to pay 10,000Rp to enter before you can park and walk to the top of the hill and those 360-degree views. Expect a crowd before sundown, though you'll have plenty of open space to roam.

Kuta

KUTA

Jalan Raya Kuta

Jalan Mawun

Jalan Mawun

0   200 m
0   0.1 miles

INDIAN OCEAN

Batuputih

Tanjung Aan

Gili Anakjina

Benjon

See Kuta

Pantai Kuta

Laut Lombok

Tanjung Tampa Nahera Recreation Park

Dandang

Gili Nusa

Pengengat

Tanakbeak

Makamnyato

Sengkol

Pendungendo

Rembitan

Silak

Ngolang

Kambalmuluh

Lengser

Sade Sasak Village

Pengembur

Pengebit

Prabu

Tumpak

Gua

Lombok

Tele

Bongak

Sungai Berdun

Embung

Mekar Sari

Teluk Mawan

Tanjung Tampa Nature Recreation Park

Pantai Mawi

0   2 km
0   1 miles

BAU NYALE FESTIVAL

Once a year in February, people flock to the shoreline of **Pantai Seger**, right by the newly built Pertamina Mandalika International Circuit (a racetrack) with a unique quest: capturing *nyale*, a surprisingly colourful species of sea worm. Crowds and ceremonies fill the area as part of the **Bau Nyale Festival** – an age-old tradition that is believed to bring good fortune.

These are regarded as no ordinary worms – the colourful, yarn-like sea creatures are thought to bring prosperity to those who catch them. The exact date depends on the year, but expect crowds if you happen to be in town for the festival. During the other 364 days of the year, Pantai Seger is frequented by swimmers, sunbathers and surfers.

Explore Sun-soaked Beaches

Revel in the turquoise coastline

The word *pantai* means beach, and you'll find a lot of them around here. For starters, the logical first pick is **Pantai Kuta**. You'll likely notice the giant Mandalika sign before your toes hit the sand, as the area has been rapidly developed in the last few years. This bay-shaped stretch of sand is gorgeous, but you'd be remiss to visit Kuta without checking out other nearby spots that are the pinnacle of tranquility. You can essentially hop from one glittering bay to another half-moon shaped cove all the way down the south coast – plenty of the coastline's magic lies beyond Kuta.

Drive 20 minutes from Kuta's center to **Pantai Mawun**, a small cove flanked by rolling hills. Apart from a few beachside warungs (food stalls) with sunbeds and coconuts, there's not much else here, and that's what makes it lovely. Venture seven minutes further west to **Pantai Lancing**, a lengthy strip of white sand backed by grasslands, most frequented by doting groups of cattle. These westward roads have been gorgeously paved, presumably in anticipation for more developments, but the area remains rustic and fairly sparse.

Surfing for all Skill Levels

Surf solo or learn from experts

Whether you're a seasoned pro or hopping on a board for the first time, there are plenty of surf spots to accommodate all skill levels. Kuta is a year-round surfing destination, with consistent swell and a variety of different breaks. You'll find it less crowded during the rainy season (roughly from November through March).

The waves at **Pantai Seger** are suitable for all levels, with both lefts and rights. East of Kuta, surf schools dot the shorelines of Tanjung Aan (p230). West of Kuta lays **Pantai Mawi** (not to be confused with Mawun), one of Kuta's most famous surf spots, with strong currents suited for intermediate and advanced surfers. Beware of the semi-treacherous 10-minute ride leading to the beach with its many potholes and loose rocks. The end views are worth it.

 EATING IN KUTA: OUR PICKS ─────────────────────── MAP p231

Bush Radio Industrial-chic cafe on the main intersection with great coffee, healthy juice, plus burgers, wraps, salads and pizza. $

Terra Fully vegan and gluten-free restaurant with a focus on wellness. The healthy desserts are worth a visit. $$

El Bazar Shared plates and Mediterranean fare in a gorgeous setting that feels perfect for a dressier dinner or date night. $$

Herry Warung Indonesian favourites on a quieter road, including all the nasi (rice) and *mie* (noodles) classics, plus soups and curries. $

Beyond Kuta

Outside of Kuta lie sleepy fishing towns, empty white-sand beaches, rice fields with mountain views and plenty of traditional Sasak culture.

It's easy to get into the swing of life in Kuta, but venturing further along Lombok's southern coast and up north into the foothills of Gunung Rinjani offers wow-worthy scenery and a true escape from it all. West of Kuta, developments dwindle, whereas the twinkling ocean's glow only seems to strengthen. In Lombok's remote southeastern corner, the rugged landscape replete with seaside cliffs remains silent, apart from the occasional small-town hum. Drive an hour and a half north of Kuta to Tetebatu, a charming Sasak village, and you'll be immersed in a verdant landscape of rice and tobacco fields. Waterfalls, cultural experiences and fantastic Indonesian food make the decision to visit Tetebatu a no-brainer – this town is worth adding to your list.

Places

GETTING AROUND

The main east and west roads along Lombok's southern coast are well-paved. When heading westbound, expect steep hills and sharper turns – the area is hilly. Previous riding experience is advised for those who plan to take a scooter. Northbound towards the mountains, the land is fairly flat. You'll find plenty of amenities along the way, such as minimarts and larger gas stations. Arranging transportation with a driver is generally quick and easy.

Selong Belanak
TIME FROM KUTA: **30 MINS**
Surf and swim in clear waters

The picture-perfect bay of **Selong Belanak** is one of the most talked about beaches of the coast, drawing both locals and visitors to its powdery, lengthy shoreline. Upon arrival, expect to pay around 10,000Rp for parking before a narrow sandy path takes you through a gap in between two beach warungs. The view becomes panoramic – an elongated beach-front framed by rolling hills on either side. It's certainly not an empty beach, but there's plenty of room to spread out – especially at low tide. Take a stroll, grab a fresh coconut or go for a surf – it's a popular spot for beginners. You can post up with your own beach towel, or opt for a lounge chair in front of one of the warungs, so long as you make a purchase while you sunbathe. Come around 5pm, and you might see the local farmers herding their water buffalo after they've grazed in the nearby fields. It's quite a sight.

Gerupuk
TIME FROM KUTA: **20 MINS**
Surf the breaks near a traditional fishing village

The coastal fishing village of **Gerupuk** is frequented by surf-ers and overlooks a bay with five different surf breaks that can only be accessed by boat. The area remains considerably

PACKING FOR DAY TRIPS

Some things can be harder to come by once you leave Kuta, like ATMs and sunscreen. Whether you're packing for an all-day excursion to the **Southwestern Peninsula** (p249) or going to a beach 30 minutes away, packing your day bag accordingly can save some headache (or rather, heatstroke) down the line.

Most of the further beaches have plenty of small beachside warungs, but keeping a water bottle handy, plus some cash and sunscreen, is advantageous. When in smaller towns, cash payments are the norm – and that includes getting gas for your scooter everywhere you go.

CHRISTOPHER MOSWITZER/SHUTTERSTOCK ©

Rice fields, Tetebatu

untouched by foreign influence, with just a few fishing boats lining the shore and a handful of small surf shops, homestays and warungs. If arriving from Kuta, you'll pass through the massive Mandalika development's shiny new gate on the way to Gerupuk, though the contrast between the two areas remains stark. Stop by for a quick surf and a roam through the area. Either bring your own board, or rent from a nearby surf shop, such as **Rasta Surfshop & Surfschool** or **Insider Surf**.

Tetebatu

TIME FROM KUTA: **1 HR 20 MINS**

Learn about Sasak culture in a beautiful setting

Backed by a postcard-like view of Gunung Rinjani (p246), the small village of **Tetebatu** exemplifies traditional Sasak charm. Here, bright-green rice and tobacco fields form most of the landscape, and the air has a lovely lightness to it, thanks to nearby mountain mist and slightly lower temperatures. Several *air tejun* (waterfalls) gushing spring water and flowing over eroded volcanic rock formations are found around the area. In the heart of town, **Tetebatu Waterfall** is most frequently visited.

 ### EATING IN TETEBATU: LOCAL DISHES

Pondok Tetebatu Resto & Bar Excellent array of classic Indonesian plates with a Sasak lens, plus rice-field views. $

Zaeni Warung Family-run favourite offering Indonesian plates, including rice, noodles and curries, along with plenty of fresh juices. $

Oktavia Warung Sasak dishes such as *urap-urap* (vegetables with coconut) and a long list of chicken plates. $

Aqila Warung Delicious Indonesian eats in a restaurant that also offers cooking classes and local tours. $

Here, traditional architecture is neighboured by tropical flowers of all shades, and the palm-fringed streets have never seen traffic. You'll find homestays and restaurants catered towards tourists, but the overwhelming majority of businesses are locally owned – making it a much more authentic experience compared to more completely gentrified areas. Apart from cruising the serene streets of Tetebatu via scooter, the best way to explore the area is by **walking tour**. Most homestays can connect you with a local guide, often including experiences such as Lombok coffee production, spice markets and the Sasak arts, including weaving and pottery: stop by Aqila Warung (p234) to book some local-led tours of the area and cooking classes, and while you're there, enjoy a traditional meal.

You can easily take a day trip out to Tetebatu since it's only a short drive from Kuta, but it's also a great place to wake up in the morning. If you have extra time on your hands, spending a night or two in the area can be a deeply relaxing experience – especially if you're either preparing for or resting after a mountain trek up Rinjani.

Ekas
TIME FROM KUTA: **1 HR 10 MINS**

Unspoiled beach and surf along a tranquil bay

Yet another surfer's paradise on southern Lombok's broad coast, the small seaside village of **Ekas** is contrastingly tiny in comparison to the massive **Awang Bay** on its doorstep. Surfers of all skill levels ride out here year-round for two well-loved waves – **Ekas Outside** and **Ekas Inside**. If you're keen on sticking around for a night or two (or even longer), **Ekas Surf Resort** (p252) has affordably priced rooms and a surf boat to get you out to the breaks.

There's plenty of beautifully mindless lazing under the sun to be had, too. **Ekas Beach** is decorated with fishing boats and tons of open space. Drive just a few minutes south to discover its surrounding area, adorned with spectacular shorelines, some of which are bordered by towering cliffs. **Paradise Beach** and **Pantai Kura Kura** are more remote picks nearby, where you won't hear too much beyond the waves.

Sekaroh
TIME FROM KUTA: **1 HR 30 MINS**

Stroll on pink beaches in a remote area

Lombok's southeasternmost corner, **Sekaroh**, might very well be the definition of 'out there'. The coastline here is where it's at, with naturally pink beaches along the northern shores of the region. A quick Google search reveals several images with dramatically boosted saturation, but it's true: the sand really *is* a light shade of pink. This phenomenon occurs thanks to the delightful mixture of red reef particles and white sand. You'll see several 'Pink Beach' markers on the map near **Tanjung Sabui**, some of which have irked reviewers expressing ire over discrepancies from the internet's dubious imagery. Expect company and likely an entrance fee.

THE SASAK TRADITION OF STICK FIGHTING

Stick fighting, a martial art of the Sasak people in Lombok, is a local tradition. Two fighters armed with rattan sticks and a leather shield face off in front of a crowd while traditional music plays. The performance is carried out to ask for rain, as the Sasaks believe that bloodshed from stick fighting results in better rainfall for the season ahead.

Stick fighting happens all over Lombok and also on the Gilis, typically in a centrally located area of the village with enough space for onlookers to view the showdown. The fighting usually starts in July and lasts up until the rain arrives – typically in November or December. Ask your homestay or local guide about stick-fighting events.

DIVING & SNORKELLING TIPS

You can slap on some flippers and a mask at any beach that you please, but some of the best marine life experiences are further afield. The lesser-visited **Southwestern Gilis** (p250) – Gili Gede, Gili Asahan and Gili Layar – are fairly sparse when it comes to human activity, yet are teeming with coral and marine life. From Kuta, it takes about 1.5 to 2 hours to ride up to Pelangan Harbour in Sekotong, where you can organise a private boat for around 400,000Rp.

Accommodations offer day-trip packages for snorkelling and diving, but be advised: you'll likely end up paying more than average if your hotel is a fancy one. Shop around a bit.

MKAZHI/SHUTTERSTOCK ©

Ekas Beach (p235)

While pink-ish sand can be an enticing lure – there are plenty more lesser-visited beaches along the south shore featuring pristine waters lapping on sand without a single footprint. Rocky outcroppings flank the shores of **Pantai Tanjung Bloam**, next to the gorgeous **Jeeva Beloam Beach Camp** – a rustic off-grid experience. Further south, **Pantai Antak-Antak's** staggering cliffs are heavenly. Make your way down to the thin strip of land that's home to **Pantai Lemerang**: this sweeping beach is remote as can be.

While Sekaroh is only 1 hour and 30 minutes from Kuta, don't underestimate the exhaustion that can come with smaller roads in remote areas, especially if you're on a scooter. Plan a day trip.

FOR MORE PINK SAND
If you want to be tickled pink, head to the (pink) sands of Pulau Padar in **Komodo National Park** (p282).

Senggigi

FANCY RESORTS | QUIET BEACHES | MOUNTAINOUS BACKDROP

Something out of a '90s holiday time capsule, Senggigi rose to fame decades ago as Lombok's premier tourist destination. The scenery is a treat: mountains, doused in junglescape, bordering the deep blue ocean. This combination is particularly spectacular when viewed from elevated areas on the main road, giving unparalleled views of the entire landscape for vast stretches. Groves of coconut palms provide generous shade close to the water, where people gather for sunset views overlooking Gunung Agung – Bali's mighty volcano – in the distance.

These days, Senggigi is quieter. Longstanding resorts remain on bays up and down the town's coastal stretch, some of which appear empty. There's a low hum of activity, but you're unlikely to encounter anywhere particularly busy – except on the weekends, when Senggigi sees a lot of domestic tourism. The waters are prime for snorkelling, and you can easily line up a day trip to the Gilis – so if you're looking for a quiet seaside spot, this might be the one for you.

Cruise to Pura Batu Bolong

A serene temple on the water

Not to be confused with the famed Batu Bolong of Canggu, **Pura Batu Bolong** is a Hindu temple perched on a rocky outcrop looking over the sea. Ornately crafted pagodas and statues stand tall above crashing waves, with small offerings placed around the grounds daily. There's a low hum of activity throughout the day, picking up around sunset when people gather to watch the sky turn hues of sherbet orange and pastel pink. Expect to pay around 5,000Rp for parking, plus a donation amount of your choice for entry to the grounds. Come prepared with covered legs, or rent a sarong on arrival. Getting to Pura Batu Bolong takes about 10 minutes via scooter or car from central Senggigi.

GETTING AROUND

Senggigi is essentially one main road along the coast with short offshoots leading inland and to the beach. The town spans roughly 10 km from north to south, but the central area is walkable. Some accommodations are closer to Mangsit on the northern end of Senggigi, where the touristy zone begins. The hotels and resorts are fairly spread out, so you may want to rent your own vehicle or save a taxi driver's number for daily outings – unless, of course, you plan to laze beachside.

☑ **TOP TIP**

Accommodation is spread out in Senggigi, so check before booking to see you'll be within walking distance of things. Many homestays, hotels and resorts are labeled 'Senggigi', but are actually several kilometres from the town's centre.

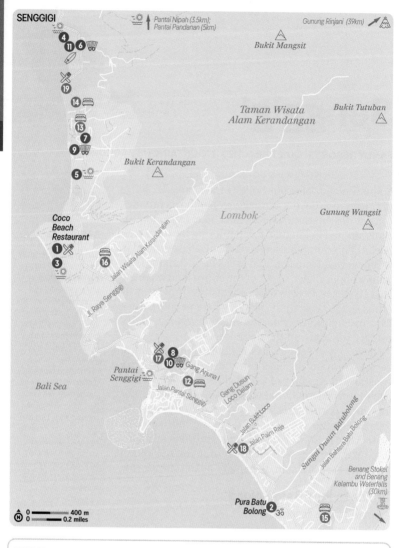

SENGGIGI

Pantai Nipah (3.5km);
Pantai Pandanan (5km)

Gunung Rinjani (39km)

Bukit Mangsit

Taman Wisata
Alam Kerandangan

Bukit Tutuban

Bukit Kerandangan

Lombok

Gunung Wangsit

Coco
Beach
Restaurant

Jalan Wisata Alam Kerandangan

JL Raya Senggigi

Pantai
Senggigi

Gang Arjuna I

Jalan Pantai Senggigi

Gang Dusun
Loco Dalam

Bali Sea

Jalan Bukit Loco

Jalan Palm Raja

Sungai Dusun Batubolong

Jalan Bahtera Batu Bolong

Benang Stokel
and Benang
Kelambu Waterfalls
(30km)

Pura Batu
Bolong

0 ——— 400 m
0 ——— 0.2 miles

HIGHLIGHTS
1 Coco Beach Restaurant
2 Pura Batu Bolong

SIGHTS
3 Coconut Beach
4 Pantai Klui
5 Pantai Senggigi

ACTIVITIES
6 Blue Marlin Dive Senggigi
7 DSM Dive
8 Lombok Scuba Dive Center
9 Scuba Froggy Senggigi
10 Sea & U Divernesia
11 Surf School Lombok Wave

SLEEPING
12 Central Inn Senggigi
13 Holiday Resort Lombok
14 Katamaran Resort
15 Makarma Resort Lombok
16 Sammy Cottage

EATING
17 Asmara Restaurant & Lounge
18 Cafe Alberto
19 The Kliff Bistro

Beach Hop around the Coast

Soak up Senggigi's laidback coastline

Walk far enough west anywhere in Senggigi, and you'll eventually hit the beach. Consider Jl Raya Senggigi your serpentine route to the surrounding region's best beaches – there's a lot more than what's within the town's limits. For starters, the aptly named **Pantai Senggigi** is the closest beach to the main tourist area, an elongated bay fit for swimming or just hanging out in the shade of a palm tree. Minutes south, **Coconut Beach** is accessible through dusty pathways that weave through a field of sky-high coconut palms. Both locals and tourists gather around the beachside **Coco Beach Restaurant** at sunset, sipping on Bintangs and fresh coconuts. The vibe is family-friendly, and you'll see groups of vacationers young and old kicking back.

For a more secluded experience, a short drive up the coast is a must. **Pantai Nipah** is a 20-minute drive from central Senggigi – a scenic route that'll have you doing double-takes at the wondrous views. This white-sand stretch is bordered by a quintessentially tropical palm-tree forest, and its shores are decorated with more beached fishing boats than tourists. Around the next bend a few minutes north, **Pantai Pandanan** is equally as quiet, commanding attention from anyone who catches a view of it. A few local vendors operate, selling snacks and drinks.

Hop on a Surfboard

Ride the waves with local experts

Most surfers flock to the southern coast of Lombok, but Senggigi has surf, too, and it's generally uncrowded. The reef break at **Pantai Klui** is suitable for beginners, and you can take lessons at **Surf School Lombok Wave**, located right on the beach. If you're already established when it comes to waves, rent a board from them and do your own thing. Sip on fresh coconuts in between lessons and stay for sunset to make a full day of it.

Wander Waterfalls Shrouded in the Jungle

Visit Benang Stokel and Benang Kelambu

Swim in crisp mountain waters tumbling down from a lush canopy of jungle vegetation. **Benang Stokel** and **Benang Kelambu** are nestled near the foothills of **Gunung Rinjani's** western side. You'll have to drive around 1 hour and 20 minutes from Senggigi, but it's worth a day trip – especially if you need a break from the muggy heat of the coastal air. Expect to pay around 90,000Rp per person for a guide– you're required to have one.

THE BEST SNORKELLING & SCUBA DIVING TRIPS

The following dive centres in Senggigi can help you arrange a great scuba diving or snorkelling adventure. Most snorkel and dive trips from Senggigi go to the Gili Islands (p255), so keep that in mind if they're already on your itinerary.

Sea & U Divernesia
All level dive courses and liveaboard boat trips.

Lombok Scuba Dive Center Snorkelling and diving trips, plus classes.

Blue Marlin Dive Senggigi
Long-standing dive centre with locations across Indonesia and the UK.

Scuba Froggy Senggigi PADI courses and accommodation, plus trips around the island.

DSM Dive Dive centre with courses from beginner to divemaster.

 EATING IN SENGGIGI: OUR PICKS

Coco Beach Restaurant	Asmara Restaurant & Lounge	Cafe Alberto	The Kliff Bistro
Chilled-out beachside joint with Indonesian food served in thatched-roof cabanas and on small tables in the sand. **$**	Both Indonesian and international cuisine in a leafy setting right in the centre of town. **$$**	Beachside restaurant plus bed and breakfast combo serving pizza, pasta, meat and seafood of various types. **$**	Mostly Italian spot located in the Katamaran Resort with great sunset views and a gorgeous setting. **$$**

Mataram

ISLAMIC CULTURE | SHOPPING & MARKETS | HINDU TEMPLES

GETTING AROUND

Once you get your bearings in Mataram, it's pretty easy to get around. Motorbikes are king here, although there are sidewalks for covering short distances. The roads are in good condition, and while there can be traffic, the wide lanes of the main avenues assuage the worst of it. Newbie motorbike riders may be intimidated by the broad streets – you should come prepared with riding experience if you're planning to ride anywhere in Indonesia.

☑ TOP TIP

Although Mataram is a coastal city, it's not really a beach destination. You can, however, check out the seaside in Ampenan and sample various local delights from the seaside vendors. Delicious scents of satay, grilled corn and *ikan bakar* (grilled fish) often fill the area.

Lombok's capital city feels like a big town – perhaps because it's the culmination of what was once several villages. Mataram has some unique experiences that provide context to the fabric of Lombok's culture, plus practical city amenities that aren't found in the island's smaller communities. Lively Indonesian markets, fascinating architecture and multi-denominational temples with centuries of history make this city rich in heritage. While the population is majorly Sasak Muslim, relics of Hindu culture are found throughout the city. Multistoried malls coexist with traditional markets on motorbike-filled avenues.

Ampenan, Mataram and Cakranegara – once villages that blended to form today's Mataram – still differentiate the city's areas. Ampenan borders the sea, and it's a port area with remnants of Dutch colonial architecture. Mataram both was and is the government centre, where you'll find administrative buildings and hotels. Cakranegara, the business district, spans the eastern side of the city. It's a commercial area with malls and shops.

Temples from Centuries Past

Explore Pura Meru and Pura Lingsar

A short 6km ride east of Mataram takes you to Lingsar, the village that's home to **Pura Lingsar**: a large temple complex regarded as Lombok's most holy. Dating back to 1714, this multi-denominational compound has temples for both Balinese Hindu and Wetu Telu – Lombok's distinct sect of Islamic beliefs. The earthy, deep-orange-hued structures are impressively crafted. Close to the heart of Mataram, **Pura Meru's** trio of tall, thatched *meru* (multi-roofed shrines in Balinese temples) can be seen on approach. Within the Hindu temple's grounds, 33 small shrines make up the interior. Come prepared with your own sarong to cover your lower body, or rent one on arrival.

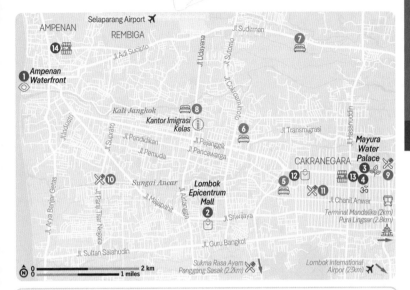

HIGHLIGHTS
1 Ampenan Waterfront
2 Lombok Epicentrum Mall
3 Mayura Water Palace

SIGHTS
4 Pura Meru

SLEEPING
5 Aston Inn Mataram
6 Dewi Sri Guesthouse
7 Lombok Astoria
8 Prime Park Hotel

EATING
9 Dapur Sayur Vegan Vegetarian Resto
10 Masterpiece of Coffee
11 Seafood and Grilled Fish 99

SHOPPING
12 Mataram Mall
13 Pasar Cakranegara
14 Pasar Kebon Roek

Stroll around Mayura Water Palace

A park in the heart of Mataram

Mayura Water Palace, also known simply as Mayura Park, is a walled-off open space in the heart of Mataram that dates back to 1744. With a temple and rectangular-shaped artificial lake, it's a good place to stretch your legs for a walk – and is contrastingly empty to the nearby busy streets. Once a royal complex of Balinese rulers in Lombok, the grounds provide a bit of insight into the island's complex political history. The Dutch and Balinese also battled here back in 1894 when the Dutch set up camp within the park's sturdy walls.

Nowadays, the lake is an interesting shade of olive green, with a walkway leading into its centre, replete with an ornate structure. It remains a site of pilgrimage for Lombok's Hindus. The parking area is on the western side of the park on Jl Purbasari – you'll likely be confused if you try to enter from any other side, as you'll be faced by walls.

VISA EXTENSIONS

You can extend your Indonesian visa in Mataram at **Kantor Imigrasi Kelas**, located in the centre at the intersection of Jl Udayana and Jl Mahoni. If you entered the country on a 30-day visa on arrival (VOA), you can extend it by 30 days (around 500,000Rp). It's five to seven days for the entire process, and a far less crowded experience than Bali's immigration offices. The phone number is +62 3706 32520.

LOMBOK'S BIGGEST BUS TERMINAL

Mataram's **Terminal Mandalika** is the biggest departure point in Lombok, only second to the airport. From here, you can get to transport points (ferry ports) for other islands such as Bali and Sumbawa, or get anywhere else within Lombok via bus or bemo. Many folks take the bus from here to **Lombok International Airport** in Praya, which takes around 45 minutes. If you're looking to save some Rupiah, it's a good way to go. If showing up in search of a ticket, be sure to purchase it at the official ticket counters inside the terminal. Anyone asking if you need a ride outside is unlikely to be affiliated with the actual bus companies.

Wander Ampenan's Historic Streets

Soak up the port-town vibe

Ampenan, the western district of Mataram, is an aging port town that was once used by Dutch colonisers. The port was used heavily for spice trade, and a roam around the area reveals countless weathered buildings with Dutch colonial architecture. Today, it's frequented by local foodies and families looking for fresh grilled seafood and other Indonesian plates. Local food vendors post up along **the waterfront** to neighbour established warungs and markets. **Pasar Kebon Roek**, a traditional market, has just about everything when it comes to groceries. From succulent tropical fruit, vegetables, meat and seafood to coffee and sweets – it's a grand selection. You won't find many tourists around here. Pro tip: go first thing in the morning before the heat of the day kicks in.

Get Some Shopping In

Mataram's shopping centres and markets

Whether you need warmer clothes to hit the mountains, a rogue item you forgot to pack, or you simply want to browse local handicrafts – Mataram is definitely *the* place in Lombok for shopping. **Lombok Epicentrum Mall** is the largest of the lot, with four floors of stores, plus a cinema and plenty of food options. A close second goes to **Mataram Mall**, less than 10 minutes east. Clothing, electronics, restaurants and a supermarket can all be found here with ease. As for traditional markets, they're scattered throughout Mataram and vary in size. **Pasar Cakranegara** is one of the more well-known markets, with items ranging from traditional batik fabrics (a classic Indonesian design) to household items and trinkets – authentic souvenirs, compared to more gentrified and touristy areas of Indonesia. If you're after a traditional food market with everything from fresh fruit and veggies to seafood and authentic Lombok coffee, head to Pasar Kebon Roek.

 EATING LOCAL FOOD IN MATARAM: OUR PICKS ──────── MAP p241

Sukma Rasa Ayam Panggang Sasak Traditional Sasak fare with a menu full of local delights in a comfortable setting outside the busy area. $	**Masterpiece of Coffee** Minimal yet cozy cafe with plenty of signature hot and cold drinks, top-rated coffee, and various breakfast foods and Indonesian dishes. $$	**Dapur Sayur Vegan Vegetarian Resto** A long menu of plant-based Indonesian eats, plus fresh juices, close to Mayura Park. $	**Seafood and Grilled Fish 99** A seemingly endless array of fresh-caught seafood smothered in a variety of different sauces. Arrive hungry. $

Senaru

RINJANI TREKKING | LUSH WATERFALLS | RICE TERRACES

Senaru is known for being the gateway to Gunung Rinjani: Indonesia's second-tallest volcano. While that in itself is a significant enough lure for most, the small village is also home to misty waterfalls, cultural riches and a labyrinth of lush rice fields. It's far from the buzz, providing a different experience than its coastal counterparts. Although the region faced significant damages with the 2018 earthquake, many homes and businesses have since been rebuilt. Cozy homestays, warungs and trekking organisers are once again abundant. A steady stream of trekking enthusiasts continues to fuel tourism in the area, but it remains untouched by mass commercialisation.

Even if you're not fixing for a multi-day trek up into some of Indonesia's highest territory, visiting the area is still worthwhile, especially if you're already making a round through the island. The land is lush, and the backdrop couldn't be better, all thanks to the mighty mountainscape that borders the village.

Surrender to Cascading Falls in the Forest

Discover thundering Sendang Gile and Tiu Kelep

Sendang Gile, a waterfall enveloped in a tropical thicket, isn't far off of Senaru's main road. This two-tiered fountain has impressive height with water roaring down atop black volcanic rock, and cool waters that are believed to have healing properties. Further down the same trail is the beautiful **Tiu Kelep**. This multi-stream *air tejun*, it has a wide curtain of smaller streams with a thundering cascade tumbling down the middle. The pools are too shallow for swimming, but the mist of the falls is enough to get you damp. Plus, you'll have to walk across a small river to get there.

It takes only a few minutes to drive from Senaru to the parking area for both falls. The walk in takes around 15 minutes to reach Sendang Gile and 40 minutes for Tiu Kelep. While you'll likely be asked about a tour upon arrival, you can easily walk the trail *sans* guide. Expect to pay an entry fee of around

GETTING AROUND

Senaru is a village, so most things are within walking distance. Exploring on foot is common – whether to organise a trek, grab a bite or take a stroll to one of the waterfalls. You can explore via motorbike and zip around the whole area in a matter of minutes. Some walks to the nature areas around town can take 30 minutes to 1 hour. Either way, the uncrowded streets make it easy to stroll compared to Lombok's busier towns.

☑ TOP TIP

Get to know the locals by staying at a homestay. The hospitality is warm, and most family-run accommodations can set you up with information on trekking, local guides and other up-to-date know-how. Many of the surrounding sights don't require a guide, but Gunung Rinjani (p246) does.

LOMBOK'S OLDEST MOSQUE

Denda Sukatniwati, trekking guide and founder of **Rinjani Women Adventure**, tells about Lombok's oldest mosque.

Bayan (the region around Senaru) is home to the oldest mosque in Lombok, **Masjid Kuno Bayan Beleq**. Islam in Lombok began here in the 14th century. Bayan first adopted Wetu Telu culture, combining Islam with the original Sasak religion. In the surrounding area, you can learn about culture, religion and traditional life, including weaving *sarung tenun* (traditional fabric).

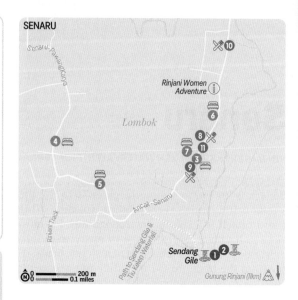

SENARU

Rinjani Women Adventure

Lombok

Sendang Gile

Path to Sendang Gile & Tiu Kelep Waterfall

Ancak-Senaru

Rinjani Track

Senaru-Pawang Karya

0   200 m
0   0.1 miles

Gunung Rinjani (11km)

20,000Rp. Since both falls are close to Senaru, it makes sense to see them both in one waterfall-filled trip.

A Tour Through Rinjani's Foothills

Stroll the Senaru Panorama Walk with Rinjani Women Adventure

Guided walking tours throughout Senaru and the foothills of Gunung Rinjani (p246) offer a deeper insight into the region's flora, fauna and local community traditions, including Sasak cooking and farming. **Rinjani Women Adventure** is a local woman-owned and operated trek and tour company that shows travellers around the area. Their **Senaru Panorama Walk**, led by local women, is a half-day excursion that meanders through small villages and rice terraces. You'll traverse irrigation channels bordered by bamboo groves, ending up at the oh-so-gorgeous waterfall nestled in the jungle, Sendang Gile (p243). Most, if not all, homestays in the area can also connect you with a local guide for tours around the area.

 EATING IN SENARU: OUR PICKS

Cafe Rifka Indonesian classics, plus Lombok-specific cuisine with vegetarian-friendly options, in the middle of town. $

Warung Poetri Delicious local eats at an unbeatable price, served in front of a sweeping jungle and waterfall view. $

Dragonfly Senaru Bar & Resto Rice, noodles and curries in a friendly little joint, often with live music, and always backed by beautiful views. $

Twin's Kitchen Rinjani A range of Indonesian favourites from chicken satay to *pisang goreng* (fried bananas), coupled with great hospitality. $

Beyond Senaru

When leaving Senaru, you're presented with two wildly different options: the wild northwest coast, or the vast mountains of the north and central region.

While there's an overwhelming amount of ground to cover (on foot, mostly) in Senaru, there is even more beyond it – most notably, Gunung Rinjani. Head south from Senaru for an evolving mountainous landscape dotted by valley towns and striking views of Indonesia's second-highest mountain. Serpentine roads loop through the varied terrain, with majestic views at countless turn-offs. Due north of Senaru lies the northwest coast of Lombok, a comparatively untravelled strip. Here, the main road snakes in and out of the ocean's view, passing numerous tranquil small towns. Further west in the Sire peninsula, a small handful of high-end, luxury resorts take up prime beachfront real estate. Apart from the honeymooner vibes, you won't find much else here.

Bukit Selong

TIME FROM SENARU: 1HR 🚗

Hike to gorgeous views from a small hill

A vibrant patchwork of varied shades of green makes the view from **Bukit Selong** unique, not to mention utterly photogenic. This viewpoint overlooks a vast stretch of fields, backed by a mountain to the east, and the town of Sembalun and Gunung Rinjani (p246) to the west. A small parking area leads to an unassuming dirt path, where you'll pay an entry fee of around 10,000Rp before continuing. Less than 10 minutes later, the uphill path leads you to the top. A wooden star-shaped platform beckons photo enthusiasts, but the attraction remains fairly quiet, despite being wildly Instagrammable. Note that Google Maps might lead you astray. Should you end up at what appears to be a dead end, ask someone to point you in the right direction – it's quite close to the map marker.

Sembalun Valley

TIME FROM SENARU: 1HR 🚗

A hillside hike to Pergasingan Hill

If Bukit Selong was the appetiser, consider **Pergasingan Hill** the main course. The ascent is often done at sunrise, leading to skyward views of the entire Sembalun Valley, plus the entirety of Gunung Rinjani (p246) in the distance.

Continues on 248

Places

GETTING AROUND

The mountain roads throughout the north and central region of Lombok are wonderfully paved – necessary for some of the steep inclines and sharp switchbacks that come with increasing elevation. If travelling with two people on one bike, beware of your collective weight against the strength of the bike on some of the steep inclines. Motorbikes with lower cubic capacity may struggle when overloaded on intense sections of the route. In contrast, the northwest coast is easy cruising.

PAT TR/SHUTTERSTOCK ©

Danau Segara Anak

Scan this QR code to book Rinjani treks and accommodation.

TOP EXPERIENCE

Gunung Rinjani

Indonesia's second-highest mountain (3726m) is both mighty and revered. Breathtaking Gunung Rinjani is sacred to the Sasak and Hindu people, and is a frequent pilgrimage site. The volcano's summit makes for a strenuous hike that isn't for the fainthearted, but the incredible views are among some of Indonesia's most lauded.

DON'T MISS

Mount Rinjani National Park

Danau Segara Anak

Senaru Crater Rim

Surya Sakti Waterfall

Rinjani Hot Springs

Mountainside Camping

Mount Rinjani National Park

The entirety of Mount Rinjani National Park spans some 413 sq km, including the greater radius of Gunung Rinjani itself. The volcano's elevation places it in a biogeographical crossroads, where the land differs from what is typical of Southeast Asian terrain, evolving into arid landscape instead. If you're not keen on lacing up your boots and hiking it, the foothills of Gunung Rinjani alone reveal a distinctly different and mesmerising ecosystem.

A Sacred & Cherished Landscape

Each year, the Balinese perform ceremonies atop Rinjani to honour the gods and spirits. It's one of three peaks they consider sacred, along with Gunung Bromo in Java and Gunung Agung in Bali. The Sasaks ascend the slopes to pray when the moon is full. Their faith, Wetu Telu, is a melange of Hindu and Islamic beliefs, as well as ancestral worship and animism.

Planning your Hike

Climbing Gunung Rinjani is not permitted from 1 January to 31 March. While that sounds like a big chunk of time, you don't want to climb it in bad or dangerous weather. If you're planning to hike, make sure your trip isn't during rainy season. April through November are typically favourable months. Finding a guide is quite easy, as tourism in the area accounts for a large part of the economy – you'll be able to join a trek fairly last-minute. Check out an independent trekking agency such as **Rudy Trekker** or ask a homestay; nearly all of them are well-connected with local guides.

The Hike

After departing from either Senaru (p243) or Sembalun (p245), trails ascend through rainforest teeming with wildlife. The route is challenging, but frequented by many people – plenty of whom aren't experienced hikers. That said, it's not exactly cruisey – this is a real trek.

The Crater Rim

Once the landscape shifts from lush to arid, the crater rim reveals a panoramic view of the skyline and summit. For less-experienced hikers, it's possible to hike for two days and one night to reach – and finish at – the crater rim.

The Summit

Loose rocks, soft ground and a steep gradient comprise the final grueling stretch to the summit. The topside views are nothing short of staggering, revealing the crater below and the landscape beyond. This prized peak takes a minimum of three days and two nights to reach, with the first night spent camping along the crater rim. Most hiking groups begin their second day before sunrise. Longer trips of three nights are also available.

Danau Segara Anak

Crescent-shaped and deeply blue, Danau Segara Anak is a volcanic lake west of Gunung Rinjani's attention-commanding massif, just below the crater rim. The word *danau* means 'lake', and *segara anak* is 'child of the sea' – alluding to the lake's similarities to the ocean.

Rinjani Hot Springs

If you decide to do the three-day, two-night hike, you can continue to the summit or head down from the crater rim to experience the natural hot springs beside Danau Segara Anak. It takes two hours to reach these natural pools – an airy downhill hike that floats through low-hanging clouds. The hot thermal waters flowing from Surya Sakti Waterfall make for a picturesque scene.

ALTERNATIVE ROUTES

Most treks begin from Senaru or Sembalun, but you can also start from Tetebatu (p234) on the southern slope. You'll meet far fewer hikers on the way up, and can reach the summit in two days. Flying in cuts travel time, as Tetebatu is just an hour away from **Lombok International Airport**.

TOP TIPS

- A local guide is required; don't try to hike without one.
- Read up on Senaru, Sembalun and Tetebatu to decide where you want to start from.
- Research trekking companies thoroughly before booking.
- Spend more time hiking the same distance if you're less experienced.
- Phone service is available in most of the park, but spotty inside the crater.
- Bring much warmer clothes than you think you'll need on a tropical island.
- Don't try to break in a brand-new pair of boots.
- Pack swimwear if you fancy a dip in the hot springs.
- There's not a lot of shade. Wear SPF like it's your job.

SEMBALUN'S SUNNY STRAWBERRIES

Sembalun Valley's mountainous climate is a perfect setting for growing strawberries: something local farmers have leveraged for sweet benefit. The rich volcanic soil and cooler temperatures mean that these juicy berries are all over the place, a source of income for the community, and a source of delight for anyone picking up a pack. You'll see farms dotted throughout the sprawling valley.

Contrary to what the Beatles might lead you to imagine, strawberry fields don't actually produce a sea of red colour. The ornate lines of these green plants are organised into rows, with most of the fruit hanging below. Whether you want to pick them yourself at a local farm or sample from a vendor, they're pretty much everywhere.

PAV-PRO PHOTOGRAPHY LTD/SHUTTERSTOCK ©

Hiking up Gunung Rinjani (p246)

Continued from p245.

It provides an impressive perspective of the landscape and can be done at a fairly steady pace in around two hours, depending on how much time you spend oohing and ahhing at the views on the way. While the soft morning light and mist make for an ethereal sight, it's also lovely at sunset. Entrance to the trailhead costs 50,000Rp. If you arrive before sunrise, expect to pay on your way back down.

Southwestern Peninsula & the Secret Gilis

SECLUDED ISLANDS | DESERTED BEACHES | LEGENDARY SURF

Rustic and mellow, Lombok's Southwestern Peninsula is full of deserted beaches, world-class surf and undisturbed local life – the type of place where passersby smile and wave at each other. The peninsula's one large road meanders along its northern shore, weaving through small villages. This ribbon-like route ascends in a circuitous nature over arid-looking hills, playing peek-a-boo with views of the aqua coastline.

While there are a handful of accommodations, ranging from chilled-out beachside bungalows to upmarket boutique hotels, most of them are offshore, on the Southwest Gilis. This series of blissfully low-key islands, often dubbed 'The Secret Gilis', remains something of a word-of-mouth phenomenon – the type of place you only hear about from locals or backpacking aficionados. They have slowly earned a reputation for their gorgeous waters and landscape. If Tom Hanks had washed up in Indonesia in *Castaway*, we're pretty sure he would've ended up on one of these secluded spots.

Explore a Tranquil Chain of Islands
Visit Gili Nanggu, Tangkong, Sudak and Kedis

While the Gili Islands (p255) have become a much-discussed experience of Southeast Asia's traveller trail, this tiny chain of partially inhabited islands epitomises off-grid at its finest. A bountiful array of marine life, including intricate corals and multi-hued fish of all sizes, surrounds each island's rim. **Gili Nanggu** – the westernmost island of the bunch, where most tours go – is known for the prime snorkelling spots. The neighbouring islands, **Gili Tangkong** and **Gili Sudak**, are also fantastic places to snorkel. **Gili Kedis** might be the tiniest island to actually make it on a map – a whimsical patch of sand emerging from the sea with only a scruff of vegetation.

GETTING AROUND

The main road of the Southwestern Peninsula, Jl Raya Sekotong, runs from Lembar to the westernmost point of Lombok, changing its name to Jl Raya Pelangan and Jl Raya Siung along the way. It's a smooth road, with hills and bends after Lembar. Further west, the road hugs the coast and flattens out. Smaller roads in the area are often dirt and gravel, which can be tricky – especially on approach to Desert Point. A few bemos run between Lembar and Pelangan.

☑ TOP TIP

There are some lodgings on the northern coast, but the Southwest Gilis – 10 minutes by boat – have the best beaches and lodgings. You could day-trip to the Southwestern Peninsula from Kuta, Senggigi or Mataram, but it's a 1- to 2-hour journey there and back.

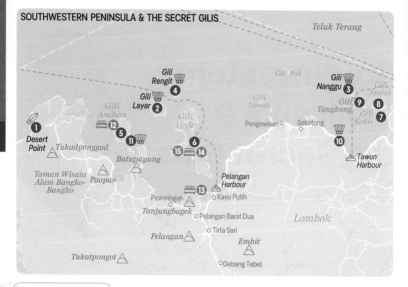

SOUTHWESTERN PENINSULA & THE SECRET GILIS

Teluk Terang

Gili Rengit 4

Gili Layar 2

Gili Asahan

Gili Gede

Gili Poh

Gili Lontar

Pengawisan   Sekotong

Gili Nanggu 3

Gili Sudak

Gili Tangkong 9   8

Gili Kedis 7

1 Desert Point   Tukadponggod   12   5   11   6   15   14

Taman Wisata Alam Bangko-Bangko   Paopao   Batupayung

Pewaringan   13   Pelangan Harbour

Kayu Putih

Tanjungbagek   Pelangan Barat Dua

Tirta Sari

Pelangan

Embit

Tukatpongot

Gebang Tebel

10   Tawun Harbour

Lombok

Many tours leaving from Kuta (p230) and labeled as 'The Secret Gilis' will take you around Gili Nanggu and its neighbours. If you're looking to venture onward to the Gilis out west (yes, there are even more – Gili Gede and its neighbours) then be sure to mention before booking. If you're already slowly roaming the Southwest Peninsula, you can organise a tour from either **Pelangan Harbour** (close to Gili Gede, Asahan, Layar, and Rengit) or **Tawun Harbour** (close to Gili Nanggu, Tangkong, Sudak and Kedis) where a few tour agencies operate. You'll also find some independent boatmen who offer their local expertise in the form of private tours. The price will depend on how many people you're with.

Snorkel in Paradise

The best of Gili Gede, Asahan, Layar and Rengit

Closer to Lombok's westernmost edge lies another collection of gorgeous isles, also referred to as the 'Secret Gilis'. **Gili Gede**, the largest of the bunch, is also the most developed. This interestingly shaped island is lined by white-sand beaches, only some of which appear to be touched by human influence. To the west, the beautiful **Gili Asahan** offers an undisturbed getaway with not much to do besides unwind on palm-shaded beaches. **Gili Layar** and **Gili Rengit** border some of the area's best off-shore snorkelling spots, where massive coral formations dominate the ocean's floor. It couldn't be more serene.

Even fewer travellers seem to make it out here, although there's a greater selection of salty beachfront stays and boutique hotels across the four quiet islands. The quintessential beach bungalows at **Yellow Coco Gili Gede** are the perfect, simple place to unplug and have a rustic digital detox. Those looking for a sumptuous 'treat yourself' type of experience will find it at **Bleu Mathis Gili Asahan** – where personal plunge pools overlook the serene shoreline. If you're coming to snorkel, gear is typically provided on tours or can be rented from your accommodation. It's definitely the go-to activity around here.

Surf the Tanjung Desert's Famous Waves

Desert Point's challenging surf

It's as far west as it gets on the Southwestern Peninsula: **Desert Point** is a famous break, albeit a temperamental one. Roughly a 15-minute drive from the fishing village of Bangko Bangko, this landscape is mostly desolate without much around (you know, besides arguably some of the world's best surf, but no big deal). Expect much better conditions during the dry season (from May to September), when offshore winds from the north create longer barrels. Even during this period, it can be an arduous waiting game when conditions suddenly go calm and leave everyone hanging for more.

Desert Point requires an advanced skill level when it comes to surfing and navigation. Getting here is a bit of a mission, but that's part of what makes it so special. While the main road along the coast (Jl Raya Siung) is in pretty good condition, once you turn off left at the fork in the road leading away from Bangko Bangko, it transforms into more of a treacherous dusty gravel path that can have even the most experienced motorbike drivers wincing over surprise potholes for 3km. So prepare for a proper road trip.

Gili Nanggu (p249)

CREATIVA IMAGES/SHUTTERSTOCK ©

THE PENINSULA'S BEST SNORKELLING & SCUBA DIVING OPERATORS

Many Kuta-based scuba and snorkelling trips head over to the Southwest Peninsula. You can also arrange trips with operators located closer to the Secret Gilis.

Scuba Froggy (Map p231) Dive courses, plus daily diving and snorkelling trips.

Blue Marlin Dive Kuta Lombok (Map p231) Dive classes and day trips to reefs.

Adventure Divers Kuta (Map p231) Diving and snorkelling excursions, plus PADI courses.

The High Dive Gili Gede Resort and PADI Scuba Dive Centre Beachfront villas on Gili Gede, combined with a dive centre.

Blow Bubbles Divers South Gilis Dive centre close to the Southwestern Gilis.

Oceanway Dive centre on Gili Asahan, with courses and accommodation.

Places We Love to Stay

$ Cheap $$ Moderate $$$ Pricey

THE GUIDE

PLACES WE LOVE TO STAY LOMBOK

Kuta   p230 (Map p231)

Kaniu Lombok Hostel $ Dorm beds with shared bathrooms, ample space to hang out by the pool and a social vibe.

Sikara Lombok $$ Modern rooms overlooking a spacious garden and pool deck, just off Kuta's main street.

Porter Lombok Hotel $$ Hillside boutique hotel with spacious rooms, a restaurant with a varied menu and a yoga shala.

Origin Lombok $$ Modern rooms with a serene feel just outside Kuta, close to the popular beach of Tanjung Aan.

LMBK Surf House $$ Centrally located surf-focused accommodation with both private and dorm rooms.

Rascals Kuta Lombok $$ Poolside cabanas, a bamboo yoga shala and well-decorated rooms in a centrally located adults-only hotel.

SIWA Resorts $$$ Clifftop resort with prime views of the south shore, impressive architecture and an upscale clubhouse-style restaurant.

Selong Belanak   p233

Singon Lombok Homestay $ Updated, modern rooms with mountain views, slightly inland from Selong Belanak beach.

Segara Lombok $$ Traditional bungalows beside a stunning beachfront pool, plus tasty food and a remarkably empty shoreline.

Amber Lombok $$ Contemporary beachside retreat with a lounge and restaurant, as well as suites, lofts and eco-friendly amenities.

Disini Lombok $$ Wooden surfaces with colourful accents in rooms perched on a hillside overlooking the sweeping shore of Selong Belanak.

Selong Selo Resort & Residences $$$ Remote hillside resort with chic and modern designs, overlooking nearby mountains and the sea.

Gerupuk   p233

Ombak Homestay $ Simple rooms near all of Gerupuk's beaches, with an upstairs restaurant; located on the town's main road.

Dome Lombok $$ nine uniquely designed dome-shaped structures in a lush setting, with healthy cuisine and hilltop views.

Roots Lombok $$$ Cheerful surf-camp-and-yoga-retreat combo with an emphasis on wellness during the week-long package stay.

Tetebatu   p234

Hakiki Bungalows & Café $ Rice-field views, basic rooms and ample space to unwind in a warm environment.

Mu Homestay $ Family-run homestay surrounded by greenery, with friendly hospitality, comfy rooms and a waterfall just up the road.

Pondok Tetebatu $ Welcoming staff and stellar Sasak eats in a guesthouse with a pool, surrounded by verdant rice fields.

Les Rizieres $$ Charming decor, views of Gunung Rinjani and a rice field as a backyard at this homestay with a cafe.

Ekas & Sekaroh   p235

Jeeva Beloam Beach Camp $$ A series of A-frame bungalows in a secluded and rustic setting, right on a private beach.

Ekas Surf Resort $$ Chilled-out surf accommodation with surf camps, kitesurfing and snorkelling for enthusiasts of all levels.

Innit Lombok $$$ Minimalist luxury on Ekas Bay with seven beach houses sat on a relatively undiscovered part of the south coast.

Senggigi   p237 (Map p238)

Sammy Cottage $ Friendly guesthouse with private rooms (breakfast included), in close proximity to Coconut Beach.

Makarma Resort $ Spacious and comfortable rooms with colourful details surrounding a pool, close to Senggigi's main area.

Central Inn $ Simple digs for good value close to Senggigi Beach and the largest supermarket in town.

Katamaran Resort $$ A glass infinity pool, private beach, and a wide gamut of wellness amenities in a classy beachside resort.

Holiday Resort Lombok $$ Longstanding beachside resort with poolside cabanas, lots of palm-tree shade, and a mountainous backdrop.

252

Mataram p240 (Map p241)

Dewi Sri Guesthouse $ Dorms and private rooms close to the heart of Mataram, with plenty of shared common space and a pool.

Prime Park Hotel $$ Upscale yet laidback hotel featuring a rooftop pool with city and mountain views, close to Mataram's centre.

Lombok Astoria $$ Large hotel with a traditionally fancy feel, featuring a rooftop garden, spa, lounge and restaurant.

ASTON Inn Mataram $$ Modern hotel part of a popular chain on Mataram's main road, close to Mataram Mall and Mayura Park.

Senaru p243 (Map p244)

Rinjani Lighthouse Cottages $ Eco-friendly guesthouse right in front of Gunung Rinjani National Park with an in-house coffee shop and bungalows amid a garden.

Dragonfly Senaru Lodge $ Volcano views, simple rooms and home-cooked meals in a guesthouse right by Senaru's waterfalls.

Tiu Kelep Homestay $ Basic rooms in a homestay with close proximity to waterfalls; helps with Gunung Rinjani trek-planning, and breakfast is included.

Rudy Trekker $ Eco-tours and guided trekking services in a guest house used as a base for trekking the lofty heights of Gunung Rinjani.

ILA Homestay $ Family-run homestay with home-cooked meals, basic rooms with small terraces and trek-planning support.

Sembalun Valley p245

Family Rinjani Bungalow $ A series of traditional bungalows with mountain views, just off the main road north of Sembalun Valley.

Bukit Tiga Lima Boutique Hotel $$ A-frame cabins right on the main road leading into the village of Sembalun, surrounded by mountain views.

Bobocabin Gunung Rinjani $$ Modern and minimalist tiny cabins with views of Gunung Rinjani and Pergasingan Hill.

Rautani Guesthouse $$ Spacious and updated cabins with small terraces and picturesque views in an open area near the foothills of Rinjani.

Southwestern Peninsula p249 (Map p250)

Yellow Coco Gili Gede $ Easygoing and unpretentious cabins with mosquito nets, on the beach facing mainland Lombok.

The High Dive Gili Gede Resort $$ Beachfront resort offering scuba diving and other water-sport activities, plus tours of the surrounding islands.

Palmyra Indah Bungalow $$ Quiet collection of bungalows with fans and mosquito nets, on the mainland facing Gili Gede.

Bleu Mathis Gili Asahan $$$ Remote and idyllic boutique resort at the end of the only road on Gili Asahan.

Segara Lombok

Above: Gili Air (p264); Right: *cidomo* (horse-drawn cart), Gili Trawangan

Gili Islands

CRYSTAL-CLEAR WATERS AND LAIDBACK LIVING

You'll have to zoom in on the map to find the Gilis, but this tiny archipelago is anything but small when it comes to nature and activities.

Reminiscent of somebody's tropical desktop wallpaper, the Gili Islands are a trio of paradise-like islands stocked with low-hanging palms and crystal-clear waters. While the outer perimeter of each island is replete with tourist-catered offerings, a quick walk down the dusty inland roads leads to traditional Sasak living. There's plenty to do onshore, but a top draw of the Gilis is the surrounding marine life, where sea turtles and colourful fish twirl around the reefs.

The only wheels on the Gilis belong to bicycles and *cidomo* (horse-drawn carts); motorbikes and cars are not allowed. While Gili Trawangan has earned a reputation for having quite the social scene, it can be thought of as a 'choose your own adventure' novel – where each page leads to something completely different. Despite the heaving parties, it's easy to slink away into the background, which, typically, includes panoramic views of both Lombok and Bali off in the distance.

Gili Meno, the middle island, remains the quietest of the three, maintaining plenty of local character and tradition. To the east, Gili Air feels like a fusion of the two – a place where you can grab a beer somewhere with a vibe, or bliss out in silence with a coconut. It's tricky to advise visiting one Gili over the other when each brings its own distinctly unique personality – far better is to see for yourself and sample each of them.

AKARAT PHASURA/SHUTTERSTOCK ©

THE MAIN AREAS

GILI TRAWANGAN	GILI MENO	GILI AIR
All-night parties and ample hangout spots.	Tranquil escape with traditional charm.	Yoga, wellness and laidback living.
p258	**p261**	**p264**

Find Your Way

A mere 15 sq km makes the collective landmass of the Gilis comparatively petite to others. But factor in surrounding turquoise waters, with a generous handful of top-notch dive and snorkel spots, and that size goes way up.

WALK

For zero dollars, the perimeter of Gili Trawangan can be walked in less than two hours – even less for Gili Meno and Gili Air. The topography of the land is flat, and you'll see people walking everywhere.

CYCLE

At the time of research, the price of 50,000Rp for a daily bicycle rental was the standard. Some may offer half-day prices at a slight discount. Expect to dodge a few carts on the way.

Gili Trawangan, p258
Where partygoers and marine enthusiasts converge, the biggest Gili island has a little bit of everything (and then some).

Gili Meno, p261
A sprinkling of larger resort developments has recently arrived, but Gili Meno remains both tranquil and traditional – a real escape.

Gili Air, p264
Neighbouring Lombok, Gili Air has a cheerful mixture of happening hangouts and quiet hideaways that take pride over their sunset views.

Gili Trawangan
Gili Meno
Gili Air
Selat Lombok
Salt Lake
West Coast
Boat Landing
Night Market
Jetty

Gili Trawangan (p258)

Plan Your Time

Zip through the Gilis like a true island-hopper, or turn down the velocity and revel in the laid-back way of living for an extended stay. For either option, start with a swim.

Three-Day Getaway

Public and private boat services make it easy to hop between the islands. Arrive at the main port on Gili Trawangan and plan a **snorkelling or scuba trip** (p259) to visit underwater sculptures, such as **Nest** (p261). Hit up the island's famous nightlife, then recover beachside. Spend the last day relaxing on Gili Air, where sipping a coconut on the beach is your only goal. Hit up **Island View Bar & Bungalow** (p266) for prime sunset views.

Week-Long Escape

Spend three days on Gili Trawangan, **diving or snorkelling** (p259) by day and sampling the **nightlife** (p258) after sundown. Next, spend two days recharging on quieter Gili Meno, where you can don some flippers to **snorkel** (p261) with the marine life. Conclude your trip with two supremely relaxing days on Gili Air, soaking up the good vibes at the many **beach hangouts** (p265) after some well-earned **yoga and wellness** (p266) activities.

SEASONAL HIGHLIGHTS

JANUARY–MARCH
It's rainy season. Nyepi, a Balinese holiday in March, causes many tourists to flock to the Gilis, where businesses remain open.

APRIL–JUNE
Right before high season, the waters are less crowded for scuba diving and snorkelling. Rainfall diminishes as the seasons shuffle.

JULY–SEPTEMBER
Dry season grants consistent sunshine. Tourism is bustling in July and August and only begins to slow by September.

OCTOBER–DECEMBER
The visitor count is up. Rainy season is looming, though. You can expect showers to start mid-November.

Gili Trawangan

SUN & SAND | WILD PARTIES | GREAT DIVING

GETTING AROUND

A ban on motorised vehicles is one of the Gilis' many awesome things. Explore on foot or rent a bicycle – the entire island is walkable and mostly flat, apart from a modest hill to the southwest. The *cidomo* operate like taxis, but we can't recommend them due to concerns over how the horses are treated. Local organisations such as Horses of Gili (horsesofgili.com) provide supplies and support to the horses through veterinary care and education, but there's still a ways to go.

☑️**TOP TIP**

Ramadan, the Muslim fasting month, takes place from March into April. This brings a quieter Gili T, with music being turned off early at bars and restaurants. You won't find any big parties during this time.

Arriving at Gili Trawangan's port, you might wonder what you've let yourself in for, with crowds of people waiting to get on the boat you just got off of. The main strip has a unique pace: bicyclists and *cidomo* (horse-drawn carts) share a dusty lane with meandering pedestrians. The first few minutes afoot Gili Trawangan might feel less than tranquil, but venture beyond the beachfront bars and hotels to an easy-going, beautiful coastline. Affectionately called 'Gili T', this island exudes friendliness and couldn't be more laid back if it tried. Coastal views of Lombok's rugged shoreline and Bali's towering Gunung Agung in the distance are simply *chef's kiss*.

If you're looking for a great party, you'll find it here. But it's also easy to escape the noise. Roam the criss-crossed pathways of the island's centre over to the west coast, where serene sands remain between looming developments. Inland, the call to prayer echoes five times a day.

Join in the Famous Party Scene

Hit the nightlife 'til sunrise

Whether you throw back a questionable volume of Bintangs with your toes in the sand or join a full-on pub crawl, Gili T's nightlife accommodates. Known for getting rowdy, Trawangan's social scene ranges from beachfront shacks to fancy resort bars and worn-in backpacker staples. **Casa Vintage**, a beachside bar and restaurant that gets buzzy, is popular for sunset libations. **Lava Bar** always draws a crowd with cheap drinks and Friday bingo. Mid-week festivities are a staple at **Tír na nÓg**, an Irish sports bar with a particular knack for throwing Wednesday bangers. Reggae music colours the scene at **Sama Sama**, a two-story reggae bar full of both locals and travellers basically every night of the week – especially Saturdays.

HIGHLIGHTS
1 Gili Trawangan Sunset Beach
2 Sama Sama Reggae Bar
3 Tír na nÓg

SIGHTS
4 Gili Trawangan Beach

ACTIVITIES
5 Blue Marlin Dive
6 Compass Divers

7 DPM Diving Gili Trawangan
8 Manta Dive
9 Shark Point
10 Trawangan Stingray Divers

SLEEPING
11 Atlas Gili Trawangan
12 Coco Cabana
13 Gili Smile Bungalows

14 Gili Teak Resort
15 Kuno Villas
16 Mad Monkey Hostel
17 Pearl of Trawangan
18 PinkCoco Gili Trawangan
19 Pondok Santi

EATING
20 Casa Vintage Beach
21 Hellocapitano Lifestyle Café
22 Jali Kitchen

23 Kayu Cafe
24 Pearl Beach Lounge
25 Regina Pizzeria
26 Samadhi Living
27 Warung Dewi
28 Warung Jaman Now

DRINKING & NIGHTLIFE
29 Lava Bar

Discover the Quieter Side of Gili T
Quiet snorkelling
Primo spots to swim and snorkel are found in droves throughout the island's quieter areas: the south, north and entire west coast. Seeing as the shoreline spans the entire perimeter, picking a specific beach isn't entirely necessary – but **Gili Trawangan Sunset Beach** lives up to its namesake, with sundowner views and lots of open space. Keep heading north for **Gili Trawangan Beach**, a long stretch of quiet sand with

GILI T'S BEST DIVING SCHOOLS

Learn from the pros at some of Gili T's most popular diving schools.

Blue Marlin Dive
The Gili T branch of a popular diving school. They're in Senggigi and Kuta, too.

DPM Diving Gili Trawangan Scuba courses and day trips for beginners and advanced divers, located steps from the east shore.

Manta Dive Dive centre and resort combo with training facilities on both Gili T and Gili Air.

Compass Divers Dive courses and accommodation, with both private and hostel dorm rooms, just steps from Gili T's ferry port.

Trawangan Stingray Divers Courses ranging from beginner to divemaster in the northeast corner of the island.

Green sea turtle

much less activity than the busy eastern coast. That said, you're not going to have a hard time finding a good place to swim around here. Do check the tides; swimming at high tide is better when the rocky coral formations are submerged.

Scuba Dive the Gilis

Discover a wealth of marine life

Roughly 25 different dive sites are located in the Gilis' greater Marine Protected Area. Tiny creatures – pygmy seahorses, mantis shrimp, pipefish – flutter about the corals. There are also plenty of large species, including whitetip and blacktip sharks. The dive sites are all over the Gili map. **Shark Point** lies west of Gili T, living up to its moniker, with sharks (and turtles) gliding around. **Turtle Heaven** is another aptly named, turtle-filled site on the east side of Meno. **Manta Point** (also referred to as Sunset Reef) is just south of Gili T, replete with mantas and plenty of smaller fish flitting between the corals. Experienced divers can venture down 45m to the **Japanese Wreck**, a shipwreck of a Japanese patrol boat off the southern coast of Gili Air.

 EATING ON GILI T: OUR PICKS ——————————————— MAP p259

Jali Kitchen Asian-fusion cuisine with Indonesian-, Thai- and Vietnamese-influenced plates, all served in a leafy setting. $$

Warung Jaman Now Indonesian fare, plus burgers, pasta and smoothie bowls, dished-up in super chilled-out surroundings. $

Kayu Cafe Healthy plates with fresh ingredients, plus a full menu of quality coffee and tea, right beside the ferry terminal. $$

Warung Dewi A classic Indonesian warung with all the favourites, such as flavour-packed curries and *nasi campur* (rice with side dishes). $

Samadhi Living Cheerfully decorated vegetarian and vegan eats located slightly inland from the main strip. $

Regina Pizzeria A top-rated staple for Italian cuisine, often crowded during the evening but well worth the wait. $$

Pearl Beach Lounge A mix of Indonesian and Western cuisine served under a massive, undulating bamboo roof. $$

Hellocapitano Lifestyle Café This bright beachside cafe serves juice and smoothies, plus plenty of Indonesian and Western plates. $

Gili Meno

PEACE & QUIET | SASAK CULTURE | SNORKELLING SPOTS

Stunningly calm and undisturbed, little Gili Meno is by far the most chill of the trio. If you're after a true escape, you'll find it here. This tiny oval-shaped island is also the most traditional of the three Gilis, where the lovely hum of local Sasak life continues on without as much tourist-catered development. Meno has all the same natural delights as the others: alabaster sand in all directions, and translucent water that glows aqua under the sun's strong rays. The small port lies on the eastern coast, where a handful of low-key accommodations and places to grab a bite dot the sand. On the west coast, a few glitzy stays change up the vibe, luring honeymooners and luxury lovers to revel in stylish solitude. Inland, coconut groves give shade to traditional Sasak homes. There's a big old saltwater lake adorned with mangroves, too – and you might just have its boardwalk all to yourself.

Snorkel around the Gilis
Underwater sculptures and intricate corals

Most snorkelling excursions sample spots across all three Gilis. You have two options: join a snorkelling trip, or rent the gear on your own. Snorkelling can be enjoyed from any Gili beach, but some of the best spots are off the northern and western coasts of Meno. Off Meno's west coast lays **Nest**: an underwater sculpture made Instagram-famous by photography-loving visitors on their snorkel sojourns. Sculpted from environmental-grade concrete, 48 human figures stand in a circle and are slowly becoming a part of the oceanscape. You'll find tour boats hovering around the area most of the day, mostly full of people from Gili T and Gili Air. Pro tip: You can DIY and swim right up to it from **BASK** on Meno's shore in just a few minutes.

Renting a snorkel set (a mask with snorkel plus fins) costs around 50,000Rp at most accommodations. Corals in shallow waters have seen better days, sadly due to bleaching. Thankfully, regeneration efforts have been strong and continue to make hopeful progress with Biorock technology –

GETTING AROUND

Walking and cycling are the ways to get around Gili Meno. You might see a rogue electric scooter – but they're silent (and typically privately owned, not for rent). It's an arduous workout to ride around the island's sandy outer edge. If you try, be prepared for an upper body workout as you walk your bike in an uncomfortably high volume of straights. It's better to walk the coast and save cycling for the inland area.

✓TOP TIP

If you're heading from Trawangan to accommodations on Meno's west coast (the opposite side of the island's public **port**), organise a private ride right to the shore. Ask some of the boatmen near the port if they'll take you, ideally with another stray traveller or two to split the cost. A private boat costs around 300,000Rp – fairly economical, and highly convenient for a group.

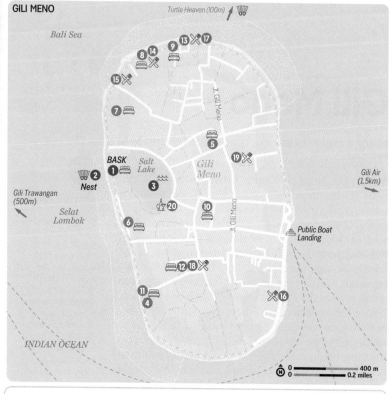

GILI MENO

Turtle Heaven (100m)

Bali Sea

Gili Air (1.5km)

Gili Trawangan (500m)

Selat Lombok

INDIAN OCEAN

Public Boat Landing

Salt Lake

Gili Meno

JL Gili Meno

N   0   400 m
    0   0.2 miles

HIGHLIGHTS
1. BASK
2. Nest

SIGHTS
3. Danau Gili Meno

SLEEPING
4. Café Gili Beach Bungalow
5. Gili Meno Escape
6. Le Pirate Gili Meno
7. Mahamaya
8. Meno House
9. Mimpi Bungalows
10. Rabbit Tree
11. Two Brothers Bungalows
12. United Colors of Gili

EATING
13. Adeng-Adeng Beach Restaurant and Bar
14. Bagno Di Gili
15. Bubbles Bar & Restaurant
16. Cemara Cafe
17. Easy Warung & Bar
18. Le Batavia
19. Rina Warung

DRINKING & NIGHTLIFE
20. Brother Hood

and there's still plenty of coral to see. The cost of snorkelling boat trips depends on how long you go for. Some excursions only last 2 hours while others can be a full-day affair. Expect to pay around 200,000Rp to join a group tour, and upwards of 700,000Rp for a private boat.

 ## EATING BEACHSIDE ON GILI MENO: OUR PICKS

Adeng-Adeng Beach Restaurant and Bar Fabulously located beach bar on the north coast, with pizza, salads, burgers and curries. **$**

Bagno Di Gili Chairs shaded by thatched roofs adorn soft sands; a menu full of pretty plates delights. **$$**

Bubbles Bar & Restaurant Good for both vegetarians and meat eaters, with beanbags to lounge on, lovingly shaded by beach umbrellas. **$$**

BASK The ultimate fancy experience with artfully crafted plates and thoughtful details in a sleek, minimalistic setting. **$$$**

Visit Meno's Saltwater Lake
Roam a quiet boardwalk

It's puzzling to see such a big old lake on such a tiny island, but Gili Meno's saltwater lake is just that. Just minutes from the western shoreline, **Danau Gili Meno** is equipped with a wooden boardwalk – although some parts need updating. It's a unique spot for the sunset, where the still waters reflect the sherbet-coloured sky with a thin strip of vegetation forming the horizon. It's the type of place where you'll likely go 'Huh, that's interesting', before carrying on with your day. A quick stop to check it out is worthwhile, but by no means should you budget a significant amount of time to visit it.

Near the entrance to the lake's boardwalk, the super friend-ly **Brother Hood** bar welcomes visitors warmly. More than a watering hole – this community hub organises rubbish collections for a greener Gili Meno and also hosts donation-based workshops centred around art and upcycling. The best way to learn what's currently going on is to simply stop by and say hello – you'll be greeted with warmth. So, come for the lake, but stay for the inevitable good vibes and post-sunset reggae jam-sesh next door.

GILI ECO TRUST

Although the underwater scenery remains awe-inspiring to this day, destructive fishing practices, coupled with an intense El Niño season back in the late 1990s, have caused significant damage to the reefs of the Gilis in the last two decades, even more evident in shallow dive sites above 18m.

Gili Eco Trust, a Trawangan-based NGO, was founded in 2002 to protect the surrounding reefs from illegal and damaging fishing. Some businesses on Gili T might ask if you're interested in making a reef donation for 50,000Rp, which goes directly to reef restoration and protective patrolling. The organisation has made significant contributions to and progress in eco-preservation across the Gilis since its inception.

Danau Gili Meno

ALI TRISNO PRANOTO/GETTY IMAGES ©

EAT INDONESIAN FOOD ON GILI MENO: OUR PICKS

Easy Warung & Bar Waterside warung (food stall) with prime sunset views, plus grilled fish and fruity cocktails. $

Le Batavia Generous portions of Indonesian staple dishes in a family-run spot with friendly service, a few minutes' walk inland. $

Rina Warung Fresh *ikan bakar* (grilled fish), chicken satay, curry and other delicious Sasak flavors. $

Cemara Cafe Indonesian classics, plus fresh seafood, piping hot soups, and even spaghetti, all on a pristine patch of Meno's beachfront. $

Gili Air

LAIDBACK VIBES | POWDERY BEACHES | DIVING & SNORKELLING

GETTING AROUND

You can walk from the top to the bottom of Gili Air in 20 minutes – strolling is easy here. Mostly paved main streets connect to smaller sandy offshoots, which comprise most of the north. Gili Air has the best conditions of all three islands for cycling, but you'll still find some beachside sections that are too sandy for riding. Gili Air is only about a 15 minute ride from Bangsal Port. Take the public boat or negotiate a private ride from one of the portside companies.

☑ **TOP TIP**

Lock your bike whenever it's not in sight. Rather than fastening the lock around a stationary object every time, you can simply loop it around the wheel so it renders the bike immobile until you're ready to roll again. This goes for all three of the Gili Islands.

Mellow yet upbeat Gili Air is the best of both worlds – fusing a bit of Trawangan's social energy with Meno's pleasant lull, the island's perimeter is full of bright and inviting beach bars, long-standing dive centres and a range of accommodation, from simple and homey to barefoot luxury. It's hard to pick favourites when it comes to beaches in the Gilis, but the overall vibe and scenery of Meno's shoreline is something special. Hushed in some corners and animated in others, you can recharge in peace but engage in tropical merriment whenever the mood arrives.

The heart of Gili Air has paved streets, unlike its neighbouring islands. While the central area is lined with tourist-catered shops and a sprinkling of Western-looking restaurants, a short walk off the main path reveals quiet palm-tree groves dotted with Sasak architecture, grazing livestock, and children playing games, often with their *ibu* (mothers) working nearby.

Wander the Cheerful Streets of Gili Air

Charming shops and inviting eateries

After stepping off the boat at Gili Air's southward-facing **port**, jovial streets entice. There's a bit of a buzz along Jl. Mojo, a central lane leading to the island's centre. You'll find everything from tour agencies to gelato shops, stores filled with handmade trinkets, and a smattering of little cafes serving both Indonesian and Western cuisine. Here, warungs with savoury Indonesian buffets border Aussie-style breakfast joints and Italian restos.

Steps from the port, **Il Gelato Damonte** beckons with fresh waffle cones and countless sweet flavors. **JUJU Zero Waste Store & Vegan Cafe** has a little gift shop with handmade goods, plus a whole menu of fresh juices, smoothies and healthy eats. **Warung Parida's** buffet-style Indonesian food is always ready, serving generous portions for as low as 25,000Rp per plate. **Kopi Susu Gili Air** and **Maxal Boulangerie** are just waiting for you to stop in for a coffee.

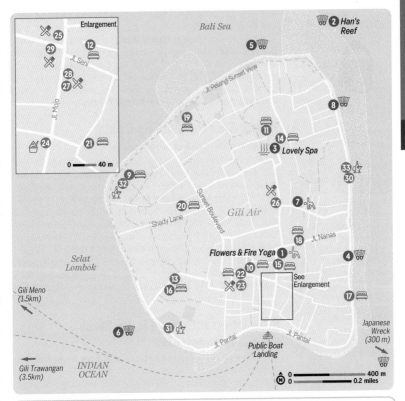

HIGHLIGHTS
1 Flowers & Fire Yoga
2 Han's Reef
3 Lovely Spa

ACTIVITIES
4 3W Dive Center
5 Frog Fish Point
6 Gili Air Wall
7 H2O Yoga
8 Next Level Scuba

SLEEPING
9 Akasia Villas
10 Café des Arts Hôtel
11 Captain Coconuts
12 Gili Air Escape
13 Gili Lumbung Bungalows and Bar
14 Island View Bar & Bungalow
15 Jago Gili Air
16 Lucy's Garden Hotel
17 Manta Dive Resort
18 Nanas Homestay
19 PinkCoco Gili Air
20 Puri Air Beach Resort
21 Slow Gili Air
22 The Koho Air

EATING
23 Flavornesia
24 Gili Martabaksss
25 Il Gelato Damonte

26 JUJU Zero Waste Store & Vegan Cafe
27 KIOSKO Café
28 Kopi Susu Gili Air
29 Maxal Boulangerie
30 Poke Gili Air
31 Warung Parida

DRINKING & NIGHTLIFE
32 Chili Bar & Segar
33 Ugem Bar

Kick Back on Gorgeous Beaches
Gili Air's beach hangouts

Like the rest of the Gilis, Gili Air is gifted with a ring of white-sand beach met by azure waters. It's arguably some of the archipelago's best shoreline, both for its condition and the lovely establishments that line the shore. The sunset views from the north coast are a point of local pride, and there's no shortage of beanbags shaded by fringed umbrellas to post up under. The east coast, lined with eateries and dive shops, is popular during the day – later on, everyone heads north

DRESS RESPECTFULLY

In the Gilis, swimwear is fully accepted on the beach and at the pool, but anywhere else is disrespectful. Throw on a cover-up if you're leaving the shoreline.

and west as the sky descends into a swirly canvas of soft pink and deep orange.

On the eastern coast, **Ugem Bar** and neighbouring **Chili Bar & Segar** draw a loyal customer base. A handful of cheerful beach cafes surround **Puri Air Beach Resort** on the north coast, all with lovely views of the neighbouring islands. Further west, you can find swings in the water at both **Gili Lumbung** and **Island View Bar & Bungalow**.

Dive & Snorkel Gili Air's Coast
Enviable waters and excellent spots

Snorkelling (and scuba diving) conditions are blissful around Gili Air, with coral reefs just off the eastern shore. **Han's Reef** is home to sea turtles and magnificent corals. Slightly north, there's **Frog Fish Point**, where sea critters such as ghost pipefish and scorpion fish flutter about. The **Gili Air Wall** lies southwest, with a solid drop-off that extends about 30m deep. If you're swimming out with snorkel gear from the shore, don't be surprised if you swim back to a different spot; the current causes some drift. You can also join a boat trip around the Gilis with a local provider such as Manta Dive (p260), **3W Dive Center** or **Next Level Scuba** – all on Air's east coast.

Slow Down with Yoga & Wellness
Unwind, stretch and relax

Get into a chill groove at **Flowers and Fire Yoga Garden**, a treehouse yoga studio shrouded in verdant foliage near Gili Air's heart. They also have a healthy cafe and cozy accommodations. A few minutes north, **H2O Yoga and Meditation Center** offers vinyasa flow, traditional hatha and various yin classes in a spacious shala, costing 130,000Rp per yoga class.

Spa seekers can find plenty of small spas throughout the island, with a one-hour massage ranging from 150,000Rp to over 300,000R (at fancier spots). **PinkCoco Gili Air's** spa is in a colourful setting fit for pampering, with floral decor and a long list of treatments. Further north, **Lovely Spa** offers Balinese massage for a great value in a simple, open-air setting.

 EATING ON GILI AIR: OUR PICKS ──────────── MAP p265

Flavornesia Indonesian classics for both veggie and meat eaters in a large bamboo structure close to Gili Air's centre. $

Gili Martabaksss Small shop exclusively dishing out *martabak* – a thick, fluffy Indonesian pancake that comes either sweet or savoury. $

Poke Gili Air Build your own poke bowls with plenty of fresh and flavourful ingredients, served in a bright, airy spot. $$

KIOSKO Café Spanish tapas, churros and classic sangria in a cozy setting, just beyond the main drag in town. $$

Places We Love to Stay

$ Cheap $$ Moderate $$$ Pricey

Gili Trawangan   p258 (Map p259)

Compass Divers $ Dive centre plus accommodation with private and dorm rooms, providing dive courses at different levels.

Mad Monkey Hostel $ Backpacker haven on the northwest coast with shared dorms, bungalows and even tents with AC.

Atlas Gili Trawangan $ Social hostel with daily activities for those who want to stay in the main area's action.

Gili Smile Bungalows $ Simple rooms with friendly vibes on the main strip, close to the action yet still quiet.

Pearl of Trawangan $$ Ocean-view rooms and cottages with bamboo roofs, right on the southeast coast.

Kuno Villas $$ Charming poolside *joglos* (traditional Javanese houses) and private villas with thoughtful details, just steps from the island's north shore.

Coco Cabana $$ Nine private rooms overlooking a pool equipped with a swim-up bar, yoga shala and restaurant.

PinkCoco $$$ Stylish adults-only hotel by the beach, living up to its namesake with rose-coloured decor in 27 all-pink rooms.

Gili Teak Resort $$$ Laid-back boutique resort on the quieter western shore with poolside gardens and a beachfront bar.

Pondok Santi $$$ Spacious resort with luxe decor, offering private villas, bungalows and rooms.

Gili Meno   p261 (Map p262)

Le Pirate Gili Meno $ Airy blue and white cabins aside a two-level pool, plus movie nights on the beach.

Rabbit Tree $ Whimsically-designed hostel quite literally in the island's middle, with unique furnishings, including a boat-shaped room.

Mimpi Bungalows $ Bungalows with hammocks on the northern shore, close to a few beachside restaurants and bars.

Two Brothers Bungalows $ Spacious guest house nestled on the edge of Meno's southwest shore, not far from the port.

Café Gili Beach Bungalow $$ Bungalows with a pool overlooking the beach, epitomising a low-key island getaway.

Mahamaya Gili Meno $$ Eco-inspired resort with beachfront villas, one- and two-bedroom suites, and family rooms that mix modern with traditional.

Gili Meno Escape $$ Cozy adults-only stay with six pool-facing bungalows, less than a ten-minute walk from the beach.

United Colors of Gili $$ Slightly inland, seven bungalows of traditional Indonesian craft accompanied by a pool and gardens.

Bask $$$ The definition of splurge and modern luxury, providing arguably the most 'treat yourself' resort experience around.

Meno House $$$ Beachfront resort with sumptuous design and an infinity pool, situated on the quiet northwest shore.

Gili Air   p264 (Map p265)

Café des Arts Hôtel $ Arty cafe and guesthouse with homemade French cuisine, plus creative workshops.

Nanas Homestay $ Thatched-roof bungalows with terraces and hammocks, close to the central road and beach.

Captain Coconuts $ Resort-style hostel with an open-air bamboo lodge, onsite cafe and eco-friendly details.

Jago Gili Air $$ Modern rooms overlooking a pool, a few minutes walk up the island's central street.

The Koho Air $$ Charming boutique hotel just steps from the port, with an eco-friendly focus.

Lucy's Garden Hotel $$ Sasak-style A-frame bungalows in a leafy setting within the island's southwestern corner.

Gili Air Escape $$ Single-level and two-storied bungalows inland towards the northern shore, tucked away from the main drag.

Manta Dive Resort $$ Scuba-centric accommodation offering myriad dive courses in a prime beachfront location.

Akasia Villas $$$ Serene and spacious villas on a quiet road, plus hanging swings and floating breakfasts.

Slow Gili Air $$$ Thoughtfully designed interiors, plus fully equipped kitchens, in the middle of a palm tree plantation.

Nusa Tenggara

TIMELESS CULTURE, EPIC NATURE, BIG WAVES

Welcome to the more remote part of Indonesia, home to rumbling volcanoes, Komodo dragons and animist culture.

Spreading west from the Wallace Line dividing Asia from Australasia, the Nusa Tenggara archipelago is Indonesia less-trodden: a verdant, volcano-studded, mountainous land of technicolour volcanic lakes, pink-sand beaches, limitless surf breaks and barrels, and traditional villages that continue to resist Balification.

On Flores, far away from crowds bristling with selfie sticks, poised to capture an Insta-ready sunset, you will encounter Komodo dragons, unspoiled underwater worlds teeming with creatures of the deep, waterfalls and hot springs hidden in the jungle, and steep volcanic slopes that throw down a gauntlet to intrepid hikers, challenging them to race to the top to watch the sun rise.

West Timor, Sumba and the smaller islands will make you forgo creature comforts as you leave behind the main towns, the bass-pumping buses, the minarets and the evening bustle of the night markets and venture inland to explore traditional villages with soaring thatched roofs. Here the spirits of the ancestors reside side-by-side with the living, animist rituals rule daily life, splatters of blood on totem poles and carvings speak of recent animal sacrifice, and Bahasa Indonesia – the lingua franca – is barely spoken. You'll find yourself stepping out of your comfort zone and coming away with experiences that will leave an indelible mark on your memory. But as everywhere, change is on the way, so step into this unique world while you still can.

B. BEUM/SHUTTERSTOCK ©

THE MAIN AREAS

FLORES	**WEST TIMOR**	**SUMBA**
Volcanoes, rice terraces, traditional villages, diving.	Traditional villages and ikat weaving.	Indigenous culture, ikat and epic surf.
p272	**p287**	**p298**

Above: Wae Rebo (p275); Left: Lake at Kelimutu volcano (p281)

Find Your Way

Nusa Tenggara comprises over 550 islands and accounts for a substantial chunk of Indonesia. We've picked the places that best capture the region's history, culture and natural landscapes.

Flores, p272

Hike up volcanoes, explore rice terraces and visit traditional villages before going island-hopping, diving and snorkelling from this all-rounder island.

West Timor, p287

Chew betel nut with royalty in traditional villages, visit the village of former headhunters and seek out intricately woven ikat.

Sumba, p298

Indonesia's best ikat weaving, traditional culture and terrific year-round surfing draw independent-minded travellers to this hilly island.

BUS, CAR & MOTORBIKE

Overland travel always takes longer than you think it will. Main roads are decent and surfaced, but minor roads can be rough. Trucks and buses connect main towns, but for everything else, rent a car or motorbike.

BOAT & AIR

An extensive and slow ferry network connects Nusa Tenggara's islands to each other, to Bali and beyond. Rough seas cause cancellations, particularly during the rainy season. Several airlines cover inter-island routes, many of which start in Denpasar, Bali.

Bena (p277)

Plan Your Time

For Komodo dragon encounters, diving, snorkelling, volcano treks and beaches, prioritise Flores. If you're into ikat weaving, animist culture and overnighting in traditional villages, head for Sumba or West Timor.

Pressed for Time

If you're a diver, head beneath the waves of **Komodo National Park** (p282) with diving outfits from **Labuan Bajo** (p284). Is Komodo dragon–spotting a deal breaker? Spot the legendary lizards on a **speedboat day trip** (p282) that incudes bouts of snorkelling. For immersion in Sumbanese indigenous culture, fly to **Tambolaka** (p303), then spend a couple of days visiting the traditional villages around **Wanokaka** (p304) and **Waikabubak** (p302).

Two-Week Tour

After two days of **Komodo dragons** (p282) and snorkelling/diving from **Labuan Bajo** (p284), head into the mountains to visit the traditional villages of **Wae Rebo** (p275) and **Bena** (p277) before ascending **Kelimutu** (p281) from Moni. Fly to **Kupang** and spend two days visiting **Tamkesi** (p291) and **Boti** (p292). Then journey between **Waingapu** (p298) and **Tambolaka** (p303), with ikat shopping and cultural immersion en route.

SEASONAL HIGHLIGHTS

MARCH–JUNE
As rains end, trek up volcanoes in Flores. Surf in Rote and Sumbawa, and search for Komodo dragons on Komodo Island.

JULY–AUGUST
Dry season, ideal for Komodo NP on a day trip from Labuan Bajo, or to the Alor archipelago aboard a liveaboard.

SEPTEMBER–OCTOBER
Surf in southwest Sumba, Sumbawa or Rote. See low-key Nusa Tenggara between downpours.

NOVEMBER–MARCH
Rainy season makes the islands lush and green. Watch warriors on horseback engage in combat during Sumba's Pasola Festival.

Flores

SPECTACULAR NATURE | TRADITIONAL VILLAGES | SUPERB DIVING

Pass through a succession of diverse topographies as you follow the serpentine, 670km-long Trans-Flores Hwy, which follows the spine of Nusa Tenggara's longest, equally sinuous island (whose original name appropriately references snakes rather than the flowery title bestowed upon it by 16th-century Portuguese colonists).

In the west, buzzy, coastal Labuan Bajo is the destination du jour of divers and dragon-seekers, and the gateway to the pink-sand beaches and gin-clear waters of Komodo National Park. Heading into the jungle-covered mountains, you pass through the highland towns of Ruteng and Bajawa, fringed by rice terraces, volcanic cones, hot springs and traditional villages, some seemingly unchanged for millennia. Further north, Riung and its offshore archipelago are another draw for divers, while east of Bajawa, rainforest gives way to verdant, vertiginous hills, white sand, beaches and busy ports. There is also the mountain town of Moni, from where you summit Kelimutu volcano with its emerald lake, and seek out ikat and Lio culture in nearby villages.

Lounge around Labuan Bajo

Explore Labuan Bajo's terrestrial attractions

Its glossy marina and ever-expanding number of restaurants aside, the jumping-off point for Komodo National Park (p282) and its famous dragons is a smidgen short on sights. Everything you need is on one-way Jl Soekarno Hatta, from Western restaurants and local *rumah makans* (eating houses) to coffee shops, accommodation, travel agents, ATMs and dive shops.

Head up to a centrally located spot on Jl Ande Bole, a block from the waterfront, for terrific sunsets. If you want to explore further afield, rent a motorbike/scooter (100,000Rp per day) from numerous outlets, and head south of Labuan Bajo to **Gua Batu Cermin** (Mirror Stone Cave; 20,000Rp

---

GETTING AROUND

The Trans-Flores Hwy is a beautiful paved drive. Secondary roads range from narrow and paved to shocking, with the latter accessible by 4WD or motorbike. Most hotels and guesthouses rent motorbikes and scooters for 80,000–100,000Rp per day. Car rental is available in Labuan Bajo and Ende. Car and driver hire is 800,000Rp–1,200,000Rp per day. Guides can arrange detailed, island-wide itineraries. Regular buses run between Labuan Bajo and Maumere. More comfortable air-con public minibuses link major towns.

☑**TOP TIP**

Visit traditional villages with a local guide to bypass the language barrier, learn about indigenous beliefs and avoid making embarrassing faux pas. Visitors must sign the guestbook in each village and make a donation.

FLORES ROAD TRIP FROM TIP TO TOE

This island-wide road trip follows the scenic Trans-Flores Hwy and takes in diverse sights. Allow a week. Begin in **❶ Labuan Bajo**, a harbour town from which you launch explorations of Komodo National Park. A four-hour drive along a picturesquely winding road through jungled hills brings you to **❷ Ruteng**, a highland market town ideal for visiting the Liang Bua Cave (p275) and detouring to Nikengto to hike Wae Rebo (p275). Heading east, you pass a scenic viewpoint overlooking terraced rice fields before the road skirts the coast at **❸ Aimere**, home to several *arak* distilleries, while the volcanic cone of Gunung Inerie (p277; 2245m) comes into view. Ignore the hairpin bends leading directly to Bajawa, and skirt the volcano along the occasionally bumpy coastal road, via the village of **❹ Bena**, to approach **❺ Baja-**

wa. Detour north from Bajawa to **❻ Riung** to snorkel and island-hop in the Seventeen Islands Marine Park (p279) before driving along the northern coast and back down south through banana plantations. The scenic coastal road brings you to **❼ Ende**, a muggy port, market town and regional transport hub, with the cones of Gunung Meja and Gunung Iya looming over it. Head up forested hills to reach **❽ Moni**, the gateway to Gunung Kelimutu (p281) and ikat-weaving villages. Passing a string of beautiful white-sand beaches at **❾ Paga**, detour to **❿ Sikka**, one of Flores's first Portuguese settlements, before proceeding to **⓫ Maumere**, an urban hub backed by layered hills, with some decent off-coast diving. A three-hour drive brings you to the port of **⓬ Larantuka**, from which you can sail to West Timor or the Alor Archipelago.

FLORES

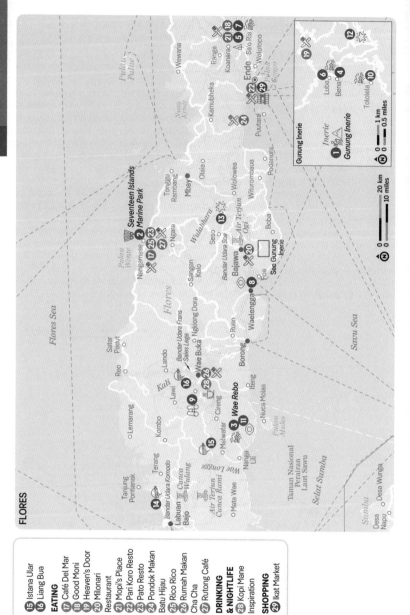

HIGHLIGHTS
1 Gunung Inerie
2 Seventeen Islands Marine Park
3 Wae Rebo

SIGHTS
4 Bena
5 Kelimutu National Park
6 Luba
7 Saʼo Ria
8 Sopi Lontar Aimere
9 Spiderweb Rice Fields
10 Tololela
11 Wae Rebo trailhead

ACTIVITIES
12 Air Panas Malanage
13 Air Panas Soa
14 Gua Rangko

15 Istana Ular
16 Liang Bua

EATING
17 Café Del Mar
18 Good Moni
19 Heaven's Door
20 Milonari Restaurant
21 Mopi's Place
22 Pari Koro Resto
23 Pato Resto
24 Pondok Makan Batu Hijau
25 Rico Rico
26 Rumah Makan Cha Cha
27 Rutong Café

DRINKING & NIGHTLIFE
28 Kopi Mane Inspiration

SHOPPING
29 Ikat Market

entry), 5km east of town. You'll need a torch to check out the large grotto with stalactites and stalagmites, while squeezing through tight spaces lets you see a fossilised turtle. To get to the more popular **Gua Rangko** (entry 25,000Rp), an oceanic cave famed for its sunlit turquoise water (visit in the afternoon for the best light), drive 12km northeast from Labuan Bajo to Rangko village, then pay around 280,000Rp for a boat to take you there.

Hang with Hobbits
Encounter tiny human remains

The Manggarai have long-told folk tales of *ebo gogo* – hairy little people with flat foreheads who once roamed the jungle. Nobody took these stories too seriously until September 2003, when archaeologists made a stunning find.

Excavating the limestone cave at **Liang Bua**, archaeologists unearthed a skeleton the size of a three-year-old child but with the worn-down teeth and bone structure of an adult. Six more remains confirmed that the team had unearthed an entirely new species of human, who reached around 1m in height. The species was named *Homo floresiensis* and nicknamed 'hobbit'.

Commandeering an *ojek* (motorbike taxi) in Ruteng, you can travel 12km north, past flooded rice paddies, and visit the vast stalactite-hung overhang looming above a small vegetable garden. Local guides, whose service is included in your 30,000Rp entry fee, will meet you at the cave's entrance, explain why Liang Bua is considered sacred and point out the excavation site where the bones of at least eight more 'hobbits' were found. The small adjacent museum tells the story of the findings (in English and Bahasa Indonesia), displays a replica 'hobbit' skeleton, explains the theories of *Homo floresiensis* evolution and, of course, quotes Tolkien.

Wander to Wae Rebo
Visit a traditional Manggarai village

The most intact of traditional Manggarai villages, **Wae Rebo** is only accessed on foot, via a 5km hike from the **trailhead** at the end of a cratered narrow road leading north from the village of Denge. The footpath climbs relentlessly up the jungle-covered mountain slope for around 3km before the greenery opens up and you catch a glimpse of the valley, Denge's tin roofs and the blue of the Savu Sea. Shortly thereafter, past the lookout tower from which you glimpse

THE MYSTERIOUS ORIGINS OF THE FLORES 'HOBBIT'

New research into the *Homo floresiensis* raises more questions. An Australian study in 2017 supposedly disproved the prevailing theory that the 'hobbits' were descendants of *Homo erectus* (who spread from Africa to Asia around two million years ago). After analysing *Homo*-related bones and dental samples from multiple countries, the research found the two had vastly different structures.

Homo floresiensis could be even more ancient than *Homo erectus*, most likely evolving from a common African ancestor. Rival anthropologists suggest that the Flores find could represent *Homo sapiens* (who travelled between Australia and New Guinea 35,000 years ago) that suffered from microcephaly – a form of dwarfism. But a 2018 study refuted any link between the 'hobbit' and *Homo sapiens*.

 EATING IN LABUAN BAJO: OUR PICKS

MadeInItaly This stylish semi-open-air Italian is known for superb pizza and imaginative, fresh pasta, with some ingredients grown on organic farms. **$$$**	**Pasar Malam** From sunset, smoky, lamp-lit waterfront stalls cook up fresh fish, prawns, squid and crab. Wash it down with BYO Bintang. **$$**	**Taman Laut Handayani** Fish steamed in banana leaf and seafood dishes served with a side of sunset views await at this lofty outdoor restaurant. **$$**	**Carpenter Coffee & Roastery** Serving superlative Flores coffee (and selling coffee beans), this friendly place also serves homemade cake and ample breakfasts. **$**

SPIDERWEB RICE FIELDS

Scramble to the viewpoint (25,000Rp) up the hill near Cara village, 20km west of Ruteng, and an extraordinary sight awaits: vast rice fields in the shape of spiderwebs. This is the last surviving vestige on Flores of the traditional communal agriculture of the Manggarai, whereby the *lingko* (land) is divided by the village headman among the village's families.

During the allocation of each segment, a buffalo sacrifice takes place at the *lodok* (ceremonial ground) in the centre of the web. The more resources the family has, the bigger its slice of the web, with choice sections owned by the headman's family. When the head of a family dies, the land segment is re-allocated.

ANNA KAMINSKI/LONELY PLANET ©

Bena

the cone-shaped houses of your destination, the trail flattens out and you descend gently to the clearing, with robusta coffee thickets, banana trees and taro plants signifying human habitation, before the much-photographed clearing with its horseshoe of conical houses comes into view.

Sitting on the woven mat of the main house, you take in the hearth in the centre, with the smoke from the cooking permeating the interior, the curtained-off living quarters, with one room per each of the eight families that live here, and the ceremonial gongs. You're welcome to wander around, taking in village life – children playing amid darting chickens, women pounding husks of rice in giant pestles, men returning from their plots of land come sundown. The only place that's off limits is the raised ceremonial ground in the centre, where ritual sacrifices are made.

The hike is best made early in the morning before the heat; simple meals of rice, cassava, tempeh and vegetables can be arranged through your guide, and you can stay overnight on a mattress on the floor in the *mbaru tembong* (traditional house) turned guesthouse (500,000Rp per night including meals), or retrace your steps before sunset. Hire guides via guesthouses in Denge or bring them with you from Labuan Bajo or Ruteng.

 EATING IN LABUAN BAJO: OUR PICKS ──────────── MAP p274

Copper Bonnet Bistro
Come for the meze, noodle bowls, Cobb salad and BBQ ribs and linger over craft beer on the terrace. **$$**

101 Barrique Paninis, aubergine lasagne and carpaccios are paired with Italian coffee and cocktails, mixed with Flores liqueurs. DJs and live music some nights. **$$**

Happy Banana Komodo
Munch on delectable sashimi, imaginative sushi rolls and handmade gyoza, slurp soupy udon noodles, or start your day with a chia bowl and poached eggs. **$$**

Wae Molas Cafe Pictures on posters help to order at this family-run spot – there's no English menu; *sop buntut* (oxtail soup) is the speciality. **$**

Summit Gunung Inerie
Tackle Flores' highest volcano

A breathtakingly beautiful, spectacularly jagged cone of a volcano looming above Bajawa, **Gunung Inerie** (2245m), 10km south of town, throws down a gauntlet to intrepid would-be climbers. The ascent is relentless but not quite as daunting as the steep sides suggest. Guided ascents are possible outside the wetter months; with an English-speaking guide and transport from Bajawa, expect to pay about 1,000,000Rp for one and 1,200,000Rp for two people. Bring plenty of water and a sun hat, since beyond the sparse eucalyptus forest at the volcano's base, the cone is shadeless. Beyond the treeline, you zigzag up its north flank to the summit; many guides prefer to do the ascent in the predawn dark, starting around 3am and arriving in time for sunrise. Depending on your fitness levels, the round-trip hike takes roughly seven hours.

Explore Bajawa's Traditional Villages
Immerse yourself in Ngada culture

Perched at 1100m above sea level, framed by forested volcanoes and blessed with a cooler climate, Bajawa is a laid-back, predominantly Catholic hill town, and a great base from which to explore dozens of surrounding Ngada villages.

One of the most traditional is **Bena**, resting on the flank of Gunung Inerie, 19km south of Bajawa (120,000Rp return by motorbike taxi). Though all villagers are now officially Catholic, traditional beliefs and customs endure. Sacrifices are held three times each year, and village elders still talk about a rigidly enforced caste system that prevented 'mixed' relationships, with those defying the *adat* (traditional law) facing serious consequences.

Bena is home to nine clans, and its houses with high, thatched roofs line up in two rows on a ridge. They're interspersed with ancestral totems, including megalithic tombs, *ngadhu* (thatched parasol-like structures) – the bases of which are splattered with animal blood from sacrifices – *bhaga* (miniature thatched-roof houses), and small sacred houses where significant relics are kept. Most houses have male or female figurines on the roofs, while doorways are decorated with buffalo horns and pig jawbones – more remnants of ritual sacrifice. Look out for wood carvings at the base of each house: roosters symbolise greatness; horses – hard work and abundant harvest; while serpents protect the inhabitants from evil powers.

After paying the entrance fee (25,000Rp) you're given a purple scarf to wear for the duration of your visit, and as you walk around, you'll see cash crops of cloves, vanilla pods and candlenut drying on the ground. It's possible to stay the night for 150,000Rp per person, which includes meals of boiled cassava and banana, but if you want a more intimate experience, walk several hundred metres uphill to the village of **Luba**.

A baker's dozen of houses and a handful of Catholic graves silhouetted against Gunung Inerie, Luba is home to four welcoming clans. You'll see four *ngadhu* and *bhaga*, and houses decorated with depictions of symbolic horses, buffalo and snakes. Leave a donation of 25,000Rp.

CACI WHIP FIGHTS

Every November, as part of the Penti harvest festival, Manggarai villages such as Wae Rebo stage **Caci** – a ritual whip fight between pairs of men. One man plays the role of aggressor and the other, the defender. The aggressor tries to hit the defender's bare upper body with a rattan whip while the defender blocks with a buffalo-hide shield.

At the beginning, the participants run towards each other to raise the tension. If the defender is struck on the back, it's considered a good sign, with the blood anointing the earth and promising bounteous harvest. The aggressor and defender switch roles after every whip lash, with a new pair stepping up after four whip strikes.

THE NGADA PEOPLE

More than 60,000 Ngada people inhabit the upland Bajawa plateau and the slopes around Gunung Inerie (p277). Most practise a fusion of animism and Christianity, worshipping Gae Dewa, a god who unites Dewa Zeta (the heavens) and Nitu Sale (the earth). The Ngada are matrilineal, meaning that kinship passes through the female line.

The most evident symbols of Ngada traditions are the pairs of *ngadhu* (male) and *bhaga* (female) structures, each associated with a particular family within a village. Some structures were built over 100 years ago to commemorate ancestors killed in battle. The *ngadhu* is a parasol-like structure about 3m high, consisting of a carved wooden pole and thatched 'roof', while the *bhaga* is a miniature thatched-roof house.

Flying foxes, Seventeen Islands Marine Park

Alternatively, a mere 4km trek from Bena, or a short drive south via Gurusina, brings you to **Tololela**, a seldom-visited Ngada settlement (donate 25,000Rp per person) consisting of three linked traditional villages.

Soak in the Hot Springs
Bajawa's mineral waters

Unofficially staffed by friendly locals who collect the 20,000Rp admission fee, and featuring basic changing rooms, the natural **Air Panas Malanage** hot springs are 6km south of Bena (p277). At the base of one of the many volcanoes in the area, two streams – one hot (up to 50°C), one cold – mix together in a temperate stream. Soak amid the greenery-covered boulders and flitting dragonflies, and don't be surprised if you're joined by locals who take the opportunity to wash their clothes while they bathe.

If you're making the journey from Bajawa to Riung along the rough road northeast of town, **Air Panas Soa** is another option. The most-serviced hot springs in the region consist of two manufactured pools (one a scintillating 45°C; the other a more pedestrian 35°C to 40°C) and one natural pool (25°C to 30°C), and can get rather busy, particularly on weekends.

EATING IN RUTENG & BAJAWA: OUR PICKS

MAP p274

Rumah Makan Cha Cha Ruteng. Homey place serving *nasi lontong* opor (chicken in coconut milk) and *nasi soto ayam* (chicken soup with glass noodles, veggies and rice). $

Kopi Mane Inspiration Ruteng. A solid spot for a Manggarai coffee. Buy some beans or order Indonesian fare. $

Heaven's Door Stellar views of Gunung Inerie, live music by staff and visitors, and a mix of Indonesian and Western dishes, 16km south of Bajawa. $$

Milonari Restaurant Bajawa. Tempeh and tofu dishes alongside myriad chicken and rice combos, sweet and sour fish, good coffee and pancakes. $

Snorkel the Seventeen Islands

Boat-tripping off Flores' north coast

Lapped at by turquoise waters and fringed with white-sand beaches, the 23 islands that make up the misnamed **Seventeen Islands Marine Park** (government authorities decided on the number 17 as a convenient tie-in with Indonesia's Independence Day, 17 August) are a worthwhile detour. The islands are accessed via a three-hour bumpy drive from Boawae, or a four-hour bone-shaking bus ride via a bumpy (but improving) road from Bajawa, or a four-hour bus journey along an arid coastal road from Ende to the laidback, coconut-fringed little fishing town of Riung – the islands' gateway.

Standard day trips tend to include lunch, snorkelling and four island stops, the first almost always being the mangrove-fringed **Pulau Ontoloe**, home to a massive colony of fruit bats and a few Komodo dragons. This is typically followed by snorkelling over the shallow reef near **Pulau Tiga**, **Pulau Laingjawa** and **Pulau Bakau** – the park's coral was impacted by El Niño bleaching of 2002, so there are patches where the reef hasn't recovered. However, the visibility is up to 15m, and you're likely to spot a variety of reef denizens, from parrotfish and clownfish to the venomous lionfish. Stops on **Pulau Rutong** (for the viewpoint) and **Pulau Tembang** (for picture-perfect white sand) are also popular.

To arrange your boat trip, hang out by the boat dock, where in high season you're likely to find fellow travellers to split day-trip fares with. Alternatively, organise a guide via your guesthouse; Al Itchan, owner of Café Del Mar (p281), comes recommended. Before going to the islands, sign in and pay 100,000Rp per person at a separate booth by the dock.

Take the Ikat Trail to Moni & Ende

Go in search of fine textiles

The mountain villages east (around Jopu) and northeast (around Lio) of the gritty port town of Ende – and around the appealing mountain town of Moni, which is fringed by rice fields and greenery-clad volcanic peaks – are still renowned for their ikat and sarong weavings, with distinctive regional patterns of triangular motifs made of continuous lines. In Ende, a block inland from the waterfront, visit the daily **ikat market**, where there's a good selection of ikat from the region and beyond; bargaining is acceptable. Alternatively, catch an *ojek* up the rough road from Ende to the village of **Wolotopo** to observe the weaving process right in front of weavers' houses and buy directly from the source.

Accessed from Moni, weaving is practised in the villages of Koanara, Jopu and further afield, in Wolonjita and Nggela. A 10-minute drive through the rice paddies south of Moni gets you to **Koanara**, with the vivid purples, oranges and electric blues of ikat cloths hanging by the roadside and weavers working their looms.

THE ART OF ARAK DISTILLATION

Approaching Aimere from the west, you'll pass **Sopi Lontar Aimere**, an *arak* distillery, marked by a display of plastic bottles containing different-coloured liquids – not to be confused with other displays of plastic bottles sold by the roadside (petrol = '*arak* for motorbike'). Coastal *arak* is made from the sap of a particular palm tree, with men scaling the tree and attaching a bucket for five days. On day six, the bucket is retrieved and stored in plastic vats to ferment.

The resulting juice is distilled over a wood fire, with the clear liquid slowly dripping through a bamboo pipe. The first dripping is the most potent (up to 50%) while the second and third go from 30 to 20%.

ADEL NEWMAN/SHUTTERSTOCK ©

Lakes on Kelimutu volcano

Visit Sa'o Ria

Delve into Lio culture

A mere 10 minutes' drive south of Moni is the village of **Sa'o Ria**, just up from the bend in the road overhung by a giant ficus tree. There, you'll be able to see its *rumah adat* (traditional house) with the traditional thatched roof. If you're lucky, the headman's effusive wife, Maria will welcome you inside the house; only other Lio headmen, their wives and visitors from outside the Lio culture are granted entry (a 20,000Rp donation is appropriate). You'll step inside the tiny doorway, decorated with intricate carvings, and sit on the springy bamboo floor inside the smoky interior while your guide translates stories of local traditions.

The **Gavi** ceremony, which accompanies the beginning of planting season in October, sees 1000 Lio from other villages come to Sa'o Ria. There are four days of dancing, imbibing of *arak* (colourless, distilled palm wine), and buffalo sacrifice. The hearts of the buffalo are cooked in the *rumah adat* and placed onto a sacred woven platform as an offering to the spirits. After the four days, the hearts mysteriously disappear. After the harvest in April, there's a two-day thanksgiving ceremony, accompanied by a pig sacrifice and the consumption of yellow rice.

EATING IN MONI & ENDE: OUR PICKS

MAP p274

Mopi's Place Moni. Start the day with local coffee, then come back for live reggae, *tapa kolo* (coconut rice cooked in a bamboo tube) and *arak* cocktails. $$

Good Moni With a friendly chef-owner and misty hill views, this open-air restaurant does Indonesian staples and the Moni potato croquette. $

Pari Koro Resto Ende. Free-range chicken rubs shoulders with sauteed pumpkin shoots and water spinach with papaya flower. $$

Pondok Makan Batu Hijau Look over the waves while scarfing down seafood and coconut water at this beachside spot 27km west of Ende. $$

Marvel at Multicoloured Lakes

Summit Indonesia's unique volcano

Waking up at 4am, you either hop on the motorbike for the solo hour-long ride from Moni to the car park near the top of **Kelimutu volcano** (1639m), or you're driven there by your guide. A gentle 15-minute ramble along the pine-fringed slope followed by a climb up some steps brings you to **Inspiration Point** at the summit.

As the first rays of the sun crest Kelimutu's western rim, filtering mist into the sky and revealing three deep volcanic lakes, there's a collective gasp of wonder from the shivering crowd.

A sacred and extinct volcano, Kelimutu is the centrepiece of the mountainous, jungle-clad national park of the same name. It is sacred to the local Lio people, who believe the souls of the dead migrate here. Young people's souls go to the warmth of **Tiwu Koo Fai Nuwa Muri** (Teal Lake); old people's to the cold of **Tiwu Ata Bupu** (Royal Blue Lake); and those of the wicked to **Tiwu Ata Polo** (Black Lake). If you happen to be up the volcano on 14 August, you'll witness the exuberant dancing on Lio ceremonial grounds en route to the summit – part of the annual Feed the Spirit of the Forefathers ceremony, after which pork, betel nuts, rice and other valuable offerings will be left on ceremonial rocks beside the lakes. Alert your guide if you have dreams about the sacred lakes prior to your ascent – apparently, siren-like spirits have lured people to their demise, which can be avoided if the right prayers and offerings are made. Resist temptation from these will-o'-the-wisps, and don't stray beyond the two official lookouts – several hikers have perished after slipping on the loose scree.

A pre-dawn visit to Kelimutu is not the meditative, tranquil experience you may hope for, since it's when you'll encounter the biggest crowds. There's a risk of clouds pulling in later on, but on a fine day, you'll find Kelimutu's summit empty and peaceful, and when the sun is high, the lakes really sparkle.

On the way down, take the shortcut (you'll need to ask locals for directions) down to Moni through steep, scenic copses of eucalyptus, and through farmland rich in banana, taro and vanilla, until you reach a gorgeous waterfall and dipping pool right below the road running through Moni.

BIRDWATCHING IN FLORES & BEYOND

Cliched as it may be to say this, but the Lesser Sunda Islands are a birdwatcher's paradise, with hundreds of feathered species spotted across varied habitats, including over 70 endemics – some very rare.

Yovie Jehabut (jagarimba.id) is a well-regarded Flores-based birdwatching guide who specialises in custom-made trips in the Wallacea bioregion (Lesser Sunda Islands, Sulawesi and Maluku). He can arrange itineraries to suit whether you want to scour the Flores lowlands for the Flores crow, the Flores green pigeon and the critically endangered Flores hawk eagle, hunt for the Timor friarbird and Timor figbird in woodlands near Kupang, or spot Sumba's apricot-breasted sunbird and the Greater Sumba boobook by night in Langgiliru National Park.

EATING IN RIUNG: OUR PICKS

MAP p274

Rico Rico Grilled fish with punchy tomato sambal is the standout at this casual pier-side spot; live music some nights, and snorkelling trips arranged. $

Pato Resto Hoover up fried noodles with vegetables, aubergine with tomato sauce and fried squid washed down with banana juice. $

Café del Mar Dine on grilled catch-of-the-day with *cah kangkung* (garlicky water spinach); stay overnight at this friendly homestay and arrange your snorkelling trips. $

Rutong Café Barbecued fish, chicken satay and an array of vegetable and noodle dishes really shine when complemented by Simeon's special sambal. $$

Beyond Flores

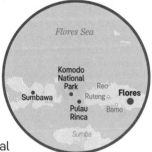

Head southeast of Labuan Bajo for primeval monster encounters, or east to Sumbawa for monster waves.

Places

Komodo National Park p282

Pulau Rinca p285

Sumbawa p285

GETTING AROUND

There's fierce competition among Labuan Bajo's boat operators and diving outfits for day- and multi-day trips to Komodo National Park. Group day trips by speedboat cost from 750,000Rp per person and allow for more time at each location than the cheaper slow boats. Multi-day liveaboards cater to divers and explorers. Rinca Island is accessible by private boat (from 1,500,000Rp) only. Fly to Bima, Sumbawa to catch a bus to Hu'u, or take a taxi from Bima (1,000,000Rp) directly to Pantai Lakey.

Arguably the single biggest reason to come to Labuan Bajo is the chance to visit Komodo National Park, centred on Komodo Island and the main home of the fearsome *ora* (Komodo dragon), the world's largest monitor lizard. Sightings are frequent but not guaranteed, particularly during the months of June and July, when the dragons disappear into the hinterland of this large island in order to mate. Dragon sightings are very common on the smaller Rinca Island, though since Rinca has been 'tamed' in recent times for cruise-ship visitors, it has become far less popular with Labuan Bajo crowds. West of Flores, the large, conservative island of Sumbawa is mostly the premise of miners, mullahs and some surfers.

Komodo National Park

TIME FROM FLORES: 1 HR

Take a day trip into the dragons' lair

Most visitors to Labuan Bajo have dragons on their mind. To see them in their most spectacular setting, you need to get yourself over to **Pulau Komodo**, the island at the heart of **Komodo National Park**.

There are various ways of doing this. Most Labuan Bajo operators run a standard day trip to Komodo, either via speedboat or slow boat, and stopping in the same six locations. The speedboat is pricier but gives you more time in each spot. If you opt for the standard day tour, the first stop is the compact, vertiginous **Pulau Padar**. A steep 15-minute hike brings you to the highest of a series of viewpoints, from which you can admire the volcanic island's scalloped bays fringed with white sand, the island's mountainous spine and the surrounding marine panorama. Next up is swimming and sunbathing on one of the national park's pink-sand beaches, on the far side of Pulau Padar.

A short boat ride away, Pulau Komodo awaits, its steep hillsides lush with greenery in the short wet season (December to March) and frazzled by sun to a rusty tan that makes its crystal waters pop the rest of the year. Ashore, you are paired with a ranger armed with a forked staff for keeping dragons at bay. The 1,355,000Rp entrance fee includes a choice of three walks:

Komodo dragons

FUN FACTS ABOUT KOMODO DRAGONS

Believed to have originated in Australia four million years ago, Komodo dragons reside on Komodo and Rinca, and parts of north and west Flores. The venom, located in glands between their teeth, is the dragons' secret weapon. One bite, loaded with toxins, promotes bleeding that slowly kills its prey (including humans). Komodos can eat up to 80% of their body weight in a single sitting. They will then retire for up to a month to digest their meal.

Dragons are omnivorous, and consume their young. Juvenile dragons live in trees to avoid becoming a meal for adults. It's estimated that there are up to 5000 dragons in the wild today, but only a few hundred or so are egg-laying females.

the short walk (1.5km, 45 minutes), which includes a stop at an artificial waterhole that attracts diminutive local deer, wild boar and of course *ora* (Komodo dragons); the medium walk (2km, 1½ hours), which includes a hill with sweeping views and a chance to see colourful cockatoos; and the long walk (4km, two hours), which includes the features of the shorter hikes and distances you from peak-season crowds.

After lunch, the boat makes a snorkelling stop at the spectacular **Taka Makassar** with its diversity of healthy coral, vast shoals of reef fish and frequent sightings of sea turtles and other pelagic life. Next, you head to **Karang Makassar** (Manta Point) in search of manta rays – often reliably present. The final stop is the rather anticlimactic **Pulau Kanawa**, for more snorkelling.

If you have more time, a rewarding way of experiencing Komodo National Park is via three-day, two-night liveaboard trips, offered by some operators. A three-day trip takes in all the day trip's highlights, and less-visited spots, such as the small, uninhabited **Siaba**, **Kalong** and **Bidadari** islands – excellent for snorkelling. It also means beating the crowds to Padar's viewpoint in the morning, and visiting Komodo Island earlier, when the dragons are more active.

Komodo Kayaking (komodokayaking.com) – the only Indonesian kayaking operator in Labuan Bajo – offers an active, eco-friendly way of exploring the park that includes dining in beachside safari tents in the evening and paddling along

LABUAN BAJO'S BEST DIVING OPERATORS

Wunderpus Liveaboard
Experienced diving and snorkelling liveaboard operator offering trips of three to seven days. There's a focus on small groups, environmentally conscious tours and uncrowded dive sites.

Manta Rhei
Specialises in themed day trips and PADI courses. Nitrox dives and *pinisi* (a Sulawesi schooner) liveaboards (from 5,000,000Rp per person, per night) also available.

Divine Diving
A supporter of environmental and wildlife non-profits, Divine Diving offers two- and three-dive day trips, PADI courses and liveaboard adventures capped at eight people.

Scuba Junkie Komodo Offshoot of award-winning diving outfit in Borneo. Excellent range of diving and snorkelling outings, and PADI courses.

Manta ray, Komodo National Park

the coastlines of various islands during the day, stopping to snorkel and occasionally catching a glimpse of the dragons – excellent swimmers – in the water. Two-day, one-night and three-day, two-night rates are US$495/695 per person.

Komodo National Park beneath the waves

Komodo's submerged seamounts – haunted by manta rays, reef sharks and turtles – its vibrant, exceptionally diverse reefs that teem with life, and its excellent underwater visibility make for an incredible diving experience, with several dozen dive sites dotted around the national park's islands. The challenging underwater topography, combined with strong, unpredictable currents, means that some of the top diving sites are for experienced divers only, though there's calmer spots for beginners. There's tremendous competition for divers in Labuan Bajo, with dozens of scuba-diving operators based there; you can also opt for a multi-day liveaboard for a more tranquil experience away from diving day-trippers. Look out for the 'DOCK' (Dive Operators Community Komodo) sticker in the window of the most conservation-minded of the diving outfits; they actively combat dynamite fishing and other harmful practices. Some also have programmes that hire and train locals and turn them into conservation ambassadors.

The best place to see Komodo's manta rays is **Karang Makassar** (Manta Point), a shallow (12m max) drift dive along a sloping rubble reed. It's a manta cleaning station and a popular feeding spot when the water is plankton-rich.

Off Pulau Komodo's northern side, **Castle Rock** is a submerged seamount, well known for its intense currents and encounters with grey, whitetip and blacktip reef sharks, as well as schooling jacks, giant trevally, tuna and huge schools of fusiliers. Another terrific site for huge shoals of fish is **Batu Bolong** – for experienced divers only due to the currents – with the shallows on the lee side of the pinnacle thick with damselfish, fairy basslets, Moorish idols, large sweetlips and sheltering lionfish, while the deep blue teems with Spanish mackerel, surgeonfish and red-toothed triggerfish.

Near Pulau Seraya Besar, **Sabolan Kecil** is great for macro diving and for beginners, with batfish, seahorses, scorpionfish and blue-spotted stingrays spotted among the gorgonian fans and barrel sponges of the sloping coral reef and sand below. The white-sand bottom of the reef on the north side of **Pulau Sabayor** (halfway between Komodo and Flores) attracts eagle rays, while the reef's ledges and overhangs house cleaner shrimp and glassfish, with hairy squat lobsters spotted between the sponge and barrel corals, and emperor fish and groupers cruising by.

Pulau Rinca

TIME FROM FLORES: **90 MINS**

Rinca's reptile residents

The slow boat hugs Flores' coast, chugging sedately past dramatically hilly, sparsely forested islets and islands, before pulling up by the dock of arid **Pulau Rinca**, where you're greeted with a larger-than-life statue of two Komodo dragons engaged in mortal combat.

A five-minute stroll along the wheelchair-accessible wooden boardwalk with a mandatory ranger brings you to the excellent **museum**, with its detailed information on Komodo dragons, and the terrestrial and marine fauna of the national park. Directly behind the museum, you're likely to find Komodo dragons resting under the trees in the daytime heat. Get here early in the day to observe them at their most active. Besides dragons, you may see tiny Timor deer, snakes, monkeys, wild boar and birds.

Long walks or overnight stays on Rinca are no longer permitted. On request, the ranger can lead you through the mangroves and up a steep, barren slope for spectacular panoramic views of the bay.

Sumbawa

TIME FROM FLORES: **60 MINS**

Ride the waves in Sumbawa

Hollow tubes break on the reefs of the white-sand **Pantai Lakey**, attracting international championship surfers year-round with its surf – the most consistent swell is between June and August. **Lakey Peak** and **Lakey Pipe** are hallowed names, both within easy paddling distance of Lakey's string of

DRAGON-SPOTTING

At Komodo and Rinca, your odds of seeing dragons are very good, with the exception of mating season on Komodo (June and July), when females go into hiding and males spread out on the vast island trying to find them. Peak months for sightings are September to December, when both sexes are out and about. Mating season is less of a problem at Rinca, where the dragons hang around near the museum.

Rangers carry a forked wooden staff as their only protection; on Komodo, they encourage tourists to get closer than the designated 5m distance for photographic purposes. Resist temptation, and treat the seemingly slow-moving dragons with respect: five deaths have been recorded, including of two tourists.

HIKING OPTIONS ON PULAU KOMODO

In Labuan Bajo, you may charter your own boat (from 2,500,000Rp per day) and choose your own itinerary according to your interests. To maximise dragon-spotting time on Pulau Komodo, you can negotiate with rangers on the island for adventure treks (from 600,000Rp for up to five people) up to 10km long (4–5 hours). One trek climbs the 538m-high Gunung Ara, with expansive views from the top. The other, through Poreng Valley, passes a memorial to 79-year-old Randolph Von Reding – who disappeared on Komodo in 1974 – then heads to Loh Sebita bay. It's challenging, the sea views are spectacular and you'll likely see ample wildlife en route. Organise your boat to pick you up.

TRUBAVIN/SHUTTERSTOCK ©

Surfing, Sumbawa

modest beach guesthouses, all linked by a sandy path studded with bars. From August to October, the wind gusts, which turns Pantai Lakey into Indonesia's best kitesurfing destination.

Grounded by reef, the A-frame Lakey Peak is the wave here, right in front of the famous tower; it's for experienced surfers only. Next to it, Lakey Pipe is a nice left-hander, best at mid-to-high tide. A five-minute drive from Lakey, less crowded **Cobblestones** is a left- and right-hander break; the gentler right-hander is good for beginners.

A short paddle from the shore, 15 minutes from Lakey, **Periscope** is a steep right-hander barrel reef-break. A similar distance away, left- and right-hander **Nangadoro** is worth seeking out at high tide, while **Nungas**, a long left-hander reef break near Lakey, is gentler than Peak or Pipe and best at low-to-mid tide, with killer sunsets from the beach.

EATING IN PANTAI LAKEY: OUR PICKS

Wreck This breezy restaurant does an Indonesian interpretation of quesadillas, fajitas and burritos, along with spicy fish in banana leaves and icy beer. $$

Fatmah's Perch in the bleached-wood house overlooking the surfing action and tuck into juices, *ayam lalapan* (fried chicken and sambal), pastas and Aussie meat pies. $$

3 Waves Fortify yourself with toast, eggs and omelettes, then roast chicken or Aussie burgers as you emerge from Lakey Peak. $$

Compass Warung Surfing footage provides entertainment while you tuck into smoothie bowls, burgers and generous *mie gorengs*. $$

West Timor

TRADITIONAL CULTURE | IKAT | CAVE DIVING

Fringed by vast, rice-growing plains and white-sand beaches, the greenery-clad hills and deep valleys of West Timor are as beguiling as the island's inhabitants. Smile at someone, and you're likely to get a smile in return, often with teeth stained a vampire-red from betel nut – an integral part of indigenous culture here.

It was the island's natural wealth – sandalwood – that brought the Portuguese here in the early 1500s, followed by the Dutch, and missionaries from both countries, who've been largely successful in Christianising the local population. Nonetheless, West Timor's ruggedly mountainous, *lontar* palm–studded topography and centuries-old division into independent, warring kingdoms has made it possible for animist traditions to persist, alongside 14 different languages and tribal dialects. After leaving the music-thumping *bemos* (minibuses) of Kupang, the capital, you enter the less-visited world of beehive-hut villages, whose chiefs preserve *adat* and whose artisans produce exquisite ikat.

Revel in the Sweet Sounds of Sasando

Mastering a Rotinese string instrument

Heading towards Soe, pull up outside **Sasandu** in Oebelo and step inside. A young man clad in a *ti'i langga* (*lontar*-leaf hat with a centre plume) – traditional headgear from the island of Rote – will treat you to an unforgettable musical repertoire as his hands fly deftly over the strings of the *sasando*, Rote's traditional 32-string zither that sounds alternately like a cross between a harp, a piano and steel pans. Used by the Rote islanders since the 17th century (though the original had bamboo or civet-gut strings rather than metal ones), the *sasando* is crafted from bamboo and teak, with a foldable palm leaf 'sail' for resonance. After the son of locally renowned Rotinese musician Pak Pah finishes serenading you, you can choose to take

---

GETTING AROUND

Bemos (5000Rp per ride) reach most of Kupang's spread-out attractions; clap loudly when you want to stop. Useful routes include 1 & 2 Kuanino–Oepura (past popular hotels); 5 Oebobo–Airnona–Bakunase (past the main post office), and 10 Kelapa Lima–Walikota (Terminal Kota, Oebobo bus terminal and Museum Nusa Tenggara Timur). Hotels rent motorbikes/scooters for 100,000Rp per day. Buses from Oebobo bus terminal, 7km from the airport, run to Soe (three hours), Kefamenanu (5½ hours) and Atambua (12 hours). You can rent a car and driver from 800,000Rp to 1,000,000Rp per day.

☑ TOP TIP

Local guides are essential for visiting traditional villages, in some of which Indonesian isn't widely spoken. They can explain local traditions and customs.

WEST TIMOR NUSA TENGGARA

THE GUIDE

Despite Kupang's scruffy waterfront, heavy traffic (only confident drivers should join in) and a lack of endearing architectural elements, there is a certain chaotic charm to West Timor's capital and regional hub. If travelling to the interior of Alor or Rote, you'll be spending time here and may find that it grows on you. England's Captain Bligh had a similar epiphany when he spent 47 days here after the mutiny on HMS *Bounty* in 1789. This day tour takes in Kupang's disparate sights. Start the morning by absorbing the clamour and pungency of **①Pasar Oeba** produce market and the adjacent fish market. Head east along the coast, then cut south to the fantastic **②Museum Nusa Tenggara**, a wonderful introduction to West Timor's history and cultural heritage. Amid displays of ceramics and kris (traditional daggers), you'll find ritual masks, warrior wear from Timor, elaborate wood carvings of statues used to ward off disease and natural disasters, and superb examples of ikat. Displays on the Pasola festival (p303), traditional music and natural history add context. Proceed to the rambling **③Pasar Inpres** to browse fresh produce and buy a *ti'i langga* (*lontar*-leaf hat with a centre plume) from Rote. Head north, then follow the coastal road to the west, past the well-signposted **④Monkey Cave**, with macaques hanging around outside. Proceed past the port to **⑤Goa Kristal Bolok** (Crystal Cave), where locals swim in turquoise water and partake in photoshoots. Nearby, **⑥Goa Uilebahan** is another cave with an aquamarine pool and interesting rock formations. Duck inland to frolic at the **⑦Air Terjun Oenesu** before finishing with sunset-watching at the white-sand **⑧Pantai Tablolong**, 25km southwest of Kupang.

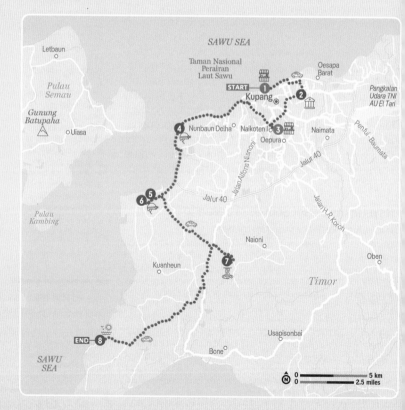

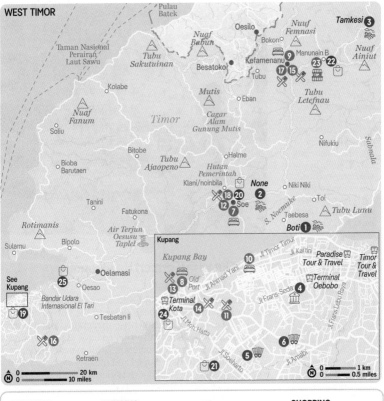

HIGHLIGHTS
1 Boti
2 None
3 Tamkesi

SIGHTS
4 Museum Nusa Tenggara Timur

ACTIVITIES
5 Cendana Dive
6 Dive Kupang Dive

SLEEPING
7 Dena Hotel
8 Lavalon Hostel
9 New Victory Hotel
10 Sotis Hotel

EATING
11 Depot Babi Se'i Aroma
12 Depot Remaja
13 Pasar Malam

14 Rumah Makan Palembang
15 Rumah Makan Pondok Selera
16 Se'i Babi Om Ba'i
17 Sisterhood Coffee & Eatery
18 Tapaleuk

SHOPPING
19 Edon Sasando Musik
20 Galeri Alekot
21 Ina Ndao
22 Maubesi Art Shop
23 Maubesi Market
24 Pak Haji Noer
25 Sasandu

lessons at **Edon Sasando Musik** on the outskirts of Kupang, if you're feeling inspired. *Sasando* virtuoso Aby Edon claims that if you have a modicum of musical talent, he'll have you coaxing out a tune within a couple of hours. Not content with playing the instrument, he also designs and builds his own, from the traditional acoustic (from 4,000,000Rp) to electric (8,000,000Rp) to hybrid (10,000,000Rp), just in case you'd like to take one home with you.

TIMOR-LESTE VISA RUN

Crossing the border to Timor-Leste is no longer complicated. It's cheapest to cross at Napan, 20km north of Kefamenanu; or Atapupu, which costs just 60,000Rp by *ojek* from Atambua. You can also make the 12-hour, one-way journey to Dili, Timor-Leste, for 250,000Rp; arrange 4am pickup with **Timor Tour & Travel** or **Paradise Tour & Travel** via your lodgings.

Short on time? Catch the 45-minute morning Wings Air flight from Kupang to Atambua, cross the border, and fly back to Kupang. Europeans from the Schengen Area may visit Timor-Leste visa-free for 30 days. Visitors from other countries are issued a visa on arrival at the border, once they pay US$30 and present proof of onward journey.

BERT DE RUITER/ALAMY STOCK PHOTO ©

None (p289)

Hang Out with (Former) Headhunters

Visit a traditional village

Near the market town of Niki-Niki, a gravel road runs for 1km past corn, pumpkin and bean fields to the village of **None**, one of the area's most compelling attractions. You'll stop by one of the *ume bubu* (beehive-shaped huts) at the roadside to greet the village chief. In some ways, this appears to be a typical Dawan village, its cramped and smoky *ume bubu* without windows and its 1m-high doorways sitting alongside modern concrete houses. At the end of the road, you reach the ceremonial grounds that end abruptly in the vine-covered sheer cliff that made the village easy to defend from enemies. It's so peaceful here that it's hard to believe they were hunting heads just two generations ago – the last conflict was in 1944.

If you have a local guide with you, they'll point out the *lopo* (village meeting place) and explain that None has a proud population of 56 families who have lived here for 10 generations and who still adhere to traditional practices.

At the cliff's edge, you'll find a 300-year-old banyan tree and totem pole where shamans once met with warriors before they left on headhunting expeditions. Nearby is a stone platform where enemy heads were once displayed. Proceed to the *ote naus*, an awning beneath which guns and spears

EATING IN KUPANG & AROUND: OUR PICKS ——————— MAP p289

Se'i Babi Om Ba'i Make the trip to the village of Baun for arguably the most authentic *se'i babi* (Rotinese smoked pork) in West Timor. $

Depot Babi Se'I Aroma Contemporary Kupang chain specialising in *se'i babi*, *sate babi* (pork satay) and other porky bites. $

Pasar Malam Come evening, head for this lamp-lit seafood market for *ikan* (fish), *cumi* (squid), *kepiting* (crab) and *udang* (prawns). $

Rumah Makan Palembang Chinese-Indonesian restaurant specialising in *ikan bakar rica rica* (grilled fish with chilli sauce), along with veg, chicken, seafood, noodle and rice dishes. $$

were stored. It is here that elders consulted chicken eggs and a wooden staff before predicting if the warriors would prevail. If there was a speck of blood in the egg, a sign of poor fortune, they'd delay their attack. The village women may break out their looms as you're leaving, with weaving demonstrations upon request (a 50,000Rp donation is appropriate) and a decent selection of ikat cloth for sale.

Drop in on Highland Royalty

Not just cats may look at a king

Some 50km northeast of Kefa, accessible via a two-hour drive along a periodically rough road and across wind-swept ridges, **Tamkesi** is one of West Timor's most isolated and best-preserved villages. Balancing on a jagged rock path, you pass through a keyhole between jutting limestone cliffs to find yourself in the middle of it all. There are two entrances: one is reserved for royalty but often used by travellers; the correct entrance has a sign reading 'Eno Fatnai Naimnune' on a stone platform, from which it's a short uphill walk along a cobblestone pathway under a canopy of trees.

The house of the *raja* (king) overlooks the village, with the east and west pillars representing the male and female, respectively. Clamber up the stone steps to meet the turbaned king and his family, where you'll offer betel nut (buy it in Manufui, the last village off the main road before turning off for Tamkesi) and make a donation (50,000Rp per person). After the obligatory respectful chewing (p292), you can shoot pictures of the low-slung beehive huts built into the bedrock and connected by red-clay paths that ramble to the edge of a precipice. Just don't take pictures of the conical hut where the village's mysterious sacred objects are stored, lest bad luck befall you. The same goes if you drop something; don't pick it up immediately and instead alert local villagers, who will first pray to the ancestors for forgiveness.

You can't miss the soaring, craggy limestone cliff. At least once every seven years, the king and the village elders climb the face of **Tapenpah**, sans rope, with a goat, rooster, branches of betel nut, bamboo, coconut, sugar cane and cotton. Depending on the size of the offering, this is done in multiples of seven. Other members of the community also ascend in multiples of seven. They slaughter the goat (but not the rooster), chew betel nut and only come down once everything has been eaten. This **Natamamausa** ritual is performed to give thanks for a good harvest, or to stop (or start) the rain.

If you want to climb the other notable rock face, **Oepuah**, enlist the help of a young villager, but only attempt it if you're a keen scrambler. The view over the village from the top, not to mention the 360-degree views, is invigorating. Tip your adventurous leader 20,000Rp.

Very little Bahasa Indonesia is spoken here, so a guide is essential. The overall mood is warm and welcoming.

BEST IKAT SHOPPING

West Timor is renowned for its ikat, whether sarong decorated with complex geometric patterns or antique *kelim* (tapestries). Quality varies, as do the dyes and yarn: pricier pieces use local cotton; others use imports from China.

Maubesi Market sells some quality ikat that a keen eye may spot.

Maubesi Art Shop stocks some truly excellent pieces that take a year to make.

Galeri Alekot is replete with options for all budgets; in Soe.

Ina Ndao sources ikat, as well as patterned espadrilles, shirts and ties; in Kupang.

Pak Haji Noer is a Kupang-based ikat expert who stocks collectors' pieces from across Nusa Tenggara, including antiques woven using ancient techniques no longer practised.

THE ART OF BETEL-NUT CHEWING

Before visiting a Dawan village, purchase a generous amount of *pinang* (dried or fresh betel nut) and *sirih* (betel nut leaves and flowers) at any market or roadside stall. It's customary to offer betel nut to the leader or king of a village as a goodwill gesture. It is avidly chewed by many in West Timor in conjunction with lime powder, which lessens the bitterness but can burn if it touches your gums. After acceptance, your host will probably offer you a chew: it's supposed to generate a warm buzz similar to a cigarette head-spin, but most first-timers will find it a bitter experience, their mouths numb and flooded with crimson saliva. Spitting is okay.

Music performance, Boti

Kupang's Underwater World
Indonesia's only freshwater cave diving

While West Timor's dive sites cannot compete with Alor, its lack of currents do make them beginner-friendly. Kupang is also the only place in Indonesia to offer freshwater cave dives, in **Kristal Cave** and **Oehani Cave**, both with up to 50m visibility, limestone tunnels, narrow swim-throughs and stalactite formations. With its fossilised, shell-encrusted walls, a 75m-long channel, a submerged chamber and an air chamber, Kristal Cave is the easier dive of the two. Oehani Cave – a 500m-long sinkhole with three air chambers – is best suited to experienced cave divers, due to difficult access and narrow tunnels. Kupang's dive operators are **Dive Kupang** and **Cendana Dive**.

Visit the Last King in West Timor
Explore the traditional village of Boti

A two-hour ride into the mountains from Soe via an undulating, unpaved road, you'll find the traditional village of **Boti**. Here, Ama Namah Benu, the charismatic *kepala suku* (chief), often referred to as the 'last king in West Timor', maintains the strict laws of *adat*.

EATING IN SOE & KEFAMENANU: OUR PICKS
MAP p289

Depot Remaja Soe. Succulent *se'i babi* (Rotinese smoked pork) and *jantung pisang* (banana flower salad) are standouts here. $$

Tapaleuk Soe. Order your *bakso* (meatballs) and *pangsit* (wontons) a myriad different ways at this neon-lit eatery. $

Sisterhood Coffee & Eatery Kefa. This fata morgana of a city cafe serves espressos, salted caramel lattes and mocktails, along with katsu sandwiches and fried rice. $$

Rumah Makan Pondok Selera Kefa. Chow down on excellent tempeh and tofu dishes, *ikan kua asam* (sour fish soup) and sweet, chunky sambal made with fresh tomato. $

Bring a guide conversant with local *adat* and the Dawan language spoken in the village. On arrival, you'll be led to the king's house, where you will offer betel nut as a gift. You'll then enjoy sweet coffee with steamed cassava cakes, served by the king's sister.

Day-trippers are expected to contribute a donation (50,000Rp); staying overnight (or longer) in the simple thatched guesthouse allows you to delve deeper into the life of a village that has resisted Christianisation, whose 300 or so inhabitants still follow ancient animist rituals, and whose king has only recently allowed just one child from each family to attend primary and middle school (but not high school, to avoid the clash between mainstream education and ancestral lore). Boti's autonomy is partially due to Dutch colonial powers failing to find the village in times past.

Boti children are named after elements in their natural surroundings; the men grow their hair from an early age – similar to Rastafarians, they view it as their connection to nature. Conversely, when a woman is pregnant, she shaves the head of her youngest daughter: a sign for the community to help out where they can. Men and women may marry outside the village, but women will be shunned if they don't bring their husbands back to live with them.

Early in the morning, you'll see the men go off to the fields to grow crops, including bananas, corn, papaya and cash crops of peanuts. The people are notoriously self-reliant, refusing government assistance (even NGO offers of food have caused offence, the implication being that outsiders think they are lazy or poor). The Boti week has nine days, with every ninth day devoted to rest, music and spiritual activities. During the day, you'll be followed around by curious children as you observe women cooking at the outdoor kitchen, going to the river to bring back bamboo 'buckets' full of water, or weaving ikat sarongs. Children as young as six are expected to help out: girls with spinning thread from locally grown cotton, boys with tending animals. Come sundown, the men return, and women serve the evening meal in coconut shell bowls. If you pay 100,000Rp, the men may perform a traditional dance, and the women may sing a haunting tune while the king strums his indigenous ukelele.

WEST TIMOR'S BEST GUIDES

West Timor's traditional villages are a minefield of cultural dos and don'ts. A local guide is essential; some charge 2,000,000Rp per day.

Edwin Lerrick
(lavalonbar@gmail.com). The irrepressible owner of Kupang's Lavalon Hostel has deep regional knowledge and connections throughout West Timor.

Ony Meda (+62 813 3940 4204) A guide with over two decades of experience organising anthropological tours and treks.

Willy Kadati
(willdk678@gmail.com) Willy specialises in cultural, botanic and ikat guides of West Timor.

Aka Nahak
(timorguide@gmail.com) Enthusiastic, Kefamenanu-based Aka has been touring Timor since 1988.

Yabes Olbata (+62 813 3894 9694) Soe-based guide conversant in the Dawan language, charging 1,200,000Rp per day.

FOR MORE IKAT
Read **Ikat Textiles** (p346) to learn more about the history, techniques and meaning behind Indonesia's famed woven cloth.

This driving loop of West Timor covers market towns, traditional villages and stunning beaches. Begin in ❶ **Kupang**, West Timor's bustling capital. Pause in ❷ **Oebelo**, a small salt-mining town 22km from Kupang on the Soe road, to visit the *sasando* workshop (p287), then proceed to the cool, leafy market town of ❸ **Soe**, the gateway to some of the fascinating traditional villages of the interior. Some 17km east of Soe, take the turnoff for ❹ **None** (p290), a former headhunting village, before passing through the market town of ❺ **Niki-Niki** – market day is Wednesday. The winding road continues through the lush interior to ❻ **Kefamenanu**, a visually unimpressive former Portuguese stronghold that's nonetheless a decent overnighter. Just 3.5km from Kefa is ❼ **Maslete**, a traditional village with a thatch-roofed *sonaf* (palace), made from wood carved with mythical birds. Nineteen kilome-

tres east of Kefa, ❽ **Maubesi** is home to the Kefa Regency's best textile market. Market day is Thursday, when, along with produce, animals and pottery, ikat is displayed beneath tamarind trees. If you're not passing by on a Thursday, Maubesi Art Shop, on the eastern outskirts, has a terrific selection of local ikat. Turn north 11km east to visit ❾ **Tamkesi** (p291), a traditional village in a lofty setting, before retracing your steps to just north of Niki-Niki. If it's Thursday, consider making the bone-shaking detour to ❿ **Ayotupas** to check out the clamour of the weekly produce market. Just south of Niki-Niki, take the minor road east into the mountains to the animist village of ⓫ **Boti** (p292). From Boti, descend to the stunning white-sand ⓬ **Pantai Kolbano**, then return to Kupang, via dune-backed ⓭ **Pantai Oetune** and West Timor's vast rice-growing plains.

Beyond West Timor

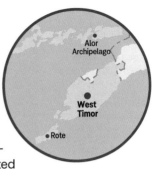

Alor Archipelago

West Timor

• Rote

Incomparable underwater worlds, a world-renowned surf break and tiny, seldom-visited islands await a mere short plane or ferry hop from Kupang.

If you're a diver, you will have heard of the Alor Archipelago, north of West Timor, and its epic dive sites such as Fish Bowl and Mike's Delight. Odds are, you're heading there right now abroad a liveaboard, all set for underwater exploration, or else staying in a diving lodge on one of its islands. But there's so much more to this tiny, isolated cluster of islands, whose 134 tribes speak 18 languages and 52 dialects, and where animist practices still thrive in fortress-like, hilltop villages. Southwest of West Timor, the parched limestone speck that is Rote draws surfers with its legendary T-Land break, relaxed vibe and white-sand beaches.

Alor Archipelago  TIME FROM WEST TIMOR: **50 MINS**

Alor Archipelago beneath the waves

One of Indonesia's most astonishing underwater archipelagos, Alor has it all: tremendous visibility, a vast array of dive sites, world-class coral reefs abuzz with shoals of reef fish, stunning walls, and frequent sightings of reef sharks, rays, turtles, and the occasional dolphin pod and whale. Best of all, you'll have it all pretty much to yourself. Strong, unpredictable currents mean that many sites are best suited to experienced divers, although correct timings open up parts of this world to novices and intermediate divers. Day dives from **Pulau Pantar** and **Pulau Kepa** aside, the Alor Archipelago is best experienced aboard a liveaboard.

One of Alor's most exhilarating drift dives is the aptly named **Fish Bowl**, in the channel between Alor and Kepa. As you float along the sloping reef covered in soft corals, look out for scorpionfish, lone titan triggerfish and midnight snappers as schools of neon-blue fusiliers stream around you and Moorish idols flit by. On the east coast of Pulau Pura, **Mike's Delight** is another excellent reef drift dive with visibility up to 40m and an abundance of hard and soft corals that are alive with parrotfish, damselfish, angelfish and Napoleon wrasse; schools of jacks, passing reef sharks and dolphin pods can be spotted in the deep blue. A stunning slope reef suitable for

Places

GETTING AROUND

There's fierce competition among Labuan Bajo's boat operators and diving outfits for day- and multi-day trips to Komodo National Park. Group day trips by speedboat cost from 750,000Rp per person and allow for more time at each location than the cheaper slow boats. Multi-day liveaboards cater to divers and explorers. Rinca Island is accessible by private boat (from 1,500,000Rp) only. Fly to Bima, Sumbawa to catch a bus to Hu'u, or take a taxi from Bima (1,000,000Rp) directly to Pantai Lakey.

ARRANGE YOUR BEST ALOR ADVENTURE

Alor Divers Operated by a French–Slovenian couple on Pulau Timur's eastern shore, Alor caters exclusively to divers, with a range of sites and courses.

Lazy Turtle Dive Alor This Kalabahi-based Australian–UK operation opposite Pulau Kepa (p295) runs daily reef- and muck-site dives aboard *Naughty Nudi* and offers accommodation packages.

Mila Salim (milasalim619@gmail.com) Mila Salim is a wonderful local guide who can arrange cultural excursions across Alor. She runs Kalabahi's first *oleh-oleh* (souvenir) shop, supporting local craftspeople.

Gabriel Tang (gabriellobangtang@gmail.com) Recommended Kalabahi-based guide who can arrange cultural itineraries of Alor, including visits to traditional houses and dugong trips.

RICH CAREY/SHUTTERSTOCK ©

Lone titan triggerfish

beginners, combined with a challenging wall dive, **Symphony No. 9** off Pulau Pantar offers tremendous coral diversity and density, along with seemingly endless schools of damselfish and basslets, and the opportunity to be suspended beneath the overhang at 15m, scanning the fathomless depths for pelagic life. **Kal's Dream**, a seamount between Pura and Kepa, is also wonderful for passing large pelagics, barracuda, Spanish mackerel, giant trevallies and schooling jacks, with octopus, morays and shrimp hiding in the 12m-deep plateau. Strong currents sweeping over the top of the pinnacle warrant a quick descent.

 EATING IN NEMBERALA: OUR PICKS

Fishbones Contrary to the name, this informal place makes great pizza, combining thin-crust pie with a *se'i babi* (Rotinese smoked pork) for that winning combo. **$$**

Narrow Resto Indonesian mains, English breakfasts big enough to get you through a siege, a chilled vibe and massages offered on the premises. **$$**

Bekky Boo's Bekky caters to all tastebuds with her crowd-pleasing menu of gnocchi, fish and veggie wraps, fried rice, and caramelised bananas. **$$**

The Pasar Enjoy excellent coffee, sourdough sandwiches, couscous and feta salads and other international dishes at this open-sided, breezy spot. **$$**

Rote

Hanging ten in Nemberala

Between March and November, the consistent southwest swell brings reliable waves to the white-sand beach of the chilled-out fishing village of **Nemberala** on the west coast of Rote Island, along with a contingent of surfers.

Unlike some other Indonesian surfing hotspots, Nemberala is a friendly place, without locals guarding their favourite surf spots. Breaking at all tides, the main wave here is the legendary **T-Land**, one of Indonesia's longest left-handers, divided into the Peak, the Pyramid and the Mountain (accessible to surfers of different abilities). Nearby is the **Bommie**, a short right-hander reef break, particularly fun at low tide with big swells. If you prefer a heavier, hollow, intense right-hander with few others in the lineup, head for **Suckie Mama's**, 3km north of Nemberala, accessed only via a 10-minute boat ride. Another hollow right, **Do'o**, breaks off an uninhabited island a 20-minute boat ride from Nemberala and is perfect for intermediate and expert surfers. Beginners take note: just north of the Nemberala fishing-boat harbour is **Squealers**, a right- and left-hander thus named for the screeches made by novices catching their first wave. About 8km south of Nemberala, **Bo'a** has a spectacular white-sand beach and a mid-tide right hander with a good tube section, accessed either by paddling out or a 10-minute boat ride. The local surf resorts can take you out to other world-class waves that fluctuate according to the wind and tide. Many resorts rent high-quality boards from about 100,000Rp per day.

THE WONDROUS LONTAR PALM

Rote remains dependent on the drought-resistant *lontar* palm. The palm is extremely versatile; its tough yet flexible leaves are woven to make sacks and bags, hats and sandals, roofs and dividing walls. *Lontar* wood is fashioned into furniture and floorboards. But what nourishes the islanders is the milky, frothy *nirah* (sap) tapped from the *tankai* (orange-stemmed inflorescences) that grow from the crown of the *lontar*. Drunk straight from the tree, the *nirah* is refreshing, nutritious and energising. If left to ferment for hours, it becomes *laru* (palm wine), which is hawked around the lanes of Rote. With further distillation, the juice is distilled into gin-like *sopi* – the power behind many a wild Rote night.

Man playing a *sasando* (p287)

ANNA KAMINSKI/LONELY PLANET ©

Sumba

TRADITIONAL VILLAGES | MEMORABLE FESTIVALS | UNTAMED NATURE

GETTING AROUND

Buses connect Waingapu with Kalala (five hours) and Tambolaka (five hours) via Waikabubak. Trucks serve Tarimbang, Wanokaka and Kerewe. Most hotels arrange motorbike or scooter rental (200,000Rp per day). Car and driver rental is around 1,000,000Rp per day; it's hard to rent a car without a driver. There are daily flights from Waingapu to Ende (Flores), Denpasar (Bali) and Kupang (West Timor). Ferries run to Ende and Kupang. There are daily flights from Tambolaka to Denpasar and Kupang, and ferries to Sape in Sumbawa (three weekly, nine hours).

☑TOP TIP

You need a guide to visit traditional villages. Some villages reject visitors if their guide has no contacts within the community. A set donation and signing the visitor book are part of village visits.

There's something truly enchanting about Sumba. Its intricately woven ikat textiles are displayed in museums worldwide as exemplars of its kind; its verdant, hilly interior – so unlike Indonesia's northern volcanic isles – is populated by roaming horses and dotted with traditional hilltop villages of tall grass roofs clustered around megalithic tombs. Its nominally Christian villagers still adhere to indigenous *marapu* (spiritual force) practices, and animal sacrifice is common. In February and March, warriors on horseback clash en masse while wielding blunt spears during the annual Pasola festival.

Culturally fascinating, Sumba is no slouch when it comes to natural attractions, either. It's encircled by pristine white-sand beaches and pounded by relentless breaks that have been drawing surfers for years, while secret swimming holes, waterfalls and caves beckon further inland. Friendly and low-key, this part of Nusa Tenggara is particularly vulnerable to change. Developers have their eye on Sumba, so go without delay.

A Perfect Day around Waingapu

Traditional villages, historic sites & viewpoint

East Sumba's transport hub, Waingapu, is a laid-back town with a leafy, dusty centre interspersed with accommodations and small *toko* (stores). It also has a busy produce market, a harbour that becomes redolent with grilled fish after sundown, and villages in the middle of it all. From Waingapu, you can launch trips along the north coast and into the interior, seeing traditional villages and archaeological sites all in one day.

Near the Praikundu Ikat Centre (p306), 6km south of Waingapu, an awning protects the small archaeological site of **Lambanapu**, whose compact size belies its considerable importance. Extensive excavations (between 2016 and 2022) have taken place here. It's the burial site of an ancient civilisation of East Sumba's prehistoric people. The physical remains of 45 individuals have been unearthed, along with weaponry,

ANGES VAN DER LOOT/SHUTTERSTOCK ©

Sumbanese men, Waingapu

SUMBANESE IKAT

Displayed in museums around the world as examples of the highest quality textile, Sumbanese ikat is recognised as the best in Indonesia. East Sumbanese ikat depicts village scenes, mythological creatures, Pasola tournaments and tribal wars. West Sumbanese ikat does not adhere to the complex ikat-making process and is much simpler, featuring geometric patterns.

The most authentic ikat is still made with natural dyes, with each strand of yarn dyed individually before being affixed to the loom. The bark and roots of the mengkudu tree produce red dye; indigo plants produce blue dye; and a mix of indigo and mengkudu produces brown and purple dyes. The ikat-weaving process is now partially mechanised, which is why vintage ikat pieces fetch collector's prices.

household items and jewellery. The jar burials, no longer practised on Sumba, are thought to date back to the earliest presence of humans in Sumba, and it is hoped that the discovery will shed light on the arrival of Austronesian speakers.

For lunch, head southeast along the coast to grab some hot-and-sour fish soup at the thatched **Amu Dahi** in Melolo village, then proceed to **Praiyawang**, a traditional Sumbanese village near Melolo. It has an imposing lineup of nine stone tombs, the largest being that of the chief of this former kingdom. Shaped like a buffalo, it consists of four stone pillars (2m high) supporting a monstrous slab (about 5m long and 2.5m wide). Two stone tablets stand atop the main slab, carved with figures. A massive Sumbanese house with concrete pillars faces the tombs, along with a number of *rumah adat* and an uninhabited ceremonial house. Within the tombs, it's permitted to bury siblings, grandchildren and grandparents together, but the deceased can't be buried alongside their parents. Crocodile statues represent the king; turtles are only seen on women's tombs; and the cockatoos and horses symbolise democracy.

On your way back to Waingapu, take the bumpy track to the **Tanau Hills** for exceptional panoramic views of Sumba's unique topography.

Do Go Chasing Waterfalls

Explore waterfalls near Waingapu

A couple of hours' drive (60km) northwest of Waingapu, along rough roads, and a further 20-minute trek through savannah or grasslands, depending on the time of year, is **Air Terjun Tanggedu**, arguably Sumba's best waterfall. What awaits will

Continues p302.

299

SUMBA

Waihula

HIGHLIGHTS

1. Air Terjun Tanggedu
2. Pantai Kerewe
3. Praikundu Ikat Centre

SIGHTS

4. Air Terjun Wai Marang
5. Laipopu Waterfall
6. Lambanapu
7. Pantai Dassang
8. Pantai Kalala
9. Pantai Marosi
10. Pantai Nihiwatu
11. Pantai Pahiri
12. Pantai Pero
13. Pantai Rua
14. Pantai Tarimbang
15. Pantai Wainyapu
16. Praigoli
17. Prailiu
18. Praiyawang
19. Sodan
20. Tanau Hills
21. Waigalli
22. Waihura

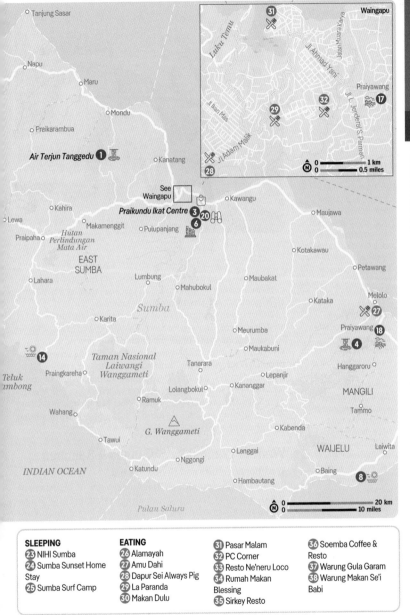

SLEEPING
23 NIHI Sumba
24 Sumba Sunset Home Stay
25 Sumba Surf Camp

EATING
26 Alamayah
27 Amu Dahi
28 Dapur Sei Always Pig
29 La Paranda
30 Makan Dulu
31 Pasar Malam
32 PC Corner
33 Resto Ne'neru Loco
34 Rumah Makan Blessing
35 Sirkey Resto
36 Soemba Coffee & Resto
37 Warung Gula Garam
38 Warung Makan Se'i Babi

KAMPUNG ADAT

Sumbanese villages were traditionally built on hillsides (to see approaching enemies) and consist of two rows of houses with their thatched roofs, or are arranged in a rough circle surrounding the tombs and *kateda* (sacrificial altars) in the centre. Villages typically have several clans living there, and each clan has its own *rumah adat*, where sacred objects are kept and ancestral spirits dwell.

Houses are constructed from bamboo tied together with vines and finished with tall traditional roofs, their bamboo scaffolding covered with dried *alang* grass. The main struts represent different elements, while the hearth in the centre represents the sun. The underfloor section is for animals; the ground floor, for humans.

CYRILLE REDOR/SHUTTERSTOCK ©

Praigoli

Continued from p299.

blow you away: two rivers run between time-layered limestone cliffs and converge into waterfall terraces that feed into multiple pools; there are dipping pools nearby.

Alternatively, get an early start and follow the north coast southeastwards in the direction of Kalala to the town of Melolo (where you sometimes see sunbathing crocodiles on the riverbanks), near Praiyawang (p299). Take the smooth, unpeopled road inland for 8km to the parking area overlooking a verdant valley, pay the 50,000Rp entrance fee and descend for around 15 minutes along some concrete steps, followed by a steep trail, to reach **Air Terjun Wai Marang**, a startlingly blue dipping pool in the middle of the jungle, surrounded by limestone walls and fed by a waterfall.

Wander Wanokaka's Villages & Beaches

Traditional culture and slivers of sand

South of **Waikabubak**, you'll encounter some of Sumba's most striking scenery, the oldest megalithic tombs, pristine beaches and world-class surfing. Taking the main road south, turn off after 8km and follow the narrower paved road west. Passing some Pasola grandstands, with rice-paddy vistas opening up and locals swimming in the river, you'll reach Hapumada, where the road forks. The rougher, partially paved northward

 EATING IN WAINGAPU: OUR PICKS ——————— MAP p300-1

Pasar Malam Head for the old wharf at dusk for wallet-friendly fish and seafood grilled by gas-lit carts. $

PC Corner Killer views, selfie-worthy murals, live music on Saturdays and dishes such as papaya flower with *kangkung* (water spinach) are big draws here. $$

Dapur Sei Always Pig Buy *se'i babi* (Rotinese smoked pork) by weight, or opt for other porky dishes (*babi rica rica, sate babi*), along with papaya blossom salad. $

La Paranda Order *ayam* (chicken), *udang* (prawns) or *cumi* (squid) in various guises, along with *cah kangkung* (garlicky water spinach) at this breezy restaurant. $$

fork leads towards the jungly trailhead to **Laipopu waterfall**. South and downhill from Hapumada is **Waigalli**, a traditional village on a promontory above the sea; further south is the fishing village of **Waihura**, at the western end of the vast, wave-battered, white-sand **Pantai Pahiri**, where the village youth practise bareback horse-riding.

A shortcut up a bumpy, unpaved road from Waigali brings you to **Praigoli**, home to Sumba's most famous megalithic statue – the fleur-de-lis *Lakaruka Jiwa Tada Bita Laka*. If you happen to be in one of the traditional villages while a traditional roof is being fixed, you may come across a roof-fixing ceremony involving a dog sacrifice and the playing of gongs, or all of the village men partaking in the fixing while the women cook for everyone in an outdoor kitchen. From Praigoli, take a bumpy, steep shortcut up a particularly scenic road with great views of Pantai Pahiri, passing the turnoff to **Pantai Rua**, a white-sand beach with a resort and some calmer spots for bathing. Further along, you pass the turnoff for the exclusive resort of NIHI Sumba (p311) before rejoining the main road towards Kerewe Beach and the Lamboya district. On your right, you'll spy the traditional roofs of the village of **Sodan** atop a steep hill (reachable by rough 4WD track). You may only visit if your guide has contacts in Sodan, as the locals are keen to preserve traditional culture. Shortly after, a turnoff south brings you to the surfing hotspot of Pantai Kerewe (p306) and Sumba's most touristy part.

Witness a Ritual Horseback Tournament

Let the battle commence

Pasola (from *pa* meaning 'game' and *sola* meaning 'wooden spear') has to be one of the most extravagant (and bloody) harvest festivals in Asia. Held annually in February and March in West Sumba, it takes the form of a ritual battle between two teams of blunt-spear-wielding, ikat-clad horsemen. The bloodier the proceedings, the better the harvest, as the blood is believed to please the spirits. Although the festival is considerably less bloody than it used to be, and blunt spears are now used, it's still a dangerous sport. Spectators should be aware of any potential animal welfare issues, including animal sacrifices.

Pasola takes place in Lamboya and Kodi villages in February and in Kodi Bangedo, Lamboya Barat and Wanokaka villages in March. A *rato* (priest) decides the exact timing based on the arrival of a sea worm called *nyale* on nearby coasts, but these days tourism comes first, and eager fans are now given up to

SUMBA'S BEST GUIDES

Erwin Pah (erwinpah9@gmail.com) Irrepressible, enthusiastic, Waingapu-based guide who seems to know everyone in Sumba. Can arrange caving, rock-climbing and village tours.

Sumba Adventure Tours & Travel (sumbaadventuretours.com) Experienced guide Philip Renggi and his team lead trips into seldom-explored villages, including his native Manuakalada and Waiwarungu. Arranges itineraries, sets you up for Pasola, rents cars and more.

Yuliana Leda Tara (+62 813 3795 7670) Expert Tarung-based English- and French-speaking guide, in demand from anthropologists and filmmakers; organises village tours throughout West Sumba.

Umba Angga (+62 813 3848 8375) Waingapu-based, recommended English-speaking driver and guide.

 EATING IN TAMBOLAKA: OUR PICKS ———————— MAP p300-1

Warung Gula Garam Run by expat Frenchman Louis, this thatched open-air cafe near the airport plays funky-fresh R&B tunes and serves surprisingly good wood-fired pizza. $$

Makan Dulu Braised lamb in coconut milk, satay dishes, and Sumbanese cassava leaf and rice cream soup are standouts at this breezy, bamboo-roofed restaurant. $$

Sirkey Resto Clean, air-conditioned diner serving grilled chicken and fish, stir-fried vegetables, and Indonesian and Indonesian-Chinese staples. $

Warung Makan Se'l Babi Place your order at the barbecue grills for Tambolaka's respectable take on smoked Rotinese-style pork. $

MARAPU BELIEFS

The basis of traditional Sumbanese religion is *marapu*, a collective term for Sumba's spiritual forces, including gods, spirits and ancestors. At death, the deceased join the invisible world of spirits, *praing marapu*, from where they can influence the world of the living. *Marapu mameti* is the collective name for all dead people. The living can appeal to *marapu mameti* for help, especially their own relatives, though the dead can be harmful if irritated.

The *marapu maluri* are the original people placed on Earth by God, and their power is concentrated in certain places or objects, which are often kept safe in the family's thatched loft. Offerings to the spirits involve betel nut and/ or animal sacrifice.

Manola (p305)

a month's warning. Dressed in full ceremonial garb, the *rato* wades into the ocean to examine the worms at dawn; they're usually found on the eighth or ninth day after a full moon.

Only in **Wanokaka**, two days before the main event, opposing 'armies' drawn from coastal and inland villages meet on deserted beaches at night for no-holds-barred, brutal boxing matches called *pajura*, with the combatants' fists bound in thorn-edged palm leaves. Teeth are lost and noses broken, but when dawn breaks, everyone sings ancestral songs of peace.

The night before the Pasola tournament, participant riders sacrifice chickens to the *rato* in the relevant village, who then consecrates the tournament ground. Early in the morning of the event, spectators gather around the Pasola stadiums, dressed in their best. There's no entrance fee; just get there on time to claim a good vantage point.

Two rows of riders of up to 50 men each, in traditional headgear and their mounts splendidly adorned, charge at each other at breakneck speed, like knights in the Middle Ages. Just when collision feels inevitable and you find yourself holding your breath, they rein in their steeds and hurl the blunt spears at one another. You'll see the most skilled riders not only evade the projectiles with ease but also pluck them out of the air, flinging them back at their opponents. In spite of the violence, the underlying purpose of Pasola battles is peace, with all inter-clan conflicts considered resolved – until the following year.

 EATING IN WAIKABUBAK & WANOKAKA: OUR PICKS ———— MAP p300-1

Soemba Coffee & Resto Score a proper espresso at this contemporary spot, or settle in for a meal of chicken sate or nasi goreng (fried rice). $$

Rumah Makan Blessing Wash down seafood-topped *mie goreng* (fried noodles), *bakso* (meatballs) or chicken with fresh juice at this family-run spot. $

Alamayah Strong cocktails, good coffee and a mix of Aussie and Indonesian dishes in refined surroundings. Open to non-guests in low season. $$

Resto Ne'neru Loco Chow down on stir-fried sweet-and-sour dishes with a side of rice-paddy views. $

TOUR WAIBAKUL & WAIKABUBAK'S TRADITIONAL VILLAGES

Those interested in Sumbanese culture will find numerous traditional villages clustered around Waikabubak and Waibakul, some with exceptional stone tombs. It's best to visit with a guide, as Bahasa Indonesia is not really spoken here. Starting in ❶ **Waibakul**, take the paved road 2.5km south through the rice fields to ❷ **Gallubakul**, home to Sumba's heaviest tomb (70 tonnes), decorated with carvings of the buried king and queen, and buffalo and cockerel motifs. Allegedly, 6000 workers took three years to chisel the Umbu Sawola tomb out of a hillside and drag it 3km, using vines and banana-tree rollers. Returning to Waibakul, proceed to tin-roofed ❸ **Pasunda**. Visible from the main road is a particularly impressive tomb with images of a chief and his wife, their hands on their hips, dating from 1926. Take the main Waikabubak road, then turn south up a steep road to ❹ **Bondomarotto**, a friendly, somewhat steep, village whose thatched roofs have been restored after a recent fire; overnight stays are possible. Take a different turnoff from the Waikabubak road to ❺ **Praijing**, where you pay a 55,000Rp entry fee. Popular with visitors from Java, it has a lofty viewpoint from which to admire the Instagrammable rows of thatched houses. Proceed to ❻ **Waikabubak**, a compact market town. Several traditional villages are walkable from Waikabubak: ❼ **Tambelar**, just off Jl Sudirman, features very impressive *kubur batu* (stone graves). Uphill, beneath a giant ficus tree, ❽ **Tarung** is known for its intricately woven palm containers and is home to a famous male model; homestays are possible. Some 17km northwest of Waikabubak, a rough road leads to ❾ **Manola**, a village so traditional it eschews electricity; it's populated by elders and children, whose parents live elsewhere.

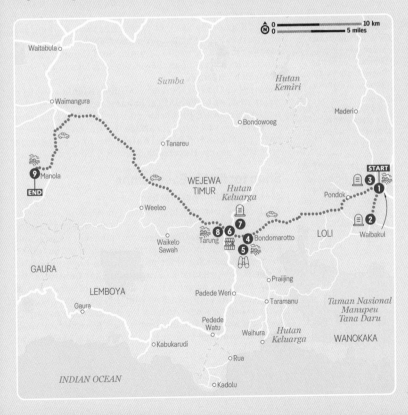

Megalithic culture on the island of Sumba goes back some 4500 years, and in numerous Sumbanese villages, you'll come across megalithic tombs, many of them highly elaborate in appearance. The tombs are rectangular and the grave is covered with a stone plate to resemble an altar or table, with the stone weighing many tonnes. The erection of these cover stones has traditionally required the sacrifice of buffalo, cows and pigs, with the stones pulled over long distances using tree trunks and lianas to the tune of rhythmic song.

Today, trucks are often used to transport the cover stones, but the ceremonies and singing still take place. Once the cover stone is in place, the grave is engraved with scenes from the life of the deceased.

Catch the Surf in Sumba

Surf's up

The beaches on West Sumba's south coast are on their way to being discovered, and not just by surfers (who've been coming here for years). In **Pantai Kerewe**, while the waves are surfable year-round, the best time is March to November, when longboarders come to ride the long, mellow right-hander out front for up to 600m. A 15-minute speedboat ride out to sea, and you have access to a dozen empty left- and right-hander reef breaks for most abilities, including some heavy barrels. North up the coast, **Pantai Pero** has nice lefts and rights on opposite sides of the river mouth, while **Pantai Wainyapu** is good for consistent and clean lefts.

A 15-minute walk from Pantai Kerewe, white-sand **Pantai Marosi** has a nice beach break, suitable for rookies. At **Pantai Dassang** – a wide sweep of white sand, fronted by a resort – there's more beachside action; drive up to the north end of the beach using a public road unless staying at the resort.

The region's legendary, world-class surf spot is **Occy's Left**, featured in the film *The Green Iguana*, off the achingly stunning **Pantai Nihiwatu**, but unless you have deep pockets and are staying at NIHI Sumba (p311), it'll remain a dream.

On Pantai Kerewe, the best digs for surfers are **Sumba Sunset Home Stay**, run by Petu, locally known as 'Raja di Laut' ('King of the Sea'); he spent eight years working as a lifeguard at NIHI Sumba and can sort out boat transport to the best breaks. Arnaud of **Sumba Surf Camp** is another expert surfer who knows the local breaks; lessons for beginners can be arranged.

Further south along the coast is **Miller's Rights** – a series of rights breaking off **Pantai Tarimbang** and arguably Sumba's most popular wave; the lineup gets busy from May to October.

On Sumba's east coast, the **Office** is a fun wave at the western end of the reef off **Pantai Kalala** – for intermediates and up – while nearby **Racetrack** is a faster, more intense ride.

Shop for Ikat in East Sumba

Seek out Sumba's best textiles

While in the past, only high-ranking members of Sumbanese society were able to afford ikat, today it's much more affordable. Near Waingapu, **Prailiu** village has numerous weavers, and prices start from 200,000Rp for small pieces; if you buy direct, the weavers get 100% of the profits. Run by English-speaking Kornelis Ndapakamang, **Praikundu Ikat Centre** on the outskirts of Waingapu is hung with some of Sumba's most prized ikat, all naturally dyed with detailed motifs. Kornelis is renowned for having some of the island's finest pieces, the largest of which go for millions of rupiah. Lengthier ikat workshops are available upon request with the help of Erwin Pah (p303).

TAMBOLAKA TO KEREWE BEACH – THE SLOW WAY

This day-long road trip goes the route less travelled from Tambolaka to Kerewe, taking in the west coast's diverse sites. On the outskirts of **1 Tambolaka**, Sumba's second city, **2 Rumah Budaya Sumba** museum is an excellent introduction to traditional Sumbanese culture, spiritual beliefs and ikat, with stone carvings and ancient ceramics on display. Next door, acquaint yourself with coffee- and cashew-nut cultivation at **3 Talasi Estate** before taking the narrow, paved road along Sumba's west coast. An hour's drive brings you to **4 Weekuri Lagoon**, where the Indian Ocean rages against the cliffs and bursts through blowholes, and where you can swim and snorkel (bring your own gear) in the sheltered lagoon popular with locals.

Further south, in Karoso village, the paved road becomes unpaved and bumpy. It is a shortcut to the main paved road and the large village of **5 Bondokodi**, the gateway to Sumba's Kodi district, renowned for its traditional houses. The best-known is nearby **6 Ratenggaro**, on a bluff above the mouth of a river, with a breathtaking view along the palm-fringed shoreline and elaborately decorated tombs at the village entrance. However, some of the residents' aggressive behaviour is off-putting. Following the bumpy main road, you pass **7 Paranobaroro**; the house of the Rajah of Kodi features Sumba's tallest (30m) roof. In **8 Wainyapu** – a Pasola (p303) site – take the bridge across the river and follow the rutted road past turnoffs to traditional waterside villages – Bwanna, WatuMalando; then gorgeous Rita, Katobo and Mambang beaches, and past a cacao plantation. At **9 Weetana**, a paved road leads you a further 29km to **10 Pantai Kerewe**.

HELP ME PICK

Nusa Tenggara Islands

Stretching east of Bali and Lombok, Nusa Tenggara comprises over 550 islands. It's dominated by three main ones: Flores, studded with volcanoes, forests and beaches; Sumba, rich in indigenous culture and covered in hills, caves and waterfalls; and West Timor, thronged with traditional villages vying for your attention alongside the brash capital. The smaller islands, some inhabited, others not, have their own appeal, from surfable waves and incredible underwater landscapes to the world's largest monitor lizard.

Where to go if you love...

Traditional Villages

Boti A picturesque Dawa village reachable from Timor's Kefamenanu, strictly practising only animist beliefs. Little electricity, and traditional dance.

Bena Bajawa-adjacent Ngada village, with a scenic ridge location, megalithic tombs and ancestral totems.

Tamkesi Thrillingly located hilltop Dawa village; scale a nearby cliff for tremendous views.

Wae Rebo Traditional Manggarai village reachable via a scenic hike; stay overnight and hike to a nearby waterfall.

Manola Take a rough track to this friendly, electricity-free Sumbanese village, populated by elders and children.

Fantastic Waves

Pantai Kerewe Good surfing year-round in Sumba, with a beach break out front, and half a dozen waves easily reachable by boat, including the legendary Occy's Left.

Nemberala Hit the consistent off-season beach break on Rote's Bo'a; ride the heavy, hollow tube at Suckie Mama's or hit the big T-Land wave.

Pantai Lakey In Sumbawa, Lakey Peak and Lakey Pipe are within paddling distance; alternatively, ride to Nungas, Cobblestone, Nangadoro and Periscope. Lakey Pipe and Nungas are top kiting destinations from August to October.

Epic Volcanoes

Gunung Inerie (pictured) Sweat your way up this spectacularly jagged cone (2245m), starting from Bajawa at 3am to catch the sunrise from the top. A six-to-eight-hour roundtrip.

Kelimutu Watch the sun's first rays illuminate the three multicoloured lakes from the summit of this volcano – unique in Indonesia – then hike down to Moni through scenic farmland.

Komodo Dragons

Pulau Komodo The main home of the world's largest monitor lizard; if you're lucky, your guide will spot some handsome specimens near the beach.

Pulau Rinca Komodo-dragon sightings practically guaranteed, since they often hang out next to the nature museum.

Underwater Landscapes

Komodo National Park Drift with manta rays at Karang Makassar, encounter reef sharks, turtles, tuna and giant trevally at Castle Rock, and brave the strong currents of the Cauldron to 'fly' over the reef.

Alor Archipelago (p295) Moorish idols, angelfish and fairy basslets awaits at the Fish Bowl reef, while Kal's Dream means barracuda and shark encounters amid schools of jacks and fusiliers.

Kristal Cave and Oehani Cave (p292) in West Timor are among Indonesia's very few freshwater cave dives, with fossil-encrusted walls, mysterious chambers and flooded tunnels to explore.

HOW TO

When to go Hiking and diving are best April to October (dry season); Komodo dragons are hardest to spot in June and July. Islands are greenest November to March.

Book ahead If visiting traditional villages, contact guides ahead of time. Book liveaboards and diving trips in advance, especially in summer.

Before you go Make sure your innoculations are up to date. Research the dive sites and traditional villages you want to explore.

Budget A guide and car will cost around 1.2–2 million rupiah per day, depending on the island and the guide. For liveaboards, budget from US$280 per day.

DIY or Guided Tour

Flores is easiest to explore under your own steam, with public transport connecting the main towns; it's also easy to rent a car, motorbike or scooter in the main towns, and to pootle around on your own, particularly along the Trans-Flores Hwy. Hotels and guesthouses in Ruteng, Bajawa, Moni and elsewhere can help arrange local guides if you want to visit traditional villages nearby.

West Timor is logistically trickier: car and scooter rental is possible to arrange in Kupang, but the main places of interest are inland, and you really need to have knowledge of the island's interior, since minor roads are often in bad condition and unlabelled. You also have to be a very good driver.

In Sumba, while cars with drivers are easy to negotiate, few individuals will rent you a car without a driver. Though most hotels can arrange scooter or motorbike rental, and you may see some of the sights off the island's main road independently, minor roads in the interior are often rough and unlabelled.

To visit traditional villages in Flores, West Timor and Sumba, you need to go with a knowledgeable local guide – both to overcome the language barrier (since there are places where Bahasa Indonesia is barely spoken) and to explain the local traditions and customs so that you don't inadvertently break the many unspoken rules.

Places We Love to Stay

$ Cheap $$ Moderate $$$ Pricey

Labuan Bajo   p272

Wae Rebo Lodge $ A lodge comprising four fan-cooled rooms and two air-con rooms sits serenely amid rice fields in Denge. Owner Martin cooks up delicious meals and offers pickup from Labuan Bajo.

Madja Edelweis Homestay $ Run by a super-helpful owner, this Bajawa homestay consists of eight colourful rooms. Guides arranged and motorbikes available for rent. Perks include breakfast and guest kitchen.

Ciao Hostel $ Labuan Bajo's best hostel has spacious ocean-view dorms with four to 12 beds; perks include a rooftop bar, free airport shuttle and nightly movies.

Bintang Tobias Lodge $ Owner Tobias is a fount of local information for Moni; simple tiled rooms come with hot water, and the cafe serves a Western/Indonesian mashup.

D-Rima Homestay $ Cosy, three-room homestay in Ruteng run by a beautiful family brimming with information about the local area; home-cooked vegetarian dinners available.

Cafe Del Mar $ Off the main road heading to the pier in Riung, these 12 air-conditioned rooms with timber furniture and private bathrooms are overseen by Riung's loveliest family.

Hobbit Hill Homestay $ Three-bedroom guesthouse near Ruteng, surrounded by rice terraces, with generous breakfasts included and home-cooked meals on request.

Wae Rebo Homestay $ Wae Rebo expert owner Blasius runs this friendly 15-room spot, right by the trailhead. If the phone signal is patchy, send him an SMS.

Scuba Junkie Komodo Beach Resort $$ Stay in breezy beach bales or seaview rooms at this fantastic dive resort in an isolated bay, an hour's boat ride south of Bajo.

Spring Hill Bungalows $$ Two storeys of deluxe rooms with plush bedding and filtered drinking water overlook a lily pond in Ruteng. Good restaurant onsite.

Manulalu B&B $$ Manulalu Jungle's more wallet-friendly sister accommodation, comprising a clutch of comfortable en suites, complimentary breakfasts and access to Heaven's Door restaurant.

Pu'u Pau Hostel $$ Spotless a/c rooms in the thick of Labuan Bajo's Jl Soekarno action, friendly staff and a great onsite cafe.

Seaesta Komodo Hostel $$ All-round crowd-pleaser with cheery blue-and-white rooms, seriously comfy dorms, a full social calendar and rooftop bar catering to backpackers and divers.

Kelimutu Crater Lakes Ecolodge $$$ Nestled by the riverside east of town in Moni are 21 rooms and villas, with solar power, outdoor sitting areas and restaurant.

Manulalu Jungle $$$ Off a scenic road 20km south of Bajawa, glassed-in bungalows feature day beds on wooden decks, perfect for admiring one of Flores' most spectacular outlooks.

Sumbawa   p285

Lakey Peak Haven $$ Hilltop Bali-style 'haven' with two-storey surf shacks overlooking a chequered pool deck and distant breaks. Reserve in advance, as walk-ups aren't accepted.

Rock Pool Home Stay $$ Set amid tropical gardens, the six air-con rooms at Rock Pool feature fabulous sea views, while the open-sided Ali's Bar serves Indonesian and Western food.

3 Waves Hotel $$ Consisting of two smart doubles with terraces overlooking Lakey Peak, this intimate spot cooks up Aussie burgers and chips and pan-Asian meals with equal aplomb.

West Timor   p287 (Map p289)

Lavalon Hostel $ A dorm and two air-con doubles, run by living Nusa Tenggara encyclopedia and former Indonesian film star Edwin Lerrick in Kepang. Guides and transport arranged.

Dena Hotel $ Unremarkable yet clean rooms in Soe with air-con and wi-fi, across the road from the market. Soe's best digs.

New Victory Hotel $ The best hotel in Kefamenanu (not that it's much of a horse race), with air-con, TV, hot water and buffet breakfast. Inspect the room first.

Sotis Hotel $$ This Kupang waterfront mid-rise features stylish rooms with pops of colour, two pools, a spa, a decent restaurant and bar.

Alor
p294

La P'tite Kepa $$ This French-owned, solar-powered dive resort consists of 11 bungalows with sea and island views, outdoor bathrooms, memorable meals and snorkelling and diving outings.

Rote
p297

Anugerah $$ Compact *lontar*-palm bungalows with outdoor bathrooms overlook the T-Land break; the restaurant shines when it comes to grilled fish.

Malole Surf House $$$ Four stylish rooms with ikat bedspreads, sublime international seafood, boat transfers to Rote's best surf breaks and island excursions when you're on dry land.

Sumba
p298

Praikundu Ikat Centre $ Two doubles and a twin share a sweet communal living and dining space at Sumba's best ikat workshop, in Waingapu. Kornelis' wife cooks traditional meals.

Sumba Sunset Home Stay $ Four traditional bungalows with mosquito nets, set up to accommodate couples, friends or families. Owner Petu familiar with nearby surf breaks; in Kerewe.

Amuya Homestay $ Run by affable Luci, this cosy central homestay in Waingapu consists of en-suite rooms fanning out around a lovely garden and pool. Indonesian breakfasts included.

Lambo Homestay $$ Four beautifully decorated rooms inside a traditional (tin-roofed) house in Wanokaka are presided over by effusive English- and Russian-speaking Azerbaijani Nailya. Meals arranged on request.

Sumba Adventure Resort $$ This secluded resort 2km east of Kalala Beach consists of basic A-frame bamboo huts, an open-walled bungalow and a spacious family option with outdoor shower.

Casa Kandara $$ Excellent, newish hotel on Waingapu's outskirts. Stylish air-con rooms with terraces, rice-paddy views from the large pool and decent restaurant.

Marthen's Homestay $$ Surfing digs near Pantai Tarimbang consist of shaggy rattan and thatch huts, with home-cooked meals on offer and surfboards for hire.

Oro Beach Houses $$ Circular thatched bungalows overlooking a white-sand beach in Tambolaka, with mosquito-netted beds and outdoor bathrooms. Meals, mountain bikes and snorkelling arranged. Occasional wildlife in rooms.

Maringi Eco Resort $$$ Beautifully designed bamboo pavilions with oval glass doors and outdoor bathrooms, powered by solar energy and run by a not-for-profit NGO that teaches hospitality; in Tambolaka.

Sumba Surf Camp $$$ Rates for four solar-powered rooms and three private bungalows in Kerewe include boat transport to a dozen surf breaks. Family-style use of produce from the organic garden.

NIHI Sumba $$$ Celebrity-favoured resort in Wanokaka with exclusive access to the virgin beach out front, myriad amenities and multi-day stays in stunning beachfront villas.

JAMES D. MORGAN/GETTY IMAGES ©

NIHI Sumba

TOOLKIT

The chapters in this section cover the most important topics you'll need to know about in Bali, Lombok and Nusa Tenggara. They're full of nuts-and-bolts information and valuable insights to help you understand and navigate the region and get the most out of your trip.

Arriving
p314

Getting Around
p315

How to Hire a Car & Driver
p316

Money
p317

Accommodation
p318

Family Travel
p319

Health & Safe Travel
p320

How to Travel Safely by Boat
p321

Food, Drink & Nightlife
p322

Responsible Travel
p324

LGBTIQ+ Travellers
p326

Accessible Travel
p327

Bali's Temple Architecture
p328

Women Travellers
p330

Nuts & Bolts
p331

Language
p332

Arriving

Most visitors to this part of Indonesia will arrive by air in Bali, but Lombok and Nusa Tenggara also have regional airports. Island hoppers catch frequent ferries between eastern Java and Bali, between Bali and Lombok, and between many destinations in Nusa Tenggara.

Passports

Make certain your passport will be valid for six months after your date of arrival in Indonesia. This regulation is strictly enforced. Also, make sure that your passport has two blank pages in the visa section.

Visas

Visas come in many types. Most tourists get a 'visa on arrival', which is good for 30 days and can be extended once. Apply in advance online (molina. imigrasi.go.id) to save waiting in airport visa lines.

Tourism Tax

Bali is introducing a new tourism tax in 2024. It costs 150,000Rp and will be payable each time an international visitor arrives in Bali. The primary point of collection will be the airport.

Money

There are ATMs at the airports. They are a better, more reliable source of rupiah than using a currency exchange. Electronic payments are widely accepted at tourism businesses.

From Airports to Popular Destinations

FROM		TO	DURATION
BALI	🚗 >	SEMINYAK	30–90MIN
BALI	🚗 >	CHANGGU	1–2HRS
BALI	🚗 >	ULU WATU	45MIN–1HR
BALI	🚗 >	NUSA DUA	20–30MIN
BALI	🚗 >	SANUR	30–45MIN
BALI	🚗 >	UBUD	1½–2HRS
LOMBOK	🚗 >	KUTA	20MIN
LOMBOK	🚗 🚤 >	GILIS	3HRS
LABUAN BAJO	🚗 >	TOWN CENTRE	10MIN
LABUAN BAJO	🚗 >	RUTENG	5HRS
MAUMERE	🚗 >	MONI	3HRS
KUPANG	🚗 >	TOWN CENTRE	15MIN
TAMBOLAKA	🚗 >	WAIKABUBAK	1HR

Getting Around

Getting around requires many modes of transit. In Bali most people use cars with drivers or rent motorbikes. Elsewhere, shared transport is more common; ferries and airplanes are inescapable between islands.

TRAVEL COSTS

Motorbike rental
75,000+ Rp/ day

Petrol
Approx
10,000Rp/litre

Ferry
75,000+ Rp

Flight
US$70+

Plane

There are regular flights between Bali's airport and airports in Nusa Tenggara and across Indonesia. Many regional flights link Lombok, Labuan Bajo, Kupang etc. Airlines include Lion Air, Batik Air, Wings Air, Air Asia, Garuda and others. Flight delays are common, so avoid tight connections. Consider staying in Bali before an international flight.

Boat

Fast boats link Bali with Lombok and the Gilis. Slow car ferries link the region's major islands. Journey times vary greatly. Liveaboards are a popular way to get from Lombok to Labuan Bajo (Flores). Shipping company Pelni (pelni.co.id) provides infrequent, long-distance services, but these trips are for the adventurous (p321).

TIP

The one reliable taxi company in Bali and Lombok is **Bluebird**. Look for blue cabs clearly branded 'Bluebird' (ersatz blue taxis abound). Drivers speak English and always use the meter.

BALI'S PUBLIC BUS

Trans-Sarbagita (@trans_sarbagita) runs air-con commuter buses, more suited to residents due to its complex route network. It is handy for the following routes: the bypass linking Sanur to Jimbaran; Denpasar to Jimbaran; or Ubud to points south to Denpasar. Other routes require transfers; airport service is inconvenient. The cheap fares require Indonesian e-payment apps.

DRIVING ESSENTIALS

Drive on the left.

An international driving permit valid for a car and/ or motorbike is essential, along with your home country licence.

Motorbike riders must use a helmet (although many residents flaunt this law).

Car & Motorbike

Renting a car (p316) or motorbike opens up the region for exploration, but driving on the islands can be harrowing and Bali's main roads are often clogged (p37). Motorbike rental is popular and cheap, but there are safety issues (wear a helmet!) and the matter of securing belongings from theft.

Taxi & Ojek

Metered taxis are common in south Bali (except Ubud) and parts of Lombok. Elsewhere, you will negotiate a fare in advance – an opaque process. Motorbike taxis *(ojek)* are common, and you'll find them available from dedicated and ad hoc drivers. Downsides are comfort and a frequent lack of helmets.

Ride Apps

The widespread adoption of ride apps has been a boon to transport in Bali. Just like Uber (which was banned), the apps allow you to summon a driver and then reach your destination for a set fare that is usually cheaper than a negotiated fare. The main apps are **Grab** and **Gojek**. Both offer cars and *ojeks*.

315

SAID SAFRI/SHUTTERSTOCK ©

Sidemen (p165)

Hire a Car & Driver

A popular and convenient way to travel around Bali and Nusa Tenggara is by a hired vehicle with a driver. This provides maximum convenience and comfort. Day trips in Bali and longer-distance transport are common reasons for having your own vehicle. There's no better way to make the fabulous multi-day trek across Flores, for instance. A local driver will be most versed in local driving conditions, whether it's finding something that's otherwise elusive on your mapping app, taking a hidden shortcut or advising on the best times to visit sights to avoid crowds and traffic. Multi-day trips allow you and the driver to become familiar with your desires and styles.

Selecting a Driver

It's easy to arrange for a vehicle and driver. Consider the following:

- Ask at your hotel, which is often a good method because it increases accountability. The person who picked you up at the airport may also be available to drive you around.
- Consult other travellers for their recommendations.
- Meet the driver to check out your chemistry. Make sure that their English is sufficient for you to communicate your wishes.
- Most vehicles used to transport tourists are some type of minivan that seats four to seven. Make certain that your driver's is modern and clean.
- If you're visiting several islands, ask your driver to recommend other drivers further along your itinerary.
- Agree on the journey and the price beforehand; know that changes may increase your cost.

Budget Considerations

If you're part of a group, it can make economic sense to hire a car and driver. Talk to other travellers at your guesthouse, hotel or at cafes popular with travellers in hubs such as Labuan Bajo.

Large public buses link the islands and go right across islands like Flores. However, there are also vans and minivans plying popular routes. These offer comfort more akin to hiring your own minivan and can be convenient with pickup and dropoff at your hotel.

WHILE ON THE ROAD

Make it clear if you want to avoid tourist-trap restaurants and shops, which offer large parking areas and possible driver kickbacks (smart drivers understand that tips depend on following your wishes).

Buy your driver lunch (they'll want to eat elsewhere to get a break from work and your company). Offer snacks and drinks.

Feel free to make requests about your driver's driving style – you're the boss. However, never ask your driver to go faster as they normally go at the speed they are comfortable driving.

Many drivers find ways to make your day delightful in unexpected ways. Tip accordingly (10% is fair).

Money

CURRENCY: RUPIAH (IDR/RP)

ATMs

There are ATMs in Bali, Lombok and larger towns in Nusa Tenggara. For small, isolated places such as Lombok's Gili Gede – and in case ATM networks go down – always carry plenty of cash. ATMs are fussy about the cards they accept, so you may need to try a few different ones.

Credit Cards

Credit and debit cards are accepted at midrange and upscale hotels and resorts. More expensive restaurants and shops will also accept them; there is often a surcharge of around 3%. Visa and Mastercard are the most commonly accepted, American Express not so much.

E-payments

Paying with your phone is popular in Indonesia as is tapping your card. From trendy cafes in Canggu to busy convenience stores, residents and visitors alike go cash-free. One wrinkle is that you may need to have an Indonesian digital wallet app on your phone; try Gopay.

HOW MUCH FOR...

Beaches
Usually free

A Bintang
40,000Rp

Warung lunch
50,000Rp

Car and driver
US$35–80

HOW TO... Avoid Ripoffs

- ATM exchange rates are usually good.
- Currency exchanges are rife with problems. Anyone approaching you on the street to change money is a scammer.
- With ATMs and credit card payments, never accept the option for conversion to your home currency; it's a ripoff.
- ATMs return your card after dispensing cash, so it's easy to forget your card.
- Card skimming is widespread – protect your PIN and look for attached skimming devices.

LOCAL TIP

In shops, change in small coins of 100Rp or less is often not given or is replaced with a small piece of candy.

TIPPING

With average wages hovering around US$150 a month, all tips are appreciated.
Restaurants Tipping a set percentage is not expected, but if service is good, 10% or more is appropriate.

Services Hand cash directly to individuals (drivers, porters, masseuses, people bringing you beer at the beach etc); 10% to 20% of the total is generous.

Hotels Most midrange and all top-end hotels add 21% to the bill for tax and service.
Spas Not mandatory, though 5% to 10% is appreciated.

Accommodation

Homestays & Guesthouses

Bali's family-run accommodation can be a delightful part of your visit. Ubud is a centre for these cheery lodgings. Rooms usually have air-con, wi-fi and some sort of terrace. You can enjoy the rhythms of the compound's life as you come and go. Best of all, prices are very cheap. Guesthouses are found across the region, but check quality as it varies.

Hostels

Found across south Bali, Ubud, the Gilis and beyond, hostels are a recent addition to Indonesia's lodging scene. Aimed at international travellers, they tend towards the flashpacker end of the scale. Look for stylish decor and amenities. Many have private rooms and organise tours and activities. Hostels are usually close to the action and can arrange transport further afield.

Hotels

Bali has hundreds of hotels in all styles, shapes and sizes. Lombok also has many, as do towns and areas across Nusa Tenggara that are popular with tourists. International budget and midrange chains are found by the score in south Bali. Older midrange hotels are often constructed in bungalow style or in two-storey blocks and are set on spacious grounds with a pool.

Resorts

Bali has some of the world's best resorts, often at lower prices than you'd pay elsewhere. You can stay on the beach or be nestled in a lush mountain valley. Service is refined and you can expect decor that astounds. Resorts such as those at Nusa Dua have hundreds of rooms. Across the region, boutique properties may have as few as two.

HOW MUCH FOR A NIGHT IN A...

Homestay
US$25

Hotel
US$30–100

Resort
US$150+

Villas

Enjoy a luxurious villa escape, private pool and even your own staff, often in a walled compound. Multi-room villas are good for groups and can become your holiday party HQ. They are found across Bali, with huge concentrations built atop the lost rice fields of Canggu and Ubud. The villa boom is controversial for environmental, aesthetic and economic reasons.

HOW TO RENT A VILLA

Renting a villa can be a challenge. Airbnb and Vrbo are popular sources of rentals. There are also many agents; some are excellent, others not. It is essential to be as clear as possible about what you want when arranging a rental. Some considerations are:

- How far is the villa from the beach, nightlife and stores?
- Is a driver or car service included?
- If there is a cook, is food included?
- Is there an electricity surcharge?
- Are there extra cleaning fees?
- What refunds apply on a standard 50% deposit?

Family Travel

Travelling with children in this part of the world is an enriching experience. Residents consider kids part of the community, and everyone has a responsibility towards them. Children of all ages will enjoy both the attention and the many diversions that will make their holiday special too. The many outdoor activities are a plus.

Staying Safe

The sorts of facilities, safeguards and services that Western parents regard as basic may not be present. For example, places with great views might not have proper railings. The main danger to kids – and adults – is traffic and bad footpaths in busy areas. Given the ongoing presence of rabies in Bali, be sure to keep children away from stray dogs and cats.

Dining with Kids

Dining as a family is one of the joys of travelling. Bali is so relaxed that kids can just be kids. At many eateries, kids romp nearby while their parents enjoy a meal. Kitchens will usually cater to fussy palates.

What to Pack

Supermarkets and stores stock almost everything you'd find at similar shops at home, including Western foods. Nappies (diapers), baby food, packaged UHT milk, infant formula and other supplies are easily purchased in Bali, but can be harder to source in Nusa Tenggara. Items to bring include a portable changing mat, car seats, favourite foods and a front or back sling or other baby carrier.

BEST REGIONS FOR KIDS

Kuta & Legian, Bali Surf lessons and souvenirs entice kids and teens, though it can be crowded, crazy and sometimes sleazy.

Sanur, Bali Beachside resorts, a reef-protected beach and many kid-friendly activities.

Nusa Dua, Bali Huge resorts with kids programs and a reef-protected beach.

Ubud, Bali There are many things to see and do (walks, monkeys, markets, dance performances).

Gili Air, Gili Islands Gentle surf, many amenities and activities such as snorkelling.

CULTURED JOY

The obvious drawcards for kids are the outdoor adventures available across the region. But there are also cultural treats that kids will love.

Markets Vendors are charmed by kids enthusiastically shopping for oddball souvenirs.

Dance Check out an evening of Barong dance at the Ubud Palace or Pura Dalem Ubud, two venues that look like sets from Tomb Raider, right down to the flaming torches. Barong has monkeys, monsters and a witch.

Temples Goa Gajah in Bedulu has a deep cavern where hermits lived and which you enter through a monster's mouth. Pura Luhur Batukau is in dense jungle.

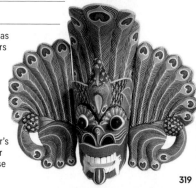

319

Health & Safe Travel

SWIMMING

Beaches in Bali and Nusa Tenggara are subject to heavy surf and strong currents, so swim between safety flags (if present). Lifeguards are on duty only at Kuta, Legian, Seminyak, Nusa Dua and Sanur. Other hazards include sharp coral and water pollution – stay away from any open streams flowing into the surf.

Drugs

High-profile drug cases in Indonesia should be enough to dissuade anyone from being involved with illicit drugs. As little as two ecstasy tabs or a bit of pot have resulted in huge fines and multi-year jail sentences (Google the 'Bali Nine'). Cops pose as dealers, and busting a foreigner for drugs, whether in a club or a private villa, is an easy bust.

Scams

Scams occur, beyond dodgy money-changers and blatant overcharging.

- Fake orphanages extract money from tourists (research online before donating).
- Scammers charge an outrageous sum to 'fix' a fake problem with your car or motorbike.
- Unofficial guides charge a fee to allow you to take a selfie at a public site.
- You get the wrong change and are hurried along.

SAFETY ON THE WATER

Ferries, ships and boats in Indonesia have a mixed safety record. Never assume any voyage will be safe.

TSUNAMI EVACUATION SIGNS

JALUR EVAKUASI TSUNAMI

In tsunami-prone coastal areas of Indonesia, look for orange signs which point the way to high ground.

Staying Safe from Disasters

Be aware of your surroundings. Note if residents are worried about a volcano erupting etc. Check your hotel for hazards (eg heavy objects near your bed) and locate fire escapes. Check whether you're in a tsunami zone. Keep bottled water and your phone handy. You may be able to call for help, and extra water can be crucial for survival.

NATURAL DISASTER AWARENESS

Gunung Agung on Bali erupted as recently as 2019. Lombok had a significant earthquake in 2018. Volcanoes continuously smoke on Flores. Over 130,000 died from the 2004 tsunami. Remember: Indonesia is prone to natural disasters. While you can't prevent these types of tragedies, you can protect yourself with a few simple precautions.

SYAIRUL HILDA/SHUTTERSTOCK ©

Fast boat, Nusa Penida

HOW TO... Travel Safely by Boat

With 17,000 islands, Indonesia relies on ocean travel to link the archipelago together. Small boats with outriggers, fast boats powered by huge outboards, smoking car ferries and well-travelled ships are part of what is all too often a shambolic fleet. Safety regulations are more theory than practice and accidents happen regularly. In 2023, there was a fatal accident on a boat linking Nusa Penida and Bali. Other recent accidents in the region have caused injuries. Yet, it is possible to improve your odds on an Indonesian boat with some simple precautions.

Many Dangers

Boating standards are low. Crews may have little or no training. In one accident, the skipper admitted that he panicked and had no recollection of what happened to his passengers. And rescue is far from assured: a volunteer rescue group in east Bali reported that they had no radio. Conditions are often rough in the waters off Bali and east through Nusa Tenggara. Although many islands are close to each other, the channels can get more turbulent than is safe for boats trying to cross.

Seeking Safety

With these facts in mind, you must take responsibility for your safety because no one else will. Two worthwhile points:

Bigger can be better It may add half an hour or more to your journey, but a larger boat deals with the open ocean better than a small overpowered speedboat. Also, trips on small boats can be unpleasant because of the ceaseless pounding through the waves and the fumes coming from the screaming outboard motors. Still, the large – and often rust-streaked – car ferries linking Bali, Lombok and other islands have all had high-profile sinkings.

Use common sense There are good operators on Indonesia's waters, but the lineup changes constantly. If a service or boat seems sketchy before you board, go with a different operator. Try to get a refund but don't risk your safety for the cost of a ticket.

SAFETY ON BOARD

Look for exits Cabins may only have one narrow entrance, making them death traps in an accident.

Don't ride on the roof It looks like fun but travellers get bounced off when boats hit swells and crews may be inept at rescue.

Avoid overcrowding Some boats leave with more people than seats and with aisles jammed with luggage. Don't use the boat if it's too full of luggage and passengers.

Check for safety equipment Make certain your boat has life preservers and that you can locate and use them. Also check for lifeboats. Don't expect the crew to be any help in an emergency.

Food, Drink & Nightlife

Ramadan

For Muslims in Bali and across Nusa Tenggara, the largest celebration is Ramadan. Each day of Ramadan, Muslims rise before sunrise to eat their only meal before sunset. At sunset, people joyously break their fast. The first thing eaten is *kolak* (fruit in coconut milk), a gentle start to the evening's feasting. After Ramadan, much of Indonesia hits the road to go home to their families and celebrate Idul Fitri (Lebaran).

MENU DECODER

Ayam: Chicken

Bakar: Barbecued

Bakso/ba'so: Meatball soup

Daging sapi: Beef

Es buah: Combination of crushed ice, condensed milk, shaved coconut, syrup, jelly and fruit

Goreng: Fried

Ikan: Fish

Jajanan: Snacks

Kelepon: Green rice flour balls with a palm-sugar filling

Krupuk: Prawn or fish cracker

Lombok: Chilli

Mie goreng: Fried wheat-flour noodles, served with vegetables or meat

Nasi: Rice

Nasi Campur: Steamed rice topped with a little bit of everything

Nasi putih: White (putih) rice, usually steamed

Nasi uduk: Rice cooked in coconut milk, served with meat, tofu and/or vegetables

Pecel: Peanut sauce

Pisang goreng: Fried banana fritters

Sate: Skewers of grilled meat, served with peanut sauce

Sayur: Vegetables

Soto: Meat and vegetable broth

Telur: Egg

Udang: Prawns

HOW TO...

Eat on the Street

As many Indonesians can't afford fine service and surroundings, the most authentic food is found at street level. Everyone dines at stalls or gets their noodle fix from vendors, who carry their victuals in two bundles connected by a stick over their shoulders: a stove and wok on one side, and ready-to-fry ingredients on the other.

Then there are *kaki lima* (roving vendors) whose carts hold a workbench, stove and cabinet. 'Kaki lima' means 'five legs': two for the wheels of the cart, one for the stand and two for the legs of the vendor – who sells every type of dish, drink and snack. Some have a permanent spot; others roam the streets, calling out what they are selling or making a signature sound, such as the 'tock' of a wooden *bakso* bell. In some places, *sate* sellers operate from a boat-shaped cart, with bells jingling to attract the hungry.

HOW MUCH FOR A...

Top-end
restaurant meal
US$20

Nasi campur
40,000Rp

Babi guling
45,000Rp

Coffee
10,000Rp

Cocktail
150,000Rp

Jamu (herbal
health drink)
10,000Rp

Fresh coconut for
drinking
5000Rp

HOW TO...

How to Be a Good Dinner Guest

In Indonesia, hospitality is highly regarded. If you're invited to someone's home for a meal, you'll be treated warmly and social miscues will be ignored. Still, here are some tips to make the experience more enjoyable for everyone.

When food or drink is presented, wait until your host invites you to eat.

Indonesians rarely eat at the table, preferring to sit on a mat or around the lounge room.

Don't be surprised if, when invited to a home, you're the only one eating. This is your host's way of showing you're special, and you should have choice pickings. But don't eat huge amounts as these dishes will feed others later. Fill up on rice and take a spoonful from each dish served (there may be many!).

Chopsticks are available at Chinese-Indonesian eateries, and a fork and spoon in restaurants, but most Indonesians prefer to eat with their hands. In a warung, it is acceptable to rinse your fingers with drinking water, letting the drops fall to the ground. Use your right hand. If left-handed, ask for a spoon.

In Islamic areas, be sure not to eat and drink in public during Ramadan. Restaurants stay open, though they usually cover the door to not cause offence. Outside of Balinese Hindu areas, pork is never served.

Just Say No

If you're invited to an Indonesian home for a meal, your hosts will no doubt insist you eat more. You may always politely pass on second helpings or refuse food you don't find appealing.

EATING IN NUSA TENGGARA

Once you board the ferry to Sumbawa from Lombok, you enter a different culinary world. Outside larger towns, cities and tourist areas such as Labuan Bajo, there are limited choices for dining out. Warungs are simple, open-air eateries that provide a small range of dishes. *Rumah makan* (eating house) or *restoran* refers to anything that is a step above a warung. Offerings may be as simple as those from a warung, but usually include a wider selection of meat and vegetable dishes and spicy accompaniments.

As Indonesia's middle class grows, the warung is also going upmarket. In urban areas, a restaurant by any other name advertises itself as a 'warung' and serves good local dishes to customers. Markets (*pasar*) have

no refrigeration, so freshness is dependent on quick turnover. You'll also find a huge range of sweet and savoury snacks. Supermarkets and convenience stores are becoming more common.

In east Nusa Tenggara, you'll eat less rice (although much is imported) and more sago, corn, cassava and taro. Fish is popular, and one local dish is Sumbawa's *sepat* (shredded fish in coconut and mango sauce). Also recommended is *sate pusut* (minced meat or fish satay, mixed with coconut and grilled on sugar-cane skewers). Look for *se'i babi* (pork smoked over kesambi wood) in non-Muslim eateries in West Timor. Non-meat dishes include *kelor* (soup with vegetables) and *timun urap* (cucumber with coconut, onion and garlic).

Responsible Travel

Climate Change & Travel

It's impossible to ignore the impact we have when travelling, and the importance of making changes where we can. Lonely Planet urges all travellers to engage with their travel carbon footprint. There are many carbon calculators online that allow travellers to estimate the carbon emissions generated by their journey; try resurgence.org/resources/carbon-calculator.html. Many airlines and booking sites offer travellers the option of offsetting the impact of greenhouse gas emissions by contributing to climate-friendly initiatives around the world. We continue to offset the carbon footprint of all Lonely Planet staff travel, while recognising this is a mitigation more than a solution.

Walking Bali

- Explore Bali without a car or motorbike.
- Walk the beaches in Kuta (p72), Canggu (p52), Sanur (p90) and Pemuteran (p207).
- Walk in Ubud (p128).
- Walk the rice terraces of Sidemen (p166).
- Hike around Munduk (p190).
- Explore north Bali's waterfalls (p204).

Saving Sea Turtles

Several turtle hatcheries work to protect eggs from poachers and predators: **Bali Sea Turtle Society** (Kuta Beach; p75), **Turtle Conservation and Education Centre** (Serangan Island; p91), and **Kurma Asih Sea Turtle Conservation Center** (Perancak; p224).

Threads of Life (threadsoflife.com) teaches about and sells traditional textiles, including beautiful works from Nusa Penida. It's one of many shops in Ubud featuring locally produced products and their designers.

Muntigunung community initiatives are working to improve lives through tourist activities in and around its namesake village in east Bali. Tours include food production, handicrafts and countryside treks.

REFILL YOUR WATER BOTTLE

Reliance on bottled water puts tens of thousands of empty plastic bottles into landfills daily. Do your part by using a refillable water bottle. In Ubud, stop by **Pondok Pekak Library & Learning Centre** (p137).

SAVING LOMBOK'S SHARKS

Southeast Lombok has long been a centre for poaching and harvesting shark fins. Project Hiu (projecthiu.com) gives shark harvesters new income protecting sharks and guiding tourists. They offer tours and you can sponsor a boat.

Cleaning Rivers

Sungai Watch (sungai.watch) has identified over 350 illegal landfills in Bali and organises river clean-ups to keep plastic trash off the beaches. It's expanding its work and you can help out.

Cleaning Nusa Lembongan's Beaches

Throughout the year, Nusa Lembongan's community holds weekly beach and town clean-ups (p107). You can join in at the French Kiss Divers (@frenchkissdiverslembongan), Tuesday; Lembongan Surf Team (@lembongansurfteam), Thursday; and Ceningan Divers (@ceningandivers), Sunday.

Seminyak's legendary club **Potato Head** (p67) details how every aspect of its functioning is dedicated to sustainability.

The **Penida Colada** (@penidacolada; p113) beach bar gives one free coconut for every bag of trash collected.

Rainy Season Blight

The density of trash on Indonesia's beaches correlates with the seasons and tides, and the rainy season (which peaks November through February) sends torrents of water through trash-filled river valleys, resulting in headline-grabbing scenes.

Sustainable Sumba

Nihi Sumba (p311) in Wanokaka pays fair wages to staff, contributes to educational programs and supports anti-malaria efforts. **Maringi Eco Resort** (p311) in Tambolaka is run by an NGO that teaches hospitality to Indonesian students.

Learning Village Life

JED (jed.or.id) organises highly regarded tours of small villages, some overnight. Working with villages off the tourist routes of Bali, the group reveals rural life, culture, farming and food. Proceeds are returned to the communities.

RESOURCES

refillmybottle.com Find places to refill water bottles in Bali.

desalescommunity center.org Teaches sustainable

tourism to villagers in East Bali.

bumisehat.org Ubud-based NGO that runs clinics for families.

LEAVE THE ANIMALS BE

Reconsider swimming with captive dolphins, riding elephants and patronising attractions where wild animals are made to perform for crowds. These interactions have been identified by animal welfare experts as harmful to the animals.

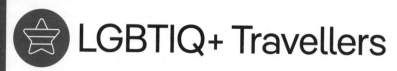

LGBTIQ+ Travellers

LGBTIQ+ travellers in Indonesia should follow the same precautions as straight travellers: no public displays of affection. This is especially important in conservative areas such as Sumba, where residents of the same sex seen hugging sparked outrage. Bali is a notable exception, but otherwise, LGBTIQ+ travellers should exercise caution in their public behaviour across the region.

Tolerant Bali

Bali is a popular spot for LGBTIQ+ travellers owing to the many ways it caters to a rainbow of visitors. There is a large gay and lesbian expat community and many own businesses that – if not gay-specific – are very gay-friendly. In south Bali and Ubud, couples have few concerns, beyond remembering that the Balinese are quite modest. Otherwise, there's a rollicking strip of very gay-friendly nightclubs in the heart of Seminyak, and there's no part of Bali that any LGBTIQ+ person should avoid.

IMPORTANT CONSIDERATIONS

Physical harassment is still uncommon, but morality police – and increasingly regular police – are known to patrol accommodation outside of tourist centres looking for unmarried couples, including same-sex ones.

Local Groups

GAYa Nusantara (gayanusantara.or.id) The national Indonesian LGBTIQ+ community group. Focuses on social issues, government policy, support services, HIV prevention and more.

Yayasan Gaya Dewata (YGD; gayadewata.com) Bali's oldest community-run LGBTIQ+ organisation works to prevent HIV and provide support services across the island.

LGBTIQ+ LEXICON

Gay men in Indonesia are referred to as *maho*, homo or gay; lesbians are *lesbi*.
Indonesia's community of transgender and transsexual *waria* – from the words *wanita* (woman) and *pria* (man) – has always had a very public profile; they are also known by the less polite term *banci*.

LGBTIQ+ STATUS IN INDONESIA

A 2016 survey showed that only 26% of Indonesians 'disliked LGBTIQ+ people'. However, after four years of anti-LGBTIQ+ rhetoric from a wide range of Indonesian politicians and clerics, a 2020 survey found that only 9% of Indonesians agreed that homosexuality should be accepted. Though same-sex sexual acts are not criminalised in Indonesian law, some districts in Java and Sumatra do criminalise consensual same-sex sexual acts between adults.

Avoid PDAs

Avoid public displays of affection. As the nation becomes more religiously conservative, any form of closeness between people of the same sex may be unwise.

Accessible Travel

Bali is the favoured destination for travellers with disabilities since it is much easier to find suitable amenities and adapted accommodation. Lombok, the Gilis and Nusa Tenggara are not well set up to cater to those with vision, mobility or hearing impairments.

Accessible Indonesia

This well-credentialled inbound travel agent (accessibleindonesia.org) welcomes clients with any kind of disability, offering tours principally to Bali, Yogyakarta and Sulawesi, as well as day cruises.

Airports

The airports in Bali, Lombok, Labuan Bajo and Kupang are modern and able to handle passengers with diverse needs. Smaller airports in the region are not as well-equipped but should be able to assist all passengers.

Accommodation

Most places to stay across the region are not equipped for people with special accessibility needs. Staff may be very willing to offer assistance, but don't expect ramps, elevators, specially equipped bathrooms etc.

INDONESIA: NOT ACCESSIBLE

This is a difficult place for those with limited mobility or vision or hearing impairment. Few buildings have disabled access, and even international chain hotels may not have fully accessible facilities.

FEW FACILITIES

Expect high kerbs, few kerb cuts, badly maintained and crowded pavements (sidewalks) and steps into many establishments. Help, however, is usually at hand even if it may not be skilled.

Accommodation Listings

Even international chain hotels may not be accessible. Always consult directly with any property.

Disabled Holidays (disabledholidays.com) UK-based travel agent lists accessible hotels and resorts in Indonesia.

Villa Sunset View (@villa_sunset_view) Comfortable villa northeast of Canggu in Bali with wheelchair-accessible facilities.

RESOURCES

Bali Access Travel (baliaccesstravel.com) Specialist wheelchair-accessible travel agent, providing tours, accommodation, transport, equipment hire and fully licensed nursing services. Arranges disabled diving and snorkelling expeditions.

Bali International Diving Professionals (bidp-balidiving.com) Offers dives for qualified disabled divers and training for people with a physical disability. They have a purpose-built boat and can accommodate many different abilities.

Temples & Sights

Stairs abound and are an integral philosophical part of every Hindu temple, thus most shrines and other sights are not accessible. Don't expect hearing aids, Braille and wheelchair-accessible walkways on beaches anywhere.

Bali's Temple Architecture

Design is part of Bali's spiritual heritage and this heritage contributes to the look of traditional homes, temples and even modern buildings. Yet it's the temples that remain paramount to the very essence of Bali's architectural and design heritage. A temple must conform to the Balinese concept of cosmic order and every aspect of the structure, from the smallest shrine in a family compound to grand complexes at Besakih and Tanah Lot, has deep meaning.

Temple Orientations

Every village in Bali has several temples, and every home has at least a simple house-temple. The Balinese word for temple is *pura*, from the Sanskrit word meaning 'a space surrounded by a wall'.

All temples are built on a mountain–sea orientation, not north–south. The direction towards the mountains, *kaja*, is the end of the temple, where the holiest shrines are found. The temple's entrance is at the *kelod* (side closest to the sea). *Kaja* may be towards a particular mountain – Pura Besakih in east Bali is pointed directly towards Gunung Agung – or towards the mountains in general.

Temple Types

There are three basic temple types found in most villages. The most important is the *pura puseh* (temple of origin), dedicated to the village founders and at the *kaja* end of the village. In the middle of the village is the *pura desa*, for the many spirits that protect the village community in daily life.

At the *kelod* end of the village is the *pura dalem* (temple of the dead). It honours the destructive sides of the gods Shiva and Parvati.

In addition to these 'local' temples (which number in the thousands), there are a smaller number of great temples. Often a kingdom would have three of these temples that sit at the top of the temple pecking order: a main state temple in the heartland of the state (such as **Pura Taman Ayun** in Mengwi, west Bali); a mountain temple (such as **Pura Besakih**, east Bali); and a sea temple (such as **Pura Luhur Ulu Watu**, south Bali).

Building New Temples

The art of temple and shrine construction in Bali is as vibrant as ever. With the island's relative wealth, more than 500 temples in all sizes are built new or renovated every month. Travelling on the backroads of east and west Bali, you'll pass numerous stone-carving sites where all the needed components for a temple are produced with power tools amidst clouds of mineral dust. The soft pumice-like stones that are used weather rapidly, which means that last year's new temple looks like this year's ancient monument.

Bottom left: Pura Ulun Danu Bratan (p190); above: Pura Taman Ayun (p218)

TEMPLE DESIGN ELEMENTS

No two temples on Bali are identical. Variations in style, size, importance, wealth, purpose and much more result in near-infinite variety. But there are common themes and elements. Use this as a guide and see how many design elements you can find in each Balinese temple you visit.

Candi Bentar The intricately sculpted temple gateway, like a tower split down the middle and moved apart, symbolises that you are entering a sanctum (unfortunately, it has become a clichéd selfie shot). It can be grand, with auxiliary entrances on either side for daily use.

Kulkul Tower The warning-drum tower, from which a wooden split drum (*kulkul*) is sounded to announce events at the temple or warn of danger.

Bale A pavilion, usually open-sided, for temporary use or storage. It may include a *bale gong,* where the gamelan orchestra plays at festivals, or a *wantilan,* a stage for dances or cockfights.

Kori Agung or **Paduraksa** The gateway to the inner courtyard is an intricately sculpted stone tower. Entry is through a doorway reached by steps in the middle of the tower.

Raksa or **Dwarapala** Statues of fierce guardian figures who protect the doorway and deter evil spirits. Above the door will be the equally fierce face of a Bhoma, with hands outstretched against unwanted spirits.

Aling Aling If an evil spirit does get in, this low wall behind the entrance will keep it at bay, as evil spirits find it difficult to make sharp turns.

Betelan Most of the time (except during ceremonies), entry to the inner courtyard is through this side gate.

Gedong These small shrines include ones to Ngrurah Alit and Ngrurah Gede, who organise things and ensure the correct offerings are made. At the *kaja* end of the courtyard, *gedong* may include a shrine to the sacred mountain Gunung Batur; a Maospahit shrine to honour Bali's original Hindu settlers (Majapahit); and a shrine to the *taksu,* who acts as an interpreter for the gods.

Padma Stone Throne for the sun god Surya, placed in the most auspicious *kaja–kangin* (sunrise in the direction of the mountains) corner. It rests on the *badawang* (world turtle), which is held by two *naga* (mythical snakelike creatures).

Meru A multiroofed shrine. Usually there is an 11-roofed *meru* to Sanghyang Widi, the supreme Balinese deity, and a three-roofed *meru* to the holy mountain Gunung Agung. However, *meru* can take any odd number of steps in between, depending on where the intended god falls in the pecking order. The black thatching is made from sugar-palm fronds. The number and height of *meru* are an easy way to discern a temple's importance.

Gedong Pesimpangan A stone building dedicated to the village founder or a local deity.

Paruman or **Pepelik** Open pavilion in the inner courtyard, where the gods are supposed to assemble to watch a festival.

♀ Women Travellers

Plenty of women travel in Indonesia either solo or in pairs, and most seem to travel through the country without problems, especially in Bali (a popular destination for female travellers). However, women travelling solo or otherwise may receive unwanted attention.

Bali

Generally, Bali is safer for women than many areas of the world, and with the usual care and common sense, women should feel secure travelling alone. Women travelling solo will get attention from Balinese men, but they are, on the whole, more relaxed and non-judgmental towards women compared to many parts of the world. Greater care should be reserved for outsiders on Bali, whether tourists or foreign workers.

In Bali, women may not enter temples if they are menstruating. And remember to behave respectfully in temples: incidents of nude yoga selfies, suggestive poses and other despicable behaviour have outraged even the otherwise mellow Balinese.

Nusa Tenggara

For the most part, Indonesia feels pretty safe for a solo female traveller. Like anywhere, however, there will always be the occasional individual trying to get your attention. Two or more women together are less likely to experience problems, and women accompanied by a man are unlikely to be harassed. There have been a small number of accounts of women being groped or followed by men in recent years, but this is not common. Watch out for touchy-feely guides.

If you're a solo female and you hire a car with a driver for several days, note that it's not culturally appropriate for a male Muslim driver to be travelling alone with you. A third party should come along as a chaperone. Traditionally, women in Lombok are treated with respect. But would-be guides, boyfriends and gigolos are often persistent in their approaches and can be aggressive when ignored or rejected.

Although it's rare, some foreign women have experienced sexual harassment and even assault while on the Gilis – don't walk home alone in the quieter parts of the islands.

COVER UP

- Nude and topless sunbathing is deeply offensive and may lead to conflict on any beach. Away from the sand, always cover up. Note the number of signs forbidding bikinis and swimming trunks away from the beach on otherwise freewheeling Gili T.
- Dress conservatively in Nusa Tenggara, especially in Sumbawa. Cover your shoulders, wear shorts and skirts that go down to the knees, and avoid showing cleavage.

Women's health

Birth-control options may be limited, so bring adequate supplies of your own form of contraception. In tourist areas and large cities, basic sanitary napkins and tampons can be purchased. However, this becomes more difficult the more rural you go, including much of Sumbawa, West Timor and Sumba. Even in Bali, the selection may be limited, so bring whatever you need – and prefer – with you.

Nuts & Bolts

OPENING HOURS

Banks 8am–2pm Monday to Thursday, 8am–noon Friday, 8am–11am Saturday

Government offices 8am–3pm Monday to Thursday, 8am–noon Friday (although these are not standardised)

Restaurants & cafes 8am–9pm daily

Shops & services catering to visitors 9am–8pm or later daily

Toilets

Toilets are porcelain holes in the floor with footrests on either side, although Western-style toilets are common in tourist areas.

During the day, look for a cafe or hotel and smile (public toilets only exist at some sights).

Tap Water

Never drink tap water in Indonesia. Most ice in restaurants is fine if it is uniform in size and made at a central plant (standard for cities and tourist areas). Avoid ice that is chipped off larger blocks (more common in rural areas).

Weights & Measures

Indonesia uses the metric system.

Wi-Fi & Internet

Wi-fi is easy to access across Bali and Nusa Tenggara.

GOOD TO KNOW

Time zone
Central Indonesian Time (GMT/UTC +8)

Country code
+62

Emergency number
Police 110; Fire 113; Medical 119

Population
14 million

Electricity
220–230V/50Hz

Type C
220V/50Hz

Type F
230V/50Hz

PUBLIC HOLIDAYS

- **Tahun Baru Masehi** (New Year's Day) 1 January
- **Tahun Baru Imlek** (Chinese New Year) Late January to early February
- **Nyepi** (day of silence when the island shuts down completely) February or March
- **Wafat Yesus Kristus** (Good Friday) Late March or early April
- **Hari Buruh** (Labour Day) 1 May
- **Hari Waisak** (Buddha's birth, enlightenment and death) May
- **Kenaikan Yesus Kristus** (Ascension of Christ) May
- **Hari Proklamasi Kemerdekaan** (Independence Day) 17 August
- **Hari Natal** (Christmas Day) 25 December

Islamic holidays:
- **Isra Miraj Nabi Muhammad** (Ascension of the Prophet Muhammad)
- **Idul Fitri** (Also known as Lebaran) End of Ramadan
- **Idul Adha** (Islamic feast of the sacrifice)
- **Muharram** (Islamic New Year)
- **Maulud Nabi Muhammad** (Birthday of the Prophet Muhammad) Around December

Language

Indonesian, or Bahasa Indonesia, is the official language of Indonesia. It has approximately 220 million speakers, although it's the mother tongue for only about 20 million. Most people in Bali and on Lombok also speak their own indigenous languages, Balinese and Sasak, respectively.

Basics

Hello. Salam. *sa·lam*
Goodbye. Selamat jalan. *se·la·mat ja·lan*
Yes. Ya. *ya*
No. Tidak. *ti·dak*
Please. Tolong. *to·long*
Thank you. Terima kasih. *te·ri·ma ka·sih*
Excuse me. Permisi. *per·mi·si*
Sorry. Maaf. *ma·af*
What's your name? Siapa namanya? *si·a·pa na·ma·nya*
My name is ... Nama saya ... *na·ma sa·ya ...*
Do you speak English? Anda bisa Bahasa Inggris? *an·da bi·sa ba·ha·sa ing·gris*
I don't understand. Saya tidak mengerti. *sa·ya ti·dak meng·er·ti*

Directions

Where's (the station)? Di mana (stasiun)? *di ma·na (sta·si·oon)*
What's the address? Apa alamatnya? *a·pa a·la·mat·nya*
Can you show me (on the map)? Bisa tunjukkan kepada saya (di peta)? *bi·sa toon·joo·kan ke·pa·da sa·ya (di pe·ta)*

Signs

Buka Open
Dilarang Prohibited
Kamar Kecil Toilets
Keluar Exit
Masuk Entrance
Pria Men
Tutup Closed
Wanitai Women
Polisi Police
Rumah Sakit Hospital

Time

What time is it? Jam berapa? *jam be·ra·pa*
It's (10) o'clock. Jam (sepuluh). *jam (se·poo·looh)*
Half past (10). Setengah (sebelas). *se·teng·ah (se·be·las)*
morning Pagi *pa·gi*
afternoon Sore *so·re*
evening Malam *ma·lam*
yesterday Kemarin *ke·ma·rin*
today Hari ini *ha·ri i·ni*
tomorrow Besok *be·sok*

Emergencies

Help! Tolong! *to·long*
Go away! Pergi! *per·gi*
Call ...! Panggil...! *pang·gil*
  ...a doctor dokter. *dok·ter*
  ...the police polisi. *po·li·si*

Eating & drinking

What would you recommend? Apa yang Anda rekomendasikan? *a·pa yang an·da re·ko·men·da·si·kan*
Cheers! Bersulang! *ber·soo·lang*
That was delicious. Ini enak sekali. *i·ni e·nak se·ka·li*

NUMBERS

1 **satu** *sa·too*
2 **dua** *doo·a*
3 **tiga** *ti·ga*
4 **empat** *em·pat*
5 **lima** *li·ma*
6 **enam** *e·nam*
7 **tujuh** *too·jooh*
8 **delapan** *de·la·pan*
9 **sembilan** *sem·bi·lan*
10 **sepuluh** *se·poo·looh*

DONATIONS TO ENGLISH

Orangutan, dugong, bamboo, papaya, satay, sarong, gong

PRONUNCIATION

Indonesian pronunciation is easy to master. Each letter always represents the same sound and most letters are pronounced the same as their English counterparts.

Street Talk

Blend in with the cool kids with the following sentences.

Alay – Tacky, garish, drama queen
Basian – Hangover
Jijay – Disgusting, grotesque
Kimpoi – Sexual intercourse
Koplak – Silly
Ndakik-ndakik – Words or phrases too hard to understand
Pansi – What the hell?

Origins

Indonesian, and its closest relative Malay, both developed from Old Malay, an Austronesian language spoken in the kingdom of Srivijaya on the island of Sumatra.

Official Language

With the Declaration of Independence in 1942, Indonesian was proclaimed the country's official language.

WHO SPEAKS INDONESIAN?

Indonesian is the official language of the Republic of Indonesia. It's used in administration, education, business and the media, although less than 10 per cent of the population claim it as their mother tongue. For the majority of speakers it's the second language, but it is a uniting force for the hundreds of ethnic groups scattered across the world's largest archipelago.

Sasak Around 2 million people speak Sasak.

Indonesia

Balinese There are 4 million speakers of Balinese.

STORYBOOK

Our writers delve deep into different aspects of Bali, Lombok and Nusa Tenggara life

Demon effigy, Ogoh Ogoh parade (p344)

A HISTORY OF BALI, LOMBOK & NUSA TENGGARA IN
15 PLACES

The Hindu Majapahit kingdom moved to Bali in the 12th century where its culture – like rice – found fertile ground. By the 20th century, the Dutch conquered the island even as the island's unique culture thrived. Westerners celebrated Balinese arts in the 1930s; surfers arrived in the 1970s and tourism has boomed ever since. By Mark Eveleigh

ISLAM SWEPT THROUGH Java in the 12th century, compelling Hindu royalty, artisans and priests to move across the narrow channel to Bali. Blessed with prodigious resources, Bali became a thriving centre of arts and faith. The priest Nirartha established landmark temples that helped develop Bali's own unique form of Hinduism. From the initial strand of seaside temples, the numbers multiplied to today's tens of thousands of temples island-wide.

The evolving Balinese culture emphasised collaboration and resourcefulness, qualities embodied in the UNESCO-recognised *subak* system that ensures fair allocation of water to every rice farmer. Various regencies formed around the island. While beneficial for funding artistic pursuits, the royalty also took to squabbling, which gave the colonial Dutch an opening.

By the 20th century, the Dutch formed alliances with some local princes while brutally suppressing others. Meanwhile, foreigners discovered the richness of Balinese arts and began collaborations in Ubud that are still felt today. Mass tourism began in the 1960s and took off in the 1970s as jets began serving the airport. Huge swaths of the island have been transformed, competition for resources like the once abundant water is fierce and material wealth has soared. Even so, Bali's extraordinary culture remains resilient.

1. Liang Bua Cave
THE MYSTERIOUS FLORES HOBBIT

Until recently it was believed that the first humanoids *(Homo erectus)* lived in Central Java around 500,000 years ago – having reached Indonesia across land bridges from Africa – before either dying off or being wiped out by the arrival of *Homo sapiens*. But the 2003 discovery in Flores of human remains, a tiny islander dubbed 'hobbit', *(Homo floresiensis)* upended that notion. Found in deep sediment in the limestone Liang Bua cave near Ruteng, the bones are around 30,000 years old. In Bali, the oldest human remains found date back to about 1000 BCE and are displayed at the Museum Manusia Purba in Gilyamanuk.

For more on Liang Bua Cave, see page 275

2. Lambanapu
ANCIENT CIVILISATION ON SUMBA

The small archaeological site of Lambanapu near Waingapu in Sumba hints more at what we don't know than what we do know about the early inhabitants in Indonesia. Just as the 'hobbit' find on Flores has caused a reevaluation of existing theories, this site – which dates to about 1000 BCE – shows that a complex Austronesian civilisation existed on Sumba earlier than previously thought. Investigations begun in 2016 have uncovered the remains of 45 individuals, along with weaponry, household items and jewellery. Evidence of jar burials shows influences from elsewhere in Southeast Asia, which supplanted the local practice of burials in megaliths.

For more on Lambanapu, see page 298

3. Boti

OVER 20 GENERATIONS OF CULTURE

Boti is an animist village in West Timor that has held out against Christianisation and still maintains a more traditional way of life. One of many isolated villages with ancient cultures in the region, Boti's 300 residents can trace their lineage back over 20 generations. Outside influences are kept at bay by tradition-minded *kepala sukus* (chiefs) who have vowed to maintain the strict laws of *adat* (customs). Yet visitors are welcomed and the populace readily shares its lifestyle and artistic creations. The people of Boti are emblematic of surviving ancient cultures found in pockets across Nusa Tenggara, especially in West Timor and Flores.

For more on Boti, see page 292

Pura Taman Ayun (p218)

LIFEINCAPTION/SHUTTERSTOCK ©

4. Gunung Kawi

EXTRAORDINARY 11TH-CENTURY MEMORIALS

Java spread its influence to Bali during the reign of King Airlangga (1019–42), one of its greatest rulers. His mother moved to Bali shortly after his birth, so when Airlangga gained the throne, there was an immediate link between Java and Bali. It was at this time that Kawi (the courtly Javanese language) came into use among the royalty of Bali; cultural and artistic influences followed. The 10 towering rock-cut memorials at 11th-century Gunung Kawi, north of Ubud, were dedicated to early royalty. They provide a clear link between Bali and 11th-century Java.

For more on Gunung Kawi, see page 337

5. Pura Rambut Siwi

A SCENIC 16TH-CENTURY LANDMARK

In the early 16th century, Java converted entirely to Islam, causing the Hindu intelligentsia on the island to flee to Bali. Notable among those who went to Bali was the priest Nirartha, who is credited with introducing many of the complexities of what became Balinese Hinduism. Among his many lasting legacies are the 'sea temples' that ring the coast and which are meant to protect against evil spirits. Notable examples include Pura Luhur Ulu Watu and Pura Tanah Lot. Locks of Nirartha's hair are said to be buried at Pura Rambut Siwi, the evocative seaside temple he built in west Bali.

For more on Pura Rambut Siwi, see page 224

6. Pura Taman Ayun

THE MAGNIFICENT TEMPLE OF SUBAK

A place of enveloping calm, this vast royal water temple in west Bali is surrounded by an elegant moat. The complex was built in 1634 and extensively renovated in 1937. Amidst the lily-pad-dappled beauty, lotus-blossoms fill the pools. The many water features symbolize the temple's role in Bali's subak system that was recognised by UNESCO in 2012. Playing a critical role in rural Bali life, the *subak* is a village association that deals with water, water rights and irrigation. Apportioning a fair share to everyone is a model of mutual cooperation and an insight into the Balinese character.

For more on Pura Taman Ayun, see page 218

7. Masjid Kuno Bayan Beleq
LOMBOK'S OLDEST MOSQUE

Wektu Telu, Lombok's animist-tinted form of Islam, was born in humble thatched mosques nestled in the Rinjani foothills. The best – and oldest – example is Masjid Kuno Bayan Beleq, next to the village of Beleq. Its low-slung roof, dirt floors and bamboo walls reportedly date from the early 1600s. Wektu Telu, a complex mixture of Hindu, Islamic and animist beliefs, has been supplanted by a more traditional form on Islam, as shown by the many new mosques financed with Middle Eastern money across the island. Balinese influence on the island faded after the Dutch victories in the late 1890s.

For more on Masjid Kuno Bayan Beleq, see page 244

8. Kertha Gosa
REMAINS OF A CONQUERED KINGDOM

In 1906, the Dutch mounted a large invasion of Bali to subdue it once and for all. The Dutch forces landed despite Balinese opposition and, four days later, had marched 5km to the outskirts of Denpasar. Thereafter, a string of military victories gave them increasing control of the island. Some of the royal families chose capitulation while others chose *puputan* (ritual suicide). Wearing their best dress and armed with 'show' daggers, the last Balinese royals and warriors in Klungkung marched into Dutch gunfire in a *puputan* in 1908. The ornate remnants of Kertha Gosa, the royal palace, are all that remain.

For more on Kertha Gosa, see page 159

9. Museum Soenda Ketjil
COLONIAL MUSEUM IN BALI'S FORMER GATEWAY

Singaraja in north Bali is the island's second-largest city. A prosperous settlement, it seems far removed from the tourism frenzy of south Bali. Many are surprised to learn that until airline travel took off in the 1970s, Singaraja was the gateway for visitors to Bali through much of the 20th century. Quiet today, the port was once busy with ships bringing Dutch administrators, tourists and cargo. The small Museum Soenda Ketjil is located in an old Dutch shipping company building and details the colonial era locally and across the island. On Lombok, the area of Ampenan west of Mataram served the same role.

For more on Museum Soenda Ketjil, see page 202

10. Ubud Palace
ARTISTIC AND CULTURAL

Ubud's royal palace is only a little over 100 years old. While it has many ornate details and a certain grandeur, it is hardly an ostentatious monument to the town's royalty, who continue to live here and exert great influence over local matters large and small. Nevertheless, the palace symbolises what Ubud has become: an internationally renowned tourism destination with a significant cultural reputation. Many of the elaborate stone carvings are the work of I Gusti Nyoman Lempad, one of the artists responsible for Ubud's acclaim. At night, the main courtyard is evocatively lit for one of the town's famous dance performances.

For more on Ubud Palace, see page 122

11. Uluwatu Surf Break
THE HEART OF BALI'S SURFING FAME

While filming scenes for what became the seminal movie about Bali surfing, *Morning of the Earth* (1972), filmmaker Albert Falzon and his crew were struck by the now legendary freight-train left-handers breaking off the cliffs at Uluwatu, on the Bukit Peninsula. All but unknown at the time, Uluwatu quickly became one of the most revered surfing spots on the planet. Amidst the myriad tourism developments and crowds today, it can be hard to grasp how inaccessible the region once was – even to Balinese surfers, who'd been introduced to the sport by Bob Koke at Kuta beach in the 1930s.

For more on Uluwatu Surf Break, see page 98

12. Jalan Sugriwa, Ubud
CULTURAL HOMESTAYS

One of several similar streets in the centre of Ubud, Jl Sugriwa is lined with simple guesthouses generically known as family homestays. Each is a traditional Balinese compound that's home to several generations. Rooms have been added for visitors and the revenue this produces has fueled

STORYBOOK

Kuta Memorial Wall

more comfortable lifestyles for homestay families. The Balinese openness to outsiders and welcoming culture make these a special cultural experience for guests, who are exposed to the daily fabric of life. Once found island-wide, family homestays have been largely supplanted by more commercial operations elsewhere on Bali, but remain a core part of the Ubud experience.

For more on Ubud homestays,
see page 141

13. Nusa Dua

INTERNATIONAL RESORTS AND PACKAGED TOURISM

Beginning in the 1970s, Nusa Dua was designed to compete with international beach resorts the world over. A gated compound of huge resorts, it's a vast and manicured place where you leave the chaos of the rest of the island behind as you pass the guards. Balinese 'culture' takes the form of attenuated shows and the odd architectural detail meant to convey a local feel. Resort construction has spread beyond Nusa Dua, marching right around the south coast of the Bukit Peninsula to Uluwatu. Trucks clog the roads, bringing water to a region that has little.

For more on Nusa Dua, see page 102

14. Kuta Memorial Wall

RECALLING THE 2002 TRAGEDY

On 12 October 2002, two bombs exploded on Kuta's bustling Jl Legian. The number of dead, including those unaccounted for, exceeded 200, although the exact num-

ber will probably never be known. Many injured Balinese made their way back to their villages, where, for lack of adequate medical treatment, they died. Authorities blamed an Islamic terrorist group; dozens were arrested and many were sentenced to jail, including three who received the death penalty. But most received relatively light terms, enraging many in Bali and Australia. Smaller bombings occurred in Bali in 2005 and there have been numerous arrests of suspected terrorists in the years since.

For more on Kuta Memorial Wall, see page 75

15. Ngurah Rai International Airport

BUSY AIRPORT WITH A HEROIC NAMESAKE

Bali's busy airport is named for I Gusti Ngurah Rai, the national hero who died leading the resistance against the Dutch at Marga in west Bali in 1946. The text of a letter he wrote in response to Dutch demands to surrender ended with 'Freedom or death!' He chose the latter, but his *puputan* slayed the Dutch colonial spirit, and soon Indonesia was independent. His namesake airport is ever-expanding as the inexorable increase in visitor numbers fuels traffic. Constrained by a short runway that precludes long-distance flights from Europe and North America, there is constant debate about building a second airport in north Bali.

For more on Ngurah Rai International Airport, see page 315

339

MEET THE BALINESE

You might think we're nosy, but we're not. We're just friendly.
NI WAYAN MURNI introduces her people.

WHERE ARE YOU going? *Ke mana?* That's the standard opening question when you meet someone in the street. To a stranger, it sounds rather nosy, but no one expects an answer. It's just a greeting in the absence of a word for 'Hello'. *Jalan, jalan* ('Walking, walking') is an acceptable reply.

You'll meet a lot of people with the same name. It's rather confusing. You get your name at birth, and it's preordained, because the name you get accords to the order in which you and your siblings are born. Everyone's position in the family is immediately clear, meaning we're all a bit pigeonholed at birth! The names are the same, regardless of whether you're a boy or girl. As you'll see below, you'll meet an awful lot of Wayans in Bali, but not so many Ketuts. I am a Wayan.

1st born: Wayan, Gede or Putu; 2nd born: Made, Nengah or Kadek; 3rd born: Nyoman, Komang or Koming; 4th born: Ketut.

In 2022, the population of Bali amounted to around 4.37 million people. About 83.5% follow Balinese Hinduism. It's evolved separately from Indian Hinduism, and the differences are clear in temple layouts, ceremonies and beliefs. Christianity, Buddhism and Islam are also practised in Bali, mostly by the Chinese community and people from other islands.

Indonesia is the largest Muslim country in the world, with 87% of the population identifying as Muslim. I often get asked why Bali is unique in Indonesia for being predominately Hindu. The reason is that Islam, which entered Sumatra in the 13th century, made headway along the coasts of Java at the beginning of the 16th century, pressing inland and dealing the great Hindu Majapahit empire a fatal blow in 1527, when the last king of Majapahit was defeated and died. The aristocracy, priests, jurists, artists, artisans and all others unwilling to convert to Islam moved to the easternmost parts of Java, and Bali.

Religion is the most important thing in Balinese life. You can see this in the numerous daily offerings – in my restaurant, hotel, shop and spa, we prepare about 200 basic offerings a day. Much of our time is taken up preparing for large religious ceremonies, staged in ornate temples full of elaborate stone carvings.

The Balinese also love food. Most meals revolve around rice. We eat the best dishes on ceremonial occasions. Bali's most famous dish – *bebek betutu* – is duck richly marinated in Balinese spices, stuffed with vegetables, wrapped in banana leaves and cooked underground – often overnight – for at least eight hours. It makes my mouth water just thinking about it!

On reflection, maybe a better answer to *Ke mana?* is *Makan, makan* ('To eat, to eat').

What's in a Name?

Bali's name reflects its Indian heritage: it's Sanskrit, and much older than the name 'Indonesia'. 'Bali' means 'offering' in Sanskrit, and in High Balinese, 'Bali' is called 'Banten', which also means 'offering' – usually to the gods.

I'M 100% BALINESE

I was born in Penestanan, now a lively suburb of Ubud that's full of yoga studios, healthy restaurants and art galleries. My parents and grandparents are from the same area. As we are Hindu, it's almost certain that our ancestors came from Java, though there are no records – it's only with my generation that birth certificates were issued. As such, many older people have no idea how old they are. It doesn't help that a Balinese year is 210 days!

I opened Ubud's first 'real' restaurant, Murni's Warung, in 1974. It came about by chance. I used to cook lunch for myself and my husband every day in my antiques shop, where I sold textiles, jewelry and other ethnic pieces. Passing tourists asked if they could eat what we were eating. And within a week, I was cooking local food for them! I started with just a couple of chairs and a bamboo table. Now, we can accommodate over a hundred people!

Demon figure, Ogoh Ogoh parade (p344)
CATWALKPHOTOS/SHUTTERSTOCK ©

AN ISLAND OF DEMONS:
THE DARK SIDE OF BALI

Known as the 'Island of the Gods' for its culture and ceremonies, Bali could also be considered the 'Island of Demons'.
By Mark Eveleigh

THE BALINESE BELIEVE that everything exists in balance and that it's impossible for a place to be the home of benevolent gods without it also being the domain of evil spirits.

Bali's demonic underworld is not for the fainthearted, and the islanders observe countless taboos in their efforts to sidestep spiritual pitfalls. After all, there are demons waiting to punish anyone who undertakes construction on inauspicious days, anyone who slaughters livestock during forbidden periods, anyone who sharpens a sacred, traditional dagger at the wrong phase of the moon...

Spirits of the Sea

Even as a tourist, you might want to reconsider those romantic strolls on moonlit beaches, and when packing for your trip, it might be a good idea to leave the green swimwear behind.

Numerous traditionally-minded Balinese consider it foolhardy to walk on a beach at night, since beaches are the lairs of *leyak* (witches). Even young Balinese might be horrified to hear you whistling on a dark beach, or in the vicinity of *pura dalem* (Balinese 'temples of the dead', where cremation ceremonies take place), since whistling is a way of summoning *hantu* (ghosts).

Times are changing, of course, but even the chilled-out beach boys might warn you against wearing green clothing in the sea: Nyai Loro Kidul, the Queen of the South Seas, sees the colour green as an open invitation to carry individuals down to her underwater realm and enslave them.

Not surprisingly, Nyai Loro Kidul is most commonly worshipped by fishermen (both Hindu and Muslim, since she also has a vast following in Java). You will find statues dedicated to her all along Bali's southern coast, and sometimes you'll notice shrines covered in green rather than the typical yellow – even in Western-style resorts. In 1966, Sukarno, Indonesia's first president, dedicated a room in the gigantic Grand Inna Bali Beach Hotel (now the Meru Sanur) to the Queen of the South Seas. To this day, room no. 327 is preserved as a shrine and is decorated in green.

Offerings to the Low Spirits

Any uninitiated traveller who imagines that appeasing demons and evil spirits is an exception to the norm would do well to notice the countless *banten* (offerings) they are likely to step over on an average morning when strolling along the streets of Bali. Those ubiquitous offerings that you see placed on the ground are invariably

intended to appease the 'low spirits', known as the *bhuta kala*. As befits these wicked demons, the offerings will frequently take the form of cigarettes, coffee, and alcohol in the form of *arak* (colourless, distilled palm wine) or *brem* (rice wine). Unsurprisingly, such vices are irresistible to these bad boys of Balinese mythology.

There's a resilient urban myth among travellers in Bali that it's a cultural faux pas to step on these offerings. While you should never deliberately cause offence by kicking or trampling such an offering, inadvertently stepping on it would not be frowned upon. The Balinese believe that once the offering has been made (and accepted, either by gods or demons), it's irrelevant what happens to it next. It's frequently the chickens or the village dogs (considered earthly manifestations of the *bhuta kala* and associated with the 'sin of lust') who benefit from these offerings.

It is well known that women who are menstruating should not enter a temple, but travellers who frown upon this as sexist would do well to remember that any man with a bleeding cut or wound is similarly banned. It is of paramount importance that blood is not spilled on sacred ground, and it is not menstruation itself that is the root of the taboo, but rather blood. Paradoxically, the demons *demand* blood and

are therefore appeased with ritual cockfights in the outer compound of the temple; the inner sanctum is kept entirely 'pure'.

The Great Spiritual Confidence Trick

While a Balinese Hindu would consider it unforgivably foolhardy to try to outwit the gods, it is entirely permissible to try to trick the demons, and there are many ways in which the islanders do this. Nyepi, the annual 'Day of Silence', featuring the parade of Ogoh Ogoh, could be described as an island-wide confidence trick that is played on the entire legion of demons. During the raucous processions – a fantastic chance to see effigies of *bhuta kala* and *leyak* in all their demonic glory – you might notice that the gigantic figures are pirouetted, shaken and generally jostled at each junction along the road. This is to disorientate the demons so that they're unable to find their way into Balinese homes and temples. After the evening's mayhem, the following 24 hours pass in a clandestine silence that aims to convince the demons that Bali is actually deserted. If all is well – and as long as everyone on the island (both locals and tourists) observe the rules – the demons will leave the 'Island of the Gods' in peace for another year.

Leyak must also be outwitted, since they, too, are constantly trying to find their

Pura Dalem Agung (p133)

way into homes and hearts. Like the demons, *leyak* are drawn to blood. When blood has been spilled – such as in a traffic accident – the Balinese will sometimes erect a *magagabag* (a small bamboo frame covered with a net) over blood-patters on the road. Any *leyak* who tries to follow the victim home will be confused by the *magagabag* and will not know which direction the victim was taken in.

Bali's Once-deserted Beaches

The ubiquitous presence of witches and demons has had a huge impact on the development of the Balinese tourism industry, ever since the first hotel was built on Kuta Beach in 1936. Bali's beautiful beaches and cliff-lined coves and capes were traditionally considered uninhabitable to the islanders. The beaches that were so paradisiacal to the island's first foreign visitors were considered close to hellish by the Balinese.

This is not to say that there were no coastal buildings prior to the construction of hotels: *pura dalem* were frequently built near beaches, where the remnants of cremations (ashes and offerings) would be deposited into the sea; the great cliff-top sea temples (Uluwatu, Tanah Lot, Rambut Siwi) were positioned akin to spiritual fortresses to protect the island from the ocean's malevolent forces. But traditional Balinese communities – even those that carved their livelihoods from the ocean – built their homes beyond the reach of the witches and demons that haunted the beaches.

So when the first international hoteliers arrived to the island, they were astounded to find vast areas of beachfront land that could be had for a song. Although the inestimable value of coastal areas is now being realised, few traditionally-minded Balinese would be comfortable sleeping in a beachfront villa.

Ghostly Marriages

Islanders will tell you it is not unusual to see ghosts on Bali's beaches. All it takes is 'the right kind of eyes'. When I was researching my first novel, I spoke to Pak Nasri – a traditional healer in an undeveloped village in west Bali. It was common knowledge in the neighbourhood that Pak Nasri had 'the right kind of eyes', and he enthralled me with his descriptions of the ghosts and spirits he would meet, almost on a nightly basis, when herding his cows home from the beachside coconut groves. The encounters varied from historic figures speaking – so he claimed – Dutch, to modern characters, including a construction labourer who'd been killed ten years previously when building a nearby bridge.

The island has a whole cast of ghostly characters: vindictive Hindu ghosts known as *banas* with human bodies and fireballs where their heads should be; white-shrouded Muslim *pocong*, who exist in a form of limbo; and dark-skinned spirits known as *wong samar*. The *wong samar* are said to be survivors of an ancient Javanese army who were condemned to a fate of perpetual roaming after defeat in battle. To some, the *wong samar* pose a dangerous threat, but to others, they are simply a fact of life. In Pak Nasri's village was one old man whom I'd assumed to be a confirmed bachelor – until I was told it was common knowledge that he was actually married to a *wong samar* who was invisible to everyone but him. After all, it was well known that Nyai Loro Kidul, Queen of the South Seas, had traditionally been the first wife of each of the Javanese Sultans of Solo. This fact was accepted as almost a delightful form of democracy – if the Sultans of Solo had married Nyai Loro Kidul, then who was to say that an elderly rice farmer couldn't marry a humble *wong samar*?

ISLANDERS WILL TELL YOU IT IS NOT UNUSUAL TO SEE GHOSTS ON BALI'S BEACHES

Nyai Loro Kidul, Queen of the South Seas

IKAT TEXTILES

Indonesia's fabled textiles, and what makes them so special.
By Anna Kaminski

INDONESIA IS RENOWNED for some of the world's most sophisticated textile art – an intrinsic part of its culture. Woven by women for adornment or ceremonies, textiles have long been essential dowry items, gifts to please ancestral spirits, or shrouds for the dead to be taken into the afterlife.

In Bahasa Indonesia, the word 'ikat' literally means 'to tie, to bind' and refers to a specific dyeing and weaving process thought to have spread from southern China to other Asian countries through the expansion of the sea trade two thousand years ago. However, ikat-weaving and -dyeing techniques are not unique to Indonesia: cultures from Uzbekistan, Iran and India to Mexico, Bolivia, Chile and Peru practise it, too. In Indonesia, it's Nusa Tenggara that excels

when it comes to ikat, with Sumba renowned for its fine cloth decorated with mythological creatures, and Flores for its intricate patterns, though West Timor, Lombok and smaller islands, such as Rote and Sawu, also produce varied, distinctive work. Ikat patterns vary from island to island and region to region. While aesthetics undoubtedly play a part, the patterns have symbolic meanings associated with social rank: traditionally, certain motifs would only have been worn by the highest-ranking members of society.

The Ikat Process

Ikat cloth is either woven from homespun cotton yarn or from imported, factory-made cotton yarn from China. Silk use is rare.

Pictured clockwise from top left: ikat, Maubesi Art Shop (p291); weaver, East Sumba (p305); Kornelis Ndapakamang, Praikundu Ikat Centre (p305), East Sumba; weavers, Boti (p292)

The threads are dyed before they are woven together in a pattern. Traditionally, dyes are made from local plants and minerals: blue comes from the indigo plant; rust-red from the bark and roots of the mengkudu tree; browns and purples are a mix of the two. You're most likely to encounter ikat produced only with natural dyes on Sumba and West Timor; elsewhere, the emerald greens, sunshine yellows, vibrant pinks and stunning aquamarines tend to come from chemical dyes.

Most ikat-related work is done by women, from planting, harvesting and cotton-spinning to dyeing and weaving using handlooms. Some of the greatest skill of ikat-making lies in figuring out the particular colour of each part of each thread, and the dyeing and tying of the threads before they're attached to the loom. A cloth may not be classed as ikat if this process is not followed.

The weaver, who has a pattern in mind, dips threads into each dye in turn. During each dipping session, the sections of the threads that are not meant to receive a particular colour are bound together with dye-resistant fibre. Once the threads are dry, they are woven together using the warp (lengthwise) or weft (crosswise) technique, or both (double ikat). On Nusa Tenggara's islands, the warp technique (associated with parts of Indonesia with no Buddhist, Hindu or Islamic influence) is the most common. The weft technique is associated with Sumatra and Java, and the double ikat technique – brought from India by Gujarati merchants – is found in just one Indonesian village: Tenganan in Bali.

Motifs, Patterns & Meaning

Ikat across Bali and Nusa Tenggara comes in an incredible array of patterns and designs, with foreign influence varying from island to island, from dragon motifs courtesy of Asian traders to the Dutch royal coat of arms. In Flores, the Dong Son (a Bronze Age culture in ancient Vietnam) influence is evident in the geometric motifs, whereas ikat design in Bali was clearly influenced by Gujarati *patola* (hand-woven silk sari), with its distinctive hexagon framing a sort of four-pronged star, with small patterns combining to form larger patterns. The Sumbanese tradition of decorating ikat with animals, birds, mythological creatures and people is believed to stem from an artistic tradition even older than Dong Son.

Across Nusa Tenggara, village leaders will often wear ikat garments with significant motifs while presiding over specific ceremonies. Large collections of ceremonial ikat are seen as status symbols, and high-quality ikat is still presented as part of the 'feminine' dowry the bride's family gives to the groom's family in return for the 'masculine' dowry, such as livestock.

Judging & Buying Ikat

The highest-quality ikat is made from hand-spun cotton, coloured with traditional dyes using the tying-and-dyeing technique, and then woven on a handloom. While factory-spun threads, coloured with eye-catching factory-made dyes, may be aesthetically pleasing, if the threads haven't undergone the tying-and-dyeing process, it's not true ikat.

You may encounter true ikat of inferior quality: woven by machine, or using the mass-production tie-dying technique that imprints an identical design onto threads for multiple cloths, which results in sloppy pattern outlines. Alternatively, you might be presented with counterfeit ikat: machine-woven fabric printed with a pattern that resembles that of genuine ikat.

Here are some things to look out for: ikat produced in villages will be hand-woven and often hand-dyed (you can often observe the weavers at work). Handspun cotton will be more uneven and have more imperfections than factory-produced cotton, and the cloth will feel rougher and stiffer to the touch. Natural dyes are more 'earthy' in colour than mass-dyed cloth, which often has specks of colour detached from the motifs.

The price of a piece of ikat depends on the materials and techniques used and how long it's taken to produce; some of the larger, best pieces take up to a year. Buying directly from weavers helps to avoid exploitative practices employed by some ikat shopkeepers, though buying from a shop often gives you greater variety. Genuine collectors in search of either antique ikat (which is very rare) or pieces of exceptional quality should seek out Kupang-based Pak Haji Noer (p291), and be prepared to pay accordingly.

Women in traditional clothes, Flores (p272)
HSU MONICA/SHUTTERSTOCK ©

NUSA TENGGARA'S
MINORITY CULTURES

How the other half lives – in Indonesia's remote reaches.
By Anna Kaminski

EAST OF BALI, and largely untouched by Bali's dominant Javanese–Hindu culture, the islands of Nusa Tenggara are a world away from typical imaginings of Indonesia as a densely populated Muslim country. While those imaginings may be true of Java and Sumatra, most of Nusa Tenggara is at least nominally Christian (either Protestant or Catholic, depending on whether the village in question was first reached by Dutch or Portuguese missionaries). The Gospel coexists with traditional beliefs that predate it by millennia, while some villages in West Timor have managed to hold out against Christianisation altogether. Megalithic cultures and animist practices exist alongside Christian churches, while ancestral spirits act as intermediaries between our world and the divine. In villages across Flores, West Timor, Sumba, Sawu, Rote and the Alor and Solor archipelagos, intricate rituals accompany all of the important events that govern one's life, including birth, marriage, death, and the planting and harvesting of crops.

The People

The people living on Nusa Tenggara's larger islands comprise an incredibly rich ethnic mix that reflects the region's seafaring history, with Flores inhabited by the Sunbawanese, Makassarese, Bugis, Bimanese, Solorese and Sumbanese, along with the indigenous Manggarai, Ngada and Lio people, among others. The West Timorese are divided roughly into the indigenous Atoni, who live in mountain villages, and the Belunese and Rotinese, who dwell on the coast. Sumba is much more homogenous, with some Timorese, Rotinese and Savunese resident in the island's two larger towns. While Bahasa Indonesia is the lingua franca, there are 86 languages spoken across Nusa Tenggara.

Throughout Nusa Tenggara, particularly in Sumba and West Timor, inland villages have essentially functioned as tiny kingdoms in their own right from their very conception, with their hilltop locations making them easier to defend from enemies, and overseen by a *raja* (king). Today, village leaders are still referred to as kings. Whether you're Manggarai, Dawa, Alorese or Sumbanese, your village has a male leader – this is true even of the matrilineal Ngada in Flores.

How the next leader is chosen varies: the Lio in Sa'o Ria, for example, have a novel way of determining who will lead them next. When the Lio headman gets married, he and his wife spend two nights in the ceremonial house to conceive a boy. The first baby has been male n 17 generations. The baby is placed on the highest platform of

348

the ceremonial house. If he cries, he will be the next headman. If not, a rooster is sacrificed. If the baby suckles on the rooster's heart, he is headman material. If not, he is carried three times around the ceremonial house and his forehead rubbed with a banana flower. If he doesn't cry, he is given up for adoption and the headman's next son becomes the successor.

Living off the Land

Nusa Tenggara's minorities, who live in houses made of natural materials in village layouts similar to one another, whether it's a Ngada village or a Sumbanese *kampung adat* (traditional village), are inextricably tied to their land. Subsistence farming – supplemented by occasional hunting and the selling of cash crops at markets – is still the way of life. Headmen typically divide the land among village families, but the Manggarai stand out due to their unique *lingko* (land) system involving the allocation of rice fields resembling giant spiderwebs.

Given the central role crops play, it's little wonder that some of Nusa Tenggara's biggest festivals and rituals revolve around planting and harvesting. In Flores, the Lio hold exuberant Gavi ceremonies at the beginning of planting season (October), complete with buffalo sacrifice, *arak* (colourless, distilled palm wine) consumption, dancing and singing. They then hold smaller thanksgiving ceremonies in April. The Ngada express their thanks for bounteous harvests during Reba, held in December. The Manggarai hold ritual Caci whip fights between pairs of men, with the spilt blood anointing the earth for the next harvest. On Sumba, the tremendous spectacle of Pasola is also rooted in the desire to appease the spirits: the more blood is spilt in the ritual battle – involving men on horseback wielding blunt spears – the better it bodes for that year's crops.

Weddings & Funerals

'It's really expensive to get married,' mused Vhendi, my twenty-something Manggarai guide. 'If I want to marry a doctor, my family has to give the woman's family 50,000,000,000Rp and two buffalo.' A wife with just a high-school education would be a more affordable prospect – perhaps a fifth of the money, and pigs and chickens instead of buffalo. While marrying for love is now more common than arranged marriage, and cross-cultural marriage is widely accepted, elaborate dowries are part of the culture across Nusa Tenggara and are paid by the man's family to the woman's.

Funerals are also an elaborate and expensive process – one that warrants buffalo sacrifice. Sumbanese funerals are perhaps the most elaborate and expensive, which is why the bodies of the dearly departed are often kept in the family home for months (even years) before being entombed. Sumba has a particularly well-developed culture of megalithic tombs, though as the recently discovered Lambanapu site testifies, jar burials were also practised.

Etiquette & Animal Sacrifice

While unspoken rules of etiquette vary between minority communities, some are a constant, regardless of which part of Nusa Tenggara you're in. Bringing the king a gift of betel nut when visiting a village is particularly important in West Timor, and guests are expected to partake. If you visit a traditional village during festivities, you will be asked to take part; refusing is impolite, as is turning down ceremonial meals, which include the parts of sacrificial animals. Some Sumbanese villages don't allow visitors during Wulla Podu (Bitter Month) ceremonies in October, and all traditional villages have sacrificial spaces where outsiders may not tread.

Whether you're in a Ngada village in the Flores' highlands or in a Sumbanese community, you will spot buffalo horns and pig jawbones affixed to the exteriors of houses and dried puddles of crimson staining wood or stone totems – testimony to ceremonies that have taken place there. Big occasions – feeding guests at a funeral, harvest festivals – call for the sacrifice of buffalos, whereas a ceremony preceding the team effort to fix the roof of a traditional house may see a goat, chicken, or, in Sumba, a dog, coming under the knife. Attending a sacrifice is not for the squeamish. In some cultures, such as the Manggarai, the colour of the sacrificial chicken is significant: white chickens are for celebrations and black chickens for appeasing the spirits when a dark event has occurred.

BALI'S
SUBAK SYSTEM

Bali's ancient and unique *subak* system is under threat.
By Elizabeth Sinclair

BALI IS BLESSED with rich volcanic soil and a tropical climate that's ideal for growing wet-field (paddy) rice. Growing rice in Bali requires irrigation, as Bali has a long dry season – from April to October. Farmers flood the fields as the rice grows and then dry them out before harvest.

Bali's landscape features several large, active volcanos with crater lakes that feed numerous rivers. These waterways cut narrow gorges into the soft rock, making most of the water inaccessible for farming. Rice irrigation first began in the lowlands, using shallow groundwater. When pressure from a growing population required more agricultural land, the Balinese cleared forests and slopes at higher elevations for farming, meaning new water sources were needed. From the 9th century, the Balinese began to dig tunnels to divert the rivers and engineered a complex network of canals, weirs, dams and channels to carry water to sites without natural water sources. Entire hillsides were flooded and terraced with rice fields, and the *subak* system was born. Rice farmers organised themselves into groups of *subaks* – farmers who shared a single water source – with all members having an equal voice, status and water rights, regardless of their position in the village.

Currently, there are 1200 *subaks* in Bali, each consisting of between 50 and 400 farmers. All functions – planning, decision-making, etc. – are made collec-

tively. *Subak* members are assigned different tasks, such as finding ways to optimise water usage, or maintaining the network of channels. In the *subak* system, nature is considered a partner rather than a resource to be exploited – there is a traditional Balinese saying that claims 'The voice of the *subak* is the voice of God.'

The Creation of Water Temples

By the 11th century, the *subak* system was so successful that its manufactured watersheds fed five interconnected irrigation systems across the entire island, as well as thousands of terraced rice fields. As water became more widely available, however, *subaks* began to clash over access. To deal with conflict and ensure water was shared equitably, the Balinese set up a system of *pura tirta* (water temples) to manage the *subak* system. These temples are strategically located near the lakes, rivers and springs of watersheds.

Pura tirta temples reflect the Balinese belief that water is a sacred symbol of fertility and prosperity. Water plays a vital role in the cultural and religious life of the Balinese, from daily offerings and cleansing ceremonies to religious rituals. As well as being places of worship, *pura tirta* play a crucial role in water management and distribution. The temple priests act as intermediaries between the spiritual realm and local agricultural communities, conducting **351**

rituals expressing gratitude to the gods – particularly Dewi Sri, the goddess of rice and fertility – and seeking their guidance for a prosperous farming season. These ceremonies are synchronised with rice planting and harvesting to ensure alignment with the Balinese lunar calendar. The priests are also involved in decisions concerning water distribution, ensuring the *subak* system operates fairly.

With the establishment of the water temples, the *subak* system became a truly democratic institution rooted in Bali's cultural and spiritual practices. The *pura tirta* and the priests maintain the interconnectedness of the spiritual, social and ecological aspects of Balinese life. The '*Subak* Landscape of Bali' was designated a UNESCO World Heritage Site in 2012, recognising its cultural and ecological significance.

IN THE SUBAK SYSTEM, NATURE IS CONSIDERED A PARTNER

The Green Revolution

In the 1970s and 1980s, the Indonesian government promoted a 'Green Revolution' to increase food yields. Farmers across the country were required to plant new high-yielding rice varieties – developed through modern bioengineering – and abandon their traditional rice varieties. The new varieties yielded two to three harvests a year but were lower in nutritional value and required the use of fertilisers and pesticides.

Farmers had to sell their rice to the government instead of storing it for their own use. The government took over water management from the temples, ignoring the traditional planting and irrigating schedules. The *subaks* clashed, as cooperative water-sharing practices were no longer maintained. Farmers experienced regular plagues of rice pests and spent more money on agricultural inputs, thus reducing their profits.

By the 1990s, the Asian Development Bank advised returning to traditional *subak* methods and putting priests back in charge of irrigation and planting. This was largely due to the research of American anthropologist Stephen Lansing, who spent decades studying Bali's *subak* system. He created a model showing that when priests determined the harvest and watering dates, damage from rice pests and water stress was minimised, and harvests maximised. Bali returned to the *subak* system, but only after hundreds of heritage rice varieties were lost, thus making farmers dependent on the new rice strains.

The Impact of Tourism & Climate Change

Tourism uses about 65 percent of Bali's total water supply, and demand from tourist facilities is depleting Bali's aquifers. According to Bali Water Protection, the island's water table has decreased 70 metres in the past decade, and many wells are going dry. In some highly developed coastal areas, saltwater seeps into the water table and contaminates it.

Climate change is another factor affecting Bali's water supply, and thus its rice cultivation. Indonesia's Ministry of Environment and Forestry estimates that over half of Bali's rivers have run dry. The island's rainfall patterns are changing, with heavier rains and flooding in the rainy season and drought in the dry season resulting in damaged crops and lower harvests. Each year, the flow of water through the *subak* system decreases, meaning most farmers can grow just one rice crop a year.

In addition to this, Bali's rice fields are a major tourist attraction. The famous rice terraces of Jatiluwih draw over 250,000 visitors annually. As tourists flock to visit these sites, restaurants, hotels and villas are built to accommodate them, paving over rice fields and pushing up local taxes and land prices. According to the Transnational Institute, Bali is losing agricultural land at the rate of 1000 hectares per year. Between the challenges of higher taxes, climate change, falling rice production and better incomes in the tourism sector, many Balinese are leaving farming behind them.

Subak has survived for millennia in the face of pests, challenging terrain, conflict and colonisation. It remains to be seen if this resilient system can survive the modern world.

Subak irrigation canal

INDEX

Map Pages **000**

"Balinese dance (p126) flows with a hypnotic grace as dancers tell stories rich with the essence of Hindu lore."

"Ubud Monkey Forest (p133) – now a top destination for day trippers – was once a shady expanse home to three temples and a resident troop of over 1000 monkeys."

Mapping data sources:
© Lonely Planet
© OpenStreetMap http://openstreetmap.org/copyright

THIS BOOK

Destination Editor
James Pham

Production Editor
Barbara Delissen

Book Designer
Virginia Moreno

Cartographers
Dorothy Davidson, Valentina Kremenchutskaya, Alison Lyall, Daniela Machová, Bohumil Ptáček

Assisting Editors
Shauna Daly, Jenna Myers, Christopher Pitts

Cover Researcher
Kat Marsh

Thanks Eve Kelly, Lauren O'Connell, Vicky Smith, Maja Vatrić

MIX
Paper from responsible sources
FSC
www.fsc.org   FSC™ C021741

Paper in this book is certified against the Forest Stewardship Council™ standards. FSC™ promotes environmentally responsible, socially beneficial and economically viable management of the world's forests.

Published by Lonely Planet Global Limited
CRN 554153
19th edition – Jul 2024
ISBN 978 1 83869 368 8
© Lonely Planet 2024 Photographs © as indicated 2024
10 9 8 7 6 5 4 3 2 1
Printed in China